D0204553

BEARING WITNESS

READERS, WRITERS, AND THE NOVEL IN NIGERIA

WENDY GRISWOLD

PRINCETON UNIVERSITY PRESS

PRINCETON, NEW JERSEY

Library of Congress Cataloging-in-Publication Data

Griswold, Wendy.

Bearing witness : readers, writers, and the novel in Nigeria / Wendy Griswold.

p. cm. — (Princeton studies in cultural sociology)

Includes bibliographical references (p.) and index.

ISBN 0-691-05828-8 (cloth : alk. paper) — ISBN 0-691-05829-6 (pbk: alk. paper)

1. Nigerian fiction (English)—History and criticism. 2. Nigeria—Intellectual life—20th century. 3. Fiction—Appreciation—Nigeria. 4. Literature and society—Nigeria. 5. Authors and readers—Nigeria. 6. Books and reading—Nigeria. 7. Nigeria—In literature. I. Title. II. Series.

PR9387.4.G75 2000 823—dc21 99-055565

To John

CONTENTS

LIST OF FIGURES

ACKNOWLEDGMENTS

NIGERIAN authors have given me both their time and their insights, and I am deeply grateful for their generosity. Tolu Ajayi and the late Ken Saro-Wiwa were enormously helpful on my research trips to Nigeria. In addition to them, I had interviews, sometimes involving several meetings over the years, with: Moses Abwa, Segun Adebanjo, Bayo Adebowale, Jare Ajayi, Valentine Alily, T. M. Aluko, I. N. C. Aniebo, Agbo Areo, Yahaya Dangana, Buchi Emecheta, the late May Ellen Ezekiel, Dibia Humphrey, Chukwuemeka Ike, Jospeh Mangut, Teresa Meniru, John Okechukwu Munonye, the late Flora Nwapa, Chuma Nwokolo, Jide Oguntoye, A. E. Ohiaeri, Nze E. C. Ohuka, Wale Okediran, Isadore Okpewho, the late Kalu Okpi, Ayodele Okuyemi, Charry Ada Onwu, Ibe Oparandu, G. O. Orewa, Bode Osanyin, Femi Osofisan, Helen Ovbiagele, Philip Phil-Ebosie, Yemi Sikuade, Victor Thorpe, the late Amos Tutuola, and Rosina Umelo. These were the authors I met face to face; a great many others filled out my surveys and corresponded with me over the course of this research, and it is my hope that this book goes some way toward repaying their kindness.

I am also indebted to the following Nigerians who shared both their personal reading experiences and their observations of Nigerian reading practices with me: Blessing F. Adeoye, Benjamin Onu Arah, Oluwatoyin Asojo, Else Bishop, Innocent Ewean Davidson, A. O. Dola-Fadun, E. O. Fagbohun, Olajide Kufoniyi, Olalekan Elufisayo Odeleye, Ikechukwuka N. A. Oguocha, Uzoma Onyemaechi, Chris Osinubi, Deji Oyewole, Kubby Rashid, John Taiwo Sanusi, and Eno Essien Ura. I interviewed Mr. Arah in Washington, D.C., and Mrs. Dola-Fadun, Mrs. Bishop, and Mr. Fagbohun in Lagos. The rest had responded to my call for readers on the Naijanet electronic mailing list; they filled out a survey of their backgrounds and reading practices, and I had a great deal of subsequent communication with many of them.

I benefited from the wisdom of numerous editors, publishers, and members of the book trade. These included: Isaac Achor and Dafe Otobo at Malthouse Press, A. I. Adelekan and E. C. Ohuka at Macmillan Nigeria, Agbo Areo at Paperback Books, Tosin Awolalu at Longman Nigeria, Francis O. Bada at CSS Bookstore, Augustina Igwe at Delta, T. C. Nwosu at Cross Continent Press, F. C. Ogbalu at University Publishing, Oluyinka Olaniran at Abiprint, Felix Onyeacholam at The Bestseller, and (in England) Rupert Parry-Jones and Pauline Tait at Macmillan Publishers Ltd, Vicky Unwin at Heinemann, and Adam Gadsby at Longman.

Along the way some Africanist scholars have tried to set me straight when

I was going off course. Bernth Lindfors allowed me to borrow from his massive library and corrected some of my errors; Fredrick Cooper and Jane Guyer helped sharpen some of my observations; Misty Bastian, at one time my co-author and research assistant, has always been my teacher regarding Nigeria. The staff of the Herskovits Africana Library at Northwestern University has been helpful well beyond the call of duty. I have also benefited from some student research assistants who went the extra mile for this project, including Ben Arah, Steve Ellingson, Kathy Hull, Anne Nye, Kristen Swenson, and Nathan Wright.

Financial support for this research, either directly or in terms of fellowship support, has come from the National Science Foundation, the Woodrow Wilson International Center for Scholars, the National Endowment for the Humanities, the University of Chicago Humanities Institute, and the Center for Advanced Study in the Behavior Sciences. I thank them all.

My family learned quite a bit about Nigeria and also about having a mother absorbed in the novels and concerns of a distant country. They shared my fascination with Nigeria and its literary culture, and they rose to the occasion when I was distracted by the demands of my research. John, Ray, and Olivia, know that you are the beginning and end of everything I do, including writing this book.

ABBREVIATIONS

ABPR	*American Book Publishing Record*
AfBPR	*African Book Publishing Record*
AFRC	Armed Forces Ruling Council, successor to SMC under Babangida regime.
ANA	Association of Nigerian Authors
CLAN	Children's Literature Association of Nigeria
CMS	Church Missionary Society; refers to the Church of England's missionary operations and the Nigerian congregations they established
CSS	Church and School Supplies, a large bookstore in Lagos, formerly CMS
ECOWAS	Economic Community of West African States, created in 1975 with goal of reducing trade barriers in the region
FESTAC	Second World Black and African Festival of Arts and Culture, held in Lagos in 1977
FMG	Federal Military Government
IBBY	International Board for Books for Young people
MOSOP	Movement for the Survival of the Ogoni People
NBA	Nigerian Booksellers Association
NCNC	National Council of Nigerian Citizens, Igbo dominated national party founded in 1940s by Azikiwe and Macauley from old NYM; originally the National Council of Nigeria and the Cameroons
NEPA	Nigerian Electric Power Authority
NNA	Nigerian National Alliance
NNDP	Nigerian National Democratic Party, nationalist party centered on Lagos, founded in 1922 by Herbert Macauley
NPA	Nigerian Publishers Association
NPC	Northern People's Congress founded in 1940s and headed by Ahmadu Bello; conservative representative of Northern regional interests.
NPN	National Party of Nigeria
NSO	National Security Organization, established in 1976; used by Buhari regime to repress critics
NYM	Nigerian Youth Movement, founded in 1930s by H. O. Davies and Nnamdi Azikiwe
OAU	Organization of African Unity
OIC	Organization of the Islamic Conference
OPEC	Organization of Petroleum Exporting Countries

PRC   Provisional Ruling Council (Abacha regime)

SAP   Structural Adjustment Program launched by Babingida in 1986

SFEM Second-Tier Foreign Exchange Market, in which foreign exchange from exports earnings and for imports was sold on auction, leading to a sharp depreciation of the naira's value; this was part of the SAP

SMC   Supreme Military Council, brought into existence by Gowon in 1967; includes top military officers, security service and police heads, state military governors

UPGA United Progressive Grand Alliance

WAEC West African Examination Council.

WAI   War Against Indiscipline, campaign during Buhari regime

KEY DATES IN NIGERIAN HISTORY

Date	Political and economic developments	Literary and cultural developments
Eighth century	Early eastern culture suggested by archaeological findings at Igbo Ukwu.	
Eleventh century	Rise of Yoruba kingdom centered in Ife under *oni* (king). In north some Hausa city-states (Kano, Katsina) build walled towns.	Urbanized Ife culture with sophisticated sculpture and metalwork; *oni* a religious as well as political leader. Islam gradually entering Hausaland via trans-Saharan caravan routes.
1400s	Oyo kingdom surpasses Ife in Yorubaland. Benin becomes major power between Yorubaland and the Niger. First European slave trade between Portuguese and Benin.	Court of *oba* (king) in Benin features sculptures, brass, bronze, ivory. Portuguese missionaries establish Roman Catholic churches in Benin; these die out by eighteenth century.
1500s	Nri Kingdom east of the Niger, considered foundation of Igbo culture. Northern Nigeria controlled by Songhai on the west, Borno on the east. Dutch, later French and British slave traders.	Islamic culture flourishes under Songhai empire.
1600s	Great expansion of transatlantic slave trade.	
1700s	Droughts in Sahel lead to political instability, collapse of Borno empire. Power struggles in Oyo kingdom. Oyo and Aro (Igbo/Ibibio) confederacy become main West African slave traders, trading with British and Americans.	
1804–8	Usman dan Fodio, Fulani (mostly) clerics leads Islamic jihad in north, overthrow Hausa states, establish Sokoto Caliphate.	Spread of Islam in north and middle belt into northern Yorubaland.
1807	Britain outlaws transatlantic slave trade, leading to increasing British	

involvement in Yorubaland and
Niger Delta.

1830s   Yoruba Wars in south, following
1817 collapse of Oyo, disruptions
of slave trade, and revolts by Muslims allied with Sokoto.

1840s   Beginning of Christian missionary activities in west
(CMS); Roman Catholic missions begin in 1860s, especially
active in east.

1861   Britain establishes Lagos colony.

1886   Royal Niger Company chartered
for trading under Georgie Goldie,
subsequently freezing out French
and German trading and thus
laying British colonial claim.

1900   Frederick Lugard named high
commissioner of Protectorate of
Northern Nigeria.

1903   Completion of British conquest.

1914   Unification of Northern and
Southern Nigeria under Lugard

1920s   Nationalist Herbert Macauley, via
Lagos *Daily News*, raises political
awareness; founds Nigerian
National Democratic Party in
Lagos in 1922.

1930s   Rise of Nigerian Youth Movement   Novels in Hausa and Yoruba
under H. O. Davies and Nnamdi   published.
Azikiwe; in 1938 defeats NNDP,
attempts to form genuinely
national political party.

1939–45 Nigerian units fight in Ethiopia,
Burma, etc. NYM reorganized as
primarily Yoruba party, Action
Group, led by Obafemi Awolowo.
Labor unions proliferate.

1940s   Party lines drawn on regional basis:
Northern People's Congress under
Ahmadu Bello (Hausa-Fulani,
north); Action Group under

Awolowo (Yoruba, west); National Council of Nigerian Citizens under Azikiwe (national, but increasingly Igbo, east).

1946   Richards Constitution establishes federalism, separate legislatures in three regions.

1951   Northern Elements Progressive Union, under Aminu Kano, breaks off from more conservative NPC. Macpherson Constitution reinforces both federalism and regionalism.

1952   Amos Tutuola's *The Palm-Wine Drinkard*, generally regarded as the first Nigerian novel in English, is published.

1954   Lyttleton Constitution creates three-region federation and paves way for independence.   Cyprian Ekwensi's *People of the City* is published. Ekwensi's and Tutoola's novels launch the first generation of Nigerian novelists. This generation includes all those who published a novel by 1970, the year the civil war ended.

1956   First commercial discovery of oil in Niger Delta.

1957   Western and Eastern regions become self-governing. Federal Executive Council formed, with Abubakar Tafawa Balewa (NPC) appointed prime minister.

1958   Export of oil begins from Port Harcourt.

1959   North becomes self-governing. Elections for enlarged House of Representatives held; NPC captures 142/312 seats; Balewa heads NPC-NCNC coalition government, Awolowo leads opposition.   Chinua Achebe's *Things Fall Apart* is published.

1960   Oct. 1 Nigeria becomes independent; Balewa heads government.

1961		Cyprian Ekwensi's *Jagua Nana* is published.
1962	Action group splits due to rift between Awolowo and Akintola, prime minister of Western Region. Akintola organizes United People's Party (later NNDP), collaborates with NPC-NCNC. Riots in Western Region produce state of emergency; legislature dissolved, many Action Group leaders arrested. Census held, but results nullified.	
1963	Nigeria becomes republic, with Azikiwe president, Balewa prime minister. Awolowo convicted of treason. Second census held, results controversial. Midwestern Region carved out of Western Region. Shifting party alignments, political disillusionment.	
Late 1964–65	Parliamentary elections: NNA (NPC, NNDP, minority parties in Midwest and East) versus UPGA (NCNC, Action Group, minority parties in North). NNA wins amid irregularities, UPGA boycott, charges of fraud; in March NNA wins Western regional elections, setting off violence. Disorder mounts.	Wole Soyinka's *The Interpreters* is published.
1966	January coup of Igbo officers, assassination of Balewa, Akintola, Bello, northern officers. General Aguiyi-Ironsi (Igbo, but not involved) restores order under Federal Military Government, suspends constitution. Mob violence in north against Igbo. July counter-coup; Aguiyi-Ironsi killed, Lt. Col. Yakubu Gowon heads military government. Violence persists in north and elsewhere; Igbo retreat to Eastern Region. Lt. Col. Chukwuemeka Ojukwu, military gov-	Flora Nwapa's *Efuru*, the first Nigerian novel by a woman, is published.

erner of Eastern Region, presses
for looser federal ties, Igbo security.

1967   Aburi Agreement in January sets
plan for loose confederation. In
May East votes to secede; Gowon,
chairing new Supreme Military
Council, proclaims abolition of
regions in favor of twelve states;
Republic of Biafra declares independence. Fighting begins in July;
early Biafran victories in Midwest, but federal forces regain
control.

1968–69   Stubborn Biafran resistance, despite overwhelming strength of
federal forces. Britain and Soviet
Union aid Nigeria; France provides
unofficial aid to Biafra. Nigerian
blockade weakens resistance, widespread starvation, December offen-
sive cuts Biafra in two. Ojukwu
flees.

1970   January: Biafra surrenders. Feared
genocide does not occur. Gowon's
program to reintegrate Biafrans
into Nigeria without reprisals
largely successful; Nigeria fails in
attempt to extradite Ojukwu from
Ivory Coast. Gowon announces
six-year plan, raising fears of continuous military rule.

Authors whose first novels were
published from 1970 through
1983 are considered
second generation.

1971   Nigeria joins OPEC.

S. Okechukwu Mezu's *Beyond
the Rising Sun,* first war novel,
published.

1972   Gowon lifts ban on political discussion; Awolowo calls for democratic socialism, antagonizing military; Gowon restores ban.

1973   Census reports 44 percent population increase; widely disbelieved,
later scrapped by Murtala Muhammed in favor of 1963 figures.
OPEC price rise sets off era of
massive oil revenues.

1974   Gowon regime widely criticized for graft, bribery, nepotism. Oil boom lasts until 1981. Between 1974 and 1979, oil revenues increase 350 percent. Massive public spending during boom years, mostly in urban areas and poorly planned. Oil becomes dominant export, eclipsing agricultural goods. Growth of urban middle class. Booming industrialization and indigenous commercial enterprises during decade. Inflation. In October Gowon backs off from 1976 date to restore democracy, triggering protests.

During oil-boom years, dramatic expansion of education. In mid-1960s Nigeria had five universities; by 1975 there were thirteen, and twenty by the 1980s. Advances in primary and secondary education, especially in north, in efforts to make regional levels of education more equal.

1975   Increasing dissatisfaction with corruption, inefficiency, epitomized by cargo ship tie-up in Lagos harbor. In July bloodless coup puts Murtala Muhammed in power. He receives broad popular support, centralizes government power, purges public officials, begins shrinking military, promises to hand over power in 1979.

Under Muhammed, federal government takes over two largest newspapers, broadcasting, universities.

1976   Muhammed assassinated in February in unsuccessful coup, country mourns loss of decisive leader; thirty-four conspirators executed after secret military trial with charges of ties to Gowon, in exile in London. Lt. Gen. Olusegun Obasanjo succeeds, continues to work toward 1979 restoration of democracy. Nineteen states created in another attempt to divide ethnic blocs and represent minority group interests. New constitution drafted, based on American system; requires political parties to have national, not just regional, support.

Universal Primary Education Scheme launched.

1977   Continued industrialization, development of infrastructure, growing number of parastatals.

Second World Black and African Festival of Arts and Culture (FESTAC) held in Lagos; a

		celebration of Nigerian affluence as well as arts, FESTAC involves huge expenditures with rampant corruption. Macmillan's "Pacesetters" series begins with publication of Agbo Areo's *Director!*
1978	Oil boom slowed by minor recession in 1978–79 but recovers until 1981. Balance-of-payments crisis. Protests at several universities over tuition increases. Move to establish Sharia Court of Appeal in constitution defeated in Constituent Assembly after passionate debate.	
1979	Following elections, FMG hands over power to civilian government under President Shehu Shagari on October 1, launching Second Republic. Elections among five parties: National Party of Nigeria (Shagari's party, successor to NPC, based in north and non-Igbo southeast); United Party of Nigeria (successor of Action Group, headed by Awolowo); Nigerian People's Party (predominantly Igbo, headed by Azikiwe); Greater Nigerian People's Party (non-Hausa-Fulani north, headed by Waziri Ibrahim); People's Redemption Party (northern, most radical party, headed by Aminu Kano). NPN minority government, in shaky coalition with NPP.	
1980	Obvious weakness of coalition government, conflict between states and federal government. Nevertheless, high expectations of continued economic growth.	Maitatsine (Muslim sect) religious riots in Kano lead to over four thousand deaths. Association of Nigerian Authors formed.
1981	Fall in oil prices in mid-1981 marks end of oil boom.	Teachers strike because not paid.
1982	Amid growing recession, heavy government spending continues, often for political reasons (e.g.,	Police crackdown on Maitatsine in Kaduna and Maiduguri leads to rioting.

heavy investment in steel industry).
Huge foreign debt increase.

1983   Two million foreign workers expelled. August elections show
massive NPN victories; Nigerians
cry fraud. On December 31 the
military, led by Major General
Muhammadu Buhari, seizes power.

1984   Buhari heads SMC; pledges to   Beginning of third generation
curb corruption and trim federal   of novelists. Buhari regime ha-
budget; launches fifteen-month   rasses journalists, arrests critics
War Agains Indiscipline, national   including popular musician
campaign promoting hard work,   Fela Ransome-Kuti. National
patriotism, cleaner environment.   Security Organization used to
Negotiations with IMF to resched-   repress criticism of government.
ule foreign debt trigger popular
resistance.

1985   Economic crisis worsens; IMF talks
fail; growing criticism of regime.
In August northern, mostly non-
Hausa officers stage coup under
Major General Ibrahim Babangida,
who heads Armed Forces Ruling
Council (successor to SMC) and
assumes title of president. Failed
countercoup in December.

1986   Babangida initiates Structural Ad-   Student demonstrations at Ah-
justment Program, which entails   madu Bello University and
much of what IMF had demanded,   Kaduna Polytechnic leads to
including greater austerity meas-   military occupation of cam-
ures, pay cuts for military and   puses, many deaths. Furor
public- and private-sector employ-   among Christians over Nige-
ees, reduction in large government   ria's entry into the Organiza-
projects, restrictions and 30 per-   tion of the Islamic Conference.
cent surcharge on imports. Unable   Wole Soyinka wins Nobel Prize
to reschedule foreign loans even   for Literature.
with SAP program. Despite resis-
tance, naira devalued.

1987   Drops in real income continue,
unemployment rising; hardships
for urban dwellers worsen. Political Bureau, set up to plan transition to civilian government,
recommends two-party system,

state involvement in economy (which AFRC was trying to decrease), creation of two new states; these were added, bringing total to twenty-one.

1988 Under loan from World Bank, foreign debt is finally rescheduled.

1989 Naira devalued again.

1990 Naira devalued again. In April coup attempt fails.

1991 Nine new states added, bringing total to thirty. Abuja replaces Lagos as federal capital.

Ben Okri's *The Famished Road* wins the Booker Prize.

1993 June 12 presidential elections, apparently won by Moshood K. O. Abiola, abruptly annulled by Babangida. In August caretaker government appointed under Chief Ernest Shonekan. In November General Sani Abacha takes over.

1994 Anniversary of annulled election sets off protests and massive strike. Abiola declares himself president, is imprisoned.

Ken-Saro Wiwa arrested in conjunction with May death of four Ogoni leaders. Wole Soyinka flees the country, works to drum up support against Abacha regime.

1995 In October speech celebrating thirty-five years of Nigerian independence, Abacha commutes death sentences passed on Obasanjo and others convicted of plotting a coup; he also announces a program for the transition to civilian rule to be completed by October 1998.

Saro-Wiwa and eight other members of MOSOP convicted of "encouraging" murder of four leaders; all nine men executed on November 10. Outcry from world leaders; Nigeria suspended from Commonwealth, other sanctions applied but no oil boycott.

1996 Abiola remains in prison. Abacha regime increases censorship of press, political repression. Number of states increses to thirty-six.

1997 In October oil prices begin to drop.

Abacha files treason charges against Soyinka, now in exile in U.S.

1998   In June Abacha dies suddenly; General Abdulsalam Abubakar becomes new head of state. About to be released from prison, Abiola suddenly dies of heart failure. Oil prices continue to fall despite OPEC reduction in production. Abubakar promises a swift return to democratic government.

In September Abubakar drops treason charges against Soyinka, who returns to Nigeria.

1999   At the end of February Nigerians elect Olusegun Obasanjo president; he takes office in May.

In August Chinua Achebe returns to Nigeria for the first time in nine years.

BEARING WITNESS

Chapter 1

TO UNDERSTAND THE NOVEL IN NIGERIA

Jagan is an aging Yoruba widow who longs to see her son married, but Tayo is balking. Though he still lives with his mother in Oko-Ibu, a village in western Nigeria, Tayo aspires to become a Lagos journalist. Marriage holds no interest for him.

Jagan negotiates with a family from a neighboring village for a bride. Though her family welcomes the match, Lenuse, the bride-to-be, runs away. Suspecting that a malevolent spirit is holding her, Jagan goes to a local oracle for help; her Christian village is scandalized, but Lenuse finally returns. This smoothed over, Jagan and the Oko-Ibu elders pressure Tayo to submit to the match.

Villagers adorn the reluctant bride and, weeping piteously, Lenuse is carried to her new home. Tayo ignores her. Jagan assumes that sooner or later nature will take its course, but Tayo heads for Lagos to work for a newspaper. In long conversations with his editor, Tayo worries about being saddled with a "bush" wife while the older man praises unspoiled village girls like Lenuse compared to the Lagos glamour girls Tayo fancies. Meanwhile back in the village Jagan frets over Tayo dying in a car crash before producing children.

Confused, Tayo goes back to Oko-Ibu for a holiday. He resists sex with Lenuse, but Jagan acquires some perfumed magic from an herbalist, and this does the trick. Lenuse quickly gets pregnant. Jagan's health begins to fail, and she dies just after seeing the birth of her twin grandchildren.

Tayo has to get back to his job in Lagos. Embarrassed by Lenuse's lack of both literacy and sophistication, he first intends to leave her in Oko-Ibu but finally agrees to take the family with him. Over time Tayo becomes increasingly successful, all the while still admiring city girls. As the novel closes, Tayo and Lenuse argue about whether a decent woman would ever wear a miniskirt.

(Francis Falemara, *The Last Chance*)

WRITING FICTION is the contemporary analogue to telling tales in the moonlit village, and Nigerian novelists see themselves as storytellers. They tell stories of a particular kind and with a particular intent, however, for these writers understand themselves to be bearing witness to Nigerian social experience. The story told in Francis Falemara's novel *The Last Chance*, which I have summarized here, displays some standard themes of Nigerian fiction: city versus village, conflict between individuals and families over marriage, Christianity versus indigenous beliefs, fertility and reproduction, the aspirations of educated young people, magic, confusion, and even traffic accidents. Jagan, Lenuse, and Tayo experience an upheaval in social relations and individual expectations. The two women resist the changes, Tayo welcomes them, and Falemara bears witness to them.

Upheaval is not the same thing as transition from one condition to another, as in some one-way movement from tradition from modernity. A jubilant crowd carrying a sobbing bride off to her husband's village is characteristic of contemporary West African culture. So is a young reporter in an air-conditioned Lagos office shooting the breeze with his boss. Falemara knows that his readers will recognize both, for he and they live in a swirling complex of older and newer, local and imported, familiar and strange; the swirling elements flow in and out of one another as they are stirred together, but they never blend into a single tone.[1] True, love and marriage, intergenerational conflict, making one's way in the world, and the tensions between individual and society are the stuff of novels everywhere. But the multiple juxtapositions of African tradition and Western modernity, the sharpness of the clash between them, and the ambivalence of people like Tayo suspended in the middle are very Nigerian.

Far and away the largest country in Africa, Nigeria has produced a huge quantity and variety of fiction since the 1950s. Nigerians have written profound meditations on politics, on gender, and on the existential dilemmas faced by postcolonial intellectuals. They have also written plenty of blood-and-sex thrillers and formulaic romances. Nigerian authors range from international literary celebrities like Wole Soyinka to ambitious students to sleep-deprived mothers writing out their stories in longhand before the children wake up; Francis Falemara wrote *The Last Chance* in the early mornings before going to work as police force marine officer for Lagos State. Nigerian publishers number in the dozens, and Nigerian readers in the millions. Moreover, many publishers and readers of Nigerian novels are nowhere near Nigeria, but instead are in London and New York, Berkeley and Stockholm. It is emblematic of this sprawling literary complex that the most prestigious prize for African literature, a prize Nigerians have walked away with several times, was established by a Japanese publisher and is administered out of Oxford.[2] Given all of this, the Nigerian novel offers an unusually good case through which to examine cultural construction as a process that is simultaneously global and local. Moreover, it is a process occurring under conditions of modernity, premodernity, postmodernity, and unmodernity, all of which characterize contemporary Nigeria.

To try to understand the novel in Nigeria is to ask, what happened when Nigerians picked up the English novel, a genre whose basic contours were established in the mid–eighteenth century, and ran with it? Run with it they did: Nigerians have written more novels in English than all other West

Africans put together. Nigerians have brought home the Nobel Prize for Literature and Britain's Booker Prize. Nigerian writers bemoan the lack of a reading public, the perfidy of publishers, and the impossibility of earning a decent living from writing, yet they keep on turning out dozens of new novels each year. Nigerian publishers (and others) keep publishing them, and Nigerian readers (and others) keep reading them. Examining the Nigerian novel in its social context, therefore, raises questions such as: What are these novels like? What local and international pressures and possibilities have influenced them? What do they mean to their authors? To their readers?

A second set of questions concerns the role that writers play in society. Why on earth would someone write a novel—or read one—in a place like Nigeria? What does this literary relic of eighteenth-century England have to do with the lives of contemporary West Africans, anyway? The novel, a relatively new genre, took its ultimate shape at a time when a growing, increasingly literate middle class in Britain constituted a rapidly expanding market for all sorts of consumer goods, including print media.[3] During this time of rampant commercialization, men of letters were no longer either bound to or supported by traditional patrons such as church, court, or aristocratic families. Their situation gave rise to "the author" as an ideal type: autonomous and beholden to no one, but at the same time forced to earn a living by selling his literary wares on an open and impersonal market.[4] The awkward combination of individualism and market dependence characterized the novel from its inception.

Individualism and the literary market, however, do not operate in Nigeria as they do in the West.[5] Nigerian individualism conflicts with communal obligations toward kinsmen, townsmen, and tribe, and it is by no means certain that an individualist orientation is displacing the collective one. Nor does the beleaguered Nigerian middle class constitute a reliable market for fiction. Yet despite these differences, by and large Nigerian authors have adopted the ideology of the Western man of letters: they regard themselves as independent intellectuals, as writing for a small-but-surely-growing reading public, and as both entertaining and instructing that public through their fiction. In this, they are very "modern," even though they are operating in a literary world that is not. What are the implications of this disjunction for their ability to bear witness to their society?

In the following chapters I try to understand the Nigerian novel by addressing these two sets of questions: What is the Nigerian literary complex like, and how does it relate to postcolonial Nigerian society?

Chapter 1 establishes some points of departure, discussing the historical background to contemporary Nigeria, the literary and sociological nature of the novel as genre, and the methods used in this study. Chapter 2 explores the social and organizational context in which writers write, publishers publish, and readers read Nigerian novels. Chapter 3 identifies the topical clusters or subgenres into which most of these novels can be assigned—village novels, city novels, novels about gender, formulaic romances, war novels, novels about academic or intellectual life, crime novels, political novels—and specifies the motifs and mythic structures of each. Along the way I hazard some explanations for these motifs and structures, explanations that, although necessarily incomplete, are rooted in a belief in connections and causality. These procedures, which involve producing readings of texts and performing comparative operations on them, represent my imperfect but determined effort to understand the novel in Nigeria.

IN NIGERIA

I have been speaking of the "Nigerian novel" as if both adjective and noun were straightforward designations, but neither one is. What does it mean to be a *Nigerian* novel? What does it mean to be a Nigerian *novel?*

To begin with, what is Nigeria? Certainly the country has all the characteristics of a contemporary state: borders, a central government, citizens bearing Nigerian passports, a seat in the United Nations. At the beginning of this book I have given a list of the key dates and events, both political and cultural, in what most people would accept as "Nigerian history."[6] Yet, although Nigeria has international political recognition and a fixed geographic demarcation, one that has stood the test of an unsuccessful secession as well as occasional skirmishing with Cameroon over some islands, what it means to be "Nigerian" or "a Nigerian" is more ambiguous.

If a nation-state is an "imagined community," as Benedict Anderson's widely accepted thesis maintains, Nigeria is about as imaginary as they come.[7] Within its boundaries are upward of 250 distinct ethnic groups (some count as many as 400), each with its distinct language. Over the colonial period, which was less than fifty years long for Nigeria as a whole, people who spoke different languages, practiced different forms of agriculture, worshiped different gods, and had no sense of common condition or fate were somehow to have undergone a collective metamorphosis and emerged as a new people called "Nigerians." To do this took a leap of the imagination indeed, and some proto-Nigerians never made the leap.

Nigeria's first fiction is its name. "Nigeria" is a Latinate evocation of the Niger River, which makes a curving T shape that divides the country into three regions, as shown on the map. The name was dreamed up by Florence Shaw, an English journalist and the fiancée of Frederick Lugard, the man who was to become the first governor of the amalgamated colony. The British colonialists considered other colorful possibilities, including

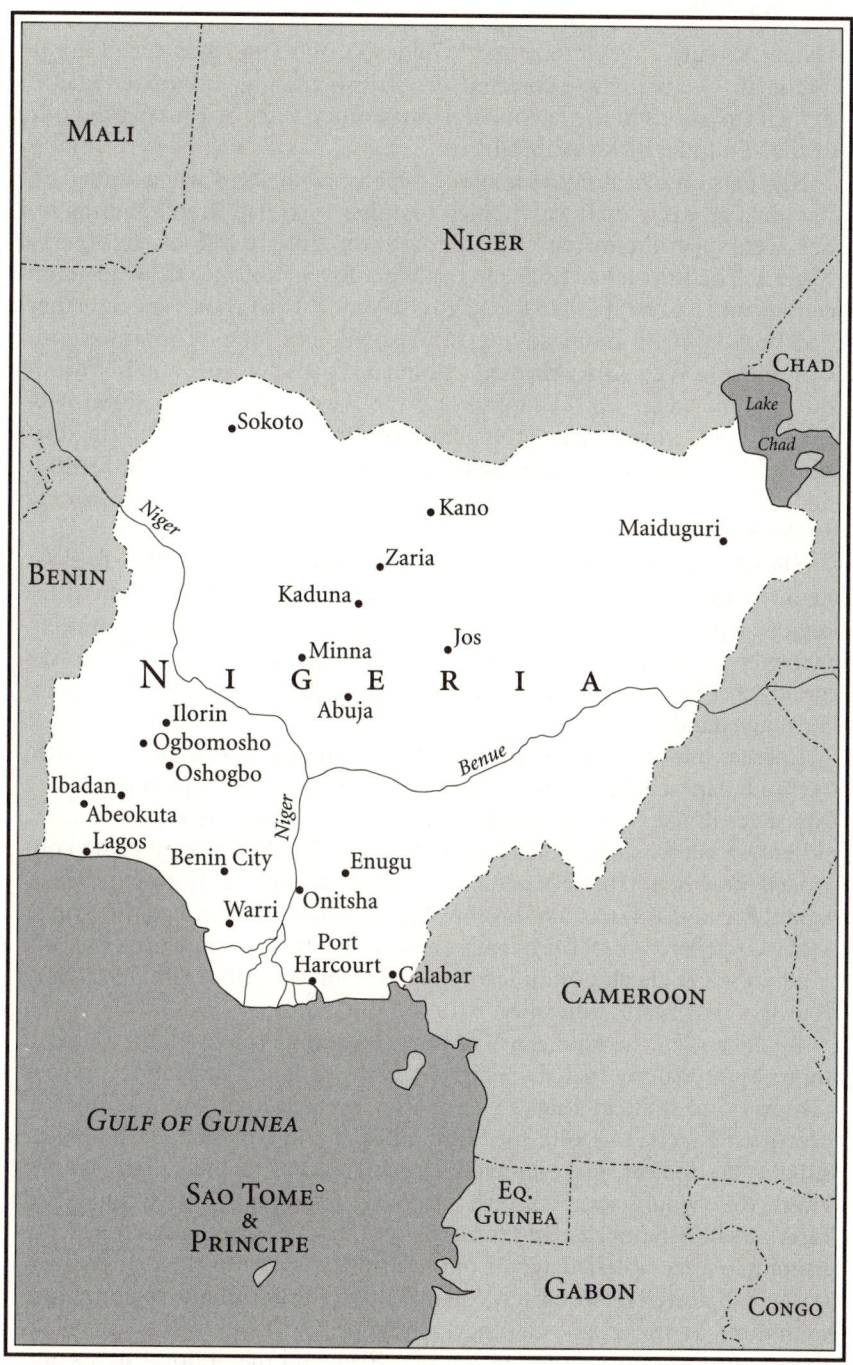

Map of Nigeria showing the largest cities

"Niger Sudan," "Negretia," and "Goldesia"; this latter was after George Taubman Goldie, who protected the British trading monopoly against French ambitions in the late nineteenth century, thereby winning the title of the "Founder of Modern Nigeria."

Nigeria's present boundaries were established in 1914 when Britain, in the usual arbitrary manner, cobbled together what had been a shifting series of colonial administrative regions into the Colony and Protectorate of Nigeria. The British had traded in the Niger River area since the eighteenth century and had established the Lagos Colony in 1861. For some time they had been hesitant about adding tropical colonies, despite their long involvement in West Africa through commerce, proselytizing, and both conducting and (after 1807) suppressing the slave trade. Competition with France and Germany over exploitation of African resources, and the division of areas of control established by the Berlin Conference of 1885, prodded the British to a more active colonialism, however, eventually leading to the 1914 unification.

The colony consisted of three regions, corresponding to the divisions made by the Niger and Benue Rivers. The British administered the three regions separately and quite differently. While it is an oversimplification to interpret Nigerian politics and culture only on the basis of differences among these three regions, they constitute the indispensable starting point for understanding.

Indirect rule was most successful in the highly centralized, Islamic north. Here a Fulani scholar, Usman dan Fodio, had led a jihad against the Hausa city-states in the early nineteenth century, establishing the Fulani Empire, otherwise known as the Caliphate of Sokoto. By 1830 the caliphate controlled most of northern Nigeria, reaching as far south as Ilorin in Yorubaland. Usman dan Fodio and his son, Muhammad Bello, unified the empire into a confederation of thirty emirates whose authority came from Sokoto. Under their leadership both learning and trade, as well as a reformed and reinvigorated Islam, flourished.

By the end of the nineteenth century, the emirs' rule was characterized more by feudalism than by religious zeal, however, making it ripe for takeover and indirect rule. Lugard, who became high commissioner of Northern Nigeria in 1900, used both military and diplomatic measures to subdue the region. He eventually struck a deal with the caliph and the emirs: they would accept British authority, abandon the slave trade, and carry out British policies. In return, they would be confirmed in office, becoming in effect salaried agents of the British. As part of their agreement, the British posted relatively few colonial administrators in the region. More significant in the long run, they also kept Christian missionaries out, thereby protecting both Islamic conservatism and the political status quo in what came to be called "the Holy North."

In the contrasting case of the Eastern Region, where the Igbo constituted the largest ethnic group, traditional political authority had been diffuse. No one higher than the village level could demand obedience, and even here village councils, not chiefs, made the key decisions. Indirect rule was far more difficult in such a decentralized situation, for the British could not find any local authorities comparable to the northern emirs. The colonial officers set up an unwieldy system of court administrators and warrant officers (i.e., those whose authority came from a British warrant). This provided a rather shaky structure of authority, for the Igbo never took the self-important warrant officers very seriously. More important, the British opened the Eastern Region to Christian missionaries and other Westernizing influences.

The Western Region, Yorubaland, fell between these two extremes of traditionalism and Westernization. The Oyo Empire, which had been a major exporter of slaves in the eighteenth century, had broken down once and for all by 1819, and for the next eighty years civil wars between the various Yoruba power centers churned up the land. The British made deals with some of the traditional rulers and propped up or revived others, thus giving some stability (with a veneer of traditional authority) to what had been a very fluid political situation. Colonial administrators used the concept of hometown to sort out the Yoruba, thus turning the multiple meanings that such towns had in Yoruba political traditions into a rigid and lasting classification system.[8] Perhaps the most significant agent of social change for the Yoruba and for Western Nigeria during the colonial period was the growth of Lagos into a commercial behemoth.

Of critical importance to Nigerian cultural change, and ultimately to the geographically uneven development of the Nigerian novel, was the varying extent of Christian missionary penetration. The first missionaries, active in the Lagos and Ibadan areas in the west by the 1840s, were the Methodists and the Church of England's Church Missionary Society (CMS). Later other Protestant denominations moved into the area, and by the 1860s several Roman Catholic orders had joined them. A rough and implicit division of the mission field took place, with the CMS especially active among the Yoruba, the Roman Catholics among the Igbo and other eastern groups. The missions established schools and promoted literacy, often translating the Bible and Christian hymns into local languages. Their emphasis on literacy and formal schooling was to have a huge influence well beyond their evangelizing, for it opened up southern Nigeria to Western ideas and institutions, and it created cadres of young men and women with Western education. The Northern Region remained closed to these changes.

Throughout the colonial period the three regions were under separate administrations, and their development differed sharply. The Western Region, especially Lagos and Ibadan, was the colony's commercial and political heart. The Eastern Region, densely populated although it had no counterpart to Lagos, was the most advanced in terms of education, with Igbo filling administrative positions and manning the growing industrial sector throughout the country. The Northern Region, still under the control of the emirs, remained relatively untouched by Western education and modernization. One ethnic group was dominant in each region—the Yoruba in the west, the Igbo in the east, and the Hausa-Fulani in the north—but all three contained dozens of minority groups jealously guarding their cultures and their political influence. Regional political rivalries were institutionalized by the constitutions of the late colonial period. Thus by October 1, 1960, when Nigeria became an independent nation, it was not at all clear what it meant to be a Nigerian.

It still isn't. During the four decades since independence, economic crises and political upheavals have both distracted Nigerians from the question of what holds the country together and made the question all the more pressing. The 1960s began with intense regional political rivalry, which led to a military coup and then a countercoup in 1966, the secession of eastern Nigeria (the Republic of Biafra) in 1967, two and a half years of civil war costing a million or more lives, and the defeat and reabsorption of Biafra. During the 1970s a reunited Nigeria benefited from the Organization of Petroleum Exporting Countries (OPEC) price hike; the consequent oil boom brought Nigeria immense but unevenly distributed affluence and triggered extravagant public expenditures. The postwar military regime, jarred but not toppled by one bloodless coup and one assassination of the head of state, handed over power to the Second Republic in 1979. Nigeria appeared headed for a more stable, if imperfect, democracy, for continued oil-based prosperity, and for preeminence in African politics.

But it was not to be. The collapse of oil prices in the early 1980s, from which the petroleum-producing countries have never recovered, launched the oil bust and years of economic crises, which undermined the shaky democracy and paved the way for the military to take over again at the end of 1983. In a series of regimes since then, punctuated by successful and unsuccessful coups, various generals have all promised to restore democracy, and have all failed to do so. In 1993 the long-prepared-for transition to democracy and the Third Republic was derailed when the generals declared the presidential election of Moshood Abiola to be invalid even before all the votes were counted. The Yoruba were incensed, and in some quarters there emerged debate over whether the country would hold together.[9] The ensuing regime of Sani Abacha was more brutal and repressive than previous ones. Abacha's death in 1998, unexpected but welcomed by most Nigerians as well as by the international community, opened the possibility for Nigeria's return to democracy. At the end of February 1999, after a series of elections for lesser offices, Nigerians went to the polls and elected as their president Olusegun Obasanjo, the military ruler who had turned the government over to civilians back in 1979. As the Third Republic dawned at the end of the nineties, Nigerians' habitual and well-earned political cynicism vied with their equally habitual optimism.

Most Nigerians continue to regard their country—as they have for the past fifty years—as being "in transition." They see it in the midst of a difficult and painful labor to deliver a modern, democratic, and prosperous society. Nigerians cling to this progressive view of their country's present and future despite considerable evidence to the contrary. Their faith that the Giant of Africa will eventually assume her rightful position as the continent's dominant power—a confidence enacted at the micro level in the Nigerian reputation for arrogance toward other Africans and at a macro level in the country's repeated demand for a seat on the United Nations Security Council—irritates other Africans and exasperates the international community. Postapartheid South Africa and Nelson Mandela's immense prestige have shaken Nigerian assumptions about their continental preeminence, and many people think this explains Nigeria's end-of-the-century regional activism in Liberia and Sierra Leone.

Writers, and novelists in particular, stand among the optimistic-in-spite-of-everything Nigerians, while at the same time they are among the most persistent chroniclers of the contemporary political, economic, and moral problems. They express vast ambivalence toward their country, given all its resources and all its corruption, its frustrations and its potential. The late Ken Saro-Wiwa put into pidgin poetry their common sentiment:

> Dis Nigeria sef,
> You too bring confusion!
> How person no like you still 'e like you
> Dis no be grade one confusion?[10]

Not liking what they see but loving their country, Nigerian authors regard themselves as bearing witness to Nigeria's confusions—they used the expression "bearing witness" repeatedly when they were talking with me about the role of the novelist—in order to help bring about the transition to a better future. In attempting to understand the Nigerian novel, I am trying to see how this literary witnessing has taken place.

I will discuss methodological issues later in this chapter, but in light of the aforementioned "confusion," it seems appropriate to address the question of why the "Nigerian novel"? If Nigeria is rather new as a geopolitical entity, and if its people's identity as Nigerians is tenuous, then why use "Nigerian" to demarcate the cultural object of my study? Why not examine the West African novel, the postcolonial novel, or—making a thematic cut—the novel about women or about African city life? Any of these categorizations would be perfectly reasonable, and all have indeed been used.

There is, however, some justification for taking the country as defining the analytic unit. The first is temporal. Nigeria has been an independent state only since 1960, and the Nigerian novel is not much older. The first novel appeared in 1952, and the overwhelming majority have been published since Nigerian independence. So it happens that the "Nigerian novel" has developed in conjunction with the country itself.

The second justification for looking at the Nigerian novel is systematic: the publication and distribution of novels in Africa is largely concentrated within the borders of a single country. Rarely does fiction from one African country find its way into another, except by way of London or Paris publication. While one might expect Nigeria and Ghana, for example, to have close literary ties, multiple contacts among authors, common literary media, and much back-and-forth, in fact they do not. And if this is the case for English-language publications and writers, it is especially true where there are linguistic differences. Nigeria's closest neighbors— Togo, Cameroon, Chad—are all French-speaking, so Nigerian books do not cross the borders. A few West African novels get translated, but only a few.

The third justification is cognitive: educated Nigerians think of themselves as Nigerians. This may not be their primary allegiance when the chips are down, but it is an everyday operative identity secured by the institutions of the Nigerian state. Moreover, this pan-ethnic, cross-regional Nigerian identity is one that the novelists themselves promote. Most Nigerian authors recognize that their books are unlikely to be read in the West, or even in Anglophone Africa, but they might hope to reach all corners of Nigeria. A hundred million people or so constitute, after all, a huge market. Therefore, most novelists avoid ethnic or regional parochialism, using techniques such as populating their novels with a heterogeneous (and sometimes unlikely) cast of Nigerian characters, having their characters use slang expressions from several local languages, or setting their novels in some generic African country (e.g., "Songhai") that mixes features from different Nigerian places and peoples. In these ways they back up their claims of writing novels for all Nigerians. Publishers and editors eschew parochialism for the same reason; even though their distribution networks may not in fact penetrate all regions of the country, they aspire to do so. Finally, Nigerian readers themselves claim that they do not favor writers of their own ethnicity or books about their home regions, for while familiarity has its charms, they are curious about other Nigerian peoples. All of these members of the Nigerian literary complex, therefore, think in terms of the "Nigerian novel," and this is the most important reason to do the same.[11]

THE NOVEL

If "Nigeria" is an artificial but operationally useful designation, so is "the novel." Most people have a working sense of the novel as being a longish, written story. We assume novels to be fictitious, made up, and we require qualification like "an autobiographical novel" or "a novel based on fact" if one is not. At the same time we assume novels to be more or less realistic in terms of everyday experience, and exceptions again require qualification as in "magical realism" or "science fiction." This rough-and-ready sense of the genre corresponds to what one finds in dictionaries of literary terms. For example, one defines the novel as "a fictional prose narrative of considerable length. . . . [Earlier long prose narratives lacked] the realism, the coherently unified plots, and the psychological consideration of character that are usually—though not all of them invariably—characteristic of the modern novel." Another states that "the term 'novel' is now applied to a great variety of writings that have in common only the attribute of being extended works of fiction written in prose." This criterion of novels being realistic, plausible, or true to everyday experience—"about recognizable characters with recognizable problems"—is routinely applied by the average reader of fiction.[12]

During the late seventeenth and early eighteenth centuries, the English novel, which was to become the universally acknowledged model for the genre, took on its ultimate form, slowly and unevenly distinguishing itself from other long prose genres such as the chivalric romance.[13] This "rise of the novel" was the subject of Ian Watt's 1957 study, which has become the point of reference for all subsequent work on the origins of the genre. Watt argued that by the mid–eighteenth century, the novel had stabilized around the convention of "formal realism," which refers to a set of narrative procedures such that

> the novel is a full and authentic report of human experience, and is therefore under an obligation to satisfy its reader with such details of the story as the individuality of the actors concerned, the particulars of the times and places of their actions, details which are presented through a more largely referential use of language than is common in other literary forms. . . . [Formal realism] allows a more immediate imitation of individual experience set in its temporal and spatial environment than do other literary forms. Consequently the novel's conventions make much smaller demands on the audience than do most literary conventions. . . . (32)

Formal realism is viable as a literary mode only in a society characterized by individualism, a society that both offers a wide variety of economic, political, and personal options and supports the belief that each person should be free to make his or her own choices. Following Max Weber's "Protestant ethic" thesis, Watt located the roots of English individualism in the ascetic Protestantism characteristic of English commercial groups during the early modern period. The ascent of the genre that embodied individualism as a formal principle thus coincided with the rise of the middle class, in particular those urban middle-class women and their servants who had sufficient leisure and literacy to partake of the novel's "smaller demands."

More recent scholarship, while paying homage to Watt with respect to his emphasis on the social context of literary forms, has tended to regard this process of separation, generic definition, and finally stabilization of the novel's characteristic features as more gradual and uneven than he suggested.[14] In addition, the stabilization may not have been around a single characteristic. J. Paul Hunter maintains that no one essential feature like realism or individualism or character separates the novel from the romance or from any other genre. Instead, novels manifest a combination of several distinguishing characteristics, with no single prerequisite. This bundle of attributes includes (1) contemporaneity; (2) credibility and probability; (3) familiarity; (4) rejection of traditional plots; (5) tradition-free language; (6) individualism and subjectivity; (7) empathy and vicariousness; (8) coherence, unity of design; (9) some degree of digressiveness, fragmentation; (10) self-consciousness innovation.[15] Works that exhibit most of these attributes are generally regarded as being novels, even though no single attribute is a prerequisite. Most Nigerian novels indeed do exhibit most of the characteristics from Hunter's list. Works that do not, such as Amos Tutuola's Yoruba fantasies, provoke the criticism that they are not *really* novels.

What is the "African" novel? Are we to think of a book as being a novel, first and foremost, but one that happens to be written by an African, or as an expression of African culture, first and foremost, but one that happens to take the form of a novel? To frame the research as investigating how Nigerian writers have transformed the novel, as I have done, implies that the Nigerian novel derives from the Western model. One could frame the issue quite differently, however, by asking, How has Nigerian narrative been transformed by its incorporation in the novel format? This would make Nigerian narrative the starting point. Even if "the novel" rather than "narrative" or "the story" is taken as the unit of analysis whose transformation is under consideration, as in this study, one needs to be aware that there is sharp disagreement over the relative influences of Western and African culture on this transformed cultural object.

Critics discussing the African-ness of the African novel divide roughly into three groups. The universalists maintain that African fiction treats the human condition and that it should be evaluated no differently than fiction from anyplace else. The traditionalists stress a specifically African aesthetic, interpreted as a cultural conjunction of racial and historical elements. And the neo-Marxists, regarding the first two as just different forms of idealism, emphasize the social and economic context of African literary production.

In his book *The Growth of the African Novel* (1979), Sierra Leonean critic Eustace Palmer makes the case for the universalists. Arguing that Western standards of literary evaluation can and should be applied to the African novel, Palmer holds that unlike poetry or drama, which were established indigenous genres, the African novel developed out of the Western novel. Disagreeing with critics who see the "African experience" as fundamental to the African novel, Palmer contends that such "sociological" viewpoints have more to do with nationalism and ideology than with literary criticism. Along the same lines, he plays down the influence of oral literature:

> A detailed examination of the forms and structures of the earliest African novels like Achebe's *Things Fall Apart*, Laye's *The Radiance of the King* or Ekwensi's *People of the City* would reveal that they could not possibly be outgrowths of the oral tale. . . . The African novel grew out of the western novel, and writers like Achebe, Laye, and Ekwensi were much more influenced by Conrad, Hardy, Dickens, Kafka and George Eliot than by the African oral tale. They had all of them been exposed to western literature during their student days. . . . African novelists have modified the genre largely in the direction of themes, language, setting and point of view. But this does not suggest that it is basically different from the western and that entirely different criteria should therefore be used in its evaluation. . . . (5–6)

Having forcefully argued that "in the business of criticism we are primarily concerned with the work in front of us, not with its background," Palmer concedes that there is no necessary opposition between sociological and artistic (formalist) criticism. The alternative to an either-or position is "a criticism which evaluates the literary quality of the work and also discusses the novelist's concern with and treatment of real issues that are relevant to the lives of the people. . . . criticism of African fiction should take into account both the relevance of the work to the human condition (the sociological, if one prefers the term) and the novelist's artistry" (8–9). This is roughly the position held by Wole Soyinka, who, while making use of traditional Yoruba folklore, denies any African essentialism, as in his well-known dismissal of Négritude that tigers didn't have to go around proclaiming their tigritude.

Indeed, the Négritude movement, developed by Senegalese Léopold Senghor and West Indian Aimé Césaire, is probably the best-known example of the traditionalist approach to African literature. Although the movement was based in the Francophone community, Chinua Achebe, Abiola Irelele, and Chinweizu are three well-known Nigerian critics who, despite their differences, share much of Négritude's emphasis on African roots, the oral tradition, and a particular African way of seeing and thinking that shapes literature. Chinweizu and his colleagues advocating the "decolonization of African literature" regard universalism as simply kowtowing to Western models. To such traditionalists, someone like Palmer is irredeemably Eurocentric. In this regard, they have scathing things to say about Soyinka, whom they see as one of the "euromodernists, who have assiduously aped the practices of 20th-century European modernist poetry."[16] Thus when a reviewer linked Soyinka's difficult language to Yoruba poetics, they retort, "Soyinka's obscurantism, however, would seem more readily explainable in terms of his fidelity to the Hopkinsian butchery of English syntax and semantics, and to his deliberate choice of Shakespearean and other archaisms as models for his poetic diction."[17] Kenyan author-critic Ngũgĩ wa Thiong'o, probably the best known scourge of cultural colonialism, goes so far as to argue that "African literature can only be written in African languages."[18] This is a point of view not all traditionalists hold, although the critic and novelist Kole Omotoso has suggested that Nigerians end their linguistic division by all learning Swahili, despite the fact that it is spoken nowhere in West Africa.[19]

On the other hand, the neo-Marxist critic Chidi Amuta rejects all such forms of traditionalism, not to mention the universalism of someone like Palmer, as idealist denial of the historical context in which literature is produced and consumed.[20] He dismisses as traditionalists all those who posit an undifferentiated African cultural past, those who embrace "a narrow ethnocentric particularism which distills the aesthetic values of a particular ethnic culture and uses information derived therefrom to pronounce on the general pre-colonial African situation." He likewise excoriates the "Neo-Négritude polemics" that sees cultural decolonization as primarily an aesthetic matter, divorcing the cultural from the political and economic. He takes "traditional rulers" as his example: "In present day Nigeria, for instance, the institution of traditional rulership has been selected and decreed into a national imperative by successive military governments since the Mohammed/Obasanjo era. Accordingly, that institution has recruited into it all manner of middlemen, petty contractors, foreign exchange racketeers, etc. and these have suddenly been consecrated by the ruling class into custodians of traditional morality whose 'fatherly' counsel is badly needed" (42). Amuta contends that the African traditionalists have inadvertently constructed their own "great tradition." This works to the disadvantage of writers like the late Senegalese feminist Mariama Bâ, whose writing not only is not derived from African tradition but also rejects much of this tradition, especially its gender roles, quite explicitly. Amuta advocates honoring the specific historical particularities, conceived of as relationships of power and class conflict, in which an African literary form is produced. In the case of the novel, for example, while Achebe and Chinweizu emphasize roots in oral tradition, Amuta argues that the novel depends on printing as its material basis. While its physical format is Western, however, its essence is not; he points out, for example, that African novels give primacy to the action of the community over that of the individual.

The three schools of thought regarding the African novel rely on somewhat different theories of cultural transformation. Fearing cultural domination from the West, traditionalists urge African writers and critics to resist foreign encroachments on an African aesthetic. While Marxists are also concerned about domination, they draw upon a modernization model in their analysis of emergent class relationships under industrialization. Universalists agree with much of modernization theory and focus on the cultural logic of what the novel can and should do, as when Palmer stresses that criticism must treat "real issues that are relevant to the lives of the people," which, as Watt and Hunter point out, has been a defining characteristic of the genre all along. Moreover, the universalists' stress on "literary quality" is itself based on an evolutionary logic.

This is not a work of literary criticism, so I have only sketched these different positions enough so they will be recognizable. Nigerian writers and readers can not help but participate in this debate, if only implicitly. Most of them, as a matter of fact, take a relaxed view that Nigerian novels respond to both Western and African influences, and that these novels have themes that are both local and universal. Nigerian novels bear witness to the Nigerian condition, they maintain, but this condition is a particular historical specification of global influences and human nature.

To Understand

Let us assume, then, that there is something we can call the Nigerian novel. How do we go about understanding it? How can we see what happens when a literary genre formed in one society is transported to and reconstructed in another?

First of all, we must recognize that the notion of a people and their culture constituting an expressive Gemeinschaft uncontaminated by outside influences, an image that has always been misleading, is blatantly untenable in the postmodern era of telecommunications, international culture markets, and the incessant mobility of intellectuals. Recall the summary of *The Last Chance* at the beginning of this chapter. In that novel, Francis Falemara may have written about a traditional Yoruba village like the one he was born in, but he also has studied marine engineering in England; has made sports tours as a champion boxer to Ghana, Tunisia, Egypt, and Finland; and is married to an Indian. He lives in an expensive area of Festac Town in Lagos, drives a Mercedes, and is a vegetarian, a Hindu, and a devotee of Hare Krishna. His view of Yoruba traditions is that of an insider, an indigene of Ondo State, but also that of a cosmopolitan, a citizen of the world. Falemara is singular, but his combination of global and local orientations is not unusual.

A global cultural transfer occurs when cultural production centers, including the capitals of former colonial empires as well as certain other metropolises of the United States, Europe, and Asia, turn out cultural objects that are exported to and appropriated by cultural consumers in the developing world.[21] Local cultural producers then re-create the cultural objects in ways that both resemble the originals and are markedly different from them. Therefore, one empirical question motivating this study is, How does an established cultural object, the English novel, get reconstructed in a new social context like Nigeria?

One may think about such a question by drawing upon theories of modernization, cultural domination, resistance, organization, and genre. Modernization holds that as a society industrializes, its members undergo certain predictable changes in their values, preoccupations, substantive concerns, and ways of living.[22] In a modernizing society, emergent cultural forms deal with individualism, entrepreneurial effort, and the defiance of traditionally prescribed social roles, for such topics reflect the new experiences that are on people's minds. Cultural convergence takes place, at least to some extent, for societies that undergo that cluster of transformations called modernization—usually taken to include industrialization, urbanization, increased literacy and education, and extensive economic and cultural interaction with the outside world—will produce similar cultural representations.

Novels do tend to appear and flourish in a modernizing society. Since becoming modern involves a population shift from the countryside to urban centers, the theory suggests that modernizing societies will produce novels about young people from the countryside struggling to succeed in the city, like Tayo bound for Lagos with his fresh degree in creative writing.[23] Here we see the convergence idea: a common process, undergone by different societies at different times, generates common literary forms and themes. Novels, from this standpoint, reflect and represent the social experience of modernization in a rather straightforward way.

Theories of cultural domination, which regard any belief in simple representation as naive, contend that the cultural impact from the West overwhelms local cultural traditions in the Third World. The terminology used by the two schools of thought is telling: Modernization theory talks about developed and developing countries, suggesting the temporal linearity of its conception, while domination theory talks about the West and the Third World, or center and periphery, suggesting asymmetrical power relationships and cultural imperialism.[24] The domination approach often asserts cultural hegemony, which holds that cultural producers and consumers freely make the choices that perpetuate their own subordination. Because Western imports mold the expectations of local audiences, because Western media inform local artists and producers, and because imported technologies carry ideological implications (e.g., that the proper place to watch television is at home, not in a community center), Third World cultural producers and consumers reproduce Western models indefinitely.

In the case of novels, while modernization theory predicts that developing societies will write fiction reflecting the social changes they are undergoing, cultural domination/hegemony theory contends that intellectual and organizational influences from the metropolitan centers have penetrated the postcolonial periphery so that they simply reproduce the centers' literary conventions.[25] Third World writers reproduce canons, practices, and fashions from the West—just like those miniskirts that Tayo and Lenuse argue about—regardless of their applicability to local conditions. This is the essence of cultural neocolonialism.

Some less pessimistic observers focus on resistance, the persistent viability of local cultural traditions and practices, and (especially) people's capacity to subvert foreign or oppressive influences.[26] In the case of Nigerian popular fiction, this approach would emphasize the autonomous roles of Nigerian creators (writers) and/or consumers (readers) in shaping the distinctive characteristics of the local fiction.[27] Postcolonial theory is a type of resistance approach that draws attention to how the interplay of neocolonial pressures and local resistance to these pressures produces new forms, mutant syntheses, in something like "the Nigerian novel."[28]

Organizational and generic influences, the fourth and fifth starting points for thinking about cultural transfers and transformations, can be called cultural logic arguments. Such approaches hold that social changes or neocolonial impositions are mediated by influences more closely related to the cultural object itself. An organizational argument maintains that the system of production and distribution of cultural products plays a key role in shaping the form and content of the cultural objects in question. Industrial and market imperatives of mass-produced cultural objects, for example, push the homogenization and standardization of such objects toward a widely acceptable, inoffensive, and noncritical norm.[29] In the case of publishing, since unit costs are low relative to the initial investment, publishers must produce and sell large quantities of a given novel in order to make a profit. This market logic would nudge Nigerian novels away from anything too local, too Nigerian, or even too African, and toward some presumably universal themes. Jagan and Tayo might be Yoruba, for instance, but they mustn't be *too* Yoruba, for they have to appeal to a non-Yoruba readership as well.

Generic approaches focus attention on the logic intrinsic to the genre itself. Different genres have different requirements, and thus the cultural transfer and transformation of one kind of genre will be different from another. In the present case, the suggestion would be that the most important influence on postcolonial writers is neither modernization per se nor pressures from international centers of power (or resistance to these), but rather the formal characteristics of "the novel." Novels everywhere respond to the genre's imperatives: novels are written, not told; prose, not poetry or drama; long, so not usually read on a single occasion; mass-produced and mass-consumed, not restricted to an elite literati; read in private, not recited in public; and read by one person at a time, not by a group.[30] Technical characteristics pertaining to print and literacy in general, and to the novel as a long, popular prose form in particular, mean that novels anywhere will focus on individual protagonists, explore the interior sensibilities of middle-class people, and have distinct narrative structures of coherent developing action leading toward a definitive conclusion.[31]

Although these theories—modernization, domination, resistance, and organizational or generic logic—are not mutually exclusive, they do offer different accounts of how the novel would be reconstructed in Africa, and they suggest different readings of a work like *The Last Chance*. Modernization theory would focus on Tayo as a "homeless mind" struggling against the claims of tradition to enter the modern sector, while postcolonial theory would focus on the wily Jagan as a trickster who can muster magic, emotion, information networks, and insight into human behavior to achieve her objectives.[32] Domination theory would claim that focusing on any one protagonist is a Western, individualistic approach to begin with, while generic determinism would reply that since novels —unlike poems, plays, riddles, songs—are individually written and read, their focus on individuals is neither surprising nor politically suspect. And organizational theorists might say that all this misses the point, for the really significant characteristics of *The Last Chance* are that the book is short, inexpensively produced, and focused on the problems of young people, who constitute the core of the Nigerian fiction market.

Taken alone, any of these theories would be both culturally crude and sociologically inadequate.[33] While they are useful for generating hypotheses about the reconstruction of the Western novel in Nigeria, we must never lose sight of the fact that Nigerians are not puppets in the hands of some cultural ventriloquist. All culture is local culture, in the sense that culture exists only through the interpretations of human minds and the practices of human actors, and this is especially the case for such concrete cultural objects as novels.[34] In other words, Nigerians tell their own tales.

To try to understand these tales and their tellers in terms of both local culture and global flows, therefore, is not to privilege transnational processes or local ones but to comprehend both. The investigator of global cultural processes and their local manifestations must move among the various levels of analysis. Understanding Nigerian fiction involves looking at an interacting complex of levels—individual (e.g., people who write novels and people who read them); organizational (e.g., Nigerian book selling); national (e.g., military regimes and their attitudes toward writers); cross-national (e.g., the impact of British publishing on Nigerian writing); worldwide (e.g., fluctuations in oil prices)—that influence cultural objects. Since my theoretical ambition has been to understand connections among the multiple and interacting contexts of the Nigerian novel, my methods have addressed these multiple levels.

I have used a framework for cultural analysis, which I set out some years ago in a journal devoted to methodological issues, that combines interpretive and institutional methods.[35] My approach involves the following:

1. Specification of the characteristics of the cultural object in question

2. Delineation of genres to which the object does and does not belong, as well as subgenres of the object itself

3. Assessment of the producers of the cultural object, their social characteristics, their organization, and their circumstances, intentions, and conventions at the time of production/creation

4. Assessment of the recipients of the cultural object, their social characteristics, and their expectations

5. Consideration of the mechanisms of production and consumption, such as markets, that connect producing and receiving agents

6. Consideration of the local culture, and of the proximate and remote historical circumstances of the various agents that may be relevant to the cultural object in question

7. Forming explanatory hypotheses and making comparisons to assess their validity[36]

I begin with the cultural object of interest: the Nigerian novel. One of the immense advantages Nigeria has for someone wishing to understand the reconstruction of the genre in a new context is its combination of newness and abundance. The first Nigerian novel in English, Amos Tutuola's *The Palm-Wine Drinkard,* was published less than half a century ago; I was able to interview Tutuola, who has since died. The vast majority of subsequent novels have been published in the past twenty-five years, and most of the authors and editors involved are active and accessible. At the same time, Nigeria has produced well over 500 novels, so the literary output is large enough to permit quantitative as well as interpretive analysis. It was feasible for me to try and look at the entire population of these novels rather than at a sample, something that would not be possible if the population had been much larger. Of course during my research the number of novels has grown; a bibliography published by myself and a colleague in 1990 included only 433 titles.[37] I have not wanted to cut off the collection of novels at any predetermined point, although my list of titles probably underrepresents books published after the early nineties.

In attempting to lay out the entire population of Nigerian novels, I have had to set some limits on what would and would not count. What is a Nigerian novel? Should one include any novel about or set in Nigeria? What about a novel written by a Nigerian-by-birth but set elsewhere? Or one written by a Briton-turned-Nigerian citizen or a Nigerian immigrant to Britain? As a practical matter I have considered any novel written by someone born or permanently resident in Nigeria to be a Nigerian novel, regardless of whether the story is about Nigeria, but one could set different criteria.

Another consideration is the age of the intended reader. In seeking adult fiction, I want to exclude books aimed at young children but not those read by secondary school students, since these largely overlap with adult reading. My rule of thumb has been to reject books that were explicitly directed toward the Nigerian primary (ages seven through twelve) or junior secondary school (thirteen through fifteen) level, or that include the paraphernalia of a reading textbook, such as study questions at the end of each chapter or a glossary of common English words. For my purposes, drawing the line between junior and senior secondary school age students had the additional advantage of corresponding roughly with the fifteen-and-over cutoff point that UNESCO uses in its estimates of "adult" readers.[38]

I consider only books that are over sixty pages in length to be novels. This rule excludes most chapbooks of the Onitsha market pamphlet sort.[39] In spite of these various inclusion criteria, a number of cases required somewhat ad hoc decisions. Okafor Azikiwe's 1977 book *Gifts for Mother*, for example, was a close call. The book is short (sixty-four pages) and concerns a wayward child and his long-suffering mother; it also has some pictures, though no study questions. On the other hand, it treats a number of adult themes, including infertility, parental frustrations leading to near infanticide, polygamy, and relationships between co-wives, between husbands and wives, and between parents and children. An introductory paragraph says it is intended for "secondary school use." I included it as a novel in my population, but such a book is clearly on the borderline.

The list of Nigerian novels I have put together is found in Appendix A. Sources for this compilation include the *African Book Publishing Record*; direct correspondence with Nigerian authors and with both English and Nigerian publishers; perusal of major African literature collections in American university libraries, particularly that of Northwestern University's Herskovits Africana Library; Professor Bernth Lindfors, a leading scholar of African literature, who generously gave me access to his extensive collection; and numerous trips to booksellers in Lagos, Ibadan, Minna, and (on the part of anthropologist Misty Bastian) Enugu and Onitsha. This list undoubtedly underrepresents novels published in Nigeria by small publishers or by the author himself or herself; this group is less likely to have been reported to Hans Zell for the *African Book Publishing Record*. The list is most comprehensive through the early 1990s, getting spottier (and more biased toward the major publishers) thereafter. I do not include any novels written in indigenous languages. As noted in the next chapter, there are only a handful of these, and they do not fit my definition of "Nigerian novels," since they are accessible to few Nigerians outside of a single ethnic group.

For each title so identified, I attempted to locate a copy. Again my success at doing so was higher for those novels published by British or the larger Nigerian publishers. In the list in Appendix A I have indicated those titles for which I never located a copy. Some of these may never have been published (e.g., some titles came from advertisements on other books by that publisher, where the line between forthcoming and actually published is sometimes obscured for promotional reasons), and of those that do exist, some might turn out not to be novels. Of the titles on my original list, a fair number turned out not to be novels. The 476 true novels I was able to locate and read, and their 261 authors, are the core of my analysis.

Once I found a copy of what was a Nigerian novel according to my criteria, I read it and summarized its content. These initial summaries recorded my impressions of the novel's plot, characters, and style. In the cases of novels that struck me as complex or especially significant in some respect, I prepared a detailed summary, ranging from a short paragraph of 200 words or so to several pages, and including both a synopsis and my own reactions to and comments on the novel. Chukwuemeka Ike's complex novel of political discussion, *The Search*, generated a 2,200-word summary, but this is one of the longest; the average was closer to 500 to 600 words. The synopses used throughout this book, for example, the summary of *The Last Chance* that opened this chapter, are edited versions of the raw summaries.[40]

After writing the summaries, I coded each novel according to a number of characteristics pertaining to the protagonist, the plot, and the central themes, so as to allow for subsequent generalizations and comparisons. The coding form is reproduced in Appendix C. Then I transferred the coding to a spreadsheet program (Microsoft Excel) to facilitate comparison and statistical analysis.

The second type of data I collected in my effort to understand the novel in Nigeria was information—direct and indirect—about the 261 novelists themselves. I pieced together published information on every novelist from biographies, published interviews, standard collections like Zell, Bundy, and Coloun's indispensable *New Reader's Guide to African Literature*, and—in many cases this was the only source of information—what was written on the back covers or in the front matter of the novels themselves.

I coded information about the authors that seemed pertinent, such as their sex, ethnicity, religion, and nonliterary occupations and again transferred this coding to an Excel spreadsheet. Appendix B lists the authors, and Appendix C shows the coding forms.

I tried to contact those authors whose locations I could determine, and I sent them a lengthy, open-ended questionnaire on their backgrounds, their literary and extraliterary careers, and their beliefs about the role of the Nigerian writer. I draw extensively on the responses to this questionnaire, for the novelists were exceedingly generous with their time and thoughts. During three trips to Nigeria, I met with over fifty writers, supplementing the previously gathered information with interviews lasting an average of two hours each. I have continued to stay in contact with some of the authors, and again they have been patient in answering my many follow-up questions.

A third type of data involves publishing, including both publishing operations within Nigeria and foreign publishers of Nigerian novels, especially in Britain. In addition to the invaluable information provided by the *African Book Publishing Record* and by a useful though short-lived periodical for the Nigerian book trade called *Books,* I corresponded with a number of Nigerian and British publishers regarding their experience with Nigerian novels. I also interviewed editors who worked with Nigerian fiction in London, Lagos, and Ibadan.

The fourth type of data was about readers: who they are, how they read, how they interpret what they read. I put together what is known about readers and reading in Nigeria and drew comparisons with what is known about reading in the West. I asked the Nigerian authors about their own reading habits, and I asked both authors and publishers about who they understood their readers to be.

Then, in my pursuit of the Nigerian reader, I did two things. First conceptually, although last in execution as it turned out, I decided to meet with some Nigerian readers in Lagos to discuss their reading habits, histories, and preferences. When my planned visit to Nigeria in the spring of 1994 had to be postponed, I put out a notice on the "Naijanet," an Internet mailing list of Nigerians living outside of Nigeria itself. This list had about six hundred subscribers at the time, and still does, although the membership is constantly changing. I asked for people who would be willing to discuss their reading histories and practices to contact me. A core group of readers replied via e-mail, answering a series of questions and numerous follow-up queries. These faithful correspondents are by no means representative of Nigerians as a whole—they are far more highly educated, for one thing, since many were graduate students or faculty at foreign universities—but they do more closely represent those adult Nigerians who continue to be readers after their youth.

In Nigeria itself I was able to conduct face-to-face interviews with readers of two types: (1) some who were directly involved in the book trade, including publishers, bookstore managers, and the authors themselves; and (2) some who were strictly consumers of fiction rather than producers. This latter group corresponds to those contacted through the Naijanet, although they represent a somewhat wider educational range. Most of these interviews were conducted in Lagos.

I have used these various sources of data and insights to put together a picture of the Nigerian literary complex. I am not calling it a literary system, for that would imply a smoothly functioning interrelationship of components, something distinctly absent in the Nigerian case. Instead it is a complex, consisting of multiple parts that do not fit together very well. It is a complex that is global as well as local, one in which a wealthy, vegetarian, retired policeman with an Indian wife writes about manipulating mothers in the village and girls wearing miniskirts in the city as he explores the transformations Nigeria has been experiencing. In this complex, Nigerians have been reconstructing the novel, using both Nigerian and Western blueprints, to make money, to entertain, to instruct, to influence, to celebrate their country's cultural diversity and potential, and to bear witness to its problems.

Chapter 2

THE NIGERIAN FICTION COMPLEX

Living with wealthy grandparents in Lagos while her parents work in the Eastern Region, Remi is the pet of her eccentric relatives and of their servants, who sometimes spirit her off on clandestine expeditions for magic charms. At a wedding someone remarks, "No snake is more sinuous than a Yoruba girl dancing." But when Grandpa dies, six-year-old Remi is torn from this privileged world and sent to England for her education.

Her school years are miserable: grim teachers, bad food, and sudden outbursts of racism. She spends her holidays with Aunt Betty's working-class family; at school her elocution teacher warns her not to say "Thornton 'eath" the way they do. Remi entertains friends with lore learned from Tarzan films—my father wears leopard skins and eats snake soup—but prefers games in which color isn't a factor ("Martians, as everybody knew, were green").

After several years, Remi's parents visit and are amazed by Remi's transformation into an English girl. Starting high school, she now spends holidays with ex-missionaries, for "my father wanted me to be in a more educative environment"; this suits Remi, who has turned into "a proper little snob." During one such visit some Jamaican women disillusion her by telling her Jamaica is like England and not at all like Africa. She goes on a student exchange to Germany, where her hosts think Africans are savages and make crude sexual overtures.

Such experiences confirm her dawning awareness that Europeans don't regard her as the typical English girl she has tried to become. After finishing school, she prepares to study law at the university. She takes up with a group of African and Indian youth, acquiring a Nigerian boyfriend and a sense of solidarity with other Commonwealth students who poke fun at English parochialism. While dancing at a party she hears a woman again remark, "Is there a sight more beautiful . . . than a Yoruba girl dancing?"

(Simi Bedford, *Yoruba Girl Dancing*)

IS *YORUBA GIRL DANCING* a Nigerian novel? Certainly: Simi Bedford is a Nigerian woman who wrote this semi-autobiographical novel about the experience of the Nigerian "been-to" (a daughter or son of an elite family who has been to Britain for schooling). In addition, the first third of the novel takes place in Nigeria. On the other hand, Bedford has lived in London since her childhood, an English publisher brought out

Yoruba Girl Dancing, the book was extensively discussed in the British and American press but not the Nigerian one, and it is virtually unavailable and unknown in Nigeria.

Most contemporary Nigerians, even the been-to elite represented in Bedford's novel, have no access to or knowledge of *Yoruba Girl Dancing.* British and American readers are more likely to have heard of the book, for it was widely reviewed. In this sense *Yoruba Girl Dancing* is a postmodern cultural object, a set of signs largely cut adrift from that which it signifies. Such a gap between culture and experience is not altogether new. Turn-of-the-century sociologist Georg Simmel worried about the separation of objective culture from subjective meanings, which he called the tragedy of modern culture. Under postmodernity, however, such a gap is no longer seen as tragic but simply as inevitable. Indeed, this type of rupture may be seen as both product and producer of the cultural hybridization celebrated by scholars of postcolonialism.[1]

It may be, however, that the notion of an increasing gap between culture and experience—for example, a novel and the social context that has produced it—derives from a misleading sense of the close relationship, the tight embrace, that normally obtains between a society and its cultural objects. ("Hybridity" also implies a preexisting state of genetic purity.) The tightness of the embrace is, after all, an empirical question. We can think of the relationship between culture and society as being relatively closed or relatively open. An image of relative closure characterizes Clifford Geertz's well-known analysis of the Balinese cockfight as "a Balinese reading of Balinese experience, a story they tell themselves about themselves." Such a story prompts in-depth interpretive analysis—"thick description"—in search of local meaning, and that meaning involves how the cultural object reflects social experience and how social practices reflect culture. While this way of viewing the culture-society relationship does not assume that relationship is frozen, it does imply a fairly steady state whereby *the* culture reflects *the* society and vice versa.[2] When a non-Nigerian thinks about the Nigerian novel, it is especially tempting to rely on a reflection model: the Nigerian novel reflects a West African worldview, or the experience of its authors, or the concerns of its readers, or the lingering cultural domination of the West, or the rejection of such domination. Indeed three of the cultural transformation theories (modernization, domination, and postcolonial resistance) strongly suggest reflection along these lines.

The idea of literature as a mirror of life has been around since Plato and is hard to avoid. Nor should we. There is undoubtedly something right about it: Distortions and all, surely novels do reflect actual or ideal social experience. At the same time, the globalization of culture means that the relationship between people and cultural objects is an obviously open one (it was probably never closed), penetrated by flows of resources, ideas, and people from outside the society, whose borders are artificial anyway. If anything is reflected, it is movement itself.

Yoruba girls dancing with fellow law students at posh London parties are just as representative of Nigerian realities as Yoruba girls dancing with their age-mates at village harvest festivals. Contemporary Nigerians live in Thornton 'eath as well as in Enugu. They seek professional careers in the city, and they seek juju charms. They are at home in a London bed-sitter and in the stalls of an open-air African market; perhaps they are not fully at home in either. While some Nigerian novels are about farmers living in villages, more are about crime in Ibadan, traffic jams in Lagos, romance in Kano, and loneliness in Hampstead.

Moreover, envisioning a simple one-to-one correspondence of the superstructure-reflects-base sort—Nigerian fiction reflects Nigerian life—takes insufficient account of agency: purposive people who as authors, editors, booksellers, or readers act as the decision makers who shape genres. These people are located in a multilevel cultural complex that spans the globe, from a reviewer in London to a printer in Hong Kong to some country cousins crowded into an Onitsha sitting room whose loud conversation is driving a reader crazy. Human actors shape all cultural objects, including Balinese cockfights—they certainly shape the Nigerian novel—and we must avoid any assumptions about mutual societal-cultural reflection that neglect human agency.

So we need to understand the actions of people and the movement of cultural objects in our exploration of the Nigerian novel. We need to ask, Who writes these books? How is the literary production—publication, markets, distribution—organized? Who reads the novels, and to what effect? These three questions organize Part II of the present study.[3] By addressing the three organizing questions—who writes Nigerian novels, how are they published and distributed, and who reads them—I am trying to map something like what Howard Becker has described as an "art world." Art worlds "consist of all the people whose activities are necessary to the production of the characteristic works which that world, and perhaps others as well, define as art." Members coordinate activities through "a body of conventional understandings embodied in common practice and in frequently used artifacts. The same people often cooperate repeatedly, even routinely, in similar ways to produce similar works, so that we can think of an art world as an established network of cooperative links among participants."[4] It is these people, their practices, their works, their understanding of what a Nigerian novel is, that I am seeking to understand. And I want to watch them working without imposing any assumptions about whether they are subjects of or insurrectionists against cultural domination; masters of or slaves to market and generic forces; agents of modernity, preservers of premodernity, outriders of postmodernity, or tricksters laughing at all such historical typifications.

I will not talk about the "world" of the Nigerian novel, however, for that suggests boundaries (the New World, the underworld, the Third World). Both as a cultural object and as set of interacting entities, the borders of Nigerian novel are too open for such an image to be apt. Likewise, I am uneasy with thinking in terms of a Nigerian literary system, for "system" implies too much integration, too smooth an articulation of parts. Instead I see the people involved with Nigerian novels as constituting a complex— what we might call the Nigerian fiction complex—made up of poorly integrated parts, of markets and organizations that are simultaneously global and parochial, with people entering and exiting all the time. They are not "a world," but they are subject to a "world culture" that defines what a novel is.[5]

The Nigerian fiction complex contains all sorts of people. It includes the teenager in Benin City reading a romance novel as a break from her studies, the doctor in Lagos wishing he could find more time for his writing, the editor in London trying to anticipate the growth of the African book market, the Ogoni author languishing in prison for advocating minority rights, the military ruler imprisoning him, the bookstore proprietor in Ibadan selling more works by Frederick Forsyth than by Buchi Emecheta, the American teacher including Emecheta's novels in a course on black women writers. It is these people and their engagement with the Nigerian novel that we seek to understand. We must look at who they are, what they are doing, and what they think about the literary complex they support.

THE NOVELS

"My father got eight children and I was the eldest among them, all the rest were hard workers, but I myself was an expert palm-wine drinkard. I was drinking palm-wine from morning till night and from night till morning. By that time I could not drink ordinary water at all except palm-wine." The son of the richest man in town, the narrator entertains his friends all day, and his indulgent father has hired him his own palm-wine tapster to provide for his gargantuan thirst. But when the tapster dies in a fall from a tree, the young man loses his former popularity and goes off searching for the tapster.

The Drinkard has a series of adventures, such as when he follows the "complete gentleman" who removes his various body parts, all rented from their rightful owners, and turns out to be nothing but a Skull. When he rescues a lady from the Skull family, her father gives her to him as a wife. She accompanies him through his travels, at one point giving birth to a monstrous baby through her thumb.

After ten years, they reach the Deads' Town, where everyone walks backward, and find the tapster. He tells them he cannot return with them because deads cannot mix with alives—"everything that [deads] were doing there was incorrect to alives and everything that all alives were doing was incorrect to deads too." On the way back home the couple acquires an egg that provides endless food. Recklessness destroys the egg; once again the Drinkard's friends abandon him when he can't provide food. A famine ensues, ending only after elaborate sacrifices.

(Amos Tutuola, *The Palm-Wine Drinkard*)

Amos Tutuola's *The Palm-Wine Drinkard*, published in 1952, was the first Nigerian novel, or so say most participants in the Nigerian fiction complex. It is a controversial claim, as we shall see, for some say it is not a novel, and others say it was not the first. Regardless of whether we accept *The Palm-Wine Drinkard*'s conventional status as the first Nigerian novel, it was hardly the first major literary work by a Nigerian.

Writing did not arrive in Nigeria with Tutuola, nor with nineteenth-century Protestant missionaries clutching their Bibles. Although the Nigerian novel is only some fifty years old, the written word has been in Nigeria for at least a thousand years. Northern Nigerian towns were the southern depots of trans-Saharan trade routes, so by A.D. 1000 Arabic was being put to religious and commercial uses in that region. While the Arabic language was confined to religious texts, local writers used Arabic letters to represent local languages, especially Hausa; such writing is called *ajami*. Poems, chronicles, and histories were written this way, although not fiction as we know it.[6]

The *ajami* tradition, although it has not completely died out to this day, was not to dominate Nigerian writing, however. During the centuries when commercial contacts, the slave trade, and, especially, colonialism pressed on West Africa, the Roman alphabet became the standard for inscribing local languages. It was here that the role of Christian missions loomed large. Protestant missionaries who wanted to win African converts made a point of learning African languages and establishing orthographies, into which they could then translate the Bible and religious literature like *The Pilgrim's Progress*. Nigerian church leaders did the same. For example, Bishop Samuel Ajai Crowther (1806–91) was an ex-slave who became a Yoruba convert to Christianity and a CMS missionary. During his long career Crowther wrote a Yoruba dictionary, five school primers, a full translation of the Bible, and a translation of *The Pilgrim's Progress*, and it was his influence that standardized written Yoruba along the line of the Oyo dialect.

Yoruba is the most widespread written indigenous language in Nigeria. By the early decades of the twentieth century, numerous Yoruba newspapers and periodicals, as well as ethnically based cultural societies, promoted reading and writing in their native tongue for the colonial elite. Most of these people spoke English as well, especially since the colonial elite was to a large extent descended from repatriated British and American slaves who had come to Nigeria via Sierra Leone, and promoters of Yoruba writing had to counter the Anglophile tendencies of this group.[7]

The first novelette in Yoruba—which we may take as the first fiction that approaches my definition of a novel —was published in 1929 after it had appeared as a serial in a Lagos newspaper.[8] Written by Isaac Babalola Thomas, it was a story of a fallen woman entitled *Sègilolá elé yinjú ege*, or *Segilola, Woman of Ensnaring Eyeballs*. The first full-length Yoruba novel, *Ogbójú ode nínú igbó irúnmalè*, was written (typically enough) by a church-school headmaster, D. O. Fagunwa, and published in 1938. This quest tale, which Wole Soyinka translated into English in 1968 as *The Forest of a Thousand Daemons*, was so well received that Fagunwa went on to write three more novels in the 1940s and 1950s.[9]

Fagunwa's was not the first novel published in Nigeria, however, for that distinction properly is shared by a set of Hausa novels published four years earlier. In 1933 the Translation Bureau in Zaria announced a fiction competition; the following year, it published five of the winning entries. The Hausa novels, like the Yoruba ones, emphasized the hero's quest (in this respect they could be considered more romances than novels), this time with Islamic twists.[10]

Hausa and Yoruba novels have continued to trickle out.[11] Recent Hausa fiction is still a mix of wild adventures, often extending into science fiction, and Islamic morality. Yoruba novels still emphasize fantasy, generally based on traditional lore, although they sometimes treat more contemporary topics such as that suggested by the title of Femi Jeboda's *Olowolaiyemo*, which translates as "Mr. People-Rally-Only-Round-the-Well-to-Do." Such fiction, which reaches a small but deeply committed audience, is the work of authors who are determined to perpetuate and enhance their native languages; there even exists a Society for Promoting the Yoruba Language (Egbe Ijinle Yoruba).

Full novels in these languages—unlike poetry or plays—are few and far between, however. Even rarer is a novel in Igbo or in any of the hundreds of minority languages because few Africans can read these languages, most of which lack a standard orthography.[12] When Nigerians write novels, they usually do so in English.

This is true for all books, not just novels. For a 1989 UNESCO tally, Nigeria reported the publication of 1,444 books in its "national languages." Of these, 1,380 were in English, 32 in Yoruba, 20 in Hausa, and 12 in Igbo.[13] A handful of books in the minority languages, nonnational by definition, may have come out as well. Be that as it may, these numbers reveal that Nigerian book publishing is overwhelmingly in English. Only books in English are accessible to literate members of all Nigerian ethnic groups, despite the fact that English is the first language of just about nobody. Therefore, only novels written in English can truly be called *Nigerian* novels. These novels, which in fact constitute the vast majority of novels by Nigerians, are the subjects of this study.[14]

So, agreeing with the conventional view, I shall take the Nigerian novel as originating in 1951 when a Yoruba government messenger wrote a fantastic tale in English—he claimed to have knocked it off in two days—and sent it off to the United Society for Christian Literature in London.[15] This worthy organization did indeed publish religious materials but not novels, let alone novels without a trace of Christianity in them. However, the USCL offered to help the young writer by sending his manuscript to Faber and Faber. That publisher recognized it had got hold of something very unusual, and a year later—on May 2, 1952—it published *The Palm-Wine Drinkard, and His Dead Palm-Wine Tapster in the Deads' Town,* by Amos Tutuola.

How was it that an obscure, semieducated colonial subject in the early 1950s came to write down a Yoruba fantasy, and to publish it with an old and established London firm? In a conversation we had in 1990, Amos Tutuola (who died in 1997) recalled the sequence of events and what motivated them. When he used to return to his village during school holidays, he recollected, there was no gramophone, no radio, no form of what would be considered entertainment in the modern sense. After work or dinner, the old people amused themselves and everyone else by telling tales. Tutuola began writing down these stories down, and when he went back to school, he would tell them to other children. His teachers encouraged him, so he kept collecting the stories when back home for holidays.

When his father died, young Amos could not continue with his education. In World War II he joined the Royal Air Force as a coppersmith, but after the war he went back to his village. By this time so many of the old men had died that Tutuola was shocked: now he couldn't get as many tales as he wanted, for much of the traditional lore had died with them. Back in Lagos working as a messenger, he saw a magazine ad put out by a missionary society for "manuscripts wanted." He decided to write up some of the folktales in story form, and he sent the resulting manuscript to London. When it came to Faber and Faber, via the United Society for Christian Literature, the editors "were keen to publish it." At the time some Yoruba living in London were opposed to the book's publication because it used "bad English" and was "old-fashioned"—complaints that have continued to dog Tutuola's work—but his editor supported the project, and Faber and Faber went ahead. Tutuola continued to publish with Faber and Faber thereafter.

"I write about my tribe," Tutuola asserted. He used Yoruba proverbs, folktales, beliefs, and behavior, all of which depicted how the Yoruba lived in the old days. He regarded this as being pure Yoruba material; there are no intentional mixtures with the lore or customs of other groups, no attempt to be "Nigerian" or pan-African. As premodern as *Yoruba Girl Dancing* is modern, The *Palm-Wine Drinkard* simply records the adventures of the twenty-five-year-old eponymous narrator, who had been "a palm-wine drinkard since I was a boy of ten years of age." In *The Palm-Wine Drinkard* one thing happens, and then another thing happens, and so on; the episodes follow one another, Bernth Lindfors has remarked, "like boxcars on a freight train."[16] There is no development of a plot, just a sequence of episodes, but the adventures are, to a Western reader, extraordinary in content and in telling.

They are, in fact, the products of the West African collective imagination. As he himself often explained, Tutuola based his writing on stories he had heard, not on stories he himself had created. For example, the man-reduced-to-a-skull tale appears in a number of Yoruba folktale collections as well as several adjacent folklore traditions.[17] The narrator's experience with the evanescence of popularity —essentially, nobody knows you when you're down and out—is about the only social message conveyed, and it, too, is a Yoruba commonplace, as in "Mr. People-Rally-Only-Round-the-Well-to-Do." Tutuola's creativity lay less in the stories than in their packaging in book form, in something that looks very much like a novel.

The Palm-Wine Drinkard illustrates some of the complexities of categorizing fiction. Tutuola regarded it as Yoruba ("I write about my tribe"). The present study takes it as Nigerian (it is written in English, therefore generally accessible to literate Nigerians). Lindfors has shown the contents are West African, not specifically Yoruba. And given its publisher, it must be some sort of an English novel as well.[18] Nigerians usually take *The Palm-Wine Drinkard* to be the first Nigerian novel, as I am doing here.[19] But like all firsts, this one is subject to debate. Some people point out that it was not really first; others argue that it is not really a novel.

With respect to the objection that *The Palm-Wine Drinkard* was not the first Nigerian novel, just the first one written in English, we have seen that a number of novels in indigenous languages did indeed appear before Tutuola's. Since these were accessible only to one linguistic community within Nigeria, however, they should be considered as Hausa novels or Yoruba novels, not as Nigerian novels proper. The second common objection is that *The Palm-Wine Drinkard*, and Tutuola's subsequent books as well, are not structured as novels but instead are just loosely linked collections of Yoruba folklore that have been written down. Lindfors suggests, for example, that "the content, structure, and style of *The Palm-Wine Drinkard* reveal that Tutuola is not a novelist but a writer of concatenated folktales."[20] Eustace

Palmer similarly argues that *The Palm-Wine Drinkard* is essentially a work of oral literature, for neither is it original nor does it "demonstrate some measure of psychological plausibility and consistency, thus revealing the author's control over the materials in his study."[21] In all of Tutuola's writing Palmer finds the stylized or minimal conversation and inconsistent point of view to be further evidence that the author is a teller of tales, not a novelist.

According to these rather stringent criteria, however, much popular fiction examined in the present study, such as the formulaic thrillers and romance novels, would be excluded from the genre of "novel," and Ben Okri's works of magical realism might be questioned as well. It is certainly the case that *The Palm-Wine Drinkard* lacks the formal realism, the everyday quality, that scholars like Watt and Hunter have claimed to be fundamental to the novel. In this respect it might be considered more of a romance, but the distinction between romance and novel has not been in general currency for well over a century. Works involving magical realism or postmodern manipulations of narrative, as well as formulaic entertainments, are routinely called novels, especially by their readers. So I use this somewhat looser definition and consider the history of the Nigerian novel as commencing with *The Palm-Wine Drinkard*.

If we grant that Tutuola wrote the first Nigerian novel, we must give him credit for the second one as well. *My Life in the Bush of Ghosts* (1954), which Tutuola submitted to Faber and Faber shortly after publication of *The Palm-Wine Drinkard*, begins when war comes to a village. A seven-year-old boy who does not yet know the meaning of *bad* and *good* runs off to hide in the bush while his older brother is captured. The child winds up in the bush of ghosts. The novel presents a series of fantastic episodes as the narrator is fought over by three old ghosts, captured by the vermin-covered ghost, turns into a cow, and so forth. As he moves from one ghost town to another, he has a series of narrow escapes from threatening spirits. *My Life in the Bush of Ghosts* contains some vivid images, as when the boy becomes entangled in the spiderweb bush, though it also contains more than a little repetition, as in the numerous accounts of how maggots and vermin infest a number of bad-smelling ghosts. One of these is memorable, however: the "television-handed ghost" who helps the boy make it back home after he had been lost in the bush of ghosts for some twenty-four years. Upon his return the boy is immediately sold into slavery, then bought by a rich man who turns out to be his brother, and so he is reunited with family at last. *My Life in the Bush of Ghosts* is longer than but not as consistently fresh as *The Palm-Wine Drinkard*, whose appeal it clearly tries to replicate.

The second Nigerian novelist was Cyprian Ekwensi, whose work was and is as different from Tutuola's as possible. The firm of Andrew Dakers published Ekwensi's novel *People of the City* in October 1954, eight months after *My Life in the Bush of Ghosts* came out. As the title implies, *People of the*

City—considered by some to be "the first contemporary African novel"—depicts the opportunity and excitement, along with politics, love, con games, and corruption, of the West African city during the late colonial period.[22] Since *People of the City* was first in a long line of city novels, it bears looking at its frenetic, one-thing-after-another plot.

Amusa Sango, a crime reporter for the *West African Sensation* and a dance band trumpeter, has forsaken his fiancée back in the village for the glamour of Lagos. When an old flame named Aina is arrested for theft, Sango visits her mother and is horrified by their poverty. Later at the All Languages Club where his band plays, he meets Beatrice, an Englishman's mistress.

Sango's landlord, Lajide, evicts him, so he goes to stay with First Trumpet. He runs into Bayo, a friend who is running a con game involving fake penicillin. Meanwhile, Beatrice becomes Lajide's mistress, and he sets her up in a house owned by a Lebanese named Zamil. Sango continues to investigate crimes, including the slaying of a woman and child over a gramophone. Covering a coal strike, he witnesses colonialism's brutality in the mining community and is impressed by a labor leader who is working for national unity. On the way back to Lagos, he has an awkward visit with Elina, his fiancée who has been living at convent.

Back in Lagos, Sango finds First Trumpet playing for a political party, Bayo in love with Zamil's sister, and Aina out of jail and looking for money. Because Sango plays for a rival political party, he gets fired from All Languages Club. Aina helps him, and they become intimate again; later she is furious to learn he is engaged.

Sango saves a stranger, Beatrice the Second, from being crushed in a crowd. Although she has a fiancé studying in England, they fall in love. Meanwhile, Bayo is distraught because Zamil is sending his sister back to the Middle East. When he and his lover prepare to elope, Zamil kills them. Sango writes an impassioned report of the crime, whereupon his editor, fearing a lawsuit, promptly fires him.

Sango meets Kofi, a Gold Coast truck driver who is happily living with the first Beatrice. Beatrice the Second introduces Sango to her family, but they favor her original fiancé. Meanwhile, Aina tells Sango she's pregnant and extorts money from him.

Elina comes to the city, but now Sango won't marry her, for "she did not 'belong.'" Running into Kofi, he learns that Beatrice has died of venereal disease; they discuss the tragic fates of so many "People of the City." When Aina comes after more money, Sango beats her and she miscarries. Beatrice the Second's fiancé fails his exams and commits suicide, so her parents reluctantly allow her to marry Sango. The couple heads for the Gold Coast with Kofi to seek new opportunities.

(Cyprian Ekwensi, *People of the City*)

The hectic world of the city and the timeless world of the village: these poles, established in the earliest novels, have constituted the basic dichotomy in Nigerian culture of the modern period. In Tutuola's tales we find the heroic quest among supernatural forces, the episodic structure, the pattern of going out from and returning to the familiar social world. All are characteristic of oral narrative, and of most of the Yoruba- and Hausa-language fiction that preceded *The Palm-Wine Drinkard*. Sango, on the other hand, is no epic hero, and the people of the city, while they may be bizarre, are no daemons or television-handed ghosts. Ekwensi's story has the realism, the everyday quality that has been an identifying feature of the English novel. It also has the open, ambiguous ending that is characteristic of many Nigerian novels: Sango heads for the Gold Coast, just like Remi dives into the international student community and Tayo wavers between his traditional wife and those girls in short skirts. Sango and his cronies are self-consciously and selfishly modern. In contrast, Tutuola's books represent the road not taken. While Nigerian epic romances occasionally appear, by and large the novelists have followed the realistic path mapped by Ekwensi.

In the years since Tutuola first caught the eye of Faber and Faber and Ekwensi began documenting the high life and low life of urban West Africa, Nigerians have published some 500 or so novels. Often called the Giant of Africa in terms of population and resources, Nigeria is the continent's literary giant as well, in both quality and volume. While Nobel laureate Wole Soyinka, Booker Prize winner Ben Okri, and the universally acclaimed Chinua Achebe are the best-known writers, even more telling is the sheer number of novels and novelists. Most of them—the 476 novels and 261 authors of Appendixes A and B—have been included in this study.

The four-decade history of the Nigerian novel, given graphic representation in Figure 2-1, is one of stuttering beginnings, an explosion of books in the late 1970s through the mid-1980s, and a slowdown thereafter. Beginning with Tutuola and Ekwensi, a trickle of titles appeared in the 1950s and 1960s, virtually all published in Britain. Output was increasing in the 1960s until the hiatus brought about by the civil war (1967–70). Nigerians refer to the writers whose novels appeared in this period before the civil war as the first generation.

After the war came a second generation, as emerging authors of the oil-boom years joined established figures. Publications jumped sharply during the late 1970s and early 1980s. Series like Macmillan's Pacesetters and Spectrum's Sunshine Romances offered new opportunities to aspiring writers. Nigerian novels, which were increasingly likely to have been published in Nigeria itself, poured onto the market. By the end of the 1970s, twenty or more new novels were appearing each year; the fiction boom reached its peak in 1982, with fifty novels coming out that year.

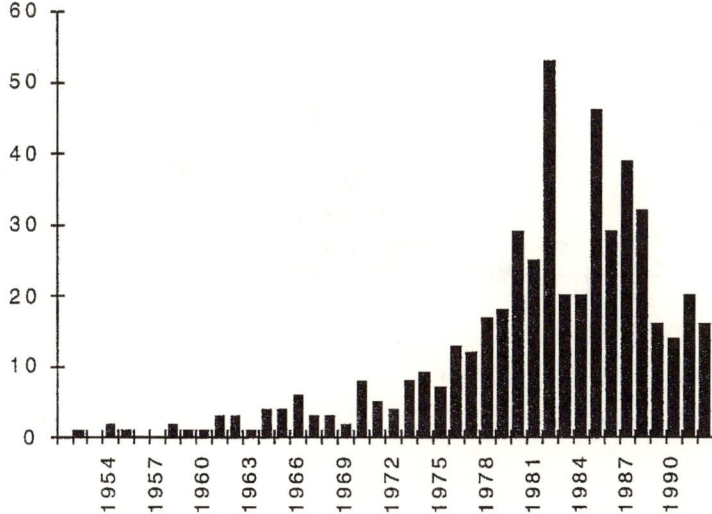

FIGURE 2-1. Nigerian novels by year 1952–92

The oil boom turned to oil bust in the 1980s, and times grew hard. In the depressed economy that has persisted from the mid-1980s up until the present, literary production slowed down. The end of the oil boom and the economic collapse that followed meant that the Nigerian market for trade fiction all but dried up; the cost of books increased as the value of the naira declined. This was a particular problem for imports, but since even locally published books depended on imported materials, all suffered. There was some lag before the impact made itself felt on the output of fiction, which remained fairly high through the late 1980s but then dropped off sharply. By the early 1990s only about twenty new novels were coming out annually. Figure 2-2 smooths out the annual variation by showing a three-year moving average of titles that appeared from the 1950s until the 1990s.[23]

British publishers beat a hasty retreat from the Nigerian market. Nigerian companies have continued to publish fiction, although at a somewhat slower pace than during the boom years. For the larger publishing houses, textbooks are the only moneymakers, but literature hangs on as a poor but prestigious adjunct, while slighter works aim for the youth market. Smaller publishers continue to put out a few novels, and authors commonly arrange their own publication; in both these cases, distribution is severely limited, and rarely do the novelists see any royalties. (Authors claim that the larger publishers seldom pay them royalties either.)

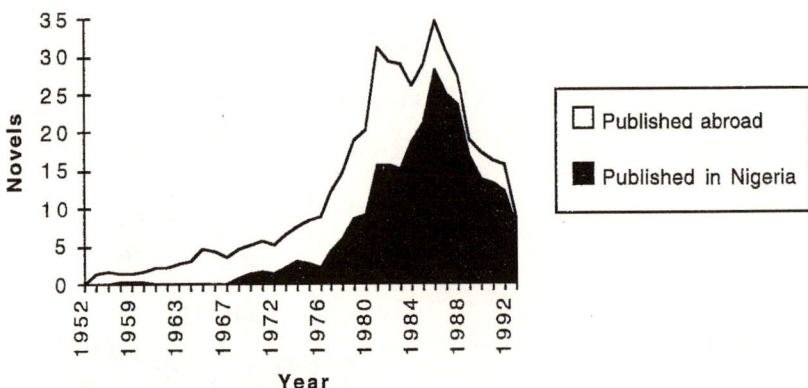

FIGURE 2-2. Novels by year and place of publication (3-year moving average)

Their financial prospects notwithstanding, however, Nigerians continue to write novels. For despite the fact that novels are and always have been market commodities, the amount of fiction published is not a simple function of market size.[24] Something else drives writers everywhere, and Nigerians, hard-pressed as they are by economic hardship and political uncertainty, are no exception. To understand the Nigerian novel, we must try to understand what motivates these people to devote so much effort to such an unprofitable, even whimsical, enterprise.

THE WRITERS

Chi-Chi and Chris are Igbos living in Ibadan; she is finishing a Youth Corps assignment and he is an engineer. They are in love, but Chi-Chi's family wants her to marry the wealthy Chief Okali, who offers a substantial bride price. Chi-Chi's roommate Cecelia and her doctor-boyfriend Lai, both very modern and impatient with their friends' concern for tradition, urge them to ignore family pressures, but neither can.

Chi-Chi becomes pregnant. Her greedy brother Agugua wants her to abort the pregnancy and marry Okali; he is opposed every step of the way by Cecelia, a vehement "women's-libber" who regards the bride price tradition as nothing but selling women. Agugua almost gets control of Chi-Chi (backed up by the cruel Okali and Uncle Iroegbulum, who thinks reluctant brides should be locked up and raped until pregnancy makes them submissive), but is foiled by Cecelia. Finally Okali is scared off. Agugua, who needs cash for a trip to America, sets a huge bride price, Chris goes into debt to pay it, and Chi-Chi's family agrees to the marriage.

Impoverished by their debt, the couple cannot afford medical care or proper food. Cecelia and Lai watch in horror as Chris's pride prevents him from accepting assistance. When Chi-Chi goes into labor, she ends up in a state hospital with no blood for transfusions. Chris begs money to buy blood but returns to find the baby stillborn and Chi-Chi dead.

Heartsick, Chris has a "metamorphosis." Bringing Chi-Chi's body to her family, he rails against old customs—"The old order changes, giving way to new; so let it be with old traditions that have ceased to fit into the modern age. If I no longer feel bound by some old traditions, it is because I've seen the harm they can do" (129)—and his passion makes an impression. Later Chris is a sadder but wiser witness to Lai and Cecelia's wedding; a postscript says they had a baby boy.

(Tolu Ajayi, *The Lesson*)

If Dr. Tolu Ajayi's novel is first and foremost a melodramatic tale of love and loss, it is an emphatically didactic one as well. Ajayi works in discussion of a number of social themes, such as the escalation of bride-price for educated girls and the dilapidated condition of government hospitals, and he leaves no doubt regarding his views on what needs to be changed. In this, Ajayi is not unusual: while not all Nigerian authors share his vehement rejection of tradition nor his unabashed feminism, by and large they do share his commitment to social improvement through literature. Ajayi is a storyteller, but a fundamentally serious one who puts enlightenment ahead of entertainment, although he believes the latter can serve the former. In this he exemplifies the view most Nigerian authors share: they see themselves in the treble roles of witnesses, teachers, and reformers. As novelists, they believe they can and should instigate social reforms by bearing witness.

What sort of person believes that writers have this kind of power? Who writes Nigerian novels, and why? While there is no such thing as a typical writer, Ajayi is unusually thoughtful about what it means to be a writer in the first place, so I will start by looking at his career.[25] With three published novels and a wealth of published poetry, screenplays, and hundreds of newspaper articles, Ajayi regards himself as a writer first and a doctor second, his successful Lagos medical practice notwithstanding. At the same time he believes that his beginnings as a writer were different from most. Although drawn to writing since childhood, he did not set out to become a professional author by getting a Ph.D. in English or attaching himself to a literary mentor at the university. Instead, following the professional role model of his parents —his mother was a lawyer and judge, his father a teacher in secondary school—and being good in science at school, he set out to become a doctor. He recalls being inspired by examples of writers such as Somerset Maugham, Anton Chekov, and A. J. Cronin, who were also doctors. At an early age he decided he, too, could do both.

While he was studying medicine at the University of Liverpool, Ajayi made heavy use of the municipal library, pursuing his goal of becoming an accomplished writer as systematically and rationally as he does everything else. He read about specific authors, and he studied reviews and discussions of what makes a good novel. Ajayi told me that he thinks writers should not just follow their instincts but should know something about literary methods and understand how theme, plot, and character work in a novel. Authors should not just imitate other writers but should develop their own literary styles. He works hard on developing his own.

As for his subjects, Ajayi writes about conflicts within Nigerian society, about social changes, and especially about the tensions between modernity and tradition. He thinks that early publishers of Nigerian literature were interested in creating an "anthropological record" of what life was like, or had been like, in Nigeria, but now this antiquarianism is not much in vogue; literary preservation of the past is, itself, "a thing of the past." While agreeing with those who say writers should depict social problems, Ajayi argues that mere documentation is not enough; the writer is a teacher and must direct readers toward social improvement. Writers should show what ought to happen, not just be chroniclers of what has happened. Bearing witness, in other words, is not a passive act.

Ajayi exemplifies the highly self-conscious decision most Nigerian novelists have made about becoming writers in the first place. There are generic reasons for this. Some forms of creative activity—writing poetry, for example, or sketching—allow a person to dabble in them for years, working in leisure moments primarily for one's own entertainment. If a poem or two is published in the local newspaper, or if friends and relatives start demanding sketches, the person gradually may come to regard himself "a poet" or "an artist," and may even be seen as such by others. The role of poet or artist gets ratified by commercial or aesthetic successes—a prize, the sale of a piece—but it is not denied in the absence of such legitimization. Becoming a novelist is different. Because of the sustained activity, the sheer number of hours, required to produce a single novel, a person choosing this path is more likely to make a concrete and conscious decision—"I am going to write a novel." And because novels are commodities and always have been, the legitimization of the role is clear-cut: If you write a novel that is published and offered for sale, then you are a novelist; otherwise, you are not. There can be unpublished novels, but no unpublished novelists.

The authors in the present study are all novelists by definition, for they have all published novels. In the following discussion I consider what kinds of Nigerians make the decision, successfully executed in these cases, to become novelists. I will look at their backgrounds, literary careers, and aspirations about what "becoming a novelist" should mean to themselves, their readers, and their society.

Backgrounds

Although it is true that becoming a novelist almost always is the result of a conscious and deliberate decision, not everyone is equally likely to make that decision. First and foremost, a novelist must be literate and must know something about literary forms as well; novelists everywhere are highly educated relative to other people in their societies.[26] In addition, certain groups are drawn to some genres and repelled by, or excluded from, others. Such attractions and exclusions, over and above differences in education, are associated with gender, class, religion, region, and ethnicity.

I have identified 261 Nigerian novelists, listed in Appendix B. Although these authors intend to represent their country in their writing, they are very unrepresentative themselves. Compared with the Nigerian people as a whole, they are more male, more southern, more Christian, more Igbo or Yoruba, and much more highly educated.

Perhaps the most fundamental imbalance is that of sex. To an overwhelming extent the Nigerians who write the novels, tell the stories, and bear witness are men. Fully 85 percent of the authors on my list are men; putting it another way, only one out of seven Nigerian novelists is a women.[27] This underrepresentation of women does not seem to vary much by ethnic group; women authors are as rare among Yoruba, where women have had considerable freedom and power historically, as among the more restrictive Hausa.[28]

While most novelists write only a single novel, a few—like Buchi Emecheta or Chukwuemeka Ike—raise the average by writing a lot. Women who do become novelists produce as many or more novels on average as their male counterparts; male novelists average 1.82 novels each, females 2.11.[29] This suggests that women face major impediments in becoming novelists in the first place, but once they have attained that status, they remain as productive as men.

We can further understand the sexual bias in Nigerian authorship by comparing it to the situation in the West, where women have been prominent as novelists from the beginning. One sociological study has suggested that women dominated the writing of English novels until the mid–nineteenth century, when increased incomes for authors attracted more men to the literary profession and women consequently were "edged out."[30] Contemporary evidence from the United States suggests that women may be even more likely than men to undertake creative writing.[31] Not all women who write fiction get published—not all men do either—but Western women seem to be successful here as well. From an American sample taken of all novels published in 1987, 39 percent of the authors were women, a figure that probably underestimates the actual proportion of women authors because the sample excludes paperback romances, whose authors are mostly female.[32] Thus, the overwhelming masculinity of Nigerian novelists is neither inherent to the genre nor a replication of a Western pattern.

If women are underrepresented, Christians are overrepresented: Four out of five Nigerian novelists are Christian, less than 15 percent are Muslim, and the rest are animist or some other religion.[33] To assess the misrepresentation involved here, it is necessary to come up with an estimate of Nigeria's religious breakdown. The country's population is roughly half Muslim, or so it is assumed. The data, however, are far from perfect. The most recent census, that of 1991, did not inquire about religion or ethnicity, since both were seen as too controversial. So one must go back to the 1963 census, itself questioned by many, to get some figures. That census reported that 47 percent of Nigerians were Muslim, 35 percent Christian, and the remaining 18 percent adherents of traditional African religions. It seems likely that the percentage of Nigerians adhering *only* to traditional religious beliefs has declined in the intervening years, since this is typical of a modernizing society and since both Islam and Christianity are aggressively proselytizing faiths. (Many Nigerian Christians and Muslims follow indigenous religious practices as well, as in the common practice of couples who celebrate both traditional or "customary" and Christian or "church" weddings.) Pentecostalism, Aladura, and other Christian cults have made inroads in the south in recent years, although it is not clear what portion of their adherents were previously Christian of a more mainstream sort. Nor is it known if the various religions have had different reproductive rates; fertility for all groups remains high, although there is some decline among the most modern groups, and these are likely to be southern Christians. Putting these bits and pieces of information together, I estimate that contemporary Nigeria is about half Islamic, 40 percent Christian, with the remaining 10 percent being animist, some other religion, or nonreligious. Nigerian novelists, therefore, are much more likely to be Christian and much less likely to be Muslim than Nigerians in general.

As is so often the case in Nigeria, the novelists' religion, ethnicity, and region—and the representational biases along these dimensions—tend to coincide. The data on ethnicity are as imperfect as the data on religion, and for similar reasons. Table 2-1 summarizes what is known of the ethnic composition of Nigeria from older census data. Extrapolating from this, it seems reasonable to estimate that of today's 110 million Nigerians, some 28 to 30 percent are Hausa and/or Fulani; almost 20 percent are Yoruba; a slightly smaller percentage, perhaps about 17 percent, are Igbo; and a bit over a third belong to one of the minority tribes. The ethnicity of the writers is very different. Igbos make up half of the novelists, three times their proportion of the population. The three most prolific authors—Buchi

TABLE 2-1
Ethnicity of Nigerian Population and Novelists (Percent)

Ethnicity	Population 1952–53	Population 1963[a]	Nigerian Novelists[b]
Hausa-Fulani	28.1	29.5	5
Yoruba	16.1	20.3	34
Igbo	17.9	16.6	49
Other	37.4	33.6	12
Total	100.0	100.0	100
N	30.4 million	55.7 million	200

[a]The 1963 census figures are generally believed to be wildly inflated as a result of manipulations undertaken to gain greater political representation. The inflation for the Northern and Western Regions is more extreme than that for the Eastern Region or the Mid-West. See Diamond (1988) for a discussion of the politics of this census; the present table is derived from his Tables 2.1 and 5.3. Most scholars regard the 1952–53 census as the last relatively reliable count.

[b]Of the 261 Nigerian novelists, I know the ethnicity of 200. Of these, 10 are Hausa-Fulani, 67 are Yoruba, 97 are Igbo, and 26 are from minority tribes.

Emecheta (twelve novels), Chukwuemeke Ike (ten), and Cyprian Ekwensi (nine)—are Igbo. Five of the nine authors who have written more than six novels are Igbo.

Yoruba are also overrepresented as novelists, although not as dramatically as the Igbo; for they constitute about a fifth of the population and a third of the novelists. Minority tribes are somewhat under-represented. And the Hausa-Fulani voices are virtually unheard, for with something approaching one-third of the total population, they have written only 5 percent of the novels.

The authors' birthplaces reveal a similar pattern. Nigerians do not consider place of birth to be the same as where they are "from," for the latter often refers to the hometown of the paternal family. Many Nigerians work and bear children in regions different from their "homes." For example, the Igbo worked in modern sector employment throughout the country prior to the civil war; many residents of Lagos maintain close ties with their home villages even though they raise their families in the city. And a few, like May Ellen Ezekiel, were born out of the country to Nigerian parents. Such caveats notwithstanding, we find that of those 140 authors born in Nigeria whose place of birth has been identified, only 10 percent come from the north, 42 percent from the east, and another 39 percent from the west (the southwest and the old "middle west"), with the remainder from the middle belt. A comparison with the 1991 census figures shown in Table 2-2 makes the underrepresentation of the north and overrepresentation of the south—both east and west—very clear.

TABLE 2-2

Nigerian Population, 1991 Census Figures, By State

As of August 1991, Nigeria was divided into thirty-one states, including the Federal Capital Territory containing Abuja. The preliminary census data reported in 1992 was broken down into these thirty-one states. I am grouping these into the generally understood divisions of North, Middle Belt, and South, with the South further divided between West and East.

Administrative Division	Population from 1991 Census (Provisional Results)	Percent of Total	Percent of Novelists (N)
Northern states			
Adamawa	2,124,049		
Bauchi	4,294,413		
Borno	2,596,589		
Jigawa	2,829,929		
Kaduna	3,969,252		
Kano	5,632,040		
Katsina	3,878,344		
Kebbi	2,062,226		
Niger	2,482,367		
Sokoto	4,392,391		
Yobe	1,411,481		
Northern states total	35,673,081	40.3	10 (14)
Middle belt states			
Benue	2,780,398		
Federal Capital Territory (Abuja)	378,671		
Kogi	2,099,046		
Kwara	1,566,469		
Plateau	3,283,704		
Taraba	1,480,590		
Middle belt states total	11,588,878	13.1	9 (13)
Southern states (West)			
Delta	2,570,181		
Edo	2,159,848		
Lagos	5,685,781		
Ogun	2,338,570		
Ondo	3,884,485		
Osun	2,203,016		
Oyo	3,488,789		
Southern states (West) total	22,330,670	25.2	39 (54)
Southern states (East)			
Abia	2,297,978		
Akwa Ibom	2,359,736		
Anambra	2,767,903		
Cross Rivers	1,865,604		

(*continued*)

TABLE 2-2 (*continued*)

Administrative Division	Population from 1991 Census (Provisional Results)	Percent of Total	Percent of Novelists (N)
Enugu	3,161,295		
Imo	2,485,499		
Rivers	3,983,857		
Southern states (East) total	18,921,872	21.4	42 (59)
Nigeria	88,514,501	100.0	100 (140)

Source: Federal Republic of Nigeria: *Census News, 1992.*

As for their schooling, while it is not surprising to learn that Nigerian authors are highly educated relative to their compatriots, the degree of the difference is stunning. According to UNESCO, only 4 percent of appropriate-age Nigerians were enrolled in tertiary education in 1995.[34] But among the novelists, fully 72 percent have completed their university education at the B.A. level, 49 percent have gone on to do postgraduate study, and 36 percent have already completed some sort of postgraduate degree (Ph.D., M.D., M.A., etc.).[35] Their extraordinary level of education relative to their fellow Nigerians—relative to anyone!—supports their self-image as teachers. One must wonder, however, at the appropriateness of what can be taught by these Nigerians, who are so male, so Christian, so southern, and so well educated compared with those they would teach.

Although one might expect the gap between novelists and the general population to be decreasing, this is not the case. Nigerian education has suffered greatly during the oil bust years. Resources have gone into building more universities in spite of the underdevelopment of the primary and secondary sectors. The proliferation of states has exacerbated the problem, for there is "an emerging tendency to make every state in the country have a Federal University, a Federal Polytechnic, and a Federal College of education,. . . . letting every section get something irrespective of whether such institutions fulfil educational objectives."[36] Meanwhile primary education has seen a gross enrollment drop from 93 percent in 1983 to 67 percent by 1990.[37]

Moreover, the educational disadvantage of the north with respect to the south is getting worse, not better. In the mid-eighties seven of the eight northern states had a fifth or less of their twelve- to seventeen-year-olds in secondary school, while Lagos had three-quarters of its youth in school.[38] The situation is especially grim for northern girls. While Lagos had girls constitute 50.7 percent of its primary school population in 1990–91 (and other southern states were about as high), the northern states lagged; girls accounted for only 29.8 percent of the primary school children in Katsina, 27.4 percent in Kebbi, and 17.4 percent in Sokoto.[39]

Thus writers and other highly educated people continue to be out of step with their fellow Nigerians, especially with northerners. Educational development is not a linear progression, a great leap made by a society once and for all, but a far more uneven and halting affair. Individuals make the leap, as have the novelists, but in doing so they have left their countrymen behind.

Careers

While all novelists may be teachers in some indirect sense, many teach in the schoolroom as well. If not teachers, they must have some other occupation, for authors can rarely earn their livings from their writing. This is true not just in Nigeria but almost everywhere. One estimate, an admittedly generous one, is that only 10 percent of bona fide (i.e., published) writers in Britain actually make their living by writing books.[40] In his social study of books drawing mainly on British experience, Peter Mann notes, "What is relatively rare in the total world of publishing is the person who is an author *and nothing else*." The "something else" that authors do varies enormously. "Adult novels seem to be written by everyone under the sun—perhaps in the belief that everyone has a book inside him (or her)," Mann comments, although academics and housewives have been especially prominent in Britain and the United States.[41]

If writers who are nothing else are rare in the West, they are even rarer in a country like Nigeria where the market for fiction is relatively small and where government or private patronage is virtually nonexistent. Indeed, Nigerian novelists have an exaggerated idea of how foreign authors live, for they assume that more earn their livings through writing than is actually the case. Few Nigerians even dream of living off their writing. So we may ask, How do these novelists earn their livings? How do they reconcile their literary and extraliterary careers? And what are the implications of their dual or treble careers for their self-assigned roles as teachers?

Education is one field where Nigerian novelists earn their keep; a quarter of the novelists work in academic settings as teachers, professors, or administrators (Table 2-3).[42] An equal number work in media, either in print journalism or in broadcasting. Others are professionals of one sort or another, like Ajayi. About 10 percent are in business, and almost as many are civil servants or military officers. A handful are still students. There were no housewives, for virtually no Nigerian women, especially in the south, are just homemakers for any period of time; urban women who lack training for a career usually engage in petty trading.

Almost half of the first-generation writers were teachers, but this proportion dropped to a quarter of the second and third generations. Almost

TABLE 2-3
Occupations of Nigerian Novelists

Occupation	Percent
Teaching, educational administration	26
Broadcasting, media, journalism	25
Profession (medicine, law)	14
Business	10
Civil service	8
Student	4
Other	13
Total	100
N = 175	

a third of the second-generation writers worked in the media; this proportion has declined to less than a quarter for the following generation, offset by small increases in the professions and civil service. Such changes, while modest, suggest that the careers of authors have shifted away from core literary and cultural venues—education, broadcasting, journalism—toward lines of work less directly involved with the production and transmission of culture.

As for the second question, that of the relationship between the literary and extraliterary careers, the key problem is that of time: When do these writers find time to write? This problem is not limited to Nigerians, of course. It is particularly pressing, however, given some of the characteristics of Nigerian middle-class life, including especially the economic insecurities, the large families and high household densities, and the large amounts of time and effort consumed by everyday business like driving to work or making a telephone call.

So Nigerian novelists must combine their creative work with jobs that put food on the table, and they must do so in a particular social context: that of a country that was a colony until 1960 and has undergone continuous political and economic upheavals ever since. A look at the careers of four authors, representing three generations, suggests the changing problems these writers have faced and the ingenious solutions they have come up with as they pursue their multiple careers. It also provides a sense of how the three generations' different economic prospects have influenced what they have written.

The first generation, the "pioneers," are the pre–civil war writers. I consider an author who published a novel before 1970 to be a first-generation writer. The second generation, the "oil boomers," includes those authors whose first novel came out between 1970 and 1983. And the third generation, the "strugglers," published their first novels in 1984 or later. My data show there to be 16 members of the first generation, 105 members of the second, and 140 members of the third.

PIONEER: JOHN OKECHUKWU MUNONYE

Like so many of the first generation, John Okechukwu Munonye is an Igbo, a Christian, and an educator. He has published six novels, all in Heinemann's African Writers Series, as well as a number of short stories; he has also been a newspaper columnist and coauthored a textbook entitled *Drills and Practice in English Language*. Born in 1929 in Akokwa, Eastern Nigeria, Munonye came from a family that revered education. He describes his father, a farmer, as "a sort of benevolent dictator, or enlightened despot, who groomed us to love schooling in those early, pioneering days, he himself being a pioneer convert to Christianity. Although he never went (could not have gone) to any school himself, he loved Western education to a degree that was infectious, and sacrificed a lot to see us remain in school. . . . I boast being a product of the very best the country could afford at that time: Christ the King College, Onitsha, and then University College, Ibadan."[43]

After a year of postgraduate study at the London Institute of Education, in 1954 Munonye began a career in education: "I am at heart a teacher." He was an education inspector, a classroom teacher, the principal of a teachers college, and eventually the chief inspector for the Imo State Ministry of Education, from which he retired in 1977. Since then he has been a columnist for *Catholic Life* (Lagos) and the *Statesman* (Owerri), has continued writing short stories, and has been an active member of the Association of Nigerian Authors. He is married and the father of grown children. Now retired to Akokwa, Munonye has traveled widely, for education and pleasure to be sure, but also to attend UNESCO meetings and to make pilgrimages to Rome, Israel, and Lourdes.

Like many Nigerian writers, Munonye was inspired by Achebe's *Things Fall Apart*, but his connection was more personal than most. "With the publication in 1958 of Achebe's first novel, I came to realize that such a venture [i.e., becoming a writer] was possible. Chinua and I happened to have been close friends in out university days and we 'lost' each other thereafter, so to say; and then the *Things Fall Apart* thing sounded. Honestly, that was how it began with me." Munonye wrote his novels during weekends and vacations while working full-time—since retirement he admits to having more time for writing but less energy—and each novel took him roughly eighteen months to finish. Munonye aims for, and in fact has reached, an international audience. He sees literature as satisfying a "spiritual need" and would choose writing a literary classic over attaining wealth or bringing about social improvement: "There lies the immortal creator, not man of wealth and not man of the people. 'An everlasting possession.' That was the term used by Thucydides. In other words, classic, not pop. Probably the others [i.e., wealth and social improvement] would come . . . in the fullness of time. If however they do not, well, there is that story of the unmarked grave—Mozart's." Munonye's favorite writers are P. G. Wodehouse and Turgenev; widely read, he also enjoys Achebe, Galsworthy, Graham Greene, Steinbeck, and classical writers, including Homer, Virgil, and Livy.

Often compared with Achebe, Munonye has similarly treated the disruption of Igbo life by the colonial encounter, but he is rather more sympathetic to the gains as well as the losses that the encounter brought, clearly viewing Western education and Christianity as positive developments for the Igbo.[44] His trilogy of the "only son" who breaks his mother's heart by converting to Christianity and embracing modernity (*The Only Son, Obi,* and *Bridge to a Wedding*) ends on an optimistic note—a reconciliation between the traditional and the modern in the next generation—but only after decades of pain for everyone. *The Oil Man of Obange* is even bleaker, for its protagonist becomes a martyr for his children's schooling.

> Jeri, an illiterate palm-oil middleman, carries oil to Otta on his old bicycle to earn money for his five children's school fees. His sister is constantly after him to return to farming and forget both the palm-oil business and education, but Jeri sets great store by schooling. His story is a series of misfortunes: his much-loved wife dies; his bike needs repairs he cannot afford; a bad accident cripples him for several years; and there is the constant scraping for money. His children excel in school, however, and the climax comes when his oldest son is accepted at an elite Catholic high school and needs more fees. Jeri finally manages to borrow money from a wealthy Otta trader who has been impressed by his integrity. Just when his problems seem solved, Jeri is robbed and beaten, his mind goes, and he soon dies. At his funeral, the oil trader celebrates his worthy life, and the book ends on a note of reconciliation; he has died in his sister's arms and is buried in the church next to his wife.
>
> (John Munonye, *The Oil Man of Obange*)

Thus in spite of the pain and estrangement experienced by individuals, in both his trilogy and *Oil Man* Munonye champions education and Christianity for the Igbo. Their introduction brings temporary social dislocation, but eventually mutual accommodation between the old and the new seems possible.

Despite his established position as a major writer of the first generation, Munonye is keenly aware of the difficulties that Nigerian novelists face. He cites three in particular: first, getting published: "A book published in London for four pounds, for example, would have to sell here for some sixty naira [at the time the exchange rate was about seven naira to one dollar] and no bookseller would go into such a venture. . . . As for local publishing, things are almost equally tight. Paper and other things cost a lot; and even after that, the market is chancy." The second problem is lack of exposure to books. Munonye mentions in particular the destruction of Igbo private libraries during the civil war, which literally tore books away from those families, like his own, that had prized education and nurtured literary talent. The third problem writers face is the cost of producing manuscripts, particularly typing and editing. While Munonye aims at as wide a readership as possible, he recognizes that in Nigeria his readers are mostly students in universities and colleges.

John Munonye, with his classical British education, his vivid memories of the dramatic cultural and economic upheavals of the late colonial period, and his firm belief in the power of fiction to provide moral instruction, is a pioneer writer of the old school. The second generation came of age in a radically different political and cultural environment, and it maintains radically different assumptions about writers and writing.

OIL BOOMER: KALU OKPI

Kalu Okpi was born in 1947, the son of an Igbo civil servant. In his youth his father's job took him throughout southern Nigeria and what later became Cameroon. He fought as an officer for Biafra. After the war he attended New York University, receiving a bachelor of fine arts degree in 1974. That same year he began his career in broadcasting, starting out as a producer for the East Nigeria Television Service; three years later he was principal producer for Nigerian Television in Enugu. In 1981 Okpi took a diploma in television drama at the Television Training Institute in London, and in 1987 he became chief writer for Nigerian Television in Lagos. Okpi is married to a businesswoman, and they have three children. He does not belong to the Association of Nigerian Authors (ANA), which he regards as a collection of "university types." While hardly a stranger to higher education, Okpi sees writing as entertainment first and foremost, and he thinks most ANA members do not share this view.

In 1977 Macmillan launched its line of popular fiction, Pacesetters, which aimed at the young, increasingly affluent African market. Kalu Okpi's first novel, *The Smugglers,* was one of the original Pacesetters, and his next six novels all came out in the series at a rate of about one per year. Most of these followed the pattern set by *The Smugglers.*

> Jonnie is a freelance journalist; formerly he was with the police, where he had captured a dangerous criminal named Kaska. Now Captain Jumbo, chief of a police Special Squad, asks Jonnie's help as independent operator "who can cut corners" to catch Kaska, newly released from prison, and his gang. Assisted

by Ada, his sharp-tongued policewoman girlfriend, Jonnie becomes a smuggler off Calabar to gather information about Kaska's smuggling operation, which involves goods, guns, and heroin. The villains kidnap the harbormaster's son and Ada; Jonnie rescues both aboard the smuggling ship and later is himself rescued by Ada.

(Kalu Okpi, *The Smugglers*)

One might call this a routine thriller, but it was far from routine in Nigeria in 1977; Okpi was breaking ground for a new type of popular entertainment. Features of *The Smugglers* that continued to characterize Okpi's thrillers include an egalitarian and bantering relationship between Jonnie and Ada, who is a very modern African woman, and less emphasis on violence and sexual sensationalism than in many of the Nigerian formulaic thrillers.

While authors such as Munonye refer to their writing careers as a lucky accident, the second generation has more of an attitude of entitlement, even inevitability. Says Okpi, "I guess I was born a writer. I only went to school to learn where to put the commas. . . . I've always been interested in writing since my father maintained a shelf full of different types of novels, when I was small." Okpi's literary heroes are very different as well. He most admires the Irish thriller writer Peter Cheyney. He reports enjoying a lively mixture of escapist and quality fiction, and firmly—if somewhat defensively—rejects European classics:

Harold Robbins. And don't say Oh God! I like him, at least the first four or so before he went overboard. Also Alistair Maclean. Also, Eddie Iroh in *Forty Nine Guns to the General* [*sic*]. William Goldman. One helluva writer. And Sidney Sheldon. Sorry to disappoint you, but I don't like Shakespeare or Shelley, or Yeats or any of those writers they taught us about in school. . . . I don't remember his name, but he wrote *The Cherry Orchard*, I don't like him either. I also don't like the one who wrote about *Hedda Gabler*. Damon Runyon is one terrific writer. He is guaranteed to cheer you up any day. And finally, Kalu Okpi. Not all the time, but once in a while, especially in his short story "The Champion Wrestler" and in his unpublished novel *The Warriors*. Terrific writing, if I say so myself.

We see here the brashness, the exuberance of a reader and writer who has thought a lot about what kind of writing he enjoys, and who has confidence in his own opinions and abilities.

With his eight published novels, his career writing for television, and his receipt of the first African Literature Prize awarded by a West German shortwave radio broadcaster in 1985 for "The Champion Wrestler," Okpi's confidence seems justified. Indeed, in the late 1970s, when he began writing as Nigeria was awash with oil money, all things seemed possible. But by the early 1990s, Okpi took a darker view of the future for Nigerian writers. The major problem was "lack of interest. If you are not Wole Soyinka or Chinua Achebe, you might just as well forget it. Also the pay is terrible. You have to have another job with which to support yourself if you want to be a writer around here."

While Okpi thinks that a writer's first obligation is to be the best writer he can be, rather than to serve society in any particular way, he is characteristically forthright when asked which he would choose: "(a) writing a novel that would be regarded throughout the world as a literary classic; (b) writing a novel that would sell so many books that you and your family would become wealthy; or (c) writing a novel that would inspire some major improvements in Nigerian society." He replied, "Are you kidding me? Give me (b) all the time! It wasn't like this before though. I can still remember when I would have said (a) all the time, but I've grown up since then, and if you can give me (b), please do not hesitate to do so." It may be that Okpi has grown up, but his generation of writers also saw a wrenching change in their prospects from the fat years of the 1970s and early 1980s to the lean years ever since. Unlike Munonye, Okpi was still developing as a writer when the change occurred, and he is acutely aware of his own altered outlook. His profound disillusionment is characteristic of second-generation Nigerian writers.

In Okpi's case, this disillusionment colors his later fiction. If the romance of Jonnie and Ada is one of derring-do and humor, consider the grim story of *Love*, Okpi's 1991 romance.

Nkem, an Igbo, and Love, an Efik, are born in the same hospital and grasp each other's hands as newborns. Years later Nkem meets Love, training to be a nurse, when he is hospitalized following an injury in a soccer match. They fall in love and plan to attend the university together and then marry, despite her being beaten up by some Igbo girls who disapprove of cross-ethnic romance. But the civil war separates them; Nkem becomes an officer for Biafra, while Love is trapped in Calabar with her family.

After months of brave but ultimately hopeless fighting, Nkem runs away to find Love. They meet and have a few romantic days together, but she cannot leave Calabar because she has agreed to marry a Nigerian major in order to save her father's life. Nkem goes back to the front and later hears Love has been killed. Unwilling to believe this, he looks for her after the war, but with no success.

In 1980 Nkem is at UCLA studying film when he meets a Nigerian woman who reminds him of Love and—all his efforts at finding Love having failed—he marries her. Ten years later he is back in Nigeria making films, with a reasonably happy marriage, two children, and a good career, although his heart still longs for Love.

One day Love walks into his Lagos office. Many explanations—she had followed her military husband to places like Alaska and Russia, and they have also had two children—but Nkem and Love are still deeply in love with each other. They plan to divorce their mates on generous terms and start life together. After writing letters to this effect, they take a plane to Enugu, vowing to never part again. But the plane crashes, and they die in each other's arms.

(Kalu Okpi, Love)

Okpi's ending for a novel that is presented as a romance in its title and its cover picture of embracing lovers may seem gratuitous, but the message seems to be that you can not fight fate, which repeatedly undermines the best-laid plans. Or as Nigerians often put it, "No condition is permanent," not even happiness. Ending a romance with this type of tragedy could be taken as a comment on Nigeria's capacity to disappoint. The second generation of writers has experienced this disappointment most keenly.

STRUGGLERS: YAHAYA SHAFII DANGANA AND MAY IFEOMA NWOYE

Just seven years younger than Okpi, though from a very different background, Yahaya Shafii Dangana speaks for the third literary generation, one that may be less disappointed because it had few illusions to begin with. Dangana is a Nupe, from Niger State in north-central Nigeria, and a Muslim. He is married to a librarian, and they have five children. Having studied architecture, civil engineering, and cartography in the United States and in Kaduna, he has worked for the Ministry of Works of Niger State since 1975, having advanced to senior technical officer by the early 1990s. He has published two novels—*Corpse as a Bridegroom* (1986) and *Blow of Fate* (1989)—as well as two plays, and also has written a number of unpublished plays. He is director of a small theater in Minna, the Dangana Educational Arts Theatre, which trains authors, actors, and actresses; the theater had thirty-five part-time students as of 1990.[45] Dangana has been president of the Niger State Chapter of the Association of Nigerian Authors and was one of the principal hosts when the ANA met in Minna in 1992. He also belongs to a number of writers' organizations such as Pen International and the Nigeria Folklore Association. In 1988 he was invited to participate in a Young Writers Program that toured eleven states in the United States, in the course of which he was made an honorary citizen of Louisville, Kentucky.

Dangana's stable employment history would be the envy of many educated Nigerians, but like many writers, he feels frustrated by his occupation outside of the literary world. "Frankly," he wrote on the author survey, "my career as a trained technician in my ministry has *never* given me a moment of artistic satisfaction for I crave nothing more than literary activities [and] affairs, which do not tally with my professional calling." Always an avid and omnivorous reader, Dangana got interested in writing when "I was reading Achebe's *Things Fall Apart* for the umpteenth time, sometime in 1975, when the inspiration started seeping in gradually into me. I later took up some magazines where, incidentally, I read about writers, their vocation, career, etcetera. I quickly decided to belong to the clique." The term *clique* suggests an image of writers as a closed circle sharing a lifestyle as well as a vocation, and Dangana has tried hard to make this image a reality.

But when, one might wonder, does he find time to write? Dangana reports devoting three or more hours a day to his literary pursuits, often at night but sometimes in his office during the day. (Nigerian writers have often told me they write when they are supposed to be doing something else.) His writing is prompted by both inspiration and convenience, and he has learned how to write even when he is not alone, an extremely valuable skill given the fact that Nigerians are rarely alone.

Like Okpi, Dangana writes to entertain. The plot of *Blow of Fate* is melodramatic but nevertheless engaging.

Flying to an Abuja conference on orphans, Ali flirts with Sala, who tells him she is engaged. The next day Ali finds a necklace and decides to sell it to help support orphans. Later he learns one of the conference delegates has been murdered, and her necklace stolen. He is afraid to go to the police because they will suspect him, but he tells Sala what has happened. She in turn shows him a letter from her fiancé, Haruna, who says he is dying and wants their marriage registered so he can leave her money in his will. Accompanied by Ali, Sala gets married in a lawyer's office "to a dead man."

After an ill-fated venture as a printer, Ali heads for Kaduna, accompanied by Sala. Their car is stolen with their belongings, including the necklace. Several days later Ali runs into Brigitte, a wealthy white woman, who tries to persuade him to help deliver illegal goods. He is drugged and taken to meet a criminal tycoon and his girlfriend—who is wearing the stolen necklace! Suddenly government security forces attack the house, and in the confusion Ali grabs the necklace and escapes.

Convinced that the necklace only brings bad luck, Ali and Sala offer to sell it to a rich man, who promptly has them arrested (he is the husband of the woman murdered at the conference). Sala and Ali are imprisoned. At their court appearance, Ali tells the truth, and in her testimony Sala stresses that they were motivated by their wish to help orphans. Both are acquitted of the murder but get short sentences for concealing the stolen necklace.

Months pass. Ali endures prison life; upon her release, Sala visits regularly. One day she shows up with the supposedly dead Haruna. He tells how he was hit by a car in India and, expecting to die, wrote to Sala about the marriage;

after coming out of a coma, he returned to Nigeria and tracked Sala down. He promises to get Ali released, and then, someday, together, the three of them will build that orphanage. Sala and Haruna leave a confused but happy Ali, who has learned that "wealth isn't everything."

(Yahaya Shafii Dangana, *Blow of Fate*)

Dangana's novel, like his earlier *Corpse as a Bridegroom*, is an action-packed, one-thing-after-another yarn, filled with implausible coincidences and loose ends, devoid of characterization or profundity. It is a good read, entertainment with a veneer of social conscience—"But, Your Honor, we only wanted to help orphans"—and in more propitious times Dangana might have made a career of churning out similar page-turners. But the times were not propitious. Dangana is old enough to have had high hopes born of the oil boom, but they have been dashed by the succeeding years of austerity. As an artistic entrepreneur, he regrets the financial squeeze that has constrained the operations of his theater. As a writer, he can reel off a host of problems that Nigerian writers face: "Lack of capital to purchase necessary stationeries (quite expensive) and to aid publishers in their work. Low readership quality. Exploitativeness of publishers (not all). Low quality of publicity, absence of adequate distribution formula, indifference of book shops and libraries, near-absence of royalties." Dangana pursues his literary career with energy, soliciting patrons and publicity for his enterprises and hoping to someday bring his theatrical troupe to the United States, but he is acutely aware of the obstacles he and other writers now face.

Strugglers like Dangana do not have the confidence once held by the oil boomers, but they share the earlier generation's commitment to literature.[46] May Ifeoma Nwoye exemplifies both the commitment and the difficulties. She is an Igbo, born in 1955 to a conservative Catholic family in Onitsha; as befits that traditional market city, both of her parents were traders. She attended Catholic schools and then traveled to Washington, D.C., for business studies, receiving a bachelor's degree in accounting from George Washington University and a master's degree in finance from Southeastern University. In the 1990s she was working on her doctorate in business. Since 1986 she has worked for the University of Benin in Benin City, currently as the head of budgets, projects and management information in the Bursary Department. Married to a senior lecturer in linguistics, she has a daughter and a son. She is active in the ANA, serving as secretary for the Edo/Delta chapter.

Despite her advanced degrees and her career success in recent years, Nwoye, like so many Nigerians of her generation, has had to cope with unemployment. After she and her husband returned from their studies in the United States, she spent a stint in the Youth Service but then was unable to find a job. Part of the problem may have been that she was job-seeking along American lines (she has held several accounting positions in the United States), not Nigerian ones. As she put it, "I was not able to find a job. I used to write my job application and put it in the mail, but I was later told that I had to lobby to get appointed to a position. [Such "lobbying" involves giving money and sometimes sexual favors.] That, I could not do, so I spent my unemployed period reading, and jotting down a lot of things I observed about people within the society. Sometimes I would stay indoors just reading and writing." In addition to developing her writing skills, Nwoye studied a number of small business entrepreneurs during this period. She also became increasingly sympathetic to the condition of women. As she noted, "Many of the people I came in contact with, especially women, were often dying in silence as culture and tradition are repulsive to the idea of women's liberation." The problems specific to Nigerian women, especially educated ones, became a theme in her writing. Of the three writers she admires—Flora Nwapa, Chinua Achebe, and Buchi Emecheta—it is notable that two are Nigerian women of a distinctly feminist cast.

Nwoye has published three books: a novel in 1993 called *The Endless Search*, a collection of short stories in 1994 entitled *Tides of Life*, and a social science text on small businesses, now in its second edition. She regards herself first of all as an observer. "I have personally observed a lot of goings-ons in terms of human interactions and social activities in Nigerian society and felt the need to document the behavior of people, their characteristics and their wishes even if they can be viewed as fiction. So what I do is to mirror the society to entertain and to create awareness." In other words, she bears witness. Her writing chronicles some of the frustrations of Nigerian daily life—a story about an attempted shakedown by the widely detested Nigerian Electric Power Authority (NEPA) is a comic gem[47]—as well as the more deeply rooted tensions between women and men in a rapidly changing society.

The Endless Search explores a theme that a number of women authors have treated: the Nigerian husband who maintains an egalitarian relationship with his wife while the couple lives abroad but treats her cruelly, aided and abetted by his family, when they return to Nigeria.

> Having supported Chuma in the United States while he earned his Ph.D., Nkoli plans to complete her own education now that they are back in Nigeria, but Chuma, a university lecturer, won't hear of it. Mama Grace, Nkoli's mother-in-law, who despises her because she has borne only two daughters, urges Chuma to take a second wife, as does his sister Arima. Nkoli finds support from her American friend Sally, who is married to a Nigerian named Mike in what seems to be a loving partnership.

When Chuma's domineering attitude and Mama Grace's meddling become intolerable, Nkoli leaves home and moves in with Sally and Mike. Chuma, now sexually involved with a student named Rose, tries to get Nkoli fired and seizes their common property. Starting over as an independent woman, Nkoli applies to the university. She also grows infatuated with Mike and they kiss, much to his chagrin. Ashamed, Nkoli begins missing Chuma.

Weeks pass. Rose turns out to be a drug smuggler. Shaken, Chuma also begins to miss the life he had shared with Nkoli. A sick daughter brings husband and wife back together; they reconcile, and Nkoli moves back home (to Mike's relief).

Mama Grace and Arima try to undo things again. Mama gets a potion to make Chuma hate Nkoli, but when she slips it into his food, he falls deathly ill. He is hospitalized, and Mama Grace runs away. Arima schemes to get Nkoli blamed, but Chuma recovers and the family is reunited. They find Mama Grace starving herself through guilt. They take her back home and nurse her; recovering, she begs Nkoli's forgiveness.

(May Ifeoma Nwoye, *The Endless Search*)

Nwoye intended "the endless search" to refer to the educated African woman's search for security, but the title could refer to third-generation writers' search as well. It is significant that her novel and the short stories were put out by different publishers (Kraft in Ibadan and UTO in Lagos), neither of which seems to have published any other Nigerian novels; novelists of this generation, even well-connected ones, have difficulty establishing lasting relationships with publishers of fiction. They are lucky if they get published at all, and Nwoye herself has written many unpublished works. She sees getting published as the main problem for writers: "You can see a lot of manuscripts flying around, crying for attention, and finally the authors are discouraged. I personally have two unfinished manuscripts but I am in no hurry to finish them because the publishers are crying for hard times." And this from a writer who has already enjoyed considerable success and attention—an endless search indeed.

Typical of the strugglers is a certain bleakness of outlook, a social and personal pessimism that gives rise to an occasional note of resignation. In her short introduction to *Tides of Life*, Nwoye says, "We are cluttered up in a society bound by hypocrisy, inconsistencies and general confusion. . . . I labour not to condemn, not to criticize, only to comprehend and later recall. For, ultimately, we are human." Such a statement is notably at odds with her expressed desire to make things better. Like virtually all third-generation novelists, Nwoye writes to contribute to social improvement, for "the people are suffering and many roam about with no clear direction. If there is anything I can do to contribute in straightening out issues, I will not hesitate in doing it." She seems balanced between this wish for her writing to make a difference and her fatalistic acceptance that the ills of Nigerian society are rooted in some "human" condition.

Aspirations

Authors like Munonye, Okpi, Dangana, and Nwoye are highly educated members of a social elite. It is not the only Nigerian elite—there is little overlap, for example, between the northern military leaders who run the government and the southern university graduates who write the novels[48]—but there can be no question that these are a privileged group of people. And one aspect of privilege is the ability to make choices. These Nigerians are fortunate enough to have many ways to spend their time and energy. So, in light of their plenitude of options, why do they choose to write novels?

Money is definitely not the motivation. As we have seen, it is virtually impossible to earn a living from writing in Nigeria. Probably only three writers have even come close over the course of their careers: Wole Soyinka, greatly helped by his winning the Nobel Prize; Chinua Achebe, but much of his income has come from teaching and being a writer-in-residence; and Buchi Emecheta, who augments her income with teaching and lecturing. Booker Prize winner Ben Okri has become a fourth, at least recently. These exceptions aside, most writers receive little or no income from their novels. If they publish in Nigeria, their only real hope for profit is to have one of their books selected as a "set book," a required text for students. Otherwise, only those who publish with a British or American company can expect to see much by way of royalties. In fact, the authors I spoke with often said something like, "Well, you know I'm not *really* a writer," for they felt that real writers ought to be able to live off their writing.

Although novelists grumble about not earning any money, blaming cheating publishers and an apathetic public, money is not what motivates them to write in the first place. Under 10 percent of the novelists describe money as their principal goal. Not surprisingly, these are concentrated in the second generation, the group that thought it might be possible to live off one's earnings as a writer. Over twice as many are motivated by the desire to create great literature. Again, it is not surprising to find that this literary emphasis is strongest among writers of the first generation. The great majority of Nigerian novelists, however, write to inspire some form of social improvement.[49] They see writers as having a responsibility to serve society; they see Nigeria as deeply troubled; and they argue that the writer must document social problems. Anything else is "art for art's sake," an idea they consistently reject.

Viewed through this lens of social concern, even thrillers become vehicles for the exploration of social problems. When I spoke with third-generation novelist Dibia Humphrey (the pen name used by Umunna Humphrey Orjiako), he stressed that the writer must "codify" Nigerian social problems so that they become available for inspection. Humphrey believes that a Nigerian crime writer can not just entertain and "be a Jeffrey Archer" but must expose corruption. Given its vast resources, Nigeria could be and do anything, Humphrey contends, if only its people could learn to forgo the excessive materialism and conspicuous consumption that the precolonial social hierarchy established for the elite and the oil-boom years encouraged in everyone else. Such materialism must be rejected in favor of the development of human resources.

Thus he described *Drop of Mercy* (1987) as a critical and didactic treatment of the "oil doom," the moral decay the accompanied the wealth of the oil-rich years.

> Miki meets Jordana, a half-Arab sexpot, while both are students at the University of Lagos. Ambitious for big money, they become lovers and partners in crime. Their scam: smuggling dope into Spain using tourists and students as the unwitting carriers. Miki and Jordana hold rather Darwinian attitudes about social winners and losers and don't show "a drop of mercy" for the carriers left rotting in Spanish prisons.
>
> As the two make a fortune and climb the social ladder, they are aided and abetted by various corrupt politicians, civil servants, and businesspeople. When they finally decide to marry and retire, they are double-crossed by Jordana's uncle, who almost succeeds in stealing their money. They manage to slaughter him and his family, but they in turn are tortured and killed by two released prisoners whom they had previously conned.
>
> (Dibia Humphrey, *Drop of Mercy*)

Standard pulp fiction, one might say—*Drop of Mercy* can be read as a routine thriller about a poor boy who turns to crime, lives the fast life, and gets his just desserts—but Humphrey sees it as bearing witness to the moral cesspool that oil-rich Nigeria had become by the early 1980s. Toward the end of the novel a bank manager, as corrupt as everyone else, reads an editorial prompted by the fall in oil prices that celebrates: "No more luxury trips for the kids, or the mistress to pick up the latest Paris fashion. No more round-the-world-in-eighty-days tours to find solutions to indigenous Nigerian problems. Hurrah! The petronaira decade is over! Extravagant living, padding of government payrolls and contracts, contracts, and more contracts! They are all gone with the wind." While the bank manager, whose own mistress is headed for a Paris shopping spree, fumes about why the police don't crack down on irresponsible journalists, the reader sees the possible dawn of a new era—as does Humphrey, who regards his novel as a jeremiad preaching new values to a rotten society.

Humphrey is a writer of the third generation, which has particularly insisted on the writer's social responsibility, but the belief that the writer should be a witness to what's wrong and a guide to making it right is shared by writers of all three generations. Tolu Ajayi, who straddles the second and third generations, contends that writers should be social and moral leaders, not just reporters. He points out that many people who have come to power in Africa are not well educated, so it is up to the educated ones to offer guidance. Everything from family planning to superstition should be subject to scrutiny, and in some cases advocacy, by the novelist-cum-teacher. Ajayi reiterates that Nigeria can not afford "art for art's sake." This is a matter not of parochialism—Ajayi is widely traveled and very knowledgeable about European and American literature[50]—but of commitment. Ajayi is hardly naive, for he recognizes that "Nigerian society's problems are so inveterate it is highly improbable a novel could inspire any major improvements." Nevertheless, he sees himself as an "explainer," using his scientific knowledge to help his countrymen understand the world around them. While his message is more complex than Dibia Humphrey's lurid depiction of the wages of sin, both authors are committed to social reform and see their writing as serving this end. In this they are like the vast majority of their counterparts: bearing witness, teaching lessons, endlessly searching for a better society.

THE BUSINESS

Dazzled by the bright lights of Ibadan, Akin contrives to go to secondary school there. He bamboozles his parents into thinking he is doing well, but he gets expelled and they disown him. Akin becomes a bus driver's apprentice but is eager for bigger things. After witnessing a terrible accident on the Ibadan-Lagos expressway, he seems to lose his nerve, quits being a driver, and decides to go into business for himself.

He starts up "Rising Star Enterprises" with Akpan, a shady ex-policeman. Impressed by his chutzpah, Akin's friends can't figure out where he got the start-up capital. Akin is successful as the director of his company, which trades in commodities like cement and beer. He throws lots of money around, thereby attracting the glamorous Bimpe.

The high living is costly, however, and when Akin and Akpan push their luck and hijack a cement shipment, they are arrested. Newspapers report that Akin had robbed a briefcase full of money at the scene of the traffic accident on the Ibadan-Lagos road, and that was where the young entrepreneur had obtained the capital for Rising Star. The papers also report Bimpe's attempted suicide.

(Agbo Areo, *Director!*)

Director! is another thriller-cum-social-jeremiad of the type seen earlier. The plot is the product of Agbo Areo's mind, but the book is the product of a set of literary institutions. *Director!* marks a significant turning point in the publishing history for Nigerian fiction, as we shall see, but all novels depend upon and are influenced by the publication context of their first appearance. No matter how intense their social concerns or how juicy their thrillers, Nigerian novelists do not just press their manuscripts into the hands of waiting readers. Publication and distribution mediate between novel writer and novel reader; its commercial quality is a distinguishing characteristic of the genre. At the very least publishing means printing multiple copies of a novel; at the most it involves bringing the novel into being by encouraging would-be writers and, at the other end, promoting and distributing the finished work. Without publication and sales, there is no novel.

As is typical of postcolonial countries, Nigerian publishing is bipolar, divided between London and Nigeria. The following sections will examine the British publishers of Nigerian novels first, because they came first in fact; the Nigerian publishers; and then book distribution in Nigeria today. These commercial factors are essential to the Nigerian literary complex because they influence what stories get told and who bears witness to whom.

British Publishers

Although conceived in Nigeria, the Nigerian novel was born in London. As described earlier, Faber and Faber took a chance on Amos Tutuola, and Andrew Dakers followed with Cyprian Ekwensi. Six of the seven Nigerian novels that came out during the 1950s were published in London: four by Tutuola, Ekwensi's *People of the City* (Dakers), and Chinua Achebe's *Things Fall Apart* (Heinemann). The single exception was T. M. Aluko's *One Man, One Wife*, which he published himself in Lagos in 1959. The situation was the same during the 1960s: every one of the twenty-seven Nigerian novels published came out in London.

British publishers were old hands at publishing for the African market.[51] The large, multinational publishing houses collectively known as the "Big Six"—Heinemann, Macmillan, Longman, Evans, Oxford University Press, and Nelson—produced the texts used in colonial African schools. Throughout the 1950s and beyond, these books were the same as the ones used in European schools; only in such areas as history and geography did books specifically deal with Africa, and even these were written by expatriates with a British point of view until independence and after. The Big Six have continued their influence in the publishing of school texts, both from the United Kingdom and through independent African companies like Macmillan Nigeria, but only Heinemann, Macmillan, and Longman have published much fiction.

The flagship publisher for African literature has been Heinemann. For forty years Heinemann's African Writers Series has been the most prestigious line for African fiction, drama, and poetry in English. Heinemann Educational Books directors Van Milne and Alan Hill conceived of the series in 1959, when rapidly approaching African independence and anticipated educational advances suggested new opportunities. Trade lore has it that one reason they decided to launch the series was to keep *Things Fall Apart* in print, and in a less expensive format than the original hardback edition. Be that as it may, Milne and Hill saw supply and demand converging: a generation of writers educated after World War II, often at the new African universities, coincided with the educational ambitions and cultural aspirations of the new nations. They asked Achebe to serve as editor in chief of the new series. He agreed, and in 1962 the African Writers Series was launched with Cyprian Ekwensi's *Burning Grass,* new editions of *Things Fall Apart* and *No Longer at Ease,* and Kenneth Kuanda's nonfictional *Zambia Shall Be Free.*

By the end of 1979, the African Writers Series had published 225 titles. One hundred fifty of these were works of fiction, and over a quarter (thirty-nine) were by Nigerians. New novels by previously published writers like Aluko and Ekwensi, and new writers like Flora Nwapa, Elechi Amadi, and John Munonye, appeared in the series during the 1960s; all of these writers would go on to prolific careers with Heinemann. This group of early Nigerian writers, the "first generation," is notable both for its talent and because most were Igbo. This would continue to be the case well into the second generation; of the fifteen Nigerian novelists published in the AWS before 1980, only five were not Igbo.[52]

Heinemann was not the only player. Other London publishers were similarly impressed by the new voices from postcolonial Africa, and by the possibilities of profiting from the expanding market there. In the early sixties Hutchinson published Onuora Nzekwu's three novels in rapid succession; it also published a couple by Ekwensi, including the notorious *Jagua Nana.* Andre Deutsch published a handful of Nigerian novels, most notably Wole Soyinka's first novel, *The Interpreters.* And Faber and Faber continued to bring out Tutuola's books, with four new titles between 1955 and 1967.

Publication accelerated, and by the mid-sixties British publishers were averaging a half dozen new Nigerian novels each year. Immediately after the civil war the pace picked up again, with eight novels coming out in 1970. No doubt these publishing houses were committed to encouraging the development of African literature, but with ever greater numbers of African youth growing ever more literate, they were also intent on doing well by doing good. The Nigerian market was the prize as the country moved into the oil-rich seventies, for Nigeria had the numbers, the naira, and the burgeoning educational system.

Throughout the decade, Britain continued to dominate the publication of Nigerian novels. A few firms published the work of only one Nigerian author, as in the case of Adaora Lily Ulasi with Michael Joseph; such a publisher was not specializing in African fiction or exporting to an African market but just happened to have a Nigerian author. The same could be said of Andre Deutsch, which brought out a second novel by Nwankwo but was not destined to be a major Nigerian publisher, and of Faber and Faber, which mainly stuck with Tutuola (the company had published one additional Nigerian novel, Obi Egbuna's *Wind versus Polygamy,* later retitled *Elina,* in 1964). Allison and Busby, publisher of Buchi Emecheta's works, represents a niche publisher; one of its founders, Margaret Busby, is a Ghanaian who has a special commitment to African women writers.[53] Far and away the most active publisher continued to be Heinemann; seventeen novels by Nigerians came out under the imprimatur of the African Writers Series in the 1970s. Longman was influential as well. This firm had long emphasized Commonwealth writers, and although it published only four Nigerian novels during the seventies, these included works by such important second-generation writers as Isidore Okpewho and Festus Iyayi. Fontana brought out a half dozen titles in the second half of the 1970s, including three by Chukwuemeka Ike.

If the high quality African Writers Series was the significant publishing development in the 1960s, the key event of the seventies was of a more popular sort: in 1977 Macmillan launched its Pacesetters series. Inaugurated with the publication of Areo Agbo's *Director!,* Pacesetters aimed at those young Africans whose accelerating numbers and increasing years of education created an enticing new market. Unlike at Heinemann, the Pacesetters editors did not see themselves as fostering fine writing so much as producing a product—books—for an emerging readership. Unabashedly commercial, they sought writers, like Kalu Okpi, who could tell a good story and hold the African readers' interest.

The Pacesetters' appeal for leisure-time reading marked a considerable shift. British publishers had hitherto concentrated on producing textbooks as well as a limited amount of serious literature, but they had not gone in for popular entertainment. A year after Pacesetters began, a Macmillan Education editor described the multinational firm's position as one of trying to move beyond school texts without moving beyond a good-sized market. Many people had believed that multinationals like Macmillan "concentrate too much on the obviously profitable lines—the main course books—and that they neglect those books which are immediately less profitable, but which also are important educationally. Such books can be those in the mother tongue, books for children and creative writing. It seems obvious, however, that if a publishing firm operating in Africa is to appear credible, it should publish across the educational board."[54] She went on to note that Macmillan Nigeria was taking care of the mother tongue and children's books, while back in England the editors had turned their attention to creative writing. After acknowledging that Heinemann had blazed the trail here, she went on to defend Macmillan's decision to move in a more popular direction: "There are, no doubt, many African novels in manuscript form which deserve to be published but if they are too sophisticated in style their readership may be small. Macmillan have [*sic*] chosen to enter the field of African popular fiction, believing that well-written novels in English, written in a simple style, will help to promote reading fluency. We believe also that the production of books at this level may help to encourage creative writing generally."[55]

Although Pacesetters authors came from throughout Anglophone Africa, and although the books were distributed just as widely, Nigeria was the key to the series. Nigeria had more young people than any other African country by far, these youth were staying in school longer, and they had money to spend. During the oil boom of the seventies it seemed that there would be ever-increasing numbers of educated young Nigerians seeking diversion through paperback novels with contemporary themes. Macmillan aimed to satisfy that demand, and to make a profit in doing so.

It would do so with books that told a good tale and told it well. The editor described the company's criteria to me thus:

> We chose the Pacesetter manuscripts for publication on the basis of (a) a good story, (b) the general "feel" of the style. Many of these manuscripts come in written in poor English, but there is something special about the style. . . . We can improve the English, but can't add to the magic which is entirely African! In the Pacesetters we look for a variety of subjects—love stories are the most popular, but we look for ones with a different twist. The readers are very varied, so we need to vary the themes. The series was originally started with the needs of reluctant young adult readers in mind, for whom there was nothing in the market except Western pulp fiction. While their needs are still catered for, we have come to realize how many other sorts of people are passionate about the series.[56]

Many Pacesetters offer moral instruction as well as excitement. Attracting readers with consumption, violence, and sex, they then go on—in a form of hypocrisy dear to creators of popular culture—to show why these are false idols. Areo's *Director!*, which charts the rise and fall of the ambitious but unscrupulous Akin who founds his business empire on stolen money, established the pattern. Areo's novel is hardly profound, nor did he intend it to be. The plot moves briskly, unencumbered by much characterization or a sense of the protagonist being torn between two worlds as in Achebe's *No Longer at Ease*; Akin knows what he wants. Some of the book's appeal—the sexy Bimpe, the urban high life that Akin longs to enter—recalls Ekwensi's portraits of urban decadence. *Director!* appeals to young readers who share Akin's ambitions, if not his methods; such ambitions were especially keen in the heady 1970s atmosphere in which anything seemed possible.

Macmillan Nigeria handled the distribution of the Pacesetters novels and aggressively promoted the series. One scheme for raising product awareness was the annual Pacesetters quiz, wherein readers competed for cash prizes by answering questions like "Where does Inspector Nur find the incriminating papers which list the names of the members of *The Black Temple* ?"[57] The series recruited new authors with the same energy. The back of the Pacesetters 1981–82 catalog called for aspiring writers to submit manuscripts: "If you've ever seen yourself as a best-selling paperback novelist, this could be the lucky break you've been waiting for." Such promotional devices, accompanied by the slogan "Pick Up a Pacesetter," were new in the African book trade, and they raised expectations in both writers and readers.

For several years Pacesetters flourished, largely on the strength of the Nigerian market. But the high hopes for the series—like so many others in Nigeria—were to be dashed in the 1980s. The oil-bust years saw Nigerian disposable income dry up, and books (both imported and domestic) became luxuries that few could afford. Macmillan pulled back. By the end of the decade it was publishing fewer Pacesetters, and those that were published were likely to have Kenyan or other non-Nigerian authors. The turnaround was dramatic. By 1989 Macmillan had published eighty-nine Pacesetters. Of the first twenty, from Areo's *Director!* (1977) through Yemi Sikuade's *Sisi* (1981), only two were written by authors who were not Nigerians. But of the last twenty, from Dede Kamkondo's *Truth Will Out* (1986) to Andrew Sesinyi's *Rassie* (1989), only two were by Nigerians. When second- and third-generation writers speak of the current lack of publishing opportunities, the rise and fall of Pacesetters epitomizes what they feel they have lost.

As a whole, British firms retreated. Heinemann and Longman, less dependent on the African market, continued to bring out Nigerian novels but at a slower pace. Figure 2-2, which shows the relative position of novels published in Nigeria and outside (mostly in Britain), suggests that, although some absolute decline in Nigerian novels has taken place since the early eighties, by and large Nigerian publishers have replaced British ones. This replacement has had a number of consequences, some of them deleterious to authors and readers. It is to these that I shall now turn.

Nigerian Publishers

In the 1950s an Ijesha Yoruba who had studied engineering in London was working as executive engineer for the Nigeria Public Works Department and then as the town engineer for the Lagos Town Council. A career in engineering was not enough for Timothy Mofolofunso Aluko, however. He had a story to tell, about an African torn between the two worlds of the West and his local community, a story he knew firsthand. Writing had been Aluko's hobby ever since his secondary school days in Ibadan, and he had published several short stories in conjunction with writing competitions organized by the British Council. He decided to try writing a novel.

The result was *One Man, One Wife*, the first Nigerian novel to be published at home. *One Man, One Wife* is a satire on the conflict between the ways of the white people (Christianity in particular, but also literacy, sanitation, ending human sacrifice, etc.) and those of a traditional Yoruba village, with Aluko poking fun at both sides. The novel presents a series of episodes involving the citizens of Isolo as they experience Christian evangelizing, smallpox epidemics, court cases, and the loves and enmities of village life. It maintains a humorous tone even though the subjects include death, madness, and long-standing feuds.

Aluko published *One Man, One Wife* himself in 1959, printing it through the Nigerian Print and Publishing Company in Lagos. Aluko's satirical fiction was not to remain a local product. Heinemann quickly discovered him, and the African Writers Series published four more of his novels between 1964 and 1972, as well as reprinting *One Man, One Wife*. Back in Nigeria, despite Aluko's early venture, local publishing of novels remained negligible until well into the 1970s.[58]

It was not that there was no local publishing: newspapers, advertising circulars, and pamphlets abounded. Local publishing during this period had a great influence on the Nigerian novel, not directly through the publication of the novels themselves but indirectly, especially through the famous Onitsha market pamphlets.

In the years following World War II, a variety of factors contributed to the Onitsha phenomenon.[59] The key seems to have been a postwar availability of obsolete printing presses in the rapidly growing commercial center of the Eastern Region, coinciding with a supply of demobilized soldiers looking for a trade to take up. Given the rise in literacy of Onitsha migrants and residents (often the ex-soldiers themselves had learned to read in the army), many would-be entrepreneurs bought a press and set up business. They printed anything—advertising posters, calling cards, invitations, and the popular pamphlets now collectively known as the Onitsha market literature.

These pamphlets may have begun in imitation of Indian models the soldiers had encountered while abroad, although popular fiction from England was not new to Nigeria. Onitsha market literature catered to the interests of the aspiring, newly (and often barely) literate urbanites, mostly young men. Some were strictly practical, such as *How to Write Business Letters and Applications*.[60] Some aimed at moral reform, such as *Money Is*

Hard to Get But Easy to Spend, or *Why Boys Never Trust Money-Monger Girls.* Some were stories that seemed to be told for sheer entertainment, although these generally had a moral message tagged on. *Mabel the Sweet Honey That Poured Away* is a lurid portrait of a girl gone wrong, but her death served as a warning against promiscuity. Many of the pamphlets, both fiction and nonfiction, dealt with love and marriage. It has been suggested that romance was an overriding concern of the returning veterans, especially when they found that in their absence, older men had taken as second or third wives many of the girls who otherwise would have been available for the young ex-soldiers.

Another striking feature of the pamphlet literature is its enthusiasm for modernity, self-improvement, and making money.

> In contrast to the novelists and intellectual playwrights who criticize material acquisition and the achievement-oriented outlook of the present time, [the pamphlet writers] are essentially materialists for whom economic prosperity is an index of progress. The popular authors extol hard work and frugality. . . . They issue advice to young men and women on how they should conduct themselves in order to make the best of their economic opportunities. Many of these advice books read like some of the eighteenth-century conduct books of Defoe and his contemporaries. (Obiechina 1972:14–15)

There is a certain double standard at work, for while the pamphlets celebrate the pursuit of wealth, they also warn young men repeatedly about money-hungry girls.

Although Onitsha was the most famous source of the pamphlet literature, and has been made more so to the outside world by the scholarly attention it has received, it was not the only place where the newly literate were providing reading material for the barely literate. In Ibadan, for example, Niyi Oniororo published a series of pamphlets beginning in the 1960s that are essentially the same as their Onitsha counterparts.[61] His *Lagos Is a Wicked Place* (1968) features another fallen woman much like Mabel the Sweet Honey. Bisi rejects poor but honest Ayo in favor of a Lagos con man who dazzles her family with his apparent wealth, and she winds up a worn-out prostitute. The pamplet ends on the usual note of warning: "Bisi was a very beautiful, dreamy lofty high minded girl who in her search for a wealthy husband was disappointed by a disastrous marriage. The whole edifice of her amorous imagination collapsed. She spent the rest of her life in suffering" (58). But Bisi is more sinned against than sinning, for Oniororo makes it clear that outmoded traditions drove Bisi to her shame. At the end of the story, her looks and money gone, Bisi writes to Ayo, now a Lagos newspaper editor, to see if she can rekindle the flame. When he writes back to say there is no hope, Ayo reviews her history:

Your parents wanted to sell you in the market to the highest bidder. It was an impossible sum for me and my poor parents. But today, reality mocks your cruelty. You see, I denounce your parents' attitude. I denounce the dictatorship of the clan which demands that a girl marry the man her parents choose for her in order to maintain the financial balance of the family budget, I denounce a custom which permits fathers to exploit their children more than any other nation has exploited this country. I denounce a tradition which threatens the individual and national liberty by the control of the young by the old. (58)

We have seen this theme of youth being ruined by the bride-price "dictatorship" in Ajayi's *The Lesson*, which came out seventeen years after Oniororo's pamphlet. The Onitsha and Onitsha-type pamphlets weighed in in favor of modernity very early on and may have influenced the expectations of those who would become the reading public for novels. Again, a double standard is at work. Bisi's leaving the village to find a wealthy husband is a twisted observance of a tradition that Ayo hints may be more destructive than colonialism itself, while Ayo's going to Lagos to pursue a journalism career is a matter of social mobility, making one's way in the modernizing sector. Pamphlet literature—double standard notwithstanding—was all about making one's way.

During the prosperous and optimistic oil-boom years, one way people could make their way was to go into publishing. The civil war had shattered the Onitsha regime, but the local production of popular literature reappeared in the postwar era on an even larger scale. Just as the Onitsha ex-soldier had done in the 1950s, Nigerian publishers emerged in the 1970s to serve the needs of, and cash in on, the growing reading public. Nigeria was not yet a nation of readers, everyone said, but it soon would be.

In Ibadan, Onibonoje became a major publisher of fiction, with books by Kole Omotoso, one of the most important writers of the second generation. In Akure, Fagbamigbe began publishing in the late seventies; the company would publish twenty novels by the end of the eighties. In Lagos, Cross-Continent was launched. In addition, a number of authors published their own books. Some were one-shot jobs, as in the case of Okafor Azikiwe, who printed his "self-published" novel *Gifts for Mother* with Bendel Newspapers. Some were more substantial enterprises: Flora Nwapa, who had been an early author with the African Writers Series (and the only woman in the pioneer generation), used her considerable means to start her own press in Enugu.

As we have seen, in the late seventies, when growing numbers of literate Nigerians with money to spend seemed to promise would-be publishers a rapidly expanding market, Nigerian publishers began to challenge the British dominance. By the middle of the eighties the majority of Nigerian novels were being published by Nigerian companies.[62] Many of these were small-scale operations that, while lacking the prestige of a Heinemann or a Longman, were more accessible to Nigerian authors. The physical and literary quality of their books often left much to be desired. Nigerian book production, binding, and illustration, especially if the publisher is small or the book is published by the author, was and usually is inferior compared to European or American books, and editing ranges from barely adequate to nonexistent.[63]

Some publishing firms have been more sophisticated enterprises and have turned out books of a higher physical and editorial quality. Spectrum, founded in 1978, became a major force in Nigerian fiction. This Ibadan firm has produced several popular fiction series, including the Sunshine Romances with Bisi Abejo's love stories and the Panti Street Crime Series of police thrillers by Louis Omotoyo Johnson. Spectrum also publishes more serious novels by writers like Ike, Ekwensi, and Omotoso, as well as Wole Soyinka's autobiographical books. Spectrum is unusual in its breadth, for it publishes academic texts, trade nonfiction, and both serious and popular literature. (The company scored a particular coup when it got Frederick Forsyth, a British writer of best-selling thrillers and a Biafran sympathizer, to write a biography of Chukwuemeka Ojukwu, Biafra's former head of state.)

Also located in Ibadan, Agbo Areo's new firm, Paperback Publishers, brought out a dozen novels in the mid-eighties, including his own political thriller *A Paradise for the Masses*. Other newcomers in the 1980s included Writers Fraternity in Lagos; Delta (notable for its annual fiction prize) and Fourth Dimension in Enugu; Northern Nigeria Publishers in Zaria; and smaller enterprises like Idodo Umeh in Benin City, Triumph in Kano, and Leadway and Jet in Onitsha. Ibadan is still considered the center of Nigerian publishing and is the home of most textbook publishers, but during the oil-boom years fiction was being published throughout the country.

But the good times were not to last. Nigerian publishing had always been beset with problems obtaining materials—ink, film, chemicals, plates, and most of all paper—as a result of high customs duties and scarce foreign exchange.[64] With only three paper mills, newsprint was both insufficient and expensive. And the expenses involved in importing foreign books added to the costs incurred by local booksellers, schools, and libraries.

These problems could be dealt with only so long as people had money to spend. With the end of the oil boom and the economic collapse that followed, capped by the Structural Adjustment Program (SAP) of 1986 and the Second-Tier Foreign Exchange Market (SFEM) that devalued the naira, the Nigerian market for books, especially trade fiction, evaporated. The cost of books went up as the value of the naira declined. All books, not just imports, were affected, since even local publishers depended heavily on imported materials. Moreover, SAP/SFEM dried up the credit Nigerian booksellers and publishers used to enjoy from overseas suppliers, which were frightened by the perilous economic situation and the sharp, and not final, devaluation of the naira. Nigerian libraries, publishers, and booksellers were left having to pay back old debts to foreign suppliers with a naira worth perhaps only a tenth of its former value. As a result, many booksellers and publishers went out of business, libraries stopped acquiring new books and journals, and books disappeared from the shelves of the few remaining book outlets.[65]

Novels became a luxury. In 1991, for example, Ben Okri's novel *The Famished Road* won the Booker Prize. Shortly afterward, at the annual meeting of the Association of Nigerian Authors in November, I observed a representative of the British Council showing a copy around, but Okri's book was unavailable in Nigeria. The following year the prizewinner was on sale in Lagos, in the British hardcover edition, for five hundred naira, at the time equivalent to about twenty-seven dollars. Only a handful of Nigerians could afford such a book.[66] Even fewer would be inclined to buy it; those Nigerians who were interested in books and had the means to buy them were scrounging around to get textbooks and other books they needed to prepare for examinations. For all but a very few Nigerians, if they had developed the habit of reading fiction at all, it was a habit recently acquired and easily broken.[67]

As the British publishers retreated in the face of the disappearing market, some Nigerian publishers managed to hang on, often putting out fewer books, and even a few new ones emerged. By the end of the decade Spectrum and Fagbamigbe had been joined by Malthouse in Ikeja (Lagos), a high-quality publisher along the lines of Spectrum. Ken Saro-Wiwa established his own publishing house in Port Harcourt (Saros International). For some of the larger houses such as the independent companies associated with British firms—Macmillan Nigeria, Heinemann Nigeria, Longman Nigeria—literature became fixed as a classy but unprofitable appendix to textbook publishing. Bayo Adebowale argues that most Nigerian publishing houses still operate under colonial assumptions, regarding publication as a "special favor to the author." He concludes, "It is not enough to talk about decolonizing African Literature, we should also begin to talk now about decolonizing African Publishing."[68]

Shaky though it may be, Nigerian publishing remains a leader in its context, for Africa is a minor player in world publishing. In 1985 sub-Saharan Africa, with roughly 9 percent of the world's population, produced only 1.3 percent of the book titles published.[69] South Africa publishing is most fully developed; the only other African countries with well-established publishing systems are Kenya, Zimbabwe, and Nigeria.[70] One Organization of

African Unity (OAU) study from 1988 estimated that Nigeria had three hundred publishing houses.[71] While such numbers must be taken with a grain of salt, all agree that within the African context Nigeria's publishing industry is impressive, as is its surrounding network of book-related activities. Nigeria has a wealth of professional literary associations: the Association of Nigerian Authors (ANA), Nigerian Publishers Association (NPA), Children's Literature Association of Nigeria (CLAN), Nigerian Booksellers Association (NBA), International Board for Books for Young people (IBBY). The country mounts several annual book fairs; the most prestigious one is the Ife Book Fair, begun in 1974, but there are prominent fairs in Enugu and Kaduna as well.[72] Thus it appears that if its economy were to improve and barriers to imports (of books and of raw materials) removed, the country would have the organizational infrastructure in place to realize the writers' dream of turning Nigeria into a "reading culture," but that remains only a dream.[73]

I have been focusing on British and Nigerian publication of Nigerian fiction because only a handful of Nigerian novels have been published anywhere else. A couple have come out of Nairobi, one from Quebec, and several from "subsidized" (i.e. vanity) publishers like Vantage Press in New York. New novels by established writers like Achebe and Emecheta, or promising new voices like Simi Bedford, get published in the United States shortly after they appear in Britain. But no publishing house outside of Nigeria or the United Kingdom has played an important role.

A book's physical qualities reveal something about its publisher's resources and expectations. It is a brutal fact that most Nigerian novels will not last very long, for most are published only in paperback form. This is the case for every novel published in Nigeria, as well as for the two major British lines: Heinemann's African Writers Series and Macmillan's Pacesetters. Reprints in more durable forms are possibilities for successful writers, and a few authors like Ben Okri and Buchi Emecheta have hardcover first editions, but most Nigerian fiction lives and dies between soft covers.

The covers are often unattractive, especially if the book is published in Nigeria. There are many exceptions: a blazing sunset behind him, a brooding bureaucrat wearing a coat and tie stands outside an ornate building gazing at his shadow, while inside a richly robed man turns away (Fig. 2-3a). Far more typical, however, is a crude line drawing (3b,c) or simply no art at all (3d). Many of the latter use only two or three colors on the cover, like *Voodoo Republic* with its red top, white middle, and strip of black at the bottom. Even the high-end publishers like Malthouse and Spectrum appear to devote little attention to making their books visually enticing. A few publishers of thrillers—notably Fagbamigbe—lure readers with a photograph of a sexy woman (3e); indeed, attractive women in modern or traditional garb are commonplace. Novels that are published in Britain have

FIGURE 2-3. Typical covers of Nigerian novels

a. Abubakar Gimba's *Sunset for a Mandarin*

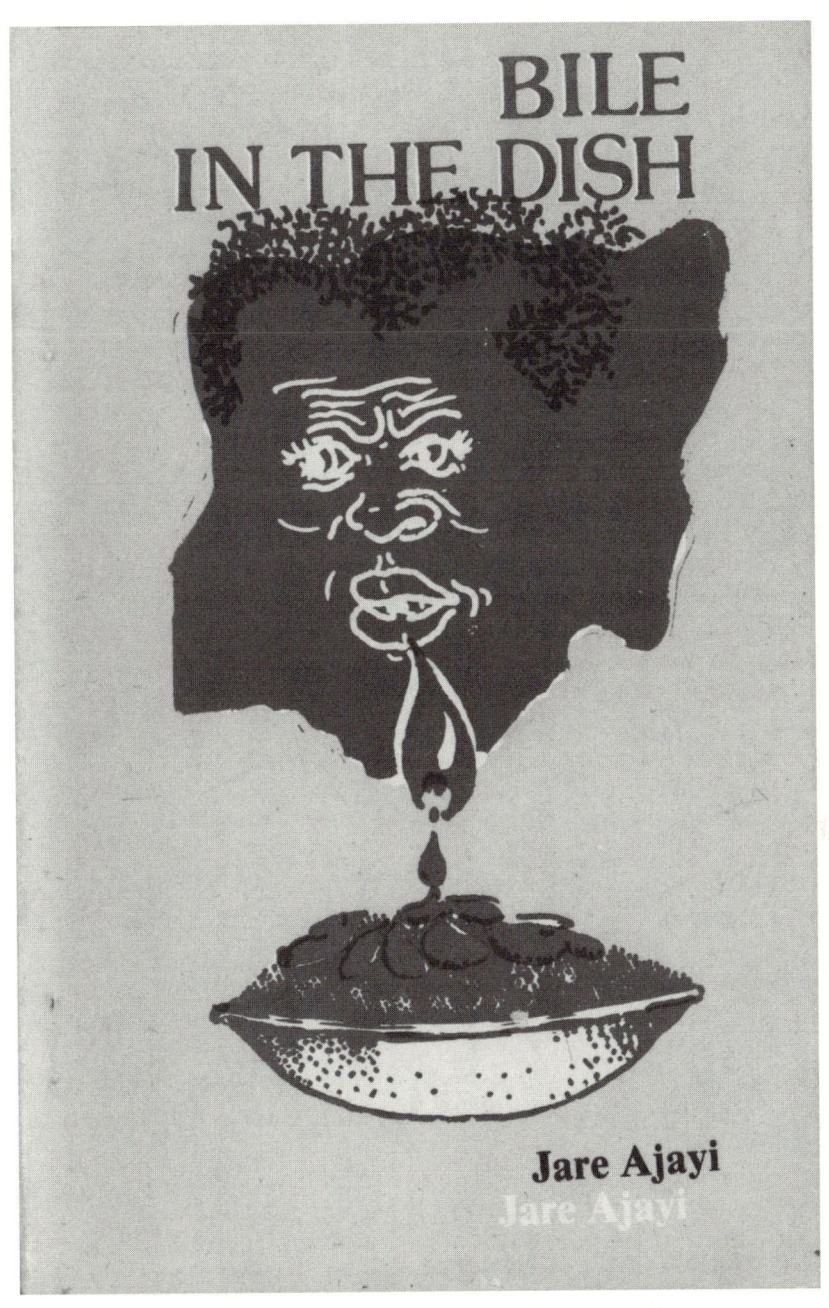

b. Jare Ajayi's *Bile in the Dish*

c. Wale Okediran's *The Boys at the Border*

d. Igbuku-Otu's *Voodoo Republic*

e. J. Obi J. Nwachukwu-Agbada's *No Need to Cry*

f. Mohmed Tukur Garba's *Stop Press: Murder!*

The Only Son
JOHN MUNONYE

g. John Munonye's *The Only Son*

AFRICAN WRITERS SERIES

KEHINDE

BUCHI EMECHETA

h. Buchi Emecheta's *Kehinde*

better cover art—realistic in the case of Pacesetters (3f), more figurative in the case of the African Writers Series (3g, 3h).

Most Nigerian novels are on the short side, typically in the vicinity of 120 pages. Those novels that are published in Nigeria are more likely to be short than those published in Britain or elsewhere. Long novels—over one hundred thousand words, or roughly 220 pages—are exceptional, constituting only about 14 percent of the total. They are much more likely to be published outside Nigeria.[74]

Editing represents a considerable challenge for the hard-pressed Nigerian publishers. Most poorly edited are the self-published books, some of which seem to have never been proofread at all. Type fonts change; sections are missing or repeated; and malapropisms— "Infatuation is consummate although deciduous while it lasts" or "she was a bundle of skeleton"—approach the poetic.[75] Fourth Dimensions, Fagbamigbe, and Delta are only slightly better than the self-published books. Higher standards are set, as usual, by Spectrum, Malthouse, and the Nigerian operations of Longman and Heinemann, although even these do not meet Western standards. The Heinemann Nigeria edition of Tolu Ajayi's *The Ghost of a Millionaire*, for example, included a set of pages from an entirely different novel, much to the author's disgust. Ajayi is one of the authors who have published novels with both British and Nigerian publishers, and thus he has had personal experience with the huge difference good editing makes. Good editing is a luxury, however, one that the Nigerian literary complex cannot afford.

Distribution and Promotion

Regardless of its physical quality, a Nigerian novel may never make its way to a potential reader. The distribution of trade fiction within Nigeria is, to put it mildly, haphazard. Books, often dirty and faded, are sold in the open markets, from sidewalk vendors in downtown centers such as the Marina in Lagos, and at small "academic" shops that sell school and stationery supplies. Inventory held by such modest operations tends to be an awkward mix of titles, all jumbled together. Finding any particular title or author would be a matter of sheer luck, although the browser may well come across unexpected gems.

A few larger bookstores do exist, such as those serving university students. When I visited the University of Ibadan Bookstore in 1990, I found its books arranged according to topic, with new titles attractively displayed. The store also offered maps, stationery items, and other supplies for scholarly work. Even this premier academic bookstore has fallen on hard times lately (as has the university in general), especially with respect to literature. A writer who had been a student at Unibad in the glory days of the late

1970s reports how what once was "a dazzling array of literary classics" has become "rows and rows of empty mournful shelves."[76]

Other bookstores cater to the affluent. One reputed to have a good selection of fiction is The Bestseller, located in the Falomo Shopping Centre in the Ikoyi section of Lagos.[77] Ikoyi is one of the city's toniest neighborhoods, and the shopping center is a hangout for fashionable young people. The Bestseller is prominently located right in front, next to a stationery store that sells imported paperbacks by the likes of Stephen King and Danielle Steel for nine nundred naira (over eleven dollars) and up.

Customers who walk into the Bestseller face a large desk that, on the day I visited the store, was manned by two clerks who seem to be as much security guards as sales assistants. Along the front wall is a large display of religious books that seem to be all Christian, representing a mixture of foreign and Nigerian authors (I spotted *The Total Woman*).[78] Across from the religion section is a good-sized section of children's books, again a mixture of Nigerian and foreign. Behind the clerks' desk is a large assortment of Mills and Boon romances, selling for 120 and 160 naira ($1.50 and $2.00).[79] Across from the children's section on the far left are law books.

In the back left corner, the most inconspicuous part of the store, is a section called "African Literature" that contains a motley collection of Nigerian titles, many published by Spectrum. I saw a new novel by Adebayo Williams (*The Remains of the Last Emperor*); a couple of Niyi Oniororo's market pamphlets, including *Persevere Dear Brother*; Soyinka's *Iskara*; Naiwu Osahon's *Sex Is a Nigger* (a soft-core pornographic novel about a Nigerian student who discovers that Scandinavian girls go crazy for African men); several short story collections, including Malthouse's *Our Wife*; some plays by Ola Rotimi; and some collections of poems. The section offered nothing by Achebe or Saro-Wiwa, no Pacesetters, no Longman or Heinemann imports nor locally published books by these publishers (although the children's section had many books from the Longman Winners series for nine- to thirteen-year-olds). The novels in the African literature section mostly sold for 120 naira, although some went up to 300 naira, or close to $4.00.

According to Felix Onyeacholam, the Bestseller store manager, Nigerians seldom read novels because they are concentrating on business and making money. Reading requires a conducive environment, and with the political and economic problems they face, most Nigerians, even educated, middle-class Nigerians, are too preoccupied with getting by from day to day. If they do have time to read, they prefer the escapism offered by foreign novels. It is the expatriates who buy the African literature! In fact, Onyeacholam estimated that foreigners buy an astonishing 80 percent of the Nigerian and other African literature that the store sells.

The Bestseller does not carry textbooks, although school librarians make some purchases. Most Bestseller customers are what Onyeacholam called "working class," by which he meant white-collar workers from the banks and ministries. In the 1990s, religious books have been the store's biggest sellers; apparently people are turning to religion for answers to Nigeria's problems and their own. Children's books also sell well, since indulgent or ambitious parents buy books for their children even if they never buy any for themselves.

Earlier I noted which publishers were active in publishing Nigerian fiction. Onyeacholam considers Spectrum the top firm, but even with that company authors had to sponsor (i.e., contribute financially to the publication of) their own books; no publishers could afford to take a chance on literature, for it simply would not sell. In his view, Malthouse shows promise but does not have a strong line of books yet. Heinemann is not publishing in Nigeria, just importing books. And Macmillan does not currently bring in Pacesetters. The youth loved them, but the foreign exchange rate is such that a new Pacesetter would now have to sell for two hundred naira or so, and since few people could afford them, Macmillan no longer finds the Nigerian market worthwhile.

As for what readers like, Onyeacholam thinks mature readers (over thirty) are interested in stories about traditional life and culture, including supernatural events, juju, and witchcraft, whereas younger readers want more contemporary stories. Old or young, readers want novels in English, period. A Yoruba himself, Onyeacholam says that he could not read Yoruba stories, and that anyone with a secondary school education or more prefers reading in English. Less educated people might read Yoruba newspapers, but he supposes that such people would not read novels anyway. Yoruba literature might be produced for use in the schools, but people who have any choice don't want it. The Bestseller does not carry any Yoruba or other indigenous-language books; even if the economic situation improved, he insists, there would be no market for them.

While the Bestseller is something of a boutique, popular with the Ikoyi trendsetters, CSS Bookstore is more of a department store.[80] Located on Broad Street in the heart of downtown Lagos, CSS claims to be both the largest and the oldest bookstore in Africa. Textbooks are prominent in its large retail area, as are maps and various educational supplies. Many of the textbooks are quite old; during my 1995 visit, CSS was selling science books with copyright dates from the 1970s. The store features a large section for religious books and tapes. Just inside the door is a religious magazine display with the provocative headline "Is It God's Will for MKO [Abiola] to Rule?" (this less than two years after Abiola's apparent victory in the 1993 presidential election was annulled by the military).[81] Spectrum has its own small display area, containing a mixture of fiction and nonfiction titles. Otherwise, literature is not prominent.

For most of its history this was the CMS Bookstore, run through the Church Missionary Society of the Anglican Church, and many Lagosians still refer to it as CMS out of habit. But in recent years the church has withdrawn from the day-to-day operations of the store—reflected in the name change to the more secular CSS, which stands for Church and School Supplies—and CSS now operates largely independently as a profit-seeking corporation. It publishes some books on its own, primarily religious titles, and sells all sorts.

All of this was explained to me by Francis O. Bada, the firm's energetic and purposeful editor in striped buttoned-down shirt and tie, who coolly juggled visitors and phone calls while we talked. His office is rather dark—a heavy curtain blocked what I assume was a window—and, by the standards of editors' offices, relatively uncluttered. Books, manuscripts, files, book jackets, dictionaries, family photos, calculators, and a notebook full of business cards cover his desk, but only two or three layers deep. On the wall are two banners from local branches of the Rotary club and book covers from *The Makers of the Church in Nigeria* and *The ABC of the Bible*, two CSS books. A small radio is playing, the phone rings often, and people are in and out constantly. Mr. Bada seems to have the ability to keep a great many things in his head at the same time, and to be firm without losing his composure. While waiting to talk with him, I hear him patiently explain to an aggrieved author why she should not receive royalties on the complimentary copies he had used for promotion. Their dispute seems good-natured, and he handles her complaints sympathetically without giving an inch.

"Who are CSS's customers?" I ask Bada when the disgruntled writer has finally left. White-collar workers in the offices and banks of the area, plus parents who buy their children textbooks there, and other customers who have long-standing loyalty toward the store and trust it. Bada believes the problem with Nigerian reading is not so much economic as the lack of anything worthwhile to read. There is demand for quality books, but no supply. Good foreign literature is almost impossible to find, as are externally published works like the African Writers Series; a reader is lucky to scrounge up a few pirated copies. While Bada acknowledges that people have less time and money for luxuries like books than they did in the past, he is convinced that reading would increase if more quality books were available; as an example of the quality missing in most Nigerian fiction, he waves around the copy of Camara Laye's *The African Child* that he is currently reading. "At least," he claims, "people like me" would read. But, he admits that economics lies at the root of the quality problem. If publishers can sell only five to six thousand copies of a book, they have to price them at five hundred naira—and since few people can afford them, they can't take many risks on quality. A larger printing of, say, thirty thousand copies would result in more affordable books, but the market is too weak. Problems of scale apply to both quality and popular books, which is why Macmillan is not bringing in any more Pacesetters.

Another problem, Bada believes, is "lazy authors." As a publisher as well as seller of books, CSS brings out some titles without author sponsorship and some with such sponsorship, as joint ventures. Bada handles the various author negotiations involved. From this perspective, he claims that local authors don't want to do the rewriting necessary to improve their books; they just want to get them in print as quickly as possible. (To the extent that this is the case, it sheds a different light on the editing problems discussed previously.)

When I ask what he thinks about the future of reading in Nigeria, Bada admits to having two sorts of answers—the personal and the professional. "Personally, I doubt if there *is* a future, and it's so sad." Interest in quality books, even foreign books, has been stifled, and Nigeria is now producing "educated illiterates" who are not interested in books or acquiring more information. Even the textbooks used in schools are out of date, so Nigerians are losing their desire for, and trust in, books. Professionally, on the other hand, with any luck the future could be bright. Publishers and booksellers need to move into other African markets and into Europe. Expanding their external markets could bring down the price of books, thus expanding the local market as well.

Despite the promise offered by foreign markets, Bada's pessimism comes through again when he worries about the impact of foreign tastes on Nigerian writers. What outsiders see as attractively exotic is familiar stuff to Nigerians. He dismisses Okri's *Famished Road*–"Abiku [the spirit-child constantly reborn] is well known to us, nothing new." Booker Prize committees in London may get excited about books with spirits roosting in trees, but "we see spirits in trees every day." The novelty that intrigues outside readers should not be confused with quality prose writing, and he fears that foreign tastes for the exotic could distort Nigerian writing.

Nor, he emphasizes, is this spirit-child type of thing what Nigerians ought to write about and read about in the first place. Nigerians don't need more writing that mourns the passing of traditional life: "Let's face it, parts of traditional culture *should* be let go." Instead, he wants to see quality prose written about contemporary issues. Writers should explore the future—what might happen, for example, how Nigeria might take over Cameroon—in their imaginations. All this writing about the past just takes Nigeria backward, he argues. Even children's stories should be contemporary: "Write about Tortoise playing his pranks with a computer, not a calabash!"

While editors like Bada are articulate and competent, the bookselling operation itself is sluggish. CSS is a Lagos fixture, and most customers come to it knowing what they want. This is just as well, for even the large book-stores like CSS are not very good at promoting their wares or creating new wants, at least not at the level of the individual purchaser. For example, in 1991 I visited the Abiola Bookshops, one of Lagos's largest bookstores. The books were well organized, though not attractively arranged for browsing. As was true of CSS, the front displays emphasized school texts and professional manuals. The staff seemed uninterested in being helpful. When I inquired if the store carried maps, the response was a curt no, with no suggestion of where I might find one. Nigerian buyers were likewise given short shrift. Several teachers in the store were buying in bulk, and their transactions involved interminable delays as well as a long wait as a clerk handwrote each title purchased. The teachers were visibly exasper-ated, the clerks unperturbed.

The section of the store devoted to fiction featured novels in an eye-catching wall display, in contrast with most other bookstores I visited. British thrillers by writers like Frederick Forsyth and Robert Ludlum dom-inated, along with a number of historical romances of the type referred to in the United States as "bodice-rippers." Ken Saro-Wiwa's books were well represented in a section of their own. Saro-Wiwa, then known as a novel-ist, newspaper columnist, creator of a popular television series, and public intellectual, was at that time president of the ANA, and his books, which he published himself, are attractive and sturdy. The Fontana African Li-brary paperbacks were well represented on the shelves, including works by both Nigerian and non-Nigerian writers such as Camara Laye. There were no Pacesetters.

While Abiola carried fiction by Nigerian authors, it was striking that there were very few Nigerian-published titles on display. I saw none from Heinemann (Nigeria), none from Longman (Nigeria), none from Spec-trum. In fact, aside from Saro-Wiwa's books, published out of Port Har-court, I spotted only one locally published novel, Ude Ikpenwa's *When Men Were Men*, marked as selling for fifteen naira. When I tried to buy it, however, the clerk told me it was not for sale, for it was a publisher's dis-play copy to see if there was any market for that book! The clerk made no attempt to help me order the book or otherwise obtain a copy, nor did he make any note that a buyer had expressed interest in it.

Such is the situation at one of the largest bookstores in the country, one far more orderly and reader-friendly than most, one that advertises widely. Most bookstores are much smaller, tucked away in obscure locations or corners of markets, with grubby stock and a catch-as-catch-can assortment of books. Even to the goal-oriented purchaser seeking a certain book, let alone to the casual browser, such stores are not inviting.

One of the distribution problems is the Nigerian reliance on booksellers and bookstores in the first place. In Europe and North America, the sales of books are kept high, and the price of books kept down, by their ubiquity. Drugstores, supermarkets, stands at airports and train stations, and chain retailers all sell vast quantities of books, most created to meet the needs of this mass market, which bypasses traditional bookstores. Such outlets have two advantages in attracting trade, over and above their economies of scale. First, they lend themselves to impulse buying, including the impulse of anyone accompanying the principal shopper, as any parent can attest who has ever purchased peace in the grocery store by letting his or her tot have the conveniently displayed Little Golden Book she has grabbed. Second, they do not carry the whiff of high-culture stuffiness still associated with some bookstores, especially the independents. Such mass retailing is nothing new; the nineteenth century had its railway novels and penny papers, to say nothing of promotional devices like newspaper serialization and "three-deckers." What is new is the Internet, where virtual bookstores like Amazon.com have become another easy and nonintimidating place where readers find books. Furthermore, contemporary European and American readers are serviced by a wealth of book clubs and libraries. In a system like this, where books are available through a wide variety of channels, books become consumer goods like any other.

Nigeria lacks book clubs—its postal service is too prone to theft for book clubs to be feasible even if there were a demand for them—and adequate libraries, but more important, it lacks outlets for mass retailing. The vast majority of Nigerians still do their shopping in markets occupied by small traders who deal in one particular type of product, rather than at the few department stores and supermarkets that do exist. Even upscale shopping centers like Falomo or the Allen Street area in Ikeja still have primarily specialty shops rather than department stores or supermarkets. Consequently, just as a Nigerian goes to a cloth trader when she wants to buy some cloth, she goes to a bookseller when she wants to buy a book. This works for teachers and students, but it does not encourage other people to "Pick up a Pacesetter," or any other kind of a book.

So one begins to see what Nigerians mean about having problems with distribution and marketing. The one promotional effort that some books do get is the institution known as a book launching, which can be orchestrated by the author or the publisher; Spectrum, which the trade journal *Books* calls "the most glamorous publishing outfit in Nigeria," is known for its lavish launchings.[82] A launching entails a gathering of notables to praise the book and its author, a public donation by individuals wishing to support the literary effort, and some food and drink. Book launchings are promoted by posters and the newspapers. The ads list the notable people on the program and invite the general public. These events raise both money and awareness of a particular author's work.

In 1990 I attended a launching for Chukwuemeka Ike's novel *Our Children Are Coming* at the Eko Hotel on Victoria Island in Lagos. Many writers attended (in fact, I went with the late Flora Nwapa). Other notables included Chukwuemeka Ojukwu, former head of state of Biafra, and various chiefs and government officials, military and civilian. A master of ceremonies introduced a series of the high and the mighty, each of whom paid fulsome tribute to the novel, although they made no pretense of actually having read it. (If they had, they might have been less enthusiastic; *Our Children Are Coming* excoriates the corruption and materialism of the older generation in power, as seen by the youth.) A cast of drama students entertained the audience by enacting a scene from the book. One by one people got up to pledge money. Refreshments and conversation followed.

While not many books receive launchings as grand as this one, more modest affairs are quite common. No doubt these launchings, especially the more glittering ones like the celebrity-studded evening at the Eko Hotel, enhance the reputation of the author. They may or may not contribute to actual sales of books, however. Ken Saro-Wiwa once told me he thought publishers like Spectrum make a mistake by holding launchings at luxurious hotels and concentrating on getting participation from wealthy people, for this creates the impression that books are only for the elite. One can imagine a rather different type of event organized for teachers and students. Such an event would not raise much initial money, might not be reported in the social columns of the newspapers, and would not contribute much to the writer's social prestige, but it might result in more books being sold, and even read.

Chukwuemeka Ike is a prominent educator, a former head of the West African Examination Council (WAEC), as well as a prolific novelist, so Spectrum's splashy launching was not surprising. Although clearly in a better position than most authors, he is only too aware of the difficulties all Nigerian writers face. In his 1996 novel, *To My Husband from Iowa,* a Nigerian woman named Iffy, already a rising young author, goes to the United States to attend the Iowa Writers' Program. While in the United States she visits various creative writing courses as well as the offices of the National Endowment for the Arts. She reports to her husband, "I cannot enumerate everything being done in this country to nurture creative writing, including the organization of public readings, the role of the various organizations which support the arts at federal, regional and state levels, the ready availability of teach-yourself books and guides to the literary marketplace, the key role of the print and electronic media as well as booksellers in the promotion of new titles." (249).

Although American authors might find Iffy's view to be rosier than the reality, the contrast between the resources available in Nigeria and those available in the West is stark. All this notwithstanding, Nigerian authors write and Nigerian readers read. One way or another, fiction makes its way into the hands of the Nigerian reading public. It is time now to look at these readers.

THE READERS

> The story takes place in the 1940s. Eze is from a family of farmers, but his father is determined that the boy should get a formal education. Eze's mother has her doubts as he begins primary school, but when her husband dies, she tries to carry on with his plans for Eze. The school fees are more than she can afford, however. To make things worse, Eze's father's family ignores the deceased man's wishes by spending lavishly on an elaborate funeral and then refusing to pay for Eze's schooling. One sympathetic elder comes to Eze's assistance, and this plus a lucky find of some money plus much hard work finally enable Eze's mother to pay his fees.
>
> Eze does well in school, motivated by one particular teacher who has great faith in him. Later, when Eze moves to town to go to a better school, he gets into a fight with the town boys who tease him for being "bush." Despite such adversity, he does well in his new school, even growing somewhat conceited because of his academic success until is knocked down a peg when a girl bests him on an exam. He eventually wins a scholarship for secondary school from his community. Although he has a serious accident that almost derails his plans, he recovers just in time to start secondary school.
>
> (Onuora Nzekwu and Michael Crowder, *Eze Goes to School*)

Every Nigerian schoolchild reads the short novel *Eze Goes to School*. Written in 1963, in the early days of independence, it is a parable showing how the mastery of books can change a child's destiny. Schooling removes Eze from the village, from the unsympathetic relatives, and from his future as a farmer. For education here does not mean learning how to grow yams and perform rituals. It means learning how to read.

Reading is highly valued, but it is not an uncomplicated good. It is costly, it involves rupturing old ties, and it can be stunningly irrelevant to Nigerian realities. Ifeoma Okoye's novel *Men without Ears* (1984), which decries Nigerians' oil-boom obsession with money, depicts the honest, book-loving Chigo as out of step with both the national passion for acquisition and his own difficulties. Chigo is working at a firm for a managing director who has just embezzled the company's funds to build an ostentatious house.

> Payday comes. When the workers don't get their money, Chigo tells them the truth, incurring the wrath of the managing director, who fires him. At the same time, Nweke, the houseboy who has been living with Chigo, disappears. Chigo meets Kenwe, "a renowned writer and nationalist," whose simple

lifestyle, hatred of "naira mania," and love of books confirm Chigo's own ideals. Kenwe ["Can we?"] asserts that reading is "the surest way to . . . preserve one's sanity in this crazy society" (152). But on his way home Chigo sees another book, *Things Fall Apart,* lying next to the body of a student who was mutilated in a ritual murder. Recalling that wicked juju men demand human parts for moneymaking charms, Chigo fears for Nweke's fate. (Ifeoma Okoye, *Men without Ears*)

As well he might: Nweke has indeed been kidnapped so that his heart may be used for moneymaking juju. Naira mania is one contemporary form of things falling apart, and the ability to read provides no protection.

Reading does not provide much help in the face of the economic and political turmoil of Nigeria at the turn of the twenty-first century. The optimism of an *Eze Goes to School* is hard for anyone to sustain. Yet Nigerians do still read, and they read in the face of obstacles that would seem all but insurmountable. This section will look at who reads and why.

Three Readers

I begin with three readers, all living in Lagos. Although these three do not represent some average Nigerian consumer of fiction—they are older, for one thing—they do represent that hard-core group of committed readers upon which any literary complex depends. Like Kenwe, they seek to preserve their sanity through books. Reading is a way of life for such people, and their tastes and habits are absolutely critical for the revival of, or even the continued existence of, the Nigerian literary complex.

READING TO LEARN ABOUT PEOPLE: MRS. A. O. DOLA-FADUN

According to Tolu Ajayi, Mrs. Dola-Fadun was an avid consumer of fiction, so I was eager to meet her. Dr. Ajayi and I visited her in her office as the Lagos State Ministry of Health in central Lagos, where she works as an accountant. As we talk, clerks come and go, showing her accounts and reports for her approval. Although her work is hectic, she keeps whatever she is currently reading at hand—at the time of our meeting she was in the middle of a hefty Judith Krantz novel—in case she can find an odd minute or two.

Mrs. Dola-Fadun gets most of her reading materials through borrowing from friends, since she can no longer afford to buy books as she used to. Unlike many Lagos readers, she does not patronize the British Council library, nor any other library for that matter. She learns about books from friends, from reviews, and from a bookstore that occasionally puts out a newsletter. Although she reads whatever she gets her hands on, she particularly enjoys thrillers, war novels, and general fiction. She liked romances in the past but now feels she has outgrown them. She reads any time she has a spare minute—"I was brought up that way"—and always has a novel with her.

About a third of the books she reads are Nigerian, the rest foreign. She enjoys popular authors like Harold Robbins and Jeffrey Archer, but she also likes Soyinka and Achebe. Nigerian books about village life appeal to her because, since she has lived her whole life in Lagos, the world they depict is unfamiliar to her. At the same time, she is not interested in books about magic or spirits, and has no use for the fantastic tales of Amos Tutuola. She reads for information—to see how people live and cope with their problems—and reads poetry for aesthetic enjoyment.

Like many educated Nigerians who enjoy reading, she fears that under the current dismal economy, the habit of reading novels and other books will die out. To become regular readers, she reasons, people need books, the money to buy them, and the time to read them. Today Nigerians lack all three. At the same time, her own practices—scrounging for books, borrowing from friends, reading whatever she gets her hands on, reading whenever and wherever she can—suggest that there is a core of readers who will remain unfazed by scarcities of books or time.

READING TO KNOW WHAT'S GOING ON: E. O. FAGBOHUN

Mr. Fagbohun is a retired confidential secretary who formerly worked for the Federal Ministry of Health and Social Services and who still does freelance secretarial work. He also grows corn, yam, greens, and other vegetables in an impressive garden across the road from his house. His small room in Yaba, where Dr. Ajayi and I visited him, contains a bed, a desk covered with dictionaries and papers, a coffee table with two chairs, a sink in the corner, a bar for hanging his clothes, and a shelf on the wall piled high with magazines and books. Many of these either are religious in content or deal with secretarial practice and improving one's English.

He reads for knowledge and entertainment, "to know what's going on in the world." Mostly he reads magazines, both Nigerian and foreign. He can read English and Yoruba, although I saw only English-language magazines and books during our visit. He prefers news magazines and religious reading—several Bibles sat on his desk—but also likes cartoons and love stories; he showed me a romance magazine, *Heart* (priced at forty naira, currently equal to about fifty cents) that he was reading. He does not like crime or detective stories because he is a devout Anglican who hates violence.

Mr. Fagbohun's reading was encouraged by his teachers at a Christian school, where he began in 1945, and by his parents, who both read. He thinks the present education Nigerian children receive is not nearly as good; there always seem to be conflicts between school authorities and students, and standards have fallen dramatically. In such an atmosphere the reading habit is not fostered, nor is the proper use of English. (Tolu Ajayi had remarked earlier on Mr. Fagbohun's perfect spelling and painstaking grammatical accuracy.)

If he could advise Nigerian writers looking to attract a broader readership, Mr. Fagbohun would urge them to use simple language that average people understand. He would tell them to write about useful things: economics, health, household management, recipes. He likes writing about village life—"rivers, ghosts, chickens"—because he comes from such a village, but he also likes to read about "cities of the world" and news items from all over.

He sings in his church choir and loves classical music. He played us a tape of the choir's Easter oratorio, which sounded very high church indeed. Convinced that religion holds the answer to Nigeria's problems, he would like to encourage more reading of the Bible and other religious books.

READING FOR CULTIVATION: MRS. ELSA BISHOP

Mrs. Elsa Bishop, a gracious middle-aged woman, is a passionate reader. Her father was a Jamaican missionary and publisher (her mother was Nigerian) who strongly encouraged his children to read. They were "baptized into reading" through the Bible. His attitude was that one can never read enough, and that people should improve themselves all their lives through reading.

Today she reads English literature, especially classics; at the time of our interview she was in the midst of Trollope's *Can You Forgive Her?* She was introduced to literature during secondary school in Jamaica. She goes to the British Council library at least once a month, and also uses the library of the Goethe Institute. She used to buy books, but since the Kingsway department store closed there have been few imported books beyond the sort of romances published by the British company Mills and Boon. As for African writers, she mentions Soyinka and Tutuola as being particular favorites.

Mrs. Bishop is the patron of the Association of West African Young Writers, which meets in "the Hive," a small library, working space, and general hangout on the ground floor of her house in the middle-class Apapa section of Lagos. Much of her reading involves reading the manuscripts of this group, which has about three hundred members, mostly male. (She admires women writers like Nwapa and Emecheta, and commented on how hard it is to get women involved in "the Hive" and its activities.) The association holds monthly readings, although sometimes only a handful of members actually attend, especially if there is a conflict with the University of Lagos schedule. Most members are either university students or journalists.

In her view the problem with Nigerian writing is not only the fault of the publishers—although they could do more promotion—but the readers themselves. Nigerian children are not encouraged to read, she maintains. Parents and teachers promote reading strictly as a tool for study and achievement, not for pleasure, so few young people pick up the habit. She draws a comparison with England, where there are so many libraries with attractive children's sections and where reading for recreation as well as for information is held in high esteem.

As for her own preferences, she likes Cyprian Ekwensi very much. In fact she will read the work of just about any Nigerian writer. She likes to read about people, and she believes literature is the best way of coming to understand others. Interested in issues involving community, she likes reading about traditional village life because of its sense of order. In her view writers who depict their own villages seem to know their subject well, whereas few writers have emerged (beyond Ekwensi) who can adequately treat the complexities of city life. Moreover, as a half-Jamaican cosmopolitan who has lived much of her life in Jamaica, Britain, and Germany, she finds village life to be "exotic." She suspects that most Nigerian readers of fiction, what few there are, care more about the quality of the writing than its setting.

Mrs. Bishop disagrees with writers who feel compelled to write about social problems, a view held by most of the young writers she sees (and most third-generation Nigerian novelists as well). She thinks they should stop worrying about politics and start writing, for the writer can do more for social reform by writing well (she cites Dickens, Tolstoi, and Trollope as examples) than by aiming explicitly at promoting political or social change. According to her, politics should be treated by journalists, not novelists; the novelist should just concentrate on getting the story out. Since she thinks that many the greatest novels have been written during times of turbulence, she wants Nigerian writers to let the present economic hardship and political discontent serve as a stimulus for their creativity.

These three readers are all highly committed to the practice of reading. The Nigerian novel depends on readers like Mrs. Dola-Fadun and Mrs. Bishop, who actually read novels. It also depends on potential readers, both the penumbra of people like Mr. Fagbohun who could and might read novels under the right circumstances and the future readers now in school. These types of people constitute Nigeria's reading culture, such as it is. To understand the present and future condition of this reading culture, four questions need to be asked about such Nigerian readers and—more broadly—about Nigerian reading:

1. Who is reading? What Nigerians are likely to be engaged in this particular activity?

2. How are Nigerians reading? What are the conditions of Nigerian reading?

3. What are Nigerians reading?

4. What interpretations are being made? What, in other words, might be considered a "Nigerian reading" of a text?

Each of these questions is fundamentally sociological. Since I am primarily interested in novels, I might rephrase these four questions as, who reads novels, how, what novels, and to what effect? In this section I will investigate these aspects of Nigerian reading, and how it compares with reading done elsewhere.

Who Reads?

Reading—and being a reader—is not some simple dichotomy along the lines of, if you can read, you are a reader, and if you can't, you aren't. Some people can read but don't, others can't read even if they want to, and some illiterates read fotonovelas, comic books, advertisements, and other texts that use pictures to put across the essence of the story or message. To be "a reader" is usually taken to mean both to have the ability to decode written communication and to use that ability regularly. Readers have various degrees of proficiency; one literate person may read complex novels or technical scientific journals, while another barely makes his way through bureaucratic forms and newspaper headlines. Furthermore, readers of whatever level of proficiency have different practices. Some people may chose to read a great deal in their leisure time, while others possessing the same level of skill may rarely read for pleasure.

Reading—both the ability and the practice—is not a value-free way of getting information, but instead is highly esteemed. Unlike most of the ways we receive cultural information—listening, viewing—reading is a respected activity in and of itself (a fact that undoubtedly leads to considerable overreporting of reading). To take an American example, in 1994 signs on city trucks and park benches in Baltimore proclaimed that this down-at-the-heels city, an industrial dinosaur in an increasingly postindustrial economy, was "Baltimore: The City That Reads." Never mind what might be being read (pornography? help wanted ads?), let alone the fact that close to 20 percent of Baltimore residents were functionally illiterate, Baltimore's urban boosters clearly believed that their city's prestige, and its economic future, would be enhanced by association with the activity of reading.[83] Along similar lines, the United States boasts about being "a nation of readers."[84] Reading is a highly respected activity over and above its utilitarian uses; parents encourage children to read as a pastime, high-status professions are distinguished by the amount of reading they entail, and literacy itself has come to be regarded as a basic human right in the mid–twentieth century.[85]

Before addressing the question of Nigerian participation in this prestigious practice, it is helpful to consider what is known about European and American reading, to provide some basis for comparison. The oldest examples of writing, Sumerian tablets from about five thousand years ago, recorded commercial transactions. Historically, literacy in the West has always been associated with commercial activities, as well as with urbanization, with the administrative needs of translocal institutions such as the church and later the state, and with Protestantism. As literacy developed in the West, the general tendency was for cities (commercial centers regardless of what else they might be) to lead rural areas in achieving widespread literacy, and for men to become literate ahead of women. The greater the overall rate of literacy, the smaller the gap between the sexes.

Italy, for example, was three-quarters illiterate at its unification in 1861. During the next century Italy's north—urban and industrialized—achieved near total literacy, while the agricultural south continued to be a quarter or more illiterate. And while the sex difference in literacy rates had shrunk in the north by the early part of this century, it remained considerable in the south; in 1911 only 9 percent of the males and 13 percent of the females in Piedmont were illiterate, while in Calabria the respective percentages were 59 percent and 78 percent.[86] Throughout the century, advances in Italian literacy were first seen among city dwellers, among males, and among the young.

While the West understands itself, and is understood by others, to possess a reading culture, surprisingly little is known about who actually reads. This is due in part to the different needs of publishers, authors, booksellers, and libraries. All are interested in readers, but they construct "the reader" differently. Publishers, booksellers, and mass-market authors care primarily about sales, so a reader is an actual or potential buyer; libraries see a reader as an actual or potential borrower. In such cases, whether or not a book is actually read is of secondary importance.

Survey data give some help with the question of who reads. We know, for example, that the habit of reading is unevenly distributed within societies as well as between them. In the United States and the United Kingdom, it is fair to say that most adults read something, at least now and then.[87] This is not to say that most people spend their time with their noses in books, for many people read magazines and newspapers only. Surveys suggest that somewhat under half the population is reading a book at any given time.[88] This may be an inflated picture of actual reading; someone who began a book a month ago but has not gotten back to it since may claim to be "reading a book." Be that as it may, reading is the favorite pastime of a significant portion—some 15 percent—of the American population, people worry that they do not read as much as they should, they regard reading books as more rewarding than watching television, and almost half expect to do more reading in the future.[89] All of this suggests a robust book-reading culture that will continue to perpetuate itself despite competition from television and other leisure-time pursuits.

In the West the single most important factor predicting whether or not a person reads is education.[90] Sex, income, and age are associated with reading; holding education constant, women, affluent people, and the young or middle-aged are somewhat more likely to read, and to read literature, than are men, the less affluent, and the elderly, but these effects are not as strong as that of education.[91] An urban-rural divide is also present, with residents of metropolitan areas more likely to be readers than their rural counterparts, although again the effect is slight compared with that for education.[92] Reading tends to be bimodal, with adults reading either a lot or very little. Readers of magazines and newspapers may or may not be book readers, but book readers invariably read magazines and newspapers as well.[93] A similar ordering is seen with respect to serious and popular fiction: readers of popular fiction may or may not read serious literature, but readers of serious literature read popular fiction—"I like to read some trash for relaxation"—as well.[94]

The global picture is very uneven. In the mid–nineteenth century fewer than one adult of every ten was literate; by the third quarter of the twentieth century, the proportion was seven out of ten.[95] Literacy levels are spotty, roughly corresponding to the affluence of the society. Thus while Europe, Japan, and America enjoy near-universal literacy, the majority of adults in sub-Saharan Africa are illiterate.[96] In addition to literacy's association with wealth, two other common patterns are seen in Africa and elsewhere in the developing world. First, literacy is generally higher and earlier among men and in urban areas. Second, the higher the overall rate of illiteracy, the greater the difference between men and women, and between urban and rural areas, exactly the same patterns Europe had experienced.

The gender gap is especially troubling, for not only do women account for two-thirds of the world's illiterates, but the gap may actually be widening.[97] Girls are less likely to be sent to school in the first place and are more likely to drop out before attaining a solid literacy. Moreover, adult women who begin literacy programs are at greater risk of lapsing back into illiteracy then are men, since reading instruction is often presented through materials that have little relevance to women's lives, and since their domestic responsibilities often interfere with their ability to stick with a training program.

Official literacy rates are notoriously inaccurate. This is in part because of the shifting definitions of the term itself, and in part because there are political and bureaucratic incentives to fudge the numbers. Nevertheless, the UNESCO reports of illiteracy for persons fifteen years old and older provide some sense of how Nigeria compares with other countries.

In 1990 Nigeria was reporting an overall adult illiteracy rate of 49.3 percent, with 38 percent of adult men and 61 percent of adult women unable to read.[98] This rate is somewhat higher than Ghana's 40 percent, and much higher than South Africa's 24 percent, yet lower than Egypt's 56 percent; Nigeria most closely resembles another giant Commonwealth country, India, which has a 51 percent illiteracy rate (38 percent male, 66 percent female).[99] While at best only about half of Nigerian adults are literate, higher rates of schooling are reducing illiteracy rates among younger cohorts.[100]

Nigeria does not report an urban-rural breakdown of literacy. In Egypt the urban rate of illiteracy is 40 percent, the rural rate, 69 percent; in India 35 percent of city dwellers are illiterate as compared with 67 percent of their rural counterparts. The Nigerian urban-rural ratio is probably similar, with city dwellers being roughly twice as likely to be able to read as rural Nigerians. Urban and rural Nigerians also vary in terms of what written materials are available and how prevalent the practice of reading is even among the literate. A survey asking Nigerians if they read popular magazines showed that urbanites were four to eight times more likely to read the most popular magazines.[101]

Informal estimates of Nigerian literacy are lower than official ones. The editors of the trade journal *Books*, whose business it is to come up with an accurate estimate rather than an inflated one, put the figure at "barely 20 percent."[102] Mere literacy, it should be remembered, does not produce a reading culture. Chidi Amuta finds the readership for the African novel has been limited to "a minority urban elite culture," and the readership for serious fiction even more limited to "university teachers and their students, professional men of culture and certificate-conscious teenagers." Moreover, the latter are likely to be reading thrillers of the James Hadley Chase ilk when not preparing for exams.[103] Amuta attributes this to the fact that, unlike in the West, the African novel preceded the development of a reading public rather than following it, and the newly developing public was quickly distracted by films, television, and other forms of mass entertainment as well as by escapist literature.

Even during the colonial period there existed a committed reading public—people like Mr. Fagbohun's parents, for example—but they were a small, and very Christian, minority. "Certainly there can be no doubt that the habit of reading for pleasure is yet to be established among the Nigerian population," Nancy Schmidt concluded in a comprehensive dissertation that examined Nigerian literature from an anthropological point of view during the first years following independence.[104] Schmidt based her conclusion on the low rate of adult literacy—she accepted a level of about 10 percent as of the mid-1950s—as well as on a variety of surveys that suggested Nigerian readers, what few there were, by and large read for practical information rather than entertainment. She found that most Nigerians who read in English during the early 1960s lived in southern cities; literate adults in the north read in Hausa or Arabic. She saw Nigerian readers as falling into three groups: (1) The new literates included schoolchildren, whose missionary-school education led them to favor Bible stories as well as fairy tales and other children's literature, and new adult literates, whose reading tended to be practical. (2) The semiliterates were mostly men who could read newspapers, magazines, and pamphlets; this group shared the practical orientation of the new literates but showed an interest in love stories, a staple of the Onitsha market pamphlets that were flourishing at the time. (3) The full literates were people capable of reading all kinds of books. This group was composed of university students and graduates, almost entirely men. Even among the full literates, few entertained themselves with books; one survey suggested, for example, that only about one-fifth of students at the University of Ibadan read for pleasure.[105]

Thus, during the early days of independence most Nigerians could not read; of the few competent readers of English, most did not read novels; the handful who did were likely to be well-educated, urban, southern men. (This is, of course, the same profile that emerged with respect to authors.) How has this picture of readers changed in the intervening decades?

Whatever the current literacy rate—let us say that roughly half of Nigerians aged fifteen and over can read to some extent—only a small percentage of readers are actually readers of novels. It seems reasonable to suppose that readers of novels would have at least some secondary education, yet in 1989 only 19 percent of Nigerian youth of the appropriate age were in secondary schools; again the figure for males (22 percent) is higher than for females (16 percent).[106] Even fewer—3.2 percent of the age-group (4.7 percent of the males, 1.8 percent of the females)—were enrolled in tertiary education. But if the percentages are small, the sheer numbers of youth capable of reading novels are high. Some three to four million Nigerian young people are able to read novels; as this group joins the established adult readers, it constitutes the present and future fiction-reading public.[107]

Nigerian publishers and authors are surprisingly vague about literacy and about who constitutes their market. When I asked them to estimate rates of adult literacy, I got guesses ranging from "almost everybody" to "maybe a quarter or so." Again it is important to remember that "literacy" can mean different things, and the higher estimates may refer merely to the ability to decode street signs or newspaper headlines. Both authors and publishers seemed to downplay regional differences in their readership, perhaps because it is in their economic interest to believe that all of Nigeria constitutes a potential market for their books. A potential market, not an actual one—here publishers admit problems of distribution, while authors cite their publishers' lack of marketing know-how.

A different picture comes from Nigerian readers themselves, who have less incentive for wishful thinking. Here I am drawing on what my sixteen "core readers" told me. Kubby Rashid, one of six daughters of a Yoruba mother and Hausa father, comes from Zaria in the north. She attended secondary school in Ibadan, and her own experience plus her family background give her a wide understanding of both north and south. Her family is Muslim, although she herself is not currently religious. She is in her late twenties, is married to a lawyer, and works as a career counselor and teacher of accounting at Gallaudet University in Washington, D.C.; Gallaudet is a university for deaf people, and Mrs. Rashid has been deaf since childhood. She and her husband had no children at the time of her survey (1994), and she was completing an M.B.A. degree at the University of Maryland. Here is what she had to say in answer to my questions about Nigerian reading:

WG: Who reads in Nigeria? What is your general impression of the typical Nigerian reader?

KR: Well, I feel that not as many people read as much as I do. I feel that the people who read are the middle or upper classes, although even that varies. Very few people seem to find as much pleasure in it as I do, although my impression could be wrong. That is changing, I think; typical Nigerian readers now are younger, college educated, and genuinely curious about what's happening in the world.

WG: Do you think that Nigerian reading habits vary according to the following. First, age?

KR: Yes, I think the younger generation, teens through thirties, read more, although in decreasing quantity as one grows older. I can't explain why this is so, that's just my general impression

WG: Sex?

KR: Females . . . I think they're more imaginative than the men.

WG: Region of the country?

KR: Southern . . . can't differentiate between East and West, though.

WG: Ethnic group?

KR: Sorry . . . I don't know . . . at a guess, I'd say it's a toss-up between Igbo and Yoruba, considering number of writers each has produced, but this is really guessing on my part.

WG: Religious group?

KR: Depends. Muslims read the Quran a lot. Would you call this recreational reading? If not, then definitely Christians.

Kubby Rashid was better informed than many readers because of her own experience in both north and south, so her responses cannot be attributed to southern stereotypes about northerners, but virtually all of the core readers said the same thing. The general consensus, related both in personal interviews and in the reader survey, was that southerners still read much more than northerners, and Christians more than Muslims. Some put this in terms of ethnicity, saying that Yoruba and Igbos read the most. Ikechukwuka Oguocha, an Igbo man currently doing graduate study in mechanical engineering at the University of Saskatchewan, gave a detailed account of the role of religion, region, and ethnicity in reading:

> Christians tend to read more novels, newspapers, and magazines than Muslims. Maybe this has to do with how each religion views education, especially Western education. Again, most Nigerian authors are Christians. Also, non-Nigerian authors whose novels are popular in Nigeria have English/Christian-like names or are Christians. So, there is this bias in our reading habit. Most important, Christians are more educated than Muslims in Nigeria, and so it is natural to see more Christians developing better reading habits than Muslims. Whether this will change with time, I cannot tell. [As for regions], Western education entered Nigeria via the south. So, in ranking, southern Nigerians (east and west) have the majority of Nigerian readers/writers, followed by the middle belters and northerners in that order. So, in effect, one's reading habits and ability to read depend mainly on which region you come from. Between east and west, I think the west has an edge over east in volume of books per person. Vernacular newspapers started much earlier in the west than in the east. But if reading is measured as the ability to communicate in English/pidgin per head, I think the east will have a slight edge over the west.
>
> Ethnic leaning has influence on an average Nigerian reader. It is very common to see books written by an author from one ethnic group not being recommended for kids in another ethnic group, no matter how good that book is. Secondly, some authors' inability to use names from other ethnic groups for their characters, especially in fictions, make matters worse. So, whichever way, this problem limits the number of available books to eager readers. So, you see a Yoruba not reading a book just because it's written by Hausa or Igbo and vice versa. Anyway, things are gradually changing, but it will take time for ethnic influence to finally disappear. If we have to rank all ethnic groups [in terms of amount of reading], I can venture: Yoruba, Igbo, southern ethnic minorities, northern ethnic minorities, and Hausa/Fulani, in descending order.

Readers like Mr. Oguocha emphasize that the disparity in educational levels between south and north, while diminishing, is still considerable. This, coupled with the Islamic emphasis on the Koran and disapproval of secular reading, perpetuates strong north-south differences in reading habits. In my face-to-face conversations specifically about reading, all of which were with southerners, discussions of why northerners *do not* read would typically lapse into discussions of why northerners *do* run the country. While some of this may have been the venting of southern prejudice and political frustration, both the reader and the author profiles support the dramatic underrepresentation of northerners in Nigeria's literary complex.

Most of the readers believe that rates of reading are highest for young Nigerians, dropping off as people attain their adult roles and responsibilities. Most think that women are more inclined to read novels than men, although some suspect that this inclination is offset by women having less leisure time as adults. Eno Urua, an Ibibio woman and a lecturer in English and linguistics at the University of Uyo in Akwa Ibom state in the extreme southeast, was one reader who thought women might actually read less than men because of their endless responsibilities.

> Some educated people in Nigeria read, but mostly people are too busy trying to earn a living to find the time to read. You read when you have leisure time. I don't suppose that most Nigerians can afford that. They read what is relevant to what they are doing, not as a leisure activity. And as a cultural thing more men than women read because women are not supposed to spend too much time on reading but in taking care of a home. And believe me in Nigeria without the benefit of laborsaving gadgets Westerners take for granted it's a full-time job. Women are supposed to be more passive and not take part in discussions traditionally (that attitude is changing, though slowly).

Helen Ovbiagele, the author of six Pacesetters, once remarked that literate northern women living in purdah (the practice of confining married women to the household) may do a surprising amount of reading simply because they have more time on their hands than their southern counterparts. A few readers thought men read more simply because there were more educated men in the first place. Men are said to favor serious writing, including non-fiction, whereas women prefer lighter entertainment, including romances, although both boys and girls enjoy love stories of either the Onitsha market pamphlet or the Mills and Boon sort.

Readers repeatedly referred to the "survival mentality," the focus on day-to-day business of living, that stood in the way of Nigerians developing the habit of reading for pleasure. In response to my question about the major problems Nigerian readers face, Olajide Kufoniyi responded bluntly, "Trying to make ends meet (not funny, I see it as a major obstacle)." His remarks and Ms. Urua's "too busy trying to earn a living" were echoed over and over again; this is the same point Felix Onyeacholam at the Bestseller had stressed. There is some irony in the fact that these readers who reported how Nigerians were too busy to read for pleasure were themselves all avid leisure-time readers, but they maintained that they were atypical, even with respect to their educated counterparts.

Over and over, authors, booksellers, teachers, librarians, and readers report their view that so far, and with a few exceptions like themselves, Nigeria has not developed a reading culture. It will, and it should, but so far it has not. This is the standard line. A librarian of the National Library in Lagos put it this way during the National Readership Promotion Campaign in 1987: "The culture of reading is not yet cultivated. Most Nigerians only read for purposes of passing examinations, for preparing seminar papers and article writing. . . . The peak periods for attendance in this library are examination periods."[108] Virtually all members of the reading class hold this view: Nigeria will develop a reading culture someday, but that day has not yet dawned.

How Do They Read?

Potential readers are not the same as actual readers. For people to acquire the novel-reading habit—to get "lost in a book" on a regular basis—two things are necessary. First, there must be social support of reading, in the form of active encouragement of reading as a highly esteemed activity ("Baltimore: The City That Reads"), or at least a tolerance of the temporary social withdrawal that reading fiction entails. Second, there must be the physical conditions —sufficient light, relative quiet, and some degree of comfortable, personal space—to make sustained reading possible.

Once again, a comparison can help us understand how Nigerians read. On the morning on which I first drafted this chapter, I was taking a commuter bus into Washington, D.C., from the southern Maryland suburbs. The bus normally takes an hour, but it was a rainy day and the trip took somewhat longer. My fellow passengers appeared to be middle-class—neither agency heads nor office cleaners—and most would have been headed for federal offices. About two-thirds were women; about one-quarter were African-American, the rest white, with a couple of Asian and Hispanic faces in the group—ordinary adults making an ordinary commute to their jobs.

I was able to observe seven fellow passengers closely during the trip. Three were reading, using the individual reading lights overhead, which were necessary on such a dark day. A black woman in her forties was reading a thick paperback; it appeared to be a novel—the cover showed a sexy woman—but I couldn't catch the title. A white man, also middle-aged, was reading a hardback Elmore Leonard thriller, *Maximum Bob*; the book had a clear plastic cover and a label with a call number on the spine, indicating it had been checked out from a library. A white woman in her early twenties was reading a Danielle Steel paperback novel; I didn't see the title. As

I got off the bus, I saw several other passengers had been reading (I spotted one other Danielle Steel romance, this time a hardback); overall I would estimate that about half of the passengers had been reading during some portion of the trip. A few were reading newspapers, but most of the rest were reading books; of the four books I saw clearly, all were novels. Most of the people who were not reading were dozing; a few were talking quietly or just gazing out the window.

Think for a minute about what is required for such a scene to be perfectly routine, as it is in the United States. First of all, a high rate of literacy must exist for half the people on the bus to be reading (presumably at least some of the nonreaders were capable of reading). The ability to read, judging from my tiny sample, is not restricted by race or sex. Reading materials have to be available, either through libraries or in affordable editions. The bus itself has to be properly equipped, in this case with comfortable seats and overhead lights. More generally still, the bus as a form of public transportation has to exist in the first place, for the commuters were riding it instead of walking or driving themselves. Certain social norms must be in place whereby reading is an understood and respected activity, and readers are given relative privacy, so they are not disturbed without good reason and an apology.

Perhaps most important, reading lengthy materials, fiction or nonfiction, means that the reader must have a considerable amount of time free from interruption. On an American or European airplane with several hours of time to pass, for example, most passengers are reading something, often a book. On a subway or city bus, in contrast, even if crowding is not a problem, people are less apt to be reading, and often they are reading newspapers or magazines, materials more conducive to being read in short blocks of time. An hour-long ride on a commuter bus falls somewhere in between.

What I am describing with these examples is part of what occurs in a reading culture, and it is a reading culture of a particular kind, one that supports the reading of novels. The "rise of the novel" in eighteenth-century England, discussed in Chapter I, was associated with the rise of a similar form of reading culture. Novels served the needs of those with leisure time to fill—including particularly middle-class women and servants—who were literate but not educated in classical languages or belles lettres. It was also associated with architectural and technological changes, such as building houses with more windows and otherwise better lighting. And it was associated with printing facilities, first used for newspapers and political or religious tracts, that made possible the publication of long books— eighteenth-century novels were even longer than most novels today, but the novel is, by definition, a prose genre of considerable length—at affordable prices. The bare-bones requirements for the novel, then, are that people must be able to read well, must be able to get their hands on novels, and must have the time, the conditions, and the peace and quiet, in which to decode the long text. While these factors are not sufficient to explain why novels deal with the subjects they do, they are necessary for anything we would want to call a reading culture.[109]

Once such a culture exists, young people are socialized into it. The ability to read a novel becomes one of their life skills and one of their pleasures as well. Most Americans who become readers are first exposed to reading for pleasure in the home.[110] Being able to read and enjoying reading are both learned through interaction with others; many young people are first exposed to reading for pleasure, as opposed to schoolwork, when a popular paperback is passed around with the "good parts" marked.[111]

While reading is a highly esteemed practice in a reading culture, reading novels does not always win approval. Eighteenth- and nineteenth-century moralists expressed their "fear of fiction" by railing against novels that wasted young girls' time and corrupted their virtue.[112] A residual antipathy against romance and thrillers is occasionally voiced today. Reading nonfiction is regarded as a somewhat more serious activity than reading fiction, although the mountain of nonfiction books that offer celebrity biographies or diet advice makes this distinction hard to defend.

Equipped with this general sense of what a "reading culture" is, I will now consider the case of Nigeria. It is helpful to differentiate among three Nigerian reading cultures: reading in Arabic, including *ajami,* reading in African languages, and reading in English. The earliest widespread reading in Nigeria came as a result of the revival of Islamic learning under Muhammad Bello following Usman dan Fodio's jihad in the early nineteenth century.[113] Freelance *malams* (religious teachers) set up Koranic schools to teach children, usually boys, to read and write Arabic and to commit to memory sections from the Koran and hadith. This initial primary level of Islamic education was widespread, and virtually any Islamic community would have Koranic instruction at the *malam*'s house, in a mosque, or under a tree. This was essentially rote learning, but students of particular talent, or those from wealthy families, might go on to further study involving the interpretation of texts, mathematics, jurisprudence, and theology under specialist teachers called *ulama.* A few of these went for further study to the traditional centers of Islamic learning outside of Nigeria.

Such a system of Islamic education produced a type of reading culture, one that was highly conservative. While the *malams* gave their students firsthand access to sacred scripture, they remained deeply suspicious of secular texts such as novels. This tendency later combined with the colonial policy of indirect rule in the Northern Region that kept out Christian missionaries and Western education. The result was an unnatural division between traditional Islamic learning, a "hidden literacy," which was in Arabic, and modern, scientific learning, which was in English.[114]

The narrow horizons associated with a traditional Islamic reading culture are captured in Chukwuemeka Ike's *The Search* (1991), in a scene where two educated women visit the young co-wives of a Hausa official on the day after a military coup has toppled the government.

> Zainab, the first wife, had been thrilled to inform Dapa that she had successfully completed the Koranic course she had been taking for months. She could now read the Koran. Maryam, who became wife number two barely a year after the marriage to Zainab, said she was making good progress. Their husband had told them about the coup. They had also heard about it on the radio. However, it meant no more to them than news of an election victory in Fiji
> (Ike, *The Search*, 156).

Zainab and Maryam are women living in purdah. Although they have secondary-level education and can speak English, they are following the socially approved role of elite Hausa women by concentrating on religious reading in Arabic (as well as on bearing children), rather than doing other forms of reading. Their husband would be more politically aware but would also have received Koranic training, and his leisure reading would likely be devoted to Islamic texts.

The second type of reading culture would be that of one of the vernacular languages. Virtually every Nigerian's first tongue is an indigenous African language, the most common being Hausa, Yoruba, and Igbo, which are spoken by perhaps two-thirds of the population. (We must remember that language is not identical with ethnicity, especially in the case of Hausa; most northerners speak Hausa, even if their ethnicity is Fulani or one of the dozens of other northern groups.) The language heard on the streets would be either the local language of the area or pidgin. Yet, as we have seen, vernacular languages make up only a tiny portion of the available reading materials. Beyond Yoruba and Hausa (including *ajami*), many minority languages have written forms, often from the labors of Christian missionaries wanting to make the Bible available, but there is little written material in most of these. Local languages are used for instruction in primary schools, but by secondary school most of the reading and instruction is in English.

Having previously seen how few non-English-language books are published in Nigeria, we can get another sense of the relative positions of the vernacular and English reading cultures at the more popular level by considering the press. In 1988 one standard yearbook listed twenty-six daily newspapers in Nigeria; of these, two were in Yoruba, one in Hausa, and the rest in English.[115] There were seventeen Sunday papers, all in English. Vernacular languages had better representation among the eighteen weekly newspapers—two of these were in Hausa, three in Yoruba, and one in English and Yoruba—but even here two-thirds were in English. As for periodicals, which included everything from news and contemporary issues (*Afriscope; New Nation*) to popular and family magazines (*Nigerian Radio/TV Times; Modern Woman; Happy Home*) to specialist periodicals (*Nigerian Journal of Economic and Social Studies; Marketing in Nigeria*, every one of the forty listed was in English.[116] A visit to any newsstand or market confirms what these numbers suggest: while some reading material in African languages is available, the overwhelming majority of papers, magazines, and books—and virtually all novels—are in English.

So when I speak of "Nigerian reading" in this book, I am speaking of the third reading culture, reading in English. As I have tried to indicate, although this is an incomplete picture of all Nigerian reading, it does represent the predominant form of secular reading in this multilingual society. Part of the answer to the question of, How do Nigerians read? must be, therefore, "By and large, they read in English."

Further information on "how they read" comes from my communication with Nigerian readers themselves. Innocent Ewean Davidson, an electrical engineer and a Bini man from Benin City in the old Middle-West region (now in Edo state), describes a typical induction into reading:

> My reading history is closely linked with my family background. Both parents underscored education as the primary requirement in life. . . . My mum was a schoolteacher (thus an educator), my dad was a government official (auditor). My reading ability was quite poor as I somewhat stuttered a bit when asked to read out loud. I recall at eight, I read pretty well, especially those bedtime stories Daddy brought us at home; that got me interested in reading, seeing the pictures, illustrations, etcetera. As a child, I read "Bedtime Stories" (it was a series, I don't recall the author or publisher); I also read selected books for primary schools then, they were mere collection of stories like *Eze Goes to School*, etcetera.

When asked about their reading practices, most of the readers like Mr. Davidson started reading heavily as youngsters. They repeatedly cited three factors that encouraged early reading: (1) books in school that captured their interest (in addition to *Eze Goes to School*, several readers mentioned Achebe's *Chike and the River* as a particular favorite); (2) a male relative who fostered their reading (fathers seem to be key, and a few mentioned uncles as well)[117]; and (3) Sunday school and/or Bible reading. Consider two very different cases. Eno Urua, the university lecturer, comes from a highly educated background, with both parents being teachers.

> My father was a schoolteacher, so I got introduced to books at quite an early age. And since I was a long-awaited child I must have been taught to read before age four. I read children's stories and primers for the early years of primary schooling, specifically I remember reading illustrated Bible stories, for example,

David and Goliath, the birth of Jesus Christ, the Good Samaritan. I remember reading children's poetry books such as the ones that contained "Mary Had a Little Lamb," Peter Piper. They were decidedly Western stuff, since ours was mostly an oral culture. But we got told great traditional stories in the evenings. So I was influenced by my father a lot in reading. My younger brother, for instance, used to read newspapers at home and give the report to his class in the early years of his primary school.

In contrast, the parents of Ikechukwuka Oguocha, the mechanical engineering student, were farmers. His early reading depended on school and on an uncle's encouragement:

> At the primary school level, our English-language texts were structured in such a way as to make one interested in reading serials—stories told in parts. In the upper primary school (at class six), our teacher and the student teachers who did their teaching practice in my school started us in short-story novels like Chinua Achebe's *Chike and the River* and *Eze Goes to School*. The majority of us could not afford to buy these books. The student teachers loaned us theirs in groups. So, we only read these stories while at school. The stories were very interesting to us. . . .
>
> My uncle was an avid reader then. He encouraged us by telling us to retell the stories we had read from our school "English readers"—the name we gave to English-language books recommended in our school. So, basically, my interest in reading storybooks sort of started in the upper primary school. But then, the aim was not very clear to us. We just thought it was part of the game—developing our skills in the language.

Once they were launched onto reading for pleasure as children, most of my informants read a great deal in their high school and undergraduate days. They still try to do so, although adult time pressures, especially from their studies and family responsibilities, have cut down time for leisure reading.

While finding time for reading is difficult for Nigerians abroad, in Nigeria the chief reported obstacle to reading was human distractions: general noise, people who want to talk with you, friends dropping in, and a lack of privacy. One reader suggested the social distractions and impediments to reading were even greater in the villages than in Nigerian cities. University students can read in their dormitories, but they share their rooms with one or more other students, and the open windows bringing in the loud music omnipresent in student housing interfere with a reader's ability to become lost in a book. Overall, both privacy and periods of more than a few minutes without interruption are hard to come by in a society of high household density, extended families, and frequent visits. Notoriously unreliable electricity—cursing NEPA is a national pastime— may discourage a habit of nighttime reading.[118] This might be a particular problem for readers of novels, as opposed to readers of magazines and newspapers, because in the United States at least, half of all book readers read their books in bed at night.[119]

If peace and quiet are hard to find in most households, they are even more scarce outside. Nigeria is a very densely populated country.[120] Tranquil public space—a park bench, a table at an outdoor cafe—is rare. What few libraries do exist, mostly in schools and universities, tend to be crowded and noisy, even though African librarians are well aware of the need for public reading space.[121] Public transportation is of the pack-'em-in sort: there is simply no counterpart to the tranquil Maryland commuter bus described earlier. In large cities commuters must fight to get on a bus, never mind getting a seat, while intercity buses and trucks equipped with benches are stuffed full of passengers by the touts and conductors who energetically work the motor parks. Wealthy people with both a car and a driver might read as they are being taken from place to place, if they can ignore the hawkers rapping at the windows during the innumerable traffic "go-slows." Probably the best spaces for reading outside the home are in offices: indeed, clerks and secretaries are sometimes seen reading novels and magazines on company time, but even the most devout—and irresponsible—bookworm is liable to be interrupted in this environment.

We have seen that books are expensive in Nigeria, and libraries, inadequate in both numbers and services, do not help much. Nigeria officially reports having 92 public libraries. By way of comparison Mexico, a bit smaller in population, has 2,269 libraries, and a fully literate country like Britain, with a little more than half the population of Nigeria, has 5,270 libraries.[122] Nigerians abroad often remark on the ease with which they can buy books or borrow them from public libraries. The Nigerian readers I studied sometimes mentioned using school libraries, but never public ones.

One library they did use, an important exception to this dismal picture, is that of the British Council. With libraries in Lagos, Enugu, Kaduna, Kano, and Ibadan, and an information center in Port Harcourt, the British Council supports educational, technical, and cultural cooperation between Britain and Nigeria, as well as promoting British life and culture. Its services to members include a lending library of books, videos, and cassettes; reference and bibliographic services, including CD-ROM databases; mobile vans run out of Enugu and Kano; support services for Nigerian libraries, providing such luxuries as on-line searches of international databases; information about education in Britain; and provision of newspapers, periodicals, and the BBC World Service Television via satellite for in-house use. Private membership is available for a nominal fee (160 naira in 1995). Several of the readers I interviewed, as well as a large number of the novelists themselves, mentioned heavy use of the British Council libraries.

The Lagos branch, located in the exclusive Ikoyi neighborhood, has 3,654 members.[123] Most members are men, and Librarian Sylvester Ogwara estimates that about two-thirds are Nigerian and one-third expatriate. On my two visits I saw mostly Nigerian patrons, with a few Indian women; the typical patron seemed to be an earnest-looking young man in Western dress. Clearly this is a haunt for the Anglophile, the aspiring, the elite, the intellectual, the socially mobile, the avid reader hungry for new books—and the homesick or bored expatriate.

Physically, the library is a series of linked rooms filled with metal shelves; the rooms are quiet, clean, and remarkably uncrowded by Lagos standards. They are also air-conditioned. Although the rooms are comfortable, seating space is scarce; a few patrons seem to settle in for study, but most just select their books and leave. Books are arranged according to the Dewey decimal system. The largest sections are the 300s, for social science, which includes books on politics, economics, law, and public administration, and the 600s, with books on medicine and health, engineering, and business management. In the literature section there are a dozen or so books on African literature, all published in Britain and the United States, including *Igbo Traditional Verse*, Gerard's *African Language Literatures*, Eustace Palmer's *Introduction to the African Novel*, and Ghanaian critic Kofi Awoonor's *The Breast of the Earth*.[124] The librarian Sylvester Ogwara estimated that 150 to 200 books are loaned each day. Of these, a quarter are fiction, while another quarter are on medicine; law books are also quite popular.

One library cannot serve a city's need for books. While some middle-class Nigerians like Mrs. Bishop (and many authors themselves) borrow heavily from the British Council Library, most readers from outside the literary-intellectual elite borrow novels from friends and relatives, like Mrs. Dola-Fadun, taking whatever happens to come along. Most readers can afford to buy only the occasional book, although they bought more before the oil bust, and when they do buy one they expect to pass it on to other readers. So the picture of "how" shows a Nigerian reading a paperback book, probably not from a library, that may be a bit grubby from having been passed from hand to hand (if it was bought at an open-air market, it may well be dusty even if newly purchased). The reader is likely to be distracted by noise and human interruptions unless he or she is reading late at night. And then the lights may go out. Under circumstances such as these, reading novels is a testament to perseverance, a heroic triumph against the odds.

The result of the barriers preventing even educated and affluent people from developing a reading habit may be illustrated with some observations I made on a flight from Amsterdam to Lagos.[125] The jetliner was full, and most—I would estimate at least four-fifths—of the passengers were

Africans. (On this flight, the majority of African passengers would have been Nigerians; the flight was going on to Lomé before looping back to Amsterdam, so there may have been some Togolese and other African nationalities on board.) Only a sprinkling of children or elderly people occupied the seats; most of the African passengers were young or middle-aged adults. Some were traveling in groups, and a few more, even though alone, seemed to know other passengers. Three-quarters of the Africans were in Western dress, one-quarter in traditional dress; in either one, passengers favored bright colors, shiny metallic fabrics, and lots of gold jewelry. This was an affluent, cosmopolitan crowd, and probably an urban one as well. I saw only one man with ritual facial scars; I saw no passenger carrying large bundles of food or dressed in an inappropriate way (e.g., wearing sandals or dirty clothing); and all passengers seemed to be familiar with the routines of international flights. Overall the Africans appeared middle-class and urbane, as is suggested by their traveling to Europe in the first place.

Neither in the airport prior to departure nor on the plane did I observe any African reading a book. They spent their time talking, dozing, or watching the film during the six-and-a-half-hour flight. Several times I walked the length of the airplane counting passengers and observing what they were doing. Of 120 people observed, of whom about 20 were white or Asian and therefore (in all likelihood) not African nationals, I saw only eleven people reading anything. Nine of the eleven were Europeans (Nigerians refer to white people as "Europeans," so I shall do the same) or Asians. Of the two Africans who were reading, one was looking at the airline magazine, the other was reading a newspaper. The contrast with the non-Africans was striking, for about half of the latter were reading.[126] The Africans on such a flight would be part of a wealthy, elite minority and would, for the most part, be literate. The fact that they did not choose to occupy themselves by reading during a lengthy airplane flight vividly illustrates the complaint so often made by Nigerian writers and publishers that "Nigeria lacks a reading culture."

What Do They Read?

Not all book readers in Europe or the United States are reading fiction, of course, but most are. Somewhere between two-thirds and three-quarters of people who read for pleasure read novels.[127] Fiction accounts for three-quarters of all public library loans, as well as some 70 percent of mass-market titles published (and since fiction has larger than average print runs, it constitutes an even higher percentage of actual mass-market books produced).[128] On the one hand, if we think in terms of all reading, the majority of books are published for educational and occupational uses, with perhaps only 15 to 25 percent of world book production being fiction.[129]

On the other hand, if we think in terms of reading for pleasure, the voluntary and often addictive reading that psychologist Victor Nell calls "ludic reading" because of its play characteristics, the sort of reading that Mrs. Dola-Fadun does, most of this is fiction.

Of those who do read fiction, most read popular fiction: contemporary or historical romances, mysteries, thrillers.[130] The readership for serious fiction is very small indeed, no more than 10 percent of all adults. For instance, Peter Mann conducted a study of the fiction read by a sample from a highly educated population, the faculty at Sheffield University. With the help of several professionals in literature and the book trade, he constructed a list of twenty works of "modern serious fiction" that had been published during the previous year and that had received numerous and generally favorable reviews. When he polled the sample of 146 couples, in only 23 of them had either spouse read anything from the list. [131] We can estimate that, in the United States and Great Britain, roughly one-third of adults may be considered to be readers of novels, and perhaps one-third of these read serious classic or contemporary fiction.

In developing countries like Nigeria, reading is inclined to be more instrumental than ludic, more aimed at acquiring the skills and knowledge needed for social and occupational mobility.[132] Fewer readers have acquired the habit of reading for pleasure. Recall Schmidt's finding that only a fifth of the students at the University of Ibadan read for pleasure; in the United States, by contrast, virtually everyone over the age of sixteen who reads for school or work reads for pleasure as well.[133] The largely instrumental character of Nigerian reading is reinforced by the system of distributing books through bookstores and academic stalls in markets, rather than through mass retailing outlets that encourage impulse purchases. Similarly, as mentioned earlier, textbooks or books on law and religion occupy the prominent front-of-the-store positions that would be given over to the latest thrillers or best-sellers in an American or European bookstore. To be sure, reading for information can shade into reading for pleasure, as the readers of Onitsha pamphlets about money-hungry girls no doubt experienced, but the Nigerian emphasis is instrumental, not ludic. As Mrs. Bishop pointed out, the very social aspirations of parents who urge their children to read more and study harder may discourage the view of reading as a pleasurable, voluntary, noninstrumental activity.

Therefore, while the percentage of readers who read novels is very likely smaller in Nigeria than in the West, Nigerian fiction readers' preference for popular genres over more serious ones is no doubt similar. Nancy Schmidt found that detective stories and love stories were the favorite popular fiction during the early years of independence, whereas university students enjoyed English writers such as Shakespeare, Arthur Conan Doyle, Marie Corelli, and Thomas Hardy.[134] While the data on African writers are sketchy, in the Enugu public library it appeared that Achebe and Ekwensi—especially *Jagua Nana*, considered to be somewhat risqué at the time—were the most frequently read. The library, however, would not have had the Onitsha market pamphlets, though it was these fictions and semifictions that the typical Enugu reader was reading at the time.

Schmidt's analysis of the themes of Nigerian literature led her to single out religion, education, love and marriage, and success and failure as being especially prominent. Novels represented all of these themes, and invariably (in all of the twenty-one novels studied) treated the topic of culture conflict or cultural differences.[135] But we must note that these are the topics of novels that had been published in London and, as Schmidt observes, had to appeal to the tastes of British publishers "who were looking for books that would appeal to European readers because they were exotic or educational, or they were going along with the fashion of being in sympathy with any manifestation of African national aspirations."[136]

The readers in the present study, when asked about their favorite novelists, most often mentioned Achebe and Soyinka. Several readers liked the Nigerian writers Elechi Amadi, Cyprian Ekwensi, Buchi Emecheta, Flora Nwapa, Ola Rotimi, and Amos Tutuola (interestingly, Booker Prize winner Ben Okri seems to have made little impact). Cyprian Ekwensi was cited as being one writer whose popular appeal transcends regional and ethnic differences. The hectic mix of personalities in *People of the City,* which set the pattern for most of Ekwensi's subsequent fiction, seems to present a contemporary reality that all Nigerian readers find interesting.

As for non-Nigerians, the most popular seem to be Ngũgĩ wa Thiong'o, Camara Laye, Shakespeare, Charles Dickens, Frederick Forsyth and Jeffrey Archer. Several readers pointed out somewhat apologetically that Archer was one of a group of popular authors—including James Hadley Chase, Danielle Steel, and the Mills and Boon romances—whose works are read for sheer entertainment. Innocent Davidson reports typically eclectic tastes:

> I always devoted my holidays to extensive novel reading. I recall reading as much as one novel of 120 pages average in two to three days. It kept me occupied since most holidays spanned ten weeks, and I often didn't have a vacation job. During those periods, I could spend six hours daily reading novels, including James Hadley Chase novels, a bit of Nick Carter, Denise Robins, etcetera. Quite some junk you'll say.
>
> Well, when I became a Christian, my reading habit did quite change, as well as my reading material. I read the Bible more extensively, I do recall reading through the whole Bible once every year. . . . Over the next five years I did that. I guess that had a profound influence on my values. Often, when reading literature, I read small pocket books while riding on the bus between campuses, trav-

eling, and on weekends. . . . I did stop reading those Hadley Chase novels, because I lost interest in them. However, I still read occasional folktales which expound past traditions (Chinua Achebe), books on history, some philosophy, and the like. But these are more like academic enlightenment than literature reading for leisure.

Availability influences tastes. Until recently, novels published by British companies, whether by Nigerian or foreign authors, were more generally available than locally published fiction. This is somewhat less true in the 1990s, when the fiction of no particular publisher, with the possible exception of Spectrum and, inevitably, Mills and Boon, can be said to be well represented on bookstore shelves. So it is not so much that Nigerian-published books have become more available as that British published books have become less so—except at the British Council.

Elite tastes are influenced by the British Council Libraries, which favor British authors of relatively high quality. In the Lagos branch, fiction is shelved separately in an area labeled "Twentieth-Century Fiction," not a strict description, for the section includes the fiction of Dickens and other earlier writers. There are roughly twelve hundred books on the shelves. Most of the fiction (I would estimate two-thirds) is by British authors, the rest by Americans, West Indians, Africans, and other Commonwealth writers. The collection is oriented toward highbrow reading; there were no Fredrick Forsyth or Jeffrey Archer thrillers, but plenty of Anita Brookner, Ruth Prawer Jhabvala, David Lodge, Margaret Drabble, Robertson Davies, and the like. A fair number of Caribbean writers were represented, mostly though Heinemann's Caribbean Writers Series, and there were quite a few South African books as well.

The fiction collection also contained a number of Nigerian novels published in Britain, particularly those of Heinemann's African Writer Series (eight copies of John Munonye's novels were there, making him the most visible Nigerian novelist), as well as several from Fontana. Very few Nigerian-published books were on the shelves, although I did see Malthouse's *Our Wife and Other Stories* by Karen King-Aribisala, a Guyanese married to a Nigerian, and Ken Saro-Wiwa's 1986 short story collection, *A Forest of Flowers*. Surprisingly, no books by either Emecheta or Tutuola were on the shelves, although some may have been checked out. By and large this looked like a collection on contemporary British fiction with a generous dash of Commonwealth writers; if the shelves had been seen out of context, it would not be obvious that the collection of fiction was located in Nigeria, or even in Africa.

An assumption that authors and publishers often make is that Nigerian readers, if given the choice, would prefer to read Nigerian books. This, however, is not the case. Recall that I caught Mrs. Dola-Fadun reading a

Danielle Steel melodrama, Mrs. Bishop reading Trollope, Mr. Bada reading Camara Laye and complaining that Nigerian writers were not as good. And at the most popular level, someone is reading all those Mills and Boon romances. That could be a matter of availability. Stronger evidence for Nigerians having catholic reading tastes comes from the fact that while the readers I surveyed were careful to distinguish African from non-African authors, they never expressed strong preferences for the former. The same was true for the Nigerian novelists themselves.

To get a more direct indication of reading tastes, I did a comparison of the number of times works of fiction had been checked out at the British Council Library in Lagos, comparing all Nigerian novels on the shelves with an equal sample of all others. I broke these non-Nigerian novels down into British, other African, and Caribbean authors. If one simply compares the Nigerian to the non-Nigerian novels, the Nigerian books were borrowed an average of 3.491 times from 1993 to May 1995, while the non-Nigerian books were borrowed 3.344 times. But when the latter group is analyzed, those novels written by Britons were checked out an average of 4.025 times; non-Nigerian African novels lagged with an average of 2.581 loans, while West Indian novels were checked out only once on average. Thus, a ranking of reader preferences would put British authors first, then Nigerian, then other African, and finally other Commonwealth writers. Perhaps we should not make too much of this apparent preference for British over Nigerian authors, given that a goodly number of the British Council members are themselves English, but recall Mr. Onyeacholam saying that most of the Bestseller customers who bought any African literature were foreigners. At the very least we can say that the avid readers who patronize the British Council Library, like their down-market counterparts reading James Hadley Chase and Mills and Boon, do not seem to favor Nigerian novelists.

Similar results come from a study of Nigerian children's reading preferences.[137] When researchers asked 216 primary school students to list some books that they "liked very much," having either read them or had them read to them, the children named 174 non-Nigerian books and 135 Nigerian ones. This could have been because non-Nigerian children's books were more available, however, and hence more familiar. One school library's circulation records showed that a random sample of local titles had a higher circulation rate (7.4 per title) than foreign ones (4.6 per title). The researchers interpret this difference as giving the "true picture"—that is. Nigerian children prefer Nigerian books—but this conclusion seems unwarranted, since teachers themselves may account for much of the library circulation. The children's stated preferences certainly do not support the assumption that they strongly favor Nigerian books, to say the least, and in this they resemble their elders. Nigerian readers of any age are in no position, and have little inclination, to be parochial.

What Do They Make of What They Read?

Reading serves many functions, in theory ranging from pure utility to pure entertainment. An instruction manual approaches one end of the continuum, a light romance the other. In practice, however, reading materials are mixtures, simultaneously serving the functions of entertainment and instruction. Readers of fiction seek information as well as pleasure. They express motives involving education (Mrs. Dola-Fadun reading for information, Mrs. Bishop for improvement, Mr. Fagbohun "to know what's going on in the world"), recreation, and participation in literary discourse, perhaps with a view to elevating status or constructing and maintaining social bonds through talk about books.[138]

Readers of all fiction expect there to be a connection between books and "real life." They evaluate a novel based on its connections to their own experience of people and how they behave.[139] The highest praise many young adults can bestow on a book is that it "seems like real life," because it either reminds them of their own experiences or makes them feel personally involved in the action.[140] If good fiction leaves a "residue," that residue seems to involve a clear link with readers' sense of what people are like and how the world works.[141] More generally, the attainment of literacy means not only acquiring practical skills but also participating in a human community that is closed to the illiterate.

Those who do not take literacy for granted, people who have become literate through adult education programs, see this very clearly. A fascinating collection of interviews with adults who had participated in the University of Ibadan Experimental Literacy Project emphasizes this point about fuller participation.[142] Now that they can read, they say, "I feel fully human" (22), or "I felt somewhat confident and human" (34). This new sense of being "fully human" seems based on enhanced prestige, the ability to get better jobs and promotions, and a sense of being in control of one's life both on the job and at home. Interviewees report how they are now able to defend themselves from being cheated and avoid making mistakes, as when one woman told how she almost killed her child in her illiterate days by not being able to read the directions on a prescription drug.

Beyond this, such adults share a sense of finally being able to participate in the discourse of those who could communicate in English:

> "My literate wife often carried on conversations in English with her friends and our literate visitors, while I looked on. I laughed when they laughed and showed signs of grief when they looked despondent, but I felt shy and less human, for I was totally ignorant of what they were saying. . . . Having passed the Primary School Leaving Certificate Examination in 1978, I felt somewhat confident and

human, for I could participate in discussions with our literate friends and business partners. (34)

Another Yoruba man reports how literacy allowed him to break some of the restrictions of tribe: "My boss and colleagues began to give me due recognitions for I held regular conversations with them in English, carried out their written instructions and attended to non-Yoruba speaking visitors" (39).

Earlier we saw how European literacy was associated with enhanced individualism. The Nigerian case is less straightforward, for the newly literate adults Okedara studied see literacy in the context of a web of mutual dependence and independence. On the one hand, being able to read means no longer relying as much on others. A Yoruba woman reports:

> I had no means of checking the accuracy of the news. For instance, immediately after the second coup in Nigeria, many friends told me that they read in some Nigerian papers that the country was about to start another civil war. I was in a state of fear and uncertainty for many weeks. I auctioned some of my goods in order to be free to move to my state should it be necessary. When nothing happened months later I discovered that all was a lie. Then I decided to learn how to read newspapers myself. Hence, I became serious about attending literacy classes. (26)

It also means the preservation of privacy, as exemplified by one Igbo man:

> My children wrote both from home and abroad about their finances and other problems. When literate friends read and wrote my letters for me, they leaked my secrets out. I heard about the incidents several times, and I was sorry and felt ashamed. In my mind there was no other solution than learning how to read and write by myself. (24)

But literacy is understood as enhancing social connections, not just allowing for individual advancement:

> I am able to read some local and national newspapers. . . . I read about a woman who was killed in the Bendel State by a mob for allegedly being a witch. I told my girl friends about the incident, and everyone of us was scared. (22)

> [When I learned to read] I could also read the Holy Koran in English [so] I became a better Muslim than before. . . . I helped interpret the Koran to illiterate Muslims. . . . I felt great that I could be of service to my Muslim brothers by using my literacy skills. . . . One day I read in the *Daily Sketch* about an accident that occurred on the Abeokuta-Ibadan Road. I learnt that the accident was due to overtaking. Since then I have been advising my relatives, friends and acquaintances to avoid excessive speeding and overtaking of other vehicles. (37)

The enhanced humanity that the interviewees felt seemed to come from increases in both individual capacities and social competence.

This sense of greater participation in society, dramatically experienced by those for whom literacy has come late, is shared by all readers of novels. While fiction is usually regarded as being weighed more heavily toward entertainment than instruction, readers emphasize how novels provide a better understanding of how people operate in society. Indeed, many readers deny the instruction-entertainment division altogether; it is common for readers of light fiction, for example, to justify their reading in terms of what they learn.[143]

This understanding comes only when the story holds readers' attention, however. Nigerian readers assume that novelists are making money from their books (Nigerian novelists deny this), and that they are trying to appeal to a readership by being entertaining, often by imitating European or American models. These readers demand, above all else, a good story, for they regard the writer as a storyteller who happens to use paper rather than the spoken word. If the story is compelling, if it succeeds in holding readers' interest, they may draw practical lessons from it—this is what life is like in Lagos, this is what happens if a boy doesn't obey his parents—although it is hard to assess how influential such messages actually are. The point is, both readers and novelists in Nigeria assume that a successful novel should teach as well as entertain.

When I asked Nigerian readers what Nigerian novelists should be aiming for, most said that novelists should strive for social improvement, serving as guides and social critics. Here again we see the teaching theme. A smaller number of readers felt it was more important for the writer to write his or her best without worrying about social import, and several remarked that it was only reasonable for writers to have making money as their goal.

Often readers pointed out that these various objectives were not mutually exclusive, contending that a fine novel is likely to have more social impact than a weak one, and might well make more money too. But this last point is debatable, and several readers expressed concern over Nigerian reading tastes being debased by the wide availability of "junk novels" by both Nigerians and foreigners.

In sum, Nigerian readers take it for granted that novels are "true," that they give insights about real life, realistic people and situations. Since fiction is true to life, and since reading is instructive and not simply entertaining, it follows that reading novels is a way of gaining information about what other people are "really like." The goal is one of understanding, of an increased capacity to grasp and participate in one's times. This corresponds to the authors' somewhat self-serving pronouncements that even the most sensational thrillers were about contemporary social problems. Nigerian readers do not see the novel as a mirror, a projection of their own experience, but as a window into the contemporary human condition.

What Is a Reading Culture, and Will Nigeria Ever Have One?

I conclude by returning to the question, What is a reading culture? In a general sense, a reading culture exists in a society with a literacy rate that is relatively high and does not exclude any particular social group. Such a culture assumes literacy for full social participation; literacy is regarded as a right, illiteracy as a personal or systemic failure. Routine communications of economic, political, and commercial life take place through writing. A popular press and other forms of mass print media, as well as perhaps more specialized publishing, and effective distribution systems make reading materials widely available. People's working lives, and their leisure time as well, routinely involve reading.

Even in this general sense, a reading culture is a considerable achievement. Societies notable for their sophistication, advanced technologies, and political dominion, such as Qing dynasty China or imperial Rome, did not have reading cultures. China had a scribal culture, where literacy was both exceedingly important and exceedingly restricted to the literati of the state bureaucracy. Despite the omnipresence of the written word on its monuments and buildings, at the height of the Roman empire Rome and Italy had only 20 to 30 percent male literacy, and less than 10 percent female.[144] On the other hand, countries that are economically underdeveloped or politically insignificant may have reading cultures; Barbados is a contemporary example. So one must not assume that having a reading culture goes with being somehow "advanced."

One might favor an even stricter definition of a true reading culture Some would say that a reading culture exists only where people are in the habit of reading relatively serious books, and when they choose reading over other forms of entertainment. By such a stringent definition, few nations could claim to have a reading culture, although there might be pockets, as in the academic community or among certain urban elites. Such pockets have existed historically, long before reading cultures in the more general sense came into being; the manuscript culture of medieval European monastic life or the Chinese bureaucratic elite ("the literati") constituted such pockets of high culture reading in the midst of unlettered societies.

Nigeria has a reading culture in this strict sense—academics, journalists, men and women of letters, people like the elite schoolgirl Remi in *Yoruba Girl Dancing* who get immersed and indoctrinated into English literature—but not in the more general sense. Most Nigerians get through their daily lives without having much occasion to read, regardless of whether they can. They conduct their commercial affairs face-to-face in the markets. They vote—when they are able to vote—by putting their marks next to a party's symbol. They keep in touch by visiting or, among the urban elite, by telephoning. They get their news from television, radio, and word of mouth. And if a letter, a bureaucratic form, or a juicy tale in one of the tabloids requires reading, they can always find someone—a young relative, a paid clerk—to read and interpret it for them.

In Nigeria, as in many places in the non-Western world, the premodern exists cheek by jowl with the postmodern. Television programs with names like *Tales by Moonlight* feature actors as storytellers and listeners in traditional village settings. These programs are broadcast to the antennae and satellite receivers throughout the country. They may be viewed in villages, in the evenings, in public spaces once occupied by storytellers. In such a situation, stories come full circle, and written literature is not part of the loop. Examples of the simultaneity of the premodern and postmodern are everywhere. Youth who leave school after the primary grades get their entertainment through VCRs. People who have lived their lives in a single village learn an emotional repertoire from Indian films on television and photo-magazines modeled after the Latin American fotonovelas.

If literacy and a reading culture are part and parcel of modernity, one might speculate that Nigeria is going to skip this reading-culture stage altogether. According to this view, the country will lurch from the premodern to the postmodern without following some developmental logic that accords reading a culturally central role. It will never develop a reading culture in the general sense because it will never need one.

This is not a possibility that Nigerian writers or readers like to contemplate, for it devalues their skills and threatens their prestige. They remain confidently whistling in the dark as they assert that, before long, Nigeria will have a reading culture. They are probably wrong; at the very least, it seems clear that a linear model whereby a society moves into literacy and a reading culture along the lines of nineteenth-century England or twentieth-century America is ill suited for comprehending the Nigerian literary complex of today and tomorrow. While literacy in English will continue to be a necessity for full social participation, postmodern Nigeria will have too many alternative sources of information and entertainment to develop into a reading culture, or a nation of readers, as understood in the West. Reading will be one discursive channel among many, and novels will be only one of the media through which stories are told.[145]

At the same time we must recognize the enormous prestige of reading in Nigeria, as well as its utility. Books may be costly, but they are a lot cheaper than VCRs, do not require additional equipment, and are more immune to the vagaries of the electric power supply than are other media. Novels may continue to compete with other modes of storytelling, other forms of instructing through entertainment, but they have some social and practical advantages in this competition. They will never dominate, and in this sense a place like Nigeria will never have a "reading culture" in the same way that the West has had one. Nevertheless, novels may be the single most influential vehicle for the stories that Nigerians—especially Nigerians in the urban, semi-industrial, modern sectors, those global citizens wrestling with local problems—need to tell and to hear.

Chapter 3

NIGERIAN NOVELS

I N THIS EXAMINATION of the Nigerian literary complex—the writers, the publishers, the readers—I have thus far looked at the novels themselves only in passing. Now it is time to move the novels to the foreground. In this chapter I examine the 476 Nigerian novels that have been published from the appearance of *The Palm-Wine Drinkard* until the mid-1990s.

When I began reading Nigerian fiction systematically some ten years ago, I had in mind a vague sense of what "the Nigerian novel" was apt to be like. The prominence of *Things Fall Apart* had shaped my expectations, as it has for many Western readers, so I supposed that the story of the colonial impact on traditional African life would constitute one of the fundamental themes of Nigerian fiction. Beyond that I had little idea what I would find. I did not anticipate the prominence of crime novels, for example, nor did I ever imagine that city life would be far more important as a theme and setting than would rural life. I might have guessed that some portion of Nigerian novels would focus on women and their particular problems and issues, but I did not expect to see the boy-meets-girl romance—that most Western of formulas—reconstructed along Nigerian lines. I expected traditions but not traffic jams. Yet to my great surprise, and there were many surprises, the single most common scene in Nigerian fiction is a traffic jam, one of Lagos's notorious "go-slows," in which the city's futuristic road system of bridges and expressways and "flyovers" grinds to a halt.

As I began reading more Nigerian novels, I saw that they seemed to fall into a number of thematic categories. I shall refer to these categories as genres, as in the war novel genre, because I want to draw attention to how each group shares internal similarities, especially with respect to a common plot structure, and how its members are different from those outside the group.[1] Some of these were formulaic, as in the crime thriller, and most were both clear and commonly used by people writing on African literature: the city novel, the civil war novel, and so forth. Eventually I came to identify eight genres to which most Nigerian novels could be assigned:

1. Stories of traditional village life
2. Tales of the city
3. Novels focusing on women's relationships with men
4. More or less formulaic romances

5. Stories about intellectuals and academic life
6. Novels treating the civil war
7. Crime stories and thrillers
8. Political novels

The categories made sense to the Nigerian authors I asked, as well as to Nigerian readers, so I am confident that I have not come up with too idiosyncratic a typology.[2] Table 3-1 gives the numbers and percentages for each genre.

Not every novel fits into one of the eight genres I have designated, however, and these other novels—some 10 percent of the population—could themselves be arranged in small groups; there are a handful of utopian fantasies, for example, and a cluster of semipornographic works. Moreover, some novels could plausibly be assigned to more than one of my eight categories; it is a judgment call as to whether Ekwensi's *Jagua Nana,* for example, should be considered a city novel or a novel about women. In the following pages I will indicate the basis for my own judgment—for example, why I regard *Jagua Nana* as a city novel—by describing both the genres and my criteria for inclusion within them. Thus the reader may assess the validity of my decisions, and perhaps make some different ones.

The eight genres fall into four pairs, which I shall treat in the following order. The first pair presents the contrasting worlds of the village and the city. This contrast, which we saw initially through Tayo and Lenuse of *The Last Chance,* is undoubtedly the most prominent theme in Nigerian fiction. Village novels and city novels are mutually constituted and cannot be understood except in relation to each other. (The actual number of city novels is somewhat misleading, for I have included only those novels that did not fall into one of the other genres. Most crime novels, and many nov-

TABLE 3-1
Nigerian Novels by Genre

Genre	Number	Percent of Total
Crime	104	22
Romance	67	14
Village	61	13
Women-and-men	50	11
Politics	44	9
Intellectuals	40	8
City	34	7
Civil war	29	6
Other, cannot be categorized	47	10
Total	476	100

els about gender and about intellectuals, also have the basic city novel structure.)

The second pair involves gender roles and the relations between the sexes. Women-and-men novels deal with problems faced by Nigerian women under either traditional social norms or under the pressures of rapid social change. Romances, which may center on either male or female characters, rearrange the Western formula to fit the Nigerian experience of love, marriage, and sexual relations. Romances are generally regarded as light reading in Nigeria, as they are in the West, while the women-and-men novels vary in their intended and actual degree of seriousness, but each member of the pair illuminates the other.

The third pair—novels about intellectual life and novels about the Nigerian civil war—is a less obvious coupling than the first two. What these genres have in common, as I will try to show, is their contrast between Western rationality and African social realities, particularly as these contrasts have been experienced by educated Nigerians. One prominent point of contact, for example, is through the experience of Igbo intellectuals who were so prominent in Nigerian academic life before the war and who were so centrally involved in the Biafran secession; from the point of view of the intellectual establishment of the Universities of Ibadan and Nsukka, "things fell apart" with the war and have never come together again. While each of these two genres may be seen strictly on its own terms rather than in relation to the other, considering them together clarifies their common theme of chaos overwhelming those Nigerians who have hitched their wagons to a certain form of rationality.

The fourth pair is crime and politics. In this instance, when I presented my preliminary genres to Nigerian authors, they forced me to reconsider. As some authors pointed out, my early classification scheme had no separate category for "political novels." While they agreed that the seven other categories made sense, and even agreed with my categorization of their own novels, a number asked, "But where are the political novels?" When I looked at how I had been treating novels dealing with political themes, I discovered that I had classified them as "crime novels" because of their emphasis on corruption. This made sense to me, but the Nigerian authors convinced me otherwise; although the highway robber with a gun and the high government minister selling contracts might both be crooks, these were different types of criminality representing different (though related) social problems. Since the authors and, I later learned, the readers saw this as a real and important distinction, I followed their advice and added an eighth genre.

While these eight genres are similar in terms of their internal consistency, they differ quite a bit in terms of size. The formulaic genres have the most members, with crime novels constituting almost one-quarter of the total, followed at some distance by the romances. The nonformulaic genres are smaller as a whole. The village novels are the most numerous of this group, with almost as many titles as the romances, while the civil war novels are the fewest. Overall the nonformulaic genres are fairly evenly balanced, with each of the six genres constituting between 6 and 13 percent of the total. None of these genres is so small that I would reconsider designating it as an independent category, nor is any so large to suggest it may be too inclusive.

VILLAGE AND CITY

Pataego is the daughter of farmers in Umona, a village in eastern Nigeria. Her parents, "kind, humble, good-natured—the peculiar good qualities of country people," urge her to marry, but Pataego is holding out for a husband who lives in the city. When courted by Dennis, a tailor from Enugu, Pataego decides not to let her chance slip by. "In the eighteen years of her life Pataego hadn't visited any township; not even on holiday. She spent her life entirely in the village with no idea of life outside Umona. Now she wanted a change and quickly too. Away from the drab life of the village to the more exciting and exhilarating life of a cosmopolitan city." So although she does not love Dennis, she agrees to marry him. Despite their misgivings, her parents send her off with warnings not to shame them.

Pataego is bored in Enugu, so she begins training as a seamstress. Soon she meets glamorous Madam Do-Good, who recruits her for work in a brothel. She conceals her double life, but soon Dennis notices her new wardrobe and hardened manner. Their relationship deteriorates until Pataego finally moves into the brothel. Delegations from her parents fail to budge her, nor does she respond when Dennis begs her to return.

Madam Do-Good dies suddenly, and the brothel residents are dispersed. Fallen on hard times, Pataego returns to Umona to confess her sins and start over. With a team of village elders testifying to her change of heart, she goes back to Enugu to beg Dennis's forgiveness. "Pataego was still kneeling for an answer when Dennis rose up and slowly left the room. And the crowd of elders wailed."

(Celsus Adinde, *Village Girl*)

Celsus Adinde's novel *Village Girl* is set in the city for the most part, but its plot depends on the protagonist being what the title proclaims her to be. The village and the city, the respectable but "drab" world of the country and the dangerous but "exhilarating" world of the town, are the two poles between which the characters of Nigerian fiction move. In the village, relatives and elders are ready to tell the young what to do, and to say

"I told you so" if their advice is ignored; in the city, Madam Do-Goods and men with cash to throw around are ready to lure the innocent to destruction. The city is the zone of freedom, novelty, opportunity, and risk; the village, the zone of constraint, tradition, entrapment, and security. Each depends on the other for its meaning.

The village-city axis is the principal dimension for differentiating among Nigerian novels, according to Nigerian writers, readers, and participants in the book trade, and it is this dimension that I explore in the present section. I begin by analyzing the structure of the village novel plot, immortalized in Achebe's *Things Fall Apart*. Later I lay out the city plot in the same way. In addition to the village and city genres, I examine the choice of setting more generally, asking why the city background is so common, the village so rare. I shall consider institutional influences, including authors, publishers, and readership, that have gone into the construction of these settings and plots. I shall end by exploring how both village and city work in Nigerian fiction as metaphors for modernity, and how the village-city axis records and shapes both the Nigerian experience of social change and the outside world's understanding of that change.

"In Peace and Harmony Like the Trees of Their Jungle": The Village Novel

Bayo Adebowale, who teaches English at the Oyo State College of Education, is a committed defender of village life.[3] Adebowale charges that rural areas are "criminally neglected" by the central government and ignored by most educated Nigerians; he would not be surprised that an urban sophisticate like Mrs. Elsa Bishop finds villages "exotic." This being the case, he argues that the African writer must explore the lives and problems of people in remote villages. To convey the true meaning of Africa, novelists should go to the village, to nature, to the problems of the people. They should leave the city or university now and then to "sleep on mats" and "explore what's going on behind the mud walls of the village."[4] While Adebowale recognizes that many of his fellow third-generation writers think village themes have been "overflogged" by earlier Nigerian novelists, he urges writers to continue their literary investigations of traditional culture. To facilitate this, he has established the African Heritage Research Library in his hometown of Ila-Orangun.

Adebowale's tragic first novel, *The Virgin*, exemplifies his "behind-the-mud-walls" commitments.

> A girl from the Yoruba village of Orita, Awero is betrothed to Odejimi, a hunter from a neighboring village. Having been seduced by a city boy when he briefly returned to the village, Awero awaits her marriage in trepidation,

afraid to tell anyone "her pot is broken." The wedding takes place according to tradition, and the hunter takes his bride home. When Odejimi discovers that Awero is not a virgin, he is infuriated and sends her back to Orita. She is shamed and ostracized, but nevertheless the Orita elders feel that Odejimi must accept his bride, broken pot or not, and relinquish his claims to the bride price he has paid. At the end, the two villages have gone to war over the dispute.

(Bayo Adebowale, *The Virgin*)

The Virgin both depicts and celebrates traditional sex roles: woman is subservient to her husband; women but not their male seducers are blamed for loss of virginity; Awero is passive in the face of social forces; Odejimi, though something of a brute (he shoots a rival; he kills forbidden animals), receives much sympathy for having been deceived. Denying any ironical or critical intention, Adebowale described the novel to me as dealing with the importance of trust in the matrimonial home and presenting a faithful portrayal of Yoruba values. He said that the story took place in the period between 1955 and 1965; after that time, urban and modern ways impinged on village life, including sexual expectations, to a greater extent than before. He sees *The Virgin* as contributing to cultural preservation.

The Virgin is an example of what I am calling the village novel—not simply any novel set in a village but one that depicts the destabilization of a traditional rural community. Plots exhibit a standard narrative pattern, what might be called a mythic structure, that include the following five stages.

1. *Traditional social order:* Village novels begin by depicting a small agricultural community and its established ways. Conflicts, tensions, and rivalries exist, but they occur among people everyone knows, and village residents do not regard conflict itself as threatening their way of life. Village social order is shown to be in sympathy with natural and/or spiritual forces; if this sympathy is disrupted, ritual actions such as sacrifices restore the balance. Thus Adebowale presented Orita as being in harmony with its natural and social surroundings.

2. *Disturbance from outside:* Some external force comes to disrupt the local tranquillity. This outside element is usually associated with the Western impact on African society, which may manifest itself in terms of modernization, urbanization, Christianity, colonial government, the expansion of trade, or the exposure of African youth to Western ways through education or travel. In *The Virgin*, it is a flashy city boy, parading his recently acquired sophistication, who seduces Awero and sets the tragedy into motion.

3. *Attempted restoration:* Responding to the disruption, the villagers attempt to reimpose social order. Community leaders debate the new sit-

uation and eventually agree upon a course of action intended to return the village to its previous state of equilibrium. Thus Orita's council of elders, while sympathetic to Odejimi and ashamed of Awero's depravity, decides that the marriage nevertheless should be considered valid. The elders from Odejimi's village come up with the opposite resolution, annulment of the marriage and return of the bride price, but they have the same desire to restore the status quo.

4. *Climax:* Unexpected resistance to the direction of the community leaders produces a crisis. The clash between the forces of restoration and the forces of change leads to the story's climax. In *The Virgin*, both villages want to restore harmony, but each on its own terms, so each resists the other's strategy for defusing the conflict.

5. *Disintegration or reintegration:* The village enters a new state of social existence. While occasionally the traditional order is restored, usually the village ends up far less stable and peaceful than it was at the outset of the novel. Traditional social relations have been overturned, and older cultural practices are shown to be incompatible with the new social context. At the close of *The Virgin*, only war can bring about some resolution, thus completing the sequence of destruction initiated by the city boy.

Repeated over and over in Nigerian village novels, this mythic structure enacts a one-way history of traditional community life disrupted, perhaps forever, by contact with the outside world. In its bare outlines, such a story constitutes an archetypal romance, a contrast between a lost past and a problematic present that appears throughout world literature.[5] Moreover, the five-part mythic structure of the village novel is a parable of the classic sociological view of modernization as a one-way leap into the future. In a work like *The Virgin*, the reader can see just how the disorientation of modernity, which Durkheim called *anomie,* replaces the conventional social order: Adebowale made this clear when he explained why the novel had to take place no later than the late colonial period. In this novel, as in the village novel genre as a whole, it is not so much an absence of norms that brings disaster as it is the inadequacy of old norms under new conditions. Such a before-and-after story of modernization, one that has been largely rejected by social scientists as too simple a dichotomy, continues to structure the popular understanding—in Nigeria and in the West—of African social change.

Here let me acknowledge that by concentrating on mythic structures, as I shall do for the remaining seven genres as well, I am giving short shrift to other characteristics of village novels such as their use of language. Village novels are studded with proverbs, what Achebe has famously referred to as "the palm oil with which words are eaten."[6] These proverbs serve two functions: They indicate how members of an oral culture pass on stored wisdom and direct behavior, and they represent that oral culture to readers who are, by definition, removed from it. In this latter capacity, since many proverbs are highly context-dependent, they exert a distancing effect.[7]

A city novel like *Village Girl* tells much the same story as a village novel like *The Virgin*, only from the urban standpoint. In both of these books the conflict involves a young woman whose sexual experience compromises her marriage prospects. This is a very common pattern: a woman's sexuality and reproductive potential constitute the arena in which conflicts between tradition and modernity, the old ways and the new, get fought out. One clear case of repeatedly putting the conflict in these terms is Olatunde Ojomo's aptly titled *The Young Brides*.

> During colonial times three girls from a Yoruba village make very different marriages. Risi forms a conventional union with a local boy. Her story illustrates traditional wedding rituals, such as the display of the bloody sheet that attests to her virginity on her wedding night.
>
> Risi's friend Ronke, on the other hand, gets pregnant by one of her teachers. He takes off, and Ronke refuses to name him, so she gives birth and raises her son on her own, facing down the villagers' scorn. Later the teacher has a change of heart and comes back to marry her. Both she and her community forgive his behavior.
>
> The third bride is Agbeke, whose parents had promised her to Wale when she was a baby. When she reaches marriageable age, however, Wale disappoints everyone by becoming a Catholic priest. Thereupon his family decides that Agbeke should be given to Oludare, Wale's uncle, despite the fact that the older man already has two wives. Agbeke is bitterly opposed to becoming Oludare's third wife, and she has to be kidnapped and dragged off to her new husband. Oludare treats her kindly, eventually wearing down her resistance to sex with him, and the book ends with the birth of their daughter.
>
> (Olatunde Ojomo, *The Young Brides*)

Typical of Macmillan's Past and Present series, *The Young Brides* celebrates tradition with detailed descriptions of the old beliefs and practices. In the parallel stories of the three young women, we see the outside disturbance/restoration pattern, with the restorations here being successful. Risi represents the first stage, that of the traditional order, and she never deviates from it. For the other two girls a series of external disturbances— the education of women, Christianity and the celibacy of its priests—pose problems with which the community must deal. Ojomo's novel is not as conservative as *The Virgin*, for it condemns neither Wale nor the teacher nor the independent-minded Ronke, but nevertheless the three plot lines all end in traditional marriages. Ronke's story simultaneously sets up and denies the conflict, thus suggesting Ojomo's wish to have it both ways. Ronke acts as a liberated woman, both in her rejection of the conventional woman's role by pursuing education and in her acceptance of single motherhood. Nevertheless, her fate is to be absorbed back into the traditional marriage relationship. An even more problematic restoration is that of Agbeke, for her eventual submission to her elderly, polygamous husband, while reintegrating her into the expectations of kin and village, at the same time constitutes a poignant defeat. The author presents Agbeke's story in a very matter-of-fact way, however, the entire affair being more a concern of the families than of the individuals themselves. Indeed, for all three of the young brides, even the go-it-alone Ronke, it is their families that ultimately ratify their marriages.

Yet the resolutions strike us as arbitrary, the reintegration as contrived. Agbeke's resignation seems a poor showing compared with Ronke's intransigence, yet both win the prize of children, husband, and social acceptance. What if Oludare had been less gentle with his young bride? What if the teacher-seducer had never come back? Ojomo raises sharp questions about the capacity of traditional sex roles to accommodate changes in the aspirations of youth, and his answers—things will work out, for while women can make their own choices, the choices will end up conforming to traditional expectations—are unconvincing. The shaky foundation of the reintegration here suggests disintegration, or at least a profound destabilization.

Destabilization received its most famous expression in Chinua Achebe's novel *Things Fall Apart.* When someone like Adebowale mentions the possibility that the traditional community has been "overflogged" by Nigerian writers, he is referring above all to Achebe. For most Nigerians as well as most Westerners, Achebe's 1958 novel about a traditional community encountering colonialism represents the key event of African literary history. Although a summary cannot capture the book's complexity, it illustrates how Achebe's masterpiece established the mythic structure of the village novel at a single stroke.

Okonkwo is a prosperous farmer from Umuofia, a large village in eastern Nigeria. Son of Unoka, a gentle, flute-playing ne'er-do-well whom he despised, Okonkwo has won respect as a hard man who scorns weakness.

In Part 1, fifteen-year-old Ikemefuna has joined Okonkwo's household. He came from a village that had offended Umuofia and had to give up the boy or face war. Everyone loves Ikemefuna, but an oracle declares that he must die. Ezeudu, a wise old man, warns Okonkwo, "That boy calls you father. Do not bear a hand in his death." Ignoring this advice, Okonkwo and other men take Ikemefuna into the forest, telling him he is going home. When one of the men goes after Ikemefuna with a machete, the boy runs to Okonkwo, who delivers his deathblow.

Okonkwo's sensitive son Nwoye is devastated by Ikemefuna's death, and Okonkwo himself is upset. His friend Obierika suggests that he should not have participated in the killing because this offended the Earth goddess. As Okonkwo ponders whether his act was justified, a small cloud appears on the horizon: a rumor of white men who have no toes.

Okonkwo has a scare. His second wife has seen all her children die because they are *ogbanje* (spirit children who will not stay). One daughter remains, whom Okonkwo cherishes. When she gets sick, Okonkwo rigs up a steam bath, and she survives. Again traditional wisdom has succeeded, confirming Okonkwo's belief in the old ways and in his own power.

Ezeudu dies, and at his funeral Okonkwo's gun explodes accidentally, killing Ezeudu's son. Custom dictates that Okonkwo must leave Umuofia for seven years to appease the Earth goddess. Okonkwo and family go to Mbanta, his mother's birthplace and home of his maternal kin.

Part 2 covers the years in Mbanta. Okonkwo prospers there but longs for home. Obierika visits with an unsettling story about white men destroying a village. Missionaries come to Mbanta and build a church in the Evil Forest. They welcome *osu* (outcasts descended from slaves), twins, and various other rejected groups. The gentle Nwoye converts; Okonkwo is furious, and his son flees, later showing up among the Christians at Umuofia. Rumors suggest that the white men are setting up a government as well as a religion. Part 2 ends with a feast Okonkwo throws to thank Mbanta, during which an old man worries that the new religion threatens the clan's future.

Part 3 starts with Okonkwo's return to Umuofia. The villagers are finding the new colonial trade attractive. Okonkwo scorns the changes that Christianity is bringing, but many villagers send their children to the mission school. Court officers (the despised warrant chiefs) implement the colonial district officer's will, while a heavy-handed evangelist begins to make trouble.

Conflict escalates. Christian zealots kill a sacred python and unmask a masquerader; thereupon the masqueraders burn the church. Okonkwo and other leaders are arrested and brutalized in prison, released only when the village pays a fine. At a town meeting to decide whether Umuofia should go to war, a court messenger rudely interrupts the deliberations. Push beyond endurance, Okonkwo kills him.

When the district officer and his retinue come to arrest Okonkwo, Obierika takes them to see his body hanging from a tree.[8] Because he has committed suicide, Okonkwo must be cut down by strangers and cannot be buried by the clan. The district officer finds all this very interesting and plans to include it in the book he is writing, "The Pacification of the Primitive Tribes of the Lower Niger."

(Chinua Achebe, *Things Fall Apart*)

A beautifully constructed tragedy, though one more social than Aristotelian, *Things Fall Apart* is by far the best-known, most widely read, and most frequently cited Nigerian novel.[9] Nigerians regard it as their national literary masterpiece, and it is the one Nigerian novel most foreigners will have heard of and many will have read.[10] It is compatible with the old sociological dichotomies, the assumptions of how traditional village life—when things were, by implication, "together"—gave way to disruptive social change.

If *Things Fall Apart* is taken as the romance of colonialism, precontact Umuofia becomes the golden age, Eden before the Fall, and Okonkwo becomes the seeker after a lost paradise. I am not suggesting that Achebe himself subscribes to such a simple view—Achebe is a subtle thinker, and his main character, Okonkwo, is psychologically complex—but the novel has entered the discourse of literary representation as a before-and-after account of traditional African life. Achebe's title, it must be said, encourages this reading, as does that of his second book, *No Longer at Ease* (the story of Okonkwo's grandson). Together they imply that traditional village life was integrated, together, at ease, and this implication has been very influential.

Things Fall Apart may have set the pattern, but other village novels continued it. *Eloghosa*, by N. A. Ologbosere, came out three years after Achebe's novel was published.

> Iyayu, a farmer and hunter from a village near Benin City, has been married for twenty years to Imade. The couple has no children, despite having consulted various herbalists and doctors. As he describes their struggle, Ologbosere tells about hunts, village festivals, and how crops are grown. He recounts the old story of how people used to eat the sky: In the old days no one had to work, for they just broke off a piece of sky and ate it when they were hungry. One day a woman got too greedy and wasted some sky; the sky withdrew, and people have had to work for their food ever since.
>
> Toward the end of the novel a young Irish priest comes in a car. Both man and car astonish the villagers, but they accept the new religion as being essentially compatible with their own. Away on a hunt, Iyayu breaks his leg; as he is recovering, he learns that Imade has given birth to a girl. The priest baptizes her as "Mary," and Iyayu calls her "Eloghosa," which means "Nothing is hard for God."
>
> (N. A. Ologbosere, *Eloghosa*)

While in the spirit of *Things Fall Apart*, Ologbosere's novel is more cheerful. Christianity is not necessarily a threat to the old ways; the baby can be both Mary and Eloghosa. Moreover, the author occasionally uses a biblical language ("And so Imade had a child after thirty years of searching for one. The fulfillment of God was upon her" [111]), emphasizing his own Christianity. There are some hints, however, that future intruders will not always be as benign as the friendly Irish priest. Early on an *obo* (doctor in Benin language) prophesied that a stranger would come in a few years. "He would make friends whenever he was welcomed and fight where he was not. The people would like his new way, but they would afterwards be fed-up with him." As for the village, it is little short of perfection: "Here was a village where two people never quarreled or fought. Throughout the year they always appeared in the same contented mood. What is known as jealousy and all sinister things adverse to decent human behaviours, were unheard of at Ugha village. They existed in peace and harmony like the trees of their jungle and like the crops in their farms" (61). By implication, any change in this agrarian paradise is going to be for the worse.

Eloghosa contains much nature imagery, unusual in a Nigerian novel, as when Ologbosere describes toucans and recounts the belief that they have big bills because the first toucan buried its parents in its beak. At the end of the first part (the book has two), the natural imagery is used to draw attention to the author-as-storyteller in an unusual way. It comes at the end of a great village festival:

> The star fades away as the night vanishes from the earth, to reappear as the night the next day.
>
> One Ogie-obo [the chief doctor] comes and one Ogie-obo goes but Ugha village will go on forever.
>
> Then what of me, the mouthpiece of this great exposition. I, too shall rise again like the star, while beneath nature continues its endless dance. Will you and I be a part of that nature? (53)

This intrusion of the authorial voice brings together the themes of natural cycles, human continuities, and the role of the storyteller in narrating both.

The peaceful hamlet, whose harmony can only be shattered by the advent of external (variously presented as Christian, Western, or urban) disruption: How realistic is this image of the West African village? While ecology, agricultural mode of production, and culture made rural life on the northern savanna different from rural life in the Niger delta swamplands, most traditional Nigerian villages had certain attributes, which they shared with much of the rest of West Africa. People lived in villages, clusters of compounds representing distinct households, rather than on individual farmsteads. A compound would house a man and his wives, in which each wife would have her own dwelling for herself and her children, and it might contain other members of the extended family such as married sons and their families. A village would consist of families from several lineages or clans, all from the same ethnic group.

The relationship of residence to farm was unlike that of the American farmstead, where the residence was in the middle of the land farmed. Nor was it like the village pattern of western Europe, where villages were surrounded by land, some farmed in common, some divided into individual, alternating strips, but with much of the labor communal. Instead, Nigerian farms would be at some distance from the village, scattered among the "bush," or unfarmed land. Farm and bush lands would alternate often, since the thin African soils meant that the land was rapidly depleted and would need to lie fallow for years to restore its fertility, so new land was constantly being cleared from the bush as older farms were abandoned. Individual families would have customary rights to their farms, although not ownership of the land per se, and by and large the farming would be done by family members rather than by paid farm labor or community-based mutual assistance.

Most of the actual farm work was done by the women of the household, with the husband and father directing the overall operations and cultivating certain crops such as yams, considered a "man's crop." The walk to the farm might take considerable time each day, as might the walk to the nearest supply of water. Fetching water and transporting it to the compound was women's work, and it engaged a great deal of wives' and daughters' energies. Farming was labor-intensive, with the hoe and the machet being the principal tools for cultivation; the plow, the wheel, draft animals, and irrigation were largely absent from precolonial West Africa and made little impact on farming technology during colonialism. Farming techniques were conservative, as befitted a fragile ecology that produced no surplus, with the fundamental goal being not profit or increase but "the maintenance of the family as a productive unit."[11]

A relatively low division of labor organized the productive life of the village. Virtually every able-bodied adult engaged in farming. Shamans, craftsmen, herbalists, and chiefs might practice their specialties, but they would be farmers as well, and their wives—whose labor was less differentiated—would engage in the same combination of farming and petty trading in farm products as would the wives of other households.

The traditional African village—a cluster of compounds, organized by patrilineal kinship, from which people go out to farm (African farms are often some distance from the village), hunt, or herd, and to which they return at evening; a collection of people engaged in identical forms of agricultural labor; a village thick with human relationships, with rivalry, jealousy, support, sanctions, desire, bitterness, respect, contempt; a village where little goes unobserved, where what is observed is commented upon, and where "transparency" is a virtue, secretiveness a sin—such a village would seem to exemplify the sociological characteristics of community, and the virtues associated with community as well.[12] In his thesis about the "imagined community," Benedict Anderson made a tentative exception: "All communities larger than primordial villages of face-to-face contact (and perhaps even these) are imagined," that is, the productions of human minds in particular historical contexts. So the African village would seem to be a candidate for nonimagined status if any place is.[13] Nigerians celebrate this idea of the village-as-community, and even the most urban ones refer to their ties to village homes. Highly educated Nigerian writers and publishers described themselves to me as "coming from" a village (or village-group), regardless of where they were actually born. Like most Africans of the urban elite, they plan to retire to the village, they return for Christmas and local festivals, they invest their money there, they support urban associations of indigenes from a particular rural community, and they sponsor the education and job training of youth from the village.[14] And many, like Professor Adebowale, maintain that the real Africa is found only in the villages, "behind the mud walls." Demography backs up this point of view: three-quarters of all Africans live in rural areas.

Of course neither Africans nor outsiders who study Africa would suggest that the African village has been static. Quite the contrary. Traditional African communities, it is well understood, changed irrevocably under colonialism, especially under the impact of Christianity and Western education. Social controls broke down, new conflicts were introduced based on proximity to Western ideas and technologies, former patterns of belief and practice were shattered. Things fell apart. Or—the other side of the colonial coin—things hardened; chiefs whose former status was provisional, depending on the consent of their fellow villagers, were permanently empowered by the colonial government. Nevertheless, the village remains the seat of traditional life, even granted the fact that it displays an attenuated and distorted tradition as well as a fading one. Writers who depict lives as lived in the village see their role as one of preservation, their fiction constituting public memory, and their very concentration on "preserving" a dynamic tradition tends to belie its dynamism.

The picture of the "timeless" African village resonates with a particular Western cast of mind regarding "the community." Nineteenth-century social thought postulated a set of dichotomies involving a former "community" of rich, economically and psychologically supportive relationships that is giving way to a "society" that is essentially a marketplace, a cash nexus, or a system of impersonal, contractual obligations.[15] This before-and-after theory of societal evolution, and the modernization paradigm that it supported, has been largely discredited in social science for several decades.[16] The image of a golden age of community, a "world we have lost," retains its hold on the popular imagination, however, and even sociologists continue to use "community" as an ideal type against which to set the inadequacies of current social life.[17] In spite of the descriptive inadequacy of the term, its continuing rhetorical power suggests that everyone knows what a "real" community would look like.[18] It would look, as a matter of fact, quite a bit like an African village. Comparable to historical accounts of the preindustrial English "village community"—a small congregation of "households in association," participation in a rural network of similar communities, a known local elite, a life ordered by agricultural rhythms, a shared set of religious beliefs—the traditional African village, as understood by Westerners and urban Africans, seems to exemplify the kind of community that flourished in Europe and colonial America in the "world we have lost."[19]

Does this image of the African village, so satisfying to Africans and non-Africans, social scientists and nonacademics, square with social reality? To raise the question is to invoke doubts that have been supported empirically. It is well known, for example, that in Nigeria the central government's emphasis on categorizing people according to their "towns" or historic community allegiances was developed by British colonial governors for their administrative convenience.[20] This same policy enhanced, or even created, the power of certain local "Big Men," as in the case of the so-called warrant chiefs, whose authority came from a warrant from the British and not from community standing. The colonial system was replaced during the nationalist period with a set of regional administrative units, the Local Government Authorities, that met certain demographic and financial criteria; nationalist political leaders intended these units to reduce the administrative importance of communities and the political importance of colonialist chiefs. Thus, the political significance of the community is not as historically rooted or self-evident as one might suppose.

But what about the smaller units, the villages themselves? In thinking about what might be called the ontological status of Nigerian villages, one must keep in mind three anthropological characteristics: residences were patrilocal, kinship and inheritance were patrilineal, and marriages were exogamous. If considered from women's viewpoints, the implications of these characteristics are unsettling. More than half of the adults in any village would be women. (This is because most Nigerian ethnic groups are polygynous, and women marry, thereby attaining adult status, at a much younger age than men. Therefore, even if the mortality rates between the sexes were the same, a typical village would have more adult women than men and more boys than girls.) Married women in a village were not from there and, in a profound sense, were not "of" that village. Women maintained strong ties to their natal villages. When a marriage broke up or trouble arose in her husband's village (e.g., if a new widow were unwilling to marry her husband's brother), a former wife usually returned to her father's compound in her home village. Unmarried adult women were even more marginal to the community, especially if they remained in the village of their former husbands; the Hausa word *karuwa* means widow, divorced woman, or prostitute, equating the social irregularity of the three groups.[21] Moreover, even women who were, at least for the time being, settled in their husband's home lacked a means of political participation that would make them effective citizens of the village; politically, they were little different from their children.

In addition to the unstable status of their women, Nigerian villages contained other outsiders, people who were unable to attain full membership in the community. Members of outcast groups such as the *osu* among the Igbo, people believed to be supernaturally contaminated like witches, the *ogbanje* or *abiku* (the Hausa term equivalent to *ogbanje*), people whose ancestors had come from outside the local community—all these were denied full social belonging. Islamic towns in the north had their *sabon gari*, the "strangers' quarter" where outsiders lived, sometimes for generations. There was even a temporal dimension to some forms of social exclusion; *ogbanje* were suspect until they attained a certain age, newborns were non-persons until their naming ceremonies, men were temporarily ostracized or exiled for violations of local laws, and women were banished from public during menstruation or, among the Hausa, before dark.

Full community membership was, therefore, a possibility only for nonmigratory adult men of impeccable ancestry and behavior. All others—the majority—were, to some extent or at some times, outsiders.[22] If, as Robert Frost put it, "Home is the place where, when you have to go there, they have to take you in," then the traditional Nigerian village was a highly qualified and unstable home to most of its residents.

In considering the village as an unstable "home," one may give *Things Fall Apart* a feminist (or, as some Nigerians would prefer it, a "womanist") reading, by which I simply mean attempting to uncover some of the premises of the novel by considering it from a woman's point of view.[23] (Such a reading by a Western woman seems quite in keeping with Achebe's own objectives, by the way, which include the breaking down of the "Other Place" exoticism with which Western readers tend to approach African fiction.)[24] If home is defined as "where, when you have to go there, they have to take you in," then Okonkwo's home could be said to be Mbanta, not Umuofia. Indeed, the whole idea of home is laid open to question: Ikemefuna, after all, is told that he is going home, but his home has come to be Umuofia, with his father and protector Okonkwo, by whom he is indeed "taken in." Moreover, like traditional communities in general, the ones depicted in the novel were filled with outsiders—the *osu*, the *ogbanje*, the mothers of twins, the Christian converts, the married women. In the most painful of the many ironies, Okonkwo himself becomes the ultimate outsider. As a suicide and abomination, this defender of tradition—the one person who seemed most firmly "at home" in Umuofia—cannot be buried in the sacred ground and will not join the temporal community of the ancestors.

Other ironies circle around the telling of the tale. Achebe presents storytellers as doomed (Ikemefuna) or highly suspect (the district officer).

The novel ends with the story in the hands of the district officer, who, given his understandings of pacification and primitiveness, will distort history in a predictable way. But it is Chinua Achebe who is telling the tale, including the telling of its mis-telling. It is Achebe's composition, not that of a fictional colonial administrator, that constitutes the recomposition of community, the literary preservation/invention/imagining of village life before the Fall. Yet further ironies appear, beyond those intended by the author. Achebe first told Okonkwo's tale to the British, not to Nigerians; *Things Fall Apart* was published by Heinemann, a British publisher. In the pattern much deplored by African intellectuals, it was the acclaim he received abroad that brought Achebe to the attention of the Nigerian reading public. For *Things Fall Apart* to have been published, it had to pass through the editorial filter of British publishing; it had to appeal to British editors, and to their sense of what their public—in Britain—was interested in reading. Echoing Foucault, we may well ask, What is an author? here, or in my terms, Who is it who is imagining the imagined community?[25]

Eating the Sky: Village Settings

To recapitulate: *Things Fall Apart* is the most prominent and influential example of the village novel genre, those novels that take place in traditional rural communities and that exhibit the five-part mythic structure of traditional stability, disturbance from outside, attempted restoration, climax, and disintegration or reintegration. Such a structure, when repeated and reproduced throughout the literary culture, both expresses and encourages a pathos based on romantic nostalgia for the vanishing traditional community. While acknowledging its mythic power, I do want to suggest that this picture of stability before "things fell apart"—the stability that constitutes the first stage of the village plot—is misleading, in that it misrepresents Nigerian village life. Nigerian villages were dynamic, churning, filled with newcomers, with marginal members, traces of exiles, and other people profoundly not "at home." The village plots obscure this social dynamic.

More than misrepresentation is at issue here, however. We do not expect fiction to mirror social life, after all, but to represent social concerns. The real question is, Why has the village plot structure emerged and persisted? If the violation/disintegration plot is what has been called a "moral fantasy," why *this* moral fantasy?[26] Moreover, why do both Westerners and Nigerians understand the village plot to be, if not a faithful portrait of Nigerian village life, at least "typical" of the Nigerian novel? To begin to understand this village genre, it is necessary to relate it both to where Nigerians actually live and to Nigerian novels as a whole.

Like their counterparts throughout the continent, most Nigerians live in rural villages. Estimates vary given the lack of reliable data, but the general consensus is that no more than a third of Nigerians live in urban areas.[27] Most Nigerians, in spite of rapid urbanization in recent times, still live in places resembling the rural villages of the village novel genre.

Nevertheless, as can be seen in Table 3-2, two-thirds of Nigerian novels are set in cities, and only one-fifth (93/476) are set in villages. The "typical novel," with its village setting is in fact quite atypical. Contrary to the standard image, the typical Nigerian novel takes place in the city, even though the typical Nigerian lives in the village.

The fact the most Nigerian novels are set in cities comes as a surprise to Western readers familiar with *Things Fall Apart* and other prominent Nigerian (or African) novels, and there is a good reason for them to be surprised. Novels with village settings are more likely to be published in Britain, and thus available in Europe and North America, than the average. As Table 3-2 shows, 59 percent of the novels set in villages have been published in Britain or the United States, whereas only 35 percent of the novels with urban or other settings are published there.[28] Most village novels are published in the United Kingdom, most city novels in Nigeria.[29] While the majority of even the British-published novels have urban settings, the British overrepresentation of village settings coupled with the prominence of *Things Fall Apart* have given rise to a mistaken impression of where the typical Nigerian novel takes place.

The reasons for the British publishers' selection bias in favor of village novels are less clear than the fact of the bias, but it is possible to identify a few likely sources of this tendency. No doubt there exists some genuine interest in the African past on the part of the British intellectual classes (only the intellectual segments of the reading public read foreign fiction of any sort). This interest may be fueled by a certain postcolonial guilt among British cultural intellectuals, who are usually left of center politically. One European and American response to colonialism has been a "Third World-

TABLE 3-2
Settings of Novels Related to Places of Publication (Percent)

	Settings			
Place Published	*Village*	*City*	*Other*	*Total*
Nigeria	41	64	61	59
Britain, U.S.	59	35	35	40
Other	—	1	4	1
Total	100	100	100	100
N =	93	311	72	476

ism" that ascribes wisdom and virtue to the traditional ways of life that were destabilized by the colonial encounter.[30] This tendency toward a rather hollow romanticism recalls the way in which eighteenth-century aristocrats used the pastoral for their entertainment, amusing themselves by dressing up as shepherdesses and reciting poetry about lovesick swains. Similarly, Western readers, secure in their modern amenities, may cultivate a sentimental nostalgia for a simpler way of life.

If the initial biases of Western publishers and readers are based on political or nostalgic sentiments, structural factors help perpetuate them. For example, as noted in Chapter 2, Achebe himself was editor of the Heinemann African Writers Series for many years. His tastes as well as the example of *Things Fall Apart,* may have encouraged authors to write about the traditional village, especially if they were aiming toward publication in this highly visible series, and it may have discouraged those who wrote different types of novels. The series and its famous editor also established in the minds of the Western reading public just what an African novel was supposed to be like. The Heinemann series was and continues to be the most readily available source for books to be used in "African literature" courses in Europe and the United States.

Second, both immigration and an increasing emphasis on diversity in British and American schools has encouraged a tendency toward a more multicultural curriculum. For educators concerned about keeping Afro-Britons or African-Americans in touch with their cultural roots, and exposing others to these cultures, novels about traditional village life would seem to fit the bill better than novels about urban anomie in Lagos. (After all, the Nigerian immigrant's child can see enough urban anomie in his hometown of Birmingham or Chicago.) Both of these factors contribute to a loop in which the selection bias of British publishers is promulgated and becomes a key factor in the very definition of the genre, especially for outsiders.

Meanwhile, second- and third-generation Nigerian authors have told me repeatedly that they want to write about contemporary social problems such as crime, corruption, and general social dislocations. They believe they can best treat these topics through fiction dealing with urban life. Because of when they arrived on the literary scene, these younger writers are far more likely to be published in Nigeria than in Britain, and therefore are far less likely to be known to Europeans or Americans.[31] Those few second- and third-generation writers who do get published in Britain have a disproportionate influence, and a disproportionate tendency to set their novels in traditional villages.

I have identified the characteristics—the mythic structure—of the Nigerian village novel and I have shown that the village novel is disproportionately published in Britain. I also have suggested that the traditional Nigerian village as imagined in literature is, to a considerable extent, the product of an unwitting collaboration between external concerns, specifically those of British editors who are themselves imagining what their readers want, and Nigerian authors seeking a market for their books and their ideas.[32]

Even within these "village novels," however, one often finds a subtext that subverts the harmonious village image. People don't always just sit around eating the sky, even in the village, and some authors want to make this clear. This subtext of conflict and the instability of the village as "home" was seen in *Things Fall Apart* itself. But this same subtext, through which Nigerian authors make problematic the social relations of village life, gets obscured by the way in which Western publishers promote the village novels.

Consider the case of Amechi Akwanya's *Orimili*, which Heinemann published in 1991 in its African Writers Series. Depicting the interplay of tradition and social change in an Igbo town during the colonial period, *Orimili* is presented as a novel in the *Things Fall Apart* tradition; as its back cover asserts, "Akwanya has created a complex community at the point of irrevocable change." Yet an attentive reading of the novel reveals that it raises issues of belonging and membership within the community before and after, indeed without necessary relation to, some "point" of change between tradition and modernity.

Ekwenzi Orimili is a wealthy, middle-aged man from Okocha who has made his fortune as a boatman on the Orimili River; his employer is a colonial trading company. He longs to join the prestigious *ozo* society, thereby affirming that he truly belongs to Okocha. For despite Orimili's wealth and goodness, everyone knows that his great-grandfather came from someplace else, so even though his grandfather died fighting for Okocha, Orimili is regarded by some as an outsider. He is pursuing his social ambition through his friend Emenogha, who acts as his advocate with the *ozo* society. He is also arranging an advantageous marriage between his son, Osita, currently studying law in England, and Emenogha's daughter.

The plot involves Orimili's attempt to join the *ozo* society, arranging the marriage with Emenogha, being insulted by the warrant chief's wife ("And *what* is Orimili? You tell me that. Who in this town knows where he comes from, if he comes from *anywhere*?"), identification with the river spirit, tension with his wife, who thinks he favors Osita (the son of a deceased wife) over their own children, and final frustration of his hopes. Orimili is prevented from joining Okocha's *ozo* society by the political machinations of his opponents and is further humiliated when Osita marries someone else while in London. In an ironic ending, Osita becomes a nationalist and wins political prominence during the late colonial period. As a favorite son of Okocha, Osita is welcomed into the *ozo* society.

(Amechi Akwanya, *Orimili*)

The complications within the novel come not just from the crisscrossing of tradition and modernity, but from the question of membership in a community that, like all communities, has never been free from change. "*What is Orimili?*" indeed. Orimili comes from outside, generations back, but is a descendant of one of the community's martyrs. He is connected with the colonial trading economy, but it is this connection to the world beyond the traditional community that has given him the wherewithal to pursue the traditional status of insider. Osita is even less tied to the local community, having moved beyond Okocha in his education, his political career, and his marriage, yet he easily gains the traditional rank—the *ozo* threads tied around his ankle—denied his father. The warrant chief holds his office only on behalf of the colonial administration, yet he and his wife most aggressively maintain traditional social demarcations by excluding Orimili.

Akwanya has written a meditation on the ambiguities of outsider/insider status in the Nigerian community. This novelist, an Igbo from Onitsha, also is a Roman Catholic priest and holds a Ph.D. in English from the National University of Ireland, where he lived during the 1980s. From his own multicultural experience, Akwanya may be assumed to have particular insight into crossed categories of belonging and the complex interplay between tradition and change.

As a literary product, however, the novel was framed by its British publisher in such a way that its ambiguities of tradition and membership, what I have referred to as its subversive subtext, are obscured. This framing takes three forms. First, the back cover suggests that the lines of tension are solely between Orimili as an individual and the community "at the point of irrevocable change."

Second, in the most flagrant indication of how the book's physical presentation manipulates reader expectations in the direction of the "things fell apart" assumptions, the front cover includes a subtitle (found nowhere else): "One Man's Struggle for Power in Pre-Colonial Nigeria." The emphasis on one man, Orimili as struggling individual, is not altogether unwarranted, although Akwanya has shown a number of struggling people. But pre-colonial? Even the back cover announces that the book takes place during World War II, in other words, rather late in the colonial period.

The point is, however, that this editorial error does not really matter at all. Precolonial, colonial, whatever: the idea is to convey an old, stable order being swept away by changes brought with the colonial encounter. There was a "before" before things fell apart, a Gemeinschaft before the Gesellschaft, and the exact historical moment of the "before" that proceded "the point of irrevocable change" is unimportant.

Third, the art on the front cover supports the ideological message (Fig. 3-1). The painting shows a figure of a single man, blue against an ocher background. On this background at one side of the man is a fish, at the

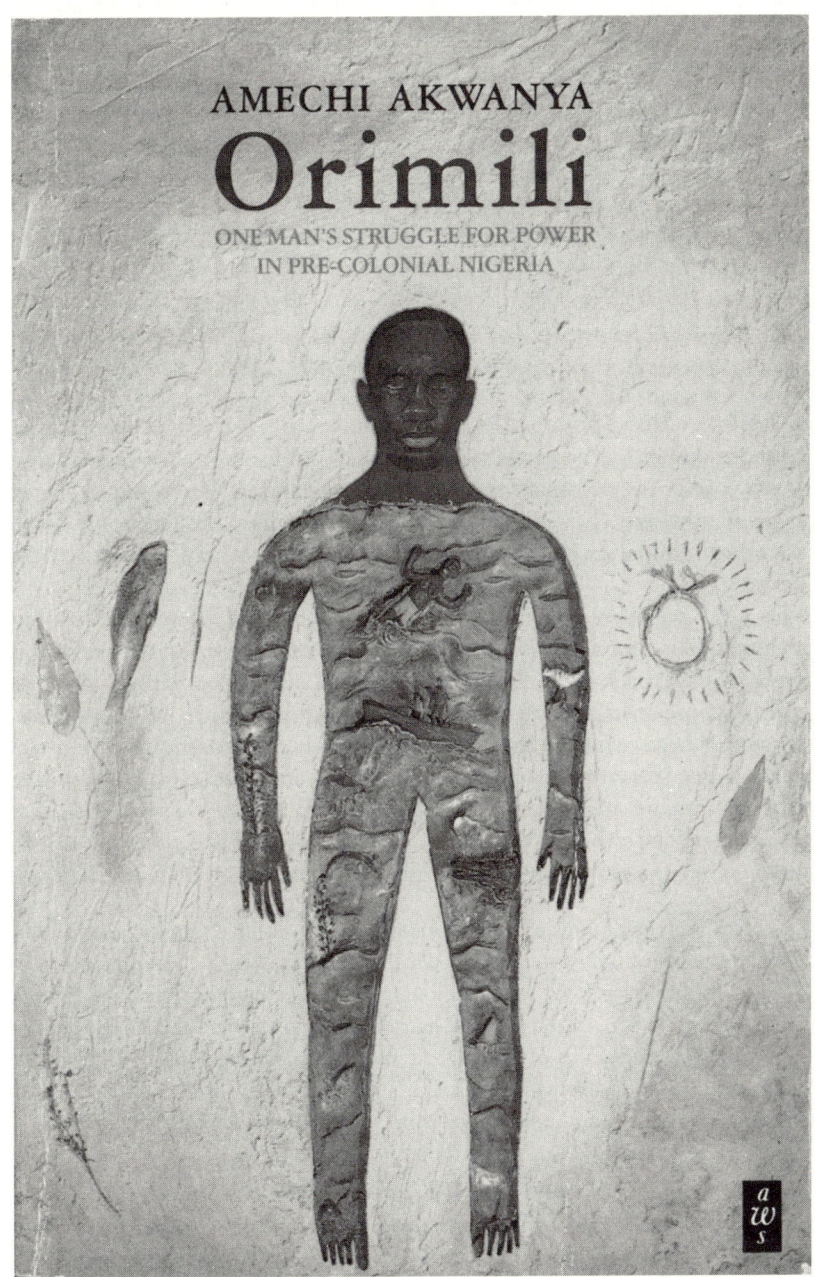

FIGURE 3-1. The cover of Amechi Akwanya's *Orimili*

other the coveted *ozo* threads, giving off an aura. Leaves and herbs scattered around the background suggest the "naturalness" of the social order against which the individual man is set. The man himself, from the neck down, is composed of churning water, filled with fish, plants, a crocodile, a boat, and—most prominently, located over the center of his chest—a man floundering, perhaps drowning. Movement, individual enterprise on the river, and individual destruction are set, literally, against the stable background of village social structure aligned with the natural world. And a closer look reveals that this background of the natural community order is painted upon (what else?) a mud wall.

Monkey Dey Work, Baboon Dey Chop: City Settings

We have seen that *Things Fall Apart,* a mainstay of African literature classes around the world, is not at all typical. British publishers and Western readers may prefer the colonial romance, the unspoiled village found in village novels if nowhere else. Nigerians, however, much as they honor Achebe and other luminaries of the first generation, want to read about the here and now.

Far more typical of the contemporary Nigerian novel, therefore, is a story of city life like Chinyere Nwogwa's *The World She Knew.* The cover of this book, in paperback like all fiction published in Nigeria, shows a young woman whose style is very Western: lipstick and nail polish, low-cut blouse, uncovered head with straightened hair. Her head and shoulders are set against a five-story urban building whose lines are softened by a palm tree or two, an image of West African Bauhaus. Such a cover clearly signals that this novel will be about an up-to-date girl in an up-to-date city. And so it is, but the plot suggests the treacherous grounding such a city offers such a girl.

> Adored but rebellious daughter of a middle-class family in the east, Vivien fails her university entrance exams and decides to go to Lagos. Her initial days there find her coping with crowds, buses, lack of privacy, and rudeness. She lives with a former schoolmate and gets a clerical job, where she is kept busy fending off the advances of her boss. At work Vivien is much impressed by the glamorous Mary. Meanwhile, money is short, her family sends irritating letters full of advice, and her relations with her roommate become strained. Finally Mary invites her to move with her.
>
> Dazzled by Mary's luxurious lifestyle, which is financed by Big Men, Vivien herself soon becomes a "buyable girl." She gets a so-called job as a confidential secretary for one of her lovers, and the money pours in. Before long she can even send money to Sonny and Prisca, her siblings back home. But regrets set in: "It was her pride and urge for independence that had put her in the mess she was in. But then where was the independence when in the real sense of it

she was living on men. She had lost respect and reputation. . . . Even some kids in the street had the guts to shower her with sand as she passed."

When her father dies, Vivien is guilt-stricken. After the funeral, she asks her family's forgiveness for bringing shame on them and vows to reform. She goes back to Lagos a changed woman, although she maintains her friendship with the wayward Mary.

A young accountant named Alpha begins courting her. Sonny and Prisca come for a visit and hit it off well with Alpha—too well, in fact, for Alpha and Prisca fall in love. Meanwhile, Mary meets a decent man who wants to marry her, but she thinks his family back in the village will scorn her; Vivien advises her to go convince his family of her contrition.

Sonny breaks the news about Prisca and Alpha. Stunned, Vivien musters the dignity to wish them well. Back after a successful visit to her future in-laws, Mary comforts her. Vivien goes to her hometown for Alpha and Prisca's wedding, then returns to Lagos having given up on men.

Three years pass. Mary and her husband are studying abroad; Prisca and Alpha have children; Sonny is married; Vivien's younger siblings are at school in the United States; and Vivien is studying law at night while working days. She is lonely but serene, having become a devout Christian.

At a company symposium she meets the exuberant Ejike. Wary, she allows him to court her. Her piety and his playfulness balance one another, and they grow close, joking about cooking for each other. After several false starts Ejike nervously proposes. Vivien puts him off for months, then tells him about her "dirty past." It doesn't matter, for he wants to marry her, not some angel. Finally she says yes, and they embrace.

(Chinyere Nwogwa, *The World She Knew*)

The World She Knew is competently written, if no masterpiece, and its Lagos setting is far more typical of Nigerian fiction than Achebe's Umuofia. The adventures of a young person like Vivien leaving the small town for the big city, a standard motif in Western fiction as well, is the single most common theme in Nigerian novels. Recurring elements, all present in Nwogwa's plot, include crowded, squalid housing; urban rudeness; transportation nightmares in traffic "go-slows" and overpacked buses; sexual predators; workplace tensions; unbroken, guilt-producing ties back home; exposure to corruption and crime; and constant temptations, which the protagonist does or does not resist. Offsetting these are the city's economic, educational, and romantic opportunities. Always there is the glamour of people who know how to get along in the city, how to succeed through savvy, through capitalizing on one's attributes, through managing connections, through urban know-how. As Nigerians say, "Monkey dey work, baboon dey chop [eat]." The baboons of the world, the "world she knew," tend to be city folk.

To explore the role of the city in Nigerian fiction, it is necessary first to distinguish between novels set in cities, which constitute the majority of Nigerian novels, and the more restrictive category of city novels as a genre. While all city novels are set in cities, not all novels set in cities are "city novels." In a city novel the city itself is paramount; the story is cast in terms of an individual's struggle in an urban milieu where the city itself, rather than some particular antagonist, is the object against which the protagonist contends. Many crime novels and romances have urban settings and young-person-comes-to-the-big-city structures, but the focus is on the fall into crime or the love story, not urban life per se. Compare, for example, Vivien with Evbu in Helen Ovbiagele's *Evbu My Love*. Evbu has come to the city because of disappointment in love, and her adventures, which include a spell of prostitution not unlike Vivien's, are put in terms of her need to find the right man. Romantic themes are only part of Vivien's story, but *Evbu My Love*, while set in the city, is—as the title suggests —first and foremost a romance.

The present section concentrates on the broader category of novels set in cities (in the next section I shall take up the city novel proper). The novelists' preference for urban settings is puzzling not just because the most famous Nigerian novel portrays village life but even more because most Nigerians don't actually live in cities. Even if British publishers have disproportionately promoted novels with village settings, the question remains, Why do Nigerians write so much about cities in the first place? It is important to explore this paradox of rural people writing and reading urban novels, this emphasis on urban life in Nigerian fiction.

I start by considering some characteristics of Nigerian cities themselves. In terms of their histories, Nigerian cities are either precolonial or colonial.[33] (The one exception is the new capital, Abuja, a postcolonial project.) Precolonial cities, established by the nineteenth century, include a number of cities in the north, Kano and Zaria being the most prominent examples, that developed from the trans-Saharan trade that connected western and northern Africa; such cities also became centers of Islamic learning. A second type of precolonial city was found in Yorubaland, now western Nigeria. In some cases, like Oyo and Ife, the ancient spiritual heart of the Yoruba that was established by A.D. 800, these cities were administrative headquarters of the Yoruba kingdoms. Others had defensive capacities—Lagos on islands, for example, or Abeokuta, whose name means "under rock"[34]—that protected them and allowed their development into trading centers. Most precolonial cities were either northern trade routes or Yoruba centers, but a few, like Benin City, were neither.

The colonial cities were developed by the British as centers of administration, extraction, and export. Examples include Kaduna, which Sir Frederick Lugard founded as the capital of the Protectorate of Northern Nigeria, the mining cities of Enugu and Jos, and the major ports such as Port Harcourt. Lagos itself can be regarded as a colonial city with respect to its immense development under British rule. These colonial cities, most of which were in the south, were less dependent on indigenous social and cultural bases than the older cities, more adapted to the needs of modern economic life (initially they were the "parasitic" cities of the colonial regime), and involved more migration and thus more mixing between rural and urban, traditional and modern ways.[35] At the same time, British colonial cities in West Africa tend to be less European in design than French ones or Spanish cities in the New World, since the British sent relatively few expatriates, and colonial administrators preferred to live in sequestered neighborhoods outside of the central city (the Government Residential Areas).

While distinguishing between precolonial and colonial cities is fundamental to most treatments of Nigerian urban life, finer distinctions have been made. In her study of eight West African cities and suburbs (four in Nigeria), Margaret Peil distinguished among three types of city formation.[36] (1) Central cities are usually national or regional capitals, with heterogeneous populations, rapid postindependence growth, and relatively high levels of education, industrialization, urban amenities, and concentration of commerce and government. Peil mentions Lagos, Ibadan, and Kaduna as examples.[37] (2) Provincial towns are commercial and administrative centers for their regions; they are growing, but at a slower rate than central cities. They are also less heterogeneous, and often are the homes of local ethnic or religious leaders. Sokoto and Ife would be precolonial examples. Some provincial towns developed during the colonial and even postcolonial periods around mining (Jos, Enugu, Sapele), oil (Warri), or transportation (Port Harcourt). Peil's study includes Aba in the east and Abeokuta in the west. (3) Suburbs and satellite towns have developed on the outskirts of the first two city types, especially the central cities. In some cases this is due to the absolute limits of the central core, as with Lagos's islands, but more generally suburban growth is the result of migrants' setting up affordable residences as close to the city as possible. Some of these suburbs are slums, like Ajegunle (one of Peil's study sites), while others have certain advantages and may even become fashionable; Ikeja, conveniently located near the airport and far from the traffic jams and bridges to Lagos Island, is an example. Regardless of their official jurisdiction—urban government in Nigeria tends to be ineffective in any case—these suburbs are essentially part of the city to which they are attached.

As with all population figures in Nigeria, the size of postindependence cities is a matter of conjecture. Here are three sources, the first two being estimates, the third a provisional figure from the 1991 census. First, using data from 1975, Jarmon found twenty-five cities with populations of one hundred thousand or more.[38] The distribution of these large cities was very imbalanced: sixteen were located in the west, five in the east, and four in the north. Lagos is by far the largest city, with over one million people in the city proper and some four million people in its metropolitan area; Ibadan, about one hundred kilometers away, is second, with three million in the metropolitan area. In the north, Kano is dominant, having twice the population (about four hundred thousand in the city proper) as Zaria, the next largest. The east is more balanced, having Port Harcourt and Onitsha at somewhat over two hundred thousand, Enugu and Aba somewhat under. While Jarmon's actual figures are not reliable, the general picture is clear: Given that the north has twice the population of the east and 60 percent more than the west (see Table 2-2), the pattern is a relatively urban west (but still with half the population living in towns of less than twenty thousand), a relatively nonurban north, and the east somewhere in between and distinguished by the newness, hence modernity, of its cities.

Second, Onibokun working ahead from the 1963 census, estimated that in 1984 there were six cities with a population of a million or more: Lagos and Ibadan with over four million each, Kano with a million and a half, Port Harcourt, Kaduna, and Ilorin with just over a million (and Enugu with just under).[39] Table 3-3 suggests both how many large cities there are and how they have swollen in the years since independence.

Third, the most recent figures come from the 1991 census; while the results published to date do not give city populations, Lagos State, covering what is generally meant by "Lagos," is reported to have a population of 5,685,781, or about 6.4 percent of the country's total population (see Table 2-2). Different sources, different numbers, but it seems clear that Nigeria has at least one megametropolis in Lagos and a number of very large (million-plus) cities, with most in the southwest but at least one in the other three regions.

Like many African countries, Nigeria has experienced overwhelming urban growth in the decades since World War II. Nigeria's urban population may be growing about 5 percent each year.[40] Estimates for the growth of Lagos alone are higher; according to one report, Lagos grew 8.6 percent annually from 1960 to 1975, while another report sees Lagos growing 12 percent annually in the early 1980s.[41] Urban growth anywhere comes from some mixture of migration from other countries (e.g., the growth of Chicago at the turn of the century), internal migration (e.g., the migration of rural southern blacks to northern cities during much of the twentieth century), and fertility rates exceeding mortality rates in the city. International migration to Nigerian cities takes place but is not a factor in their growth. While urban birth rates are high, two-thirds of the urban growth is due to net internal migration (i.e., rural-to-urban movement exceeding urban-to-rural).[42] Rural-to-urban migration in Nigeria and elsewhere in Africa tends to accelerate because of what has been called

TABLE 3-3
Estimated Populations of Nigeria's Largest Cities (in thousands)[a]

Rank (1963)	City	1963 Census	Onibokun (1984 est.)
1	Lagos	665	4,486
2	Ibadan	627	4,230
3	Ogbomosho	320	891
4	Kano	295	1,654
5	Oshogbo	209	582
6	Ilorin	209	1,167
7	Abeokuta	187	689
8	Port Harcourt	180	1,005
9	Zaria	166	463
10	Onitsha	163	454
11	Iwo	159	442
12	Ila[b]	158	439
13	Ado-Ekiti	158	439
14	Kaduna	150	1,011
15	Maiduguri	140	783
16	Enugu	138	934
17	Ede	134	375
18	Aba	132	365
19	Ile-Ife	131	362
20	Oyo	112	313
21	Ikere-Ekiti	107	320
22	Ilesha	106	462
23	Benin City	101	564
24	Katsina	99	252
25	Iseyin	95	265
26	Jos	90	506
27	Sokoto	90	503
28	Calabar	76	428
29	Akure	71	262
30	Minna	27	221

[a]The first column is from the 1963 Nigerian census as reported by Oni-bokun (1989: Table 4.3); I have ranked these cities in the order of this census. the second column is also from Onibokun (1989: Table 4.3). I have rounded off Onibokun's figures to the nearest hundred thousand.
[b]Onibokun reports identical numbers for Ila and Ado-Ekiti (157,579 in 1963; 438,851 in 1984), so undoubtedly there is some error here.

the "urban bias": governments fear the potential for trouble from swelling urban populations, so they establish pro-urban policies such as price controls to protect city dwellers from inflation. Such policies, combined with unrealistic exchange rates, encourage imported foods while making domestic farming less and less profitable. The decline in the rural economy pushes more young people to seek their fortunes in the city.[43] Monkeys, in other words, want to become baboons.

Rural-to-urban migration, particularly as stimulated by the Nigerian oil wealth of the seventies and the attendant employment opportunities, has shaped the demographic characteristics of the cities. Migrants come to the city looking for economic opportunities and for excitement; the two are intertwined. The typical migrant has been a teenage or young adult male, often just having finished his formal schooling; he may be migrating to improve his skills instead of merely seeking a job, as is the case with the many unpaid apprentices.[44] The disproportion of male to female migrants results in an urban sex ratio of 115 males to 100 females, although this imbalance is likely to decline as the gap between male and female education decreases.[45] Stories of "Dick Whittington and His Cat" notwithstanding, migrants usually come from the most educated and successful groups of their rural areas. Urban populations as a whole are better educated than rural ones. Not only is the urban migrant better educated that his rural peers, he is also apt to be better educated than the city-born urbanite.[46] Thus the migrant does not fit the image of the rural hick coming to a big town and being overwhelmed by its sophistication (although this occurs in some accounts, especially in the moral sense). A more accurate image of the migrant is that of the rural entrepreneur, the hustler, the striver who already has considerable human capital such as education (and, in the case of women, sexual attractiveness), coming to "make it" in the city. Nigerian novelists have told this story many times, and it appears grounded in demographic fact.[47]

The modernized sectors of the urban economies (i.e., those that offer regular employment for fixed salaries or wages) have been unable to absorb this tremendous growth in available labor, so the surplus has been taken up by the informal sector. The informal sector involves small-scale economic activities that require minimal capital and often are "off the books" in terms of incorporation into the state (taxation, regulation, and so forth). Beyond this definitions vary, but Sethuraman's seems about right: The informal sector "consists of small-scale units engaged in the production and distribution of goods and services with the primary objective of generating employment and incomes to their participants notwithstanding the constraints on capital, both physical and human, and know-how."[48] The informal sector includes both legitimate activities, such as trading, crafts, and services, and illegitimate activities, including prostitution, smuggling, and theft. Work in the informal sector is episodic, low-paid, and highly vulnerable to disruption. In Nigerian cities the informal sector dominates all economic sectors in terms of numbers of people involved; this is true throughout Africa wherever extensive urban migration has taken place.[49] One study estimates that 50 percent of the Lagos workers are in this sector, while a study of Benin estimates the ratio of informal to formal at an astonishing seven to one.[50] This informal sector, especially those lower levels not dominated by indigenous ethnic groups, thus contains many educated and severely disappointed migrants whose expectations regarding urban opportunities have been far grander than their actual experience proves to be.[51]

While many wealthy Nigerians live in cities, life for most urban residents can only be described as hellish. "The rapid rate of uncontrolled and unplanned urbanization has brought with it complex urban problems in the form of stiff competition for land, long journeys to work, traffic difficulties (congestion), acute shortage of housing, rapid growth of slums and accompanying health hazards, qualitative and quantitative depopulation of rural areas, the high incidence of crimes of all types, to name just a few."[52] Water shortages, electricity failures, and inadequate waste disposal, as well as the inability of local government to provide basic urban services, impinge on rich and poor, but the former can buffer themselves to some extent through purchasing water, private generators, and so on, just as their hired security guards provide some protection from crime.[53]

It might be expected, following a "rising expectations" line of reasoning, that less affluent urbanites, especially this group of dissatisfied young male migrants, would be socially and political volatile, engaging in spontaneous and perhaps organized protest activity. This seems not to have happened to any great extent so far.[54] One reason may be the "urban bias" policies, which are designed to dampen urban unrest (and which are challenged by structural adjustment programs). Another reason may be that Nigerians, like most Africans, exhibit a noticeable lack of class consciousness; Coquery-Vidrovitch calls African class consciousness "embryonic, due to the necessity of individualistic survival strategies and the influence of social and cultural conservatism, that, for example, make ethnic ties have a far stronger claim than class position."[55]

The Disappointed Young Man, politically aroused or not, constitutes a prominent social type in Nigerian fiction.[56] Often he first appears as a Johnny-Just-Come, the callow migrant newly arrived in from the country. Johnny-Just-Come's female counterpart is the Village Girl whose head is turned by the material glitter of the city and who becomes a Big Man's mistress or takes up prostitution. Both the Johnny-Just-Come and the Village Girl are monkeys who aspire to be baboons. If they fail, fiction has the Johnny-Just-Come becoming a Disappointed Young Man who may turn to crime, while the failed Village Girl sinks into total degradation and often suicide.

Migrants who survive their initial introduction to urban life vary in their attachments to the city. In Lagos, according to one humorist, some become Lagosians, others Lagosmen.[57] Lagosians (or their counterparts in other cities) are fully committed to the city, spending their time and money in it, and their attitudes are indistinguishable from those of indigenes. Lagosmen, on the other hand, earn their livings in a city but spend much of their time and fortune outside it; their identification remains with their areas of origin. The two groups are less distinct than the labels imply, but urbanites do exhibit a wide range of urban and rural ties. Making a similar point, Coquery-Vidrovitch has identified three social types in African cities: city dwellers proper (the most integrated, nascent middle class, who disregard ethnic relationships and feel little connection with the village); new city dwellers (who maintain a dual allegiance to village and city; this group works in the modern economic sector, but generally with lower salaries than the first); and proletarianized rural migrants (working in the informal sector, this group achieves little integration into city life and tries to replicate traditional ethnic and religious environments). While these analytical levels must be seen as ideal types that imperfectly represent the Nigerian case—for example, Nigerian elites of even the most cosmopolitan circles maintain village and ethnic ties—Coquery-Vidrovitch is surely correct in pointing out that it is the more successful urban workers, those integrated into the capitalist sector as opposed to an informal economy, who are the most likely to cultivate connections with villages by maintaining rights to land, participating in rural life, and holding membership in ethnic associations. This social formation is something new, not simply different points on a one-way movement from traditional to modern: "Beyond an appearance of modernity manifested in property, salary, and lifestyle, the most integrated city dwellers are giving rise to original (African?) syncretic urban practices that can no longer be associated simply either with residual rural customs or a Westernization of manners."[58]

Despite the rapid urbanization that has been taking place for several decades, three-quarters of sub-Saharan Africans still live in rural villages. Nigeria may be more urban than most other African countries—some estimate as many as a third of Nigerians are city dwellers—but is still predominantly rural. Educated and sophisticated Nigerians will tell an outsider that to know the real Nigeria, one must go to the villages and glimpse the lives conducted "behind the mud walls." And yet, as we have seen, most Nigerian novels—three-fifths of them—are set in cities (Table 3-2). Lagos is far and away the most popular choice, with Ibadan and Enugu next; Onitsha, Kano, Benin, and others are occasionally used, as are fictitious cities. In some of these novels the city itself plays a causal role, becoming an indispensable determinant of the characters' personalities and actions; these are the "city novels" that I will discuss in the next section. Most of the time, however, an urban setting is just that: the background to the action, perhaps problematic but not central to the plot. But if cities are not integral to the narrative, it is important to return to the question, Why should urban settings be routine in the fiction of a country that is, in fact, predominantly nonurban?

Recall the history of the Nigerian novel: the slow beginnings of novel production in the 1950s and 1960s; the dramatic takeoff in the late 1970s, and the precipitous decline beginning in the mid-1980s; the shift from British publishers to Nigerian ones in the late 1970s and early 1980s. The urban settings, considered against this historical background, have two important features. First, an increasing proportion of the novels appearing over the years have had urban settings.[59] Since the number of novels was itself increasing over time, this meant that the city changed from being a minority setting for a handful of novels to the dominant setting for a large number of novels. Only about one-quarter of the novels published during the 1950s and 1960s had urban settings. But in the 1970s over half of Nigerian novels were city-based; in the 1980s the urban proportion rose to about seven out of ten, where it seemed to be remaining in the 1990s. Second, as we have seen, the novels published in Nigeria are even more likely to have urban settings than those published in Britain.

Most Nigerians live in rural villages, but most Nigerian novels are set in cities. It is true that those novels published in Britain are more likely to have rural settings than novels published in Nigeria, but in both places urban settings are the rule. Village or bush settings dominated the first two decades of the Nigerian novel but have dropped to only 13 percent in the novels published in the past two decades.[60] This is the "how" of the urban transformation. The "why" remains to be investigated.

It is true that the novel has always been *the* urban genre because of its formal characteristics. Because the novel is a long prose narrative, it lends itself not to oral, group presentation but to individual, silent reading. Its inappropriateness for declamation and its sheer length make it poorly suited for political or aristocratic celebration, so it has never received much by way of private or public patronage. Instead, novels have been commercial from the beginning. To become established the genre requires substantial rates of literacy; a concentration of publishing (paper production, editorial expertise, printing); networks of people, typically overeducated and underpaid, that constitute the publishing world; an infrastructure allowing for effective book distribution; and a relatively leisured group of literate people, usually but not always middle-class, who constitute its readers. All these elements are found in cities.

One might suppose, therefore, that because publishers, writers, and readers—in Nigeria and everywhere else—are predominantly urban, all populations of novels will have settings that are disproportionately urban. This is not the case, however. Both American and English novels continued to emphasize rural or small-town settings well after the countries themselves had become urbanized, and despite the fact that their publishing, writing, and reading had been urban enterprises from the beginning.[61] When the United States was undergoing rapid and highly visible urbanization in the late nineteenth and early twentieth centuries—an urbanization that gave rise to Progressivism and to American sociology, among other things—only one-third of the novels written by Americans and published during that period had urban settings.[62] This was the case despite the fact that writers and publishers were concentrated in the urban centers of New York, Chicago, Boston, and Philadelphia, and also despite the fact that many of the canonical novelists of that period—Dreiser, Norris, Wharton, James—focused on cities and city dwellers. To this day, small towns loom disproportionately in American fiction, as do villages in British fiction; both seem to be emblematic of some notion of national essence that fiction (and other forms of popular culture, notably films) draws on and perpetuates.

So the urban settings of Nigerian novels are not intrinsic to the genre but a true cultural innovation. They reflect neither the social geography of the Nigerian people, the ineluctable necessities of the form, the configuration of publishing, nor the British and American fictional models. Why has this innovation taken place?

Elsewhere I have suggested that in Nigeria (and no doubt in other developing countries undergoing rapid social change) the city served as a metaphor for social dislocations, including those of rural areas.[63] The Nigerian novelist Ibe Oparandu put it like this: Certain themes "have been flogged enough . . . this culture thing, village life compared with town life."[64] Masterpieces have been written on this topic, he went on, citing Achebe and the early school of anticolonial writing. This sort of theme does not need further literary elaboration according to Oparandu, who says, "I'm more concerned with our contemporary society." Corruption, the excesses of new wealth, sexual immorality: "these are things that bedevil our society at the moment." Novelists, in Oparandu's view, should spotlight corruption, bear witness, show the powerful that people know what they are doing. Most of the authors I have spoken with share his opinion; Adebowale's cultural preservationism is a minority view. For the majority of Nigerian novelists, exposing what bedevils contemporary Nigerian society is most effectively done using urban settings.

Nigerian novelists, like all members of the educated elite, are disproportionately urban in their experience. Some have been born in cities and exposed to a cosmopolitan world from their childhood. Buchi Emecheta, for example, is an Igbo whose family, hence "home," is from Ibusa, in Bendel State. But she, born in Lagos, learned to speak Yoruba before learning Igbo. Other writers, indeed the majority, were born in rural areas but came to cities for their educations and have continued to pursue their careers in urban centers. Like many Nigerians working in the modern sectors, they often plan to retire to their home villages; some, like John Munonye, have actually done so, but the bulk of their careers are spent working and living in cities.

These urban authors express no great fondness for city life, however. On the contrary, they turn to their home villages not just with nostalgia but with active involvement. In this, they are like other members of the successful middle class who gain wealth in urban pursuits but then redistribute that wealth to their natal villages by building houses, financing public works, and supporting the education and material well-being of rural relatives. As discussed previously, it is the recently urbanized middle class that maintains the closest ties to the villages; the poor cannot afford the transport and cash support necessary to perpetuate such ties, while the urban elite, especially after a generation or two, may allow such ties to languish. The Nigerian middle class, authors and otherwise, puts considerable time and energy into maintaining ties to their home areas. Victor Thorpe, author of a series of Pacesetters, offers a good example. Now retired, he spent his career as administrative assistant in the British Council Library in Ibadan, and he continues to live in a prosperous section of that city. At the same time, he is president of the Cross Rivers Association in Ibadan and is actively involved in that group's many cultural and charitable activities. Novelists whose ties to their home areas and cultures have attenuated feel considerable regret. Helen Ovbiagele, for example, thinks it a pity that her children do not speak Edo, although she regards the advantages of their Lagos upbringing as worth this price.

Keeping one eye on the village or home area, even if only in memory, Nigerian authors do not tell stories of urban life because of their desire to celebrate the metropolis. Lagos, Ibadan, Enugu, Kano—these do not constitute the cultural and spiritual centers as Paris did for nineteenth-century French authors, or as New York or London have done more recently. Writers are drawn to cities like Lagos because of the economic and intellectual opportunities they offer. But nobody has a good thing to say about Lagos—quite the contrary, in fact. Nigerians regard Nigerian cities, and Lagos in particular, with a mixture of fascination and horror. "Dis Lagos, na waa," a pidgin commonplace that Americans would translate as "This Lagos is really something else," captures the ambivalence. The city is the arena of money, crime, hustling, excitement, prostitution, anomie, opportunity, loneliness, high hopes, bitter disappointments. Ambivalence can quickly turn into loathing, as the disappointments and inconveniences outweigh the glamour.

The distaste Nigerians feel for their largest city is not irrational. In 1990 the Population Crisis Committee, a research center based in Washington, D.C., studied the world's one hundred largest metropolitan areas to see which were the most livable. "Livability" was measured in terms of ten characteristics: murder rates, food costs, people per dwelling room, percent of homes having water and electricity, telephones per 100 persons, percent of children in elementary school, infant mortality rates, levels of street noise and speed in rush-hour traffic. Melbourne, Montreal, and Seattle-Tacoma tied for the world's most livable cities. Lagos came dead last. Of course quality-of-life measures and cultural significance are not closely related. Chicago may be less "livable" than Seattle, but it has had a far greater impact on American thought and writing. The very difficulties of Nigeria's urban life offer material for its writers. The point is simply that Nigerian authors do not feel compelled to write about Nigerian cities because of their sheer attractiveness, cultural or physical.

Cities *are* attractive, however, as metaphors. Many Nigerian novelists have told me that while "most" other Nigerian authors write about village life, they themselves are different: *They* write about the contemporary urban scene. Their mistaken impression that everyone else is writing about traditional rural life is no doubt due to the prestige and visibility of the first-generation writers—Achebe, Aluko, Nwapa, Munonye—who did indeed locate their early novels in villages and whose works have become canonical through the African Writers Series. Novelists of the second and third generations assert that Nigerian writers should not focus so much on traditional life but instead should write about social changes and social problems of today. They are unaware that the change they advocate has already taken place.

For Nigerian writers, the city seems to offer an apt metaphor for political, social, technological, economic, and cultural changes taking place throughout Nigerian society. Of course, these changes are not confined to cities. Introducing a well and pump into a rural village dramatically changes relations between men and women, for example, because women, water carriers throughout Africa, suddenly have more free time. But they are most dramatic and observable in cities. Cities, because of their very social density, concentrate and accentuate trends and transformations, and the problems that accompany them. The "urban bias" in government policy exacerbates this situation in African countries. In Nigerian fiction "the city," above all Lagos, epitomizes the opportunities and dislocations brought about by rapid social change.

It seems likely that the Nigerian convention of the city being the proper setting for fiction got established because the Nigerian novel developed as the country was undergoing rapid, highly visible urbanization. This was much less true for England and America—in both cases the novel was well established before the modern commercial or industrial city became recognized as a cultural problem—so there the genre's link with cities was less obvious.

The city metaphor can be read in several ways, including the strongly positive and strongly negative. Powerful metaphors always have this capacity.[65] In fiction the Nigerian city is both the fount of all opportunities and the sinkhole of all hopes.

One of the more pessimistic views can be found in Jare Ajayi's aptly titled *Bile in the Dish*, a multigenerational story of shattered dreams. If the city repeatedly offers some people the ability to rise, social mobility that would be impossible in the village, it can also be shown as squashing all attempts to rise. In Ajayi's novel the squashing is repeated over and over.

> The story begins in the Oyo village of Ajegunle,[66] with Gbola in primary school. Although he is a good student, his family cannot afford secondary school, so Gbola goes to Lagos to earn money for further education, hoping to become a doctor eventually. Enduring the rough life of an apprentice driver, he falls in love with Amoke and gets her pregnant; their marriage puts an end to Gbola's lingering aspirations.
>
> Now Gbola pins his hopes on his children. Enjoying modest prosperity, he sends his eldest, Dele, to secondary school in Ajegunle. Dele does well, but his university entrance exam gets lost in the 1977 exam scandal.[67] Soon after he meets Funmi, and her pregnancy occasions another forced marriage. Meanwhile, Gbola's second son dies in an accident, and Gbola fears that his ambitions are coming to naught.
>
> Dele is out of work. He is a frustrated writer of unpublished manuscripts, and he and Funmi dwell on their disappointment. Dele's son Dapo is born, and Gbola prays for his grandchild's success. Eventually Dapo passes university entrance exams, but his university application is not accepted (it is not clear why not, perhaps because he didn't bribe the right people). He falls in with a bad crowd, starts using drugs, and finally vanishes.
>
> Two years later Funmi passes by the Yaba roundabout. There she sees a madman, recognizes him as Dapo, and faints. Later the police begin to question Dele about Dapo's involvement in peddling narcotics.
>
> (Jare Ajayi, *Bile in the Dish*)

Tracing the family's dashed hopes through three generations effectively portrays the cycle of poverty and how hard it is to escape it, but it also shows the unbreakable link between the city and socioeconomic aspirations. The village of Ajegunle may be safe and secure, but the family is convinced that opportunities lie in the city. Gbola and even Dele claim to prefer life in the country, but they make no move to return there.

Novels use their settings as metaphors for rampant social dislocations that occur in both the cities and the villages. Paradoxically, novelists find it easier to tell a "things fall apart" story in the city, which may be regarded as the second and more contemporary zone of social disintegration. Writers may cast the city metaphor in a positive or negative light, but Nigerians understand that city settings signal books dealing with social changes and social problems.

A plausible hypothesis, but this city-signifies-social-change interpretation needs testing. After all, the city is not always the metaphor for change; Nigeria's most famous novel depicts social change in a traditional village. American novels have regularly presented the impact of change on small towns—*Things Fall Apart* in *Winesburg, Ohio,* so to speak. Moreover, not all novelists are trying to represent social changes and social problems in the first place, but if this is not their intention, they would not establish such a metaphor, even implicitly.

One test of the metaphor hypothesis comes from looking at the relationship between time and setting. The choice between rural and urban settings was there from the beginning; as discussed earlier, the first Nigerian novel in English was Tutuola's *The Palm-Wine Drinkard,* a fantastic tale drawn from Yoruba village folklore, while the second was Ekwensi's aptly named *People of the City.* If the metaphor-for-social-change hypothesis is right, novels with contemporary settings should be more urban than novels taking place in the colonial or precolonial period. This is not inevitable: not only do over two-thirds of contemporary Nigerians still live in villages, but there was a well-established urban society in the past, particularly among the Yoruba and in the north. So there is nothing to prevent novels about the past from having urban settings, just as nothing prevents contemporary fiction from being set in villages.

Nothing prevents either one, but they don't happen often. Contemporary novels are much more urban than noncontemporary ones. Four out of five contemporary novels have urban settings, while over three-quarters of the novels set in the colonial or precolonial period have rural settings.[68] The urban setting is strongly linked to narratives of the present and future.

What about the question of whether Nigerian novelists are interested in writing about social changes? Survey questions and open interviews, as well as published statements, make the authors' intentions very clear. Over and over, writers told me that Nigerian authors couldn't afford to write "existential" fiction but had to deal with what Dibia Humphrey called "this new thing, political, economic, even the kind of crimes that arise from all these new developments in our country." Social problems, social changes, social issues: these were what the writers felt compelled to treat.

Why this near unanimity on the need for novels to have a social message? Part of the explanation may come from the history of the Nigerian novel. From the heyday of the Onitsha market pamphlets, Nigerian fiction has always been practical, addressing current and concrete problems. Moreover, the genre developed at time of rapid change: independence, civil war, oil wealth, urbanization.[69] A second historical consideration is the fact that the most visible early novel, *Things Fall Apart,* set the literary agenda of social change and social problems. Later generations of writers believe that *Things Fall Apart* and other novels by the first generation have definitively depicted village life. Newer writers should treat new topics, not break their horns challenging their elders.

So far there seems to be no reason to reject the metaphor-for-social-change hypothesis. The city has become the metaphor for, as well as the site of, the social issues that novelists feel they must treat. Social change takes place in the village as well, but its pace is faster, its impact more visible, in the city, so it is here that the novelists locate their plots. To some extent this location is a function of the very nature of "setting" as an element of the genre.

Setting is something a writer can easily change and manipulate, both because it represents a conscious decision and because a particular type of setting is usually not integral to the plot; a love story, for example, can take place just about anywhere. An extreme but telling example of the malleability of setting is provided by Rosina Umelo's *Something to Hide*. Umelo was an established author with Macmillan's Pacesetters line, but when she completed the manuscript for *Something to Hide,* the Nigerian market had dried up because of the oil bust, and Macmillan editors suggested the story be set in Kenya rather than in Nigeria. Umelo demurred—she had never been to Kenya, whereas she had lived for years in Onitsha—but the need to attract a Kenyan market to replace the depressed Nigerian one prevailed. Names of places and persons were altered, physical descriptions were downplayed, and *Something to Hide* was published as a tale set in Nairobi.

Thus, setting is something authors can change rather freely, and locating their stories in cities is an easy way to suggest that the plot deals with modern life, social changes, the here and now. How do writers treat these issues over and above the simple choice of setting? If it is true that the surprising and often unrecognized emphasis on urban settings comes from the writers' desire to treat social changes, one would expect to see an accentuation and development of this theme in those novels where "the city" is not just background but the focus of the story. It is to these city novels that I now turn.

Life Was Fast, Money Was Flowing, and There Was Much Enjoyment: The City Novel

While most plots are like *Something to Hide* in that they can be set almost anywhere, in a certain type of Nigerian novel the setting becomes the key to the story's meaning. Such novels may include romance, crime, politics, and other themes in their plots, but they impress the reader as being, first and foremost, about the city itself. These constitute the genre of "city novels," works that feature not just city settings but city plots.

In one such novel, *Cheer Up, Brother,* S. M. O. Aka presents a more optimistic version of the city plot than is found in Jare Ajayi's *Bile in the Dish.* In both novels Lagos attracts a young man through a seductive promise of opportunity and advancement, then dashes his hopes. The hopes of Wahihi Ulehu, a young man from a poor family in Bendel State, do not remain dashed, however.

> Down and out in Lagos, Wahihi is homeless, jobless, friendless, and ugly to boot. He recalls his childhood as the son of a laborer, always compared to his handsome brother (named "Child is wealth," while Wahihi was called "Tax"). Expelled from school, he suffers a series of disasters: an unfaithful wife, a spell in prison, and indirect responsibility for his father's death. Guilty and without prospects, Wahihi decided to seek his fortune in Lagos. He arrived with high hopes only to find no housing and no work other than hauling night soil. When the novel opens he is living under a bridge and contemplating suicide.
>
> Wahihi meets a girl named Grace who has only one eye, and he is moved by her kindness. While courting her, he brags to her wealthy family about his fine job and home. Her parents find out about his lies, but her brother smooths things over by praising intertribal marriage in the new Nigeria and by pointing out that snobbishness toward a poor boy does not befit the family's Christianity. The parents relent and even find Wahihi a job. Holding a society wedding, they give the newlyweds a flat and a car.
>
> Wahihi and Grace are on top of the world. They visit his hometown, Wahihi proudly parading his urban success. Wahihi's prosperity and happy marriage amaze everyone. Back in Lagos, the couple's happiness is crowned by Grace's pregnancy.
>
> Their good fortune is short-lived, for Grace is killed in an automobile accident. A friend consoles the distraught Wahihi, telling him to "cheer up brother" and to try to show his love for Grace by living a life of kindness and service, as she did. A parallel is drawn to the assassinated Murtala Mohammed: Nigeria had to carry on in spite of the grievous loss. The implication is that Wahihi, too, will carry on.
>
> (S. M. O. Aka, *Cheer Up, Brother*)

In *Cheer Up, Brother,* as in all city novels, the city is a place of ups and downs, the unexpected, the unpredictable. It is the site of catastrophe and the arena of possibility. Above all it is exciting. Wahihi regards his future in these terms: "'Yes, Lagos was the right place to go. I had never been to Lagos before but I had heard some people say that Lagos was next to London or Paris in beauty, and next to New York in wealth. Its streets, they told us, were teeming with people, happy people. There were many applicants, so too were many jobs. Real jobs with fat salaries. Life was fast, money was flowing, and there was much enjoyment'" (36). The enjoyment and the disasters of urban life make up the mythic structure of the city plot, which organizes *Cheer Up, Brother, Bile in the Dish,* and *The World She Knew.* This plot has seven parts:

1. Urban migration: The protagonist, naive but full of hope, moves from the village to the city. A common scene is a motor park, jammed with vehicles traveling to and from the countryside, where the Johnny-Just-Comes and Village Girls first experience the noise, cosmopolitanism, hustle, display, and dishonesty of urban life. Passenger lorries bear names like "God's Case, No Appeal" or "No Condition Is Permanent," ominous warnings to the newly arrived. In some cases the urban migration has taken place prior to the beginning of the novel; in these novels the city-dwelling protagonist refers to a village as "home," or other characters disparage the protagonist for not being native to the city.

2. Hardship and disappointment: Initial impressions of the city turn out to be misleading, the glamour, prosperity, and security unattainable. Promised jobs fail to materialize or are beneath the newcomer's aspirations and education. Housing is hard to find and unpleasant. The rewards of the city are tantalizing but beyond reach. Wahihi lives under a bridge; Gbola must give up on education.

3. Opportunity: The key to success appears, often in the form of a sexual or criminal temptation, and the protagonist grabs it. For young women, temptation usually takes the form of outright prostitution (Pataego) or becoming the mistresses of wealthy men (Vivien); for a young man, typical temptations are embezzlement or corruption if he is employed, theft or violent crime if he is jobless. Sometimes the opportunity is benign, a chance at salvation, as with the aptly named "Grace." Even love may thwart the migrant's economic or educational ambitions, however, as do the pregnancies in *Bile in the Dish,* but here the opportunity gets pinned onto the next generation.

4. Success: The opportunity having been seized, the protagonist experiences a period of success, riding high and finally tasting the city's material and sexual delights. If the motor park is the key scene of arrival and hope, the nightclub is the key venue signaling urban success. Vivien's career as a buyable girl is typical, and Wahihi's happy marriage is its domestic counterpart. Both have made it in the big city.

5. Visit to the village: During this period of success, the protagonist visits the village to display his or her newly acquired affluence and urban sophistication. Often the return entails bringing along a lover or spouse acquired in the city, sometimes to face the disapproval of conservative relatives. Kin and villagers, noting his clothing, cars, and largesse, are impressed by the migrant's flaunted wealth. Sometimes these returns to the rural area are brief, with the protagonist eager to get back to urban delights, but they may be extended if protagonists are drawn into family and village politics, or if childbearing, sickness, or a family crisis like a parental death delays the return.

6. *Turn of fortune:* This stage finds the protagonist back in the city and brought low by a sudden turn of events. The wealthy lover absconds, the crime is uncovered, a stroke of bad luck or an enemy wipes out all previous gain. Brought low, the protagonist is no longer a struggling Johnny-Just-Come or Village Girl but a city-wise sophisticate who sees it all slipping away. Gbola realizes he will never be a doctor. Wahihi loses Grace, whose one eye suggests the inability to see the future fully. Vivien, ashamed of her "dirty past," forswears love and happiness. The city, no longer the fount of opportunities, now seems to dash all hopes.

7. *Destruction or restoration:* The outcome for the protagonist will be either destruction or rehabilitation. Criminals sometimes are hanged, and prostitutes sometimes disappear. A helper often steps in, whether to encourage the protagonist to "cheer up, brother" or to see that a wrong is righted. Occasionally the rehabilitation involves leaving the city for a simpler rural life, although this is less common than one might expect. One story ends with an arrest, another with an embrace; in either case the urbanite's future is clear.

This seven-stage structure—urban migration, hardship, opportunity, high living, visit the village, turn of fortune, and destruction or restoration—constitutes a mobility narrative, where urban migration is the effort to realize social aspirations. The migration enterprise can succeed or fail; the monkey can become a baboon by going to the city and making the most of his opportunities despite setbacks, or the city can mock naive monkeys who try to become baboons but never can. The city's attractions often take on a sexual allure—the city as temptress, seducer. Success is first and foremost material, but it is social and sexual as well, as in stories where the city dweller restores his ruptured ties with his home village through philanthropy, or when the successful migrant wins the glamorous mate. Failure is similarly social, usually taking the form of anonymity and social disappearance, and always involving the loss of the lover.

Cyprian Ekwensi, whose *People of the City* set the pattern, is the acknowledged master of this form. *Jagua Nana,* his best-known and most notorious novel, reveals how the city metaphor works. Through a close examination of its seven parts, one can see both how the structure represents a distinctive attitude toward social change and how the city is sexualized.

Jagua, an aging Lagos prostitute named after the luxury car, decides to marry her young lover Freddie before her sexual appeal fades. When they go to a lecture, the upwardly mobile Freddie criticizes her flamboyant dress, while she feels ill at ease among the intellectual set. Later, at the Tropicana Nightclub, Jagua is in her element, although her jealousy leads to a fight and she spends the night in jail.

Jagua decides to send Freddie to England to read law before they marry. As Freddie prepares to travel, Jagua cuts through the bureaucracy to get him a passport, but they argue over her wealthy men and his growing relationship with the young Nancy. Once he has left, Jagua decides to visit Freddie's family to consolidate her claim on him. She first goes to Ogabu in the east, where Papa, her father, is pastor. After relaxing in the village, bathing in the river and seeing the moon for the first time in years, she sails to Bagana, the fishing village Freddie comes from, on the *Sweet Peace* canoe. Arriving, she finds Nancy and her mother there ahead of her.

Freddie's Uncle Namme tells her about the family's old feud with Chief Ofubara, who has settled on another island, Krinameh. Jagua fights with Nancy and drives her over to the Krinameh side of the water, where she is captured. Filled with remorse, Jagua herself goes to Krinameh. Arriving there she becomes "really Jagua," bringing her urban sophistication and sexual power to bear on Chief Ofubara; it was "like bringing the Tropicana chorus girls in a helicopter and dropping them among the mud-skippers." The Chief is fascinated both by her provocative looks and by the fact that he can talk to her about Lagos, education, anything; she, in turn, finds him to be more enlighted than she expected. She persuades him to release Nancy. Then, after ten days of sex, Jagua brings Ofubara to reconcile with Namme, thus ending a thirty-year conflict. Jagua refuses the chief's offer of marriage and leaves, promising to return someday.

Next Jagua goes to Onitsha, the commercial center where her brother Fonso is a trader. Fonso urges her to give up her wild ways and became a Merchant Princess, but she quickly gets bored. Worrying about becoming "provincial and less Jagua-ful," she returns to Lagos after three months' absence.

Jagua takes up with Dennis, a young thief. Now she is being kept by a politician named Taiwo while seeing Dennis on the side. One night Dennis tells her he has shot a policeman and flees; the police who come looking for him tell Jagua that Dennis's girlfriend has killed another woman and herself. Jagua mourns the waste of the young girl's life.

Taiwo gets her to help him campaign for office when Freddie, back from England and married to Nancy, challenges Taiwo for the election. Jagua tells Freddie she is going to help Taiwo beat him, but she also warns him about the brutality of Lagos politics. Dennis is working as Freddie's bodyguard. Freddie and Taiwo run into each other at Jagua's, and Taiwo's thugs beat Freddie up. Taiwo talks her into giving a speech to market women supporting his candidacy, and she is a big hit. She learns that Dennis has been caught and will hang.

When Taiwo's thugs fatally beat Freddie, Jagua is brokenhearted, especially when Nancy chases her away from the wake. Taiwo loses the election, and, fearing retribution from his own party, he gives Jagua a bag to hide and disappears. Jagua hides out in the Ajegunle slum. Down and out, she muses about how her fifteen years in Lagos have brought her to this. Brother Fonso comes to tell her Papa is dying. Ashamed of her squalid life, she delays leaving, and Papa is dead by the time she arrives in Ogabu. She agrees to stay and help her mother with the farming.

Bored by country life, Jagua sleeps with a visiting Lagosman. After he has departed, she discovers she's pregnant. A prostitute friend visiting from Lagos tells her about Dennis being hanged and Taiwo being murdered by his party. Only then does Jagua remember the bag, which she finds stuffed with money. Still thinking fondly of Ofubara, she travels to Krinameh, where she finds he is away but his long-dreamed-of school has been built; happy for him, she sends money for its support. She gives birth to a baby boy, who dies on his third day. Sad but always a survivor, Jagua decides to go to Onitsha and set up as a Merchant Princess.

(Cyprian Ekwensi, *Jagua Nana*)

Jagua's ups and downs follow the typical mythic structure of the city novel quite closely. Beyond just exemplifying and richly illustrating the myth, the novel helps us understand why the city has been such a powerful metaphor for general social change.

Jagua's urban lovers constitute a living catalog of the types of changes Nigeria began to experience in the late colonial period: Western education and attendant social mobility (Freddie); mass, high-stakes politics (Taiwo); crime-breeding social disorganization and anomie (Dennis); night life (at one point the explicit comparison is made between Ogabu, where everything is quiet by eight o'clock, and Lagos, where the action never stops); cosmopolitanism (Jagua's lovers include an Englishman and a Syrian); and material luxury (the Big Men who park their Mercedes outside Jagua's, much to Freddie's chagrin). One is tempted to draw a simple contrast between these urban types and Jagua's rural lover, Chief Ofubara, but the contrast is far from complete. Ofubara himself is a progressive, wanting development and Western education for his people. He is attracted to Jagua precisely because of her urban sophistication, artifice, and independence. By the end of the story he has initiated development in his village, and when she goes to see him at the end she learns that he and the Nammes "had left for Lagos two days previously. They had gone to see the Governor-General over some matter" (189). Ofubara's aspirations are identical to those of Freddie and Taiwo—education, improvement, political control, even sexual sophistication—and he is ultimately more successful.

This point is reinforced by the explicit way in which Jagua is shown to bring urban ways to Krinameh, dropping the Tropicana in the mangrove swamp, indeed. Her achievement of reconciliation between Ofubara and the Nammes is based on her urban powers—her sexuality ("I goin' to teach you about Lagos woman, to make you loss your min'" [101]); her sense of equality between men and women ("She could see that he had never really experienced the sensation of African woman as equal" [101]); her independence ("Am a business woman; I can't marry no one, Chief" [95]); and her glamor ("She had chosen the brightest lipstick in her bag . . . [her] skirt was so tight she could not take a stride of more than six inches. . . . She carried a plastic handbag and wore a wig which almost succeeded in altering her into a Malayan or an Indian lovely" [89]).

The striking thing here is that urban power solves a rural problem that had resisted solution for thirty years. It is the Lagos whore who brings the village chiefs together. This resolution sheds light on the pivotal role of the fifth stage of the city-novel myth, the return to the village. Jagua's return serves not only to contrast urban and rural ways —although it does do this—but also to dramatize a theory of mutual benefit: City woman brings peace to riverside villages; city woman finds restoration and renewed energy bathing in the river. The *Sweet Peace* canoe sails in both directions. And this is not just a peculiarity of Ekwensi's novel, for the return-as-mutual-benefit theme occurs in other city novels: Vivien's reformation and, upon a second return, her restoration of family peace; Wahihi's restored dignity, crowned by Grace's pregnancy. Even for the wayward Pataego of *Village Girl,* the visit to the village offers the hope—which she and the villagers seize upon—of reconciliation with her husband. Reconciliation does not always work out, but it is when the city reaches back to the village that new possibilities for social peace emerge.

What the city novels suggest is what might be called a "trickle-out" view of social change, a view quite compatible with the modernization theory prominent among social scientists and policy makers at the time *Jagua Nana* was written. Nigerian cities would be the crucibles of economic, political, technological, and social development. Changes wrought in the urban centers would eventually make their way to the villages, via progressive local leadership. Villages would continue to be the emotional safe havens even as they modernize. While the image of a unidirectional path to modernity has seemed simplistic for some time, the very real discrepancies between urban and rural development give the myth continuing cultural power.[70] The 1980s produced a darker version of the urban myth— the "brought low" or downfall stage is emphasized, and the final "I will go on" optimism of *Cheer Up, Brother* or *Jagua Nana* rings a bit hollow—but the mythic structure remains immensely powerful.

Two Worlds

City novels and urban settings do not represent just any set of social changes. There are no novels about the nineteenth-century Islamic jihad in Hausa cities, for example, or the impact of the 1919 influenza epidemic on Lagos, although both events triggered dramatic social change. Instead, the city-village contrast in Nigerian fiction gives symbolic form to the specific set of social changes generally referred to as "modernization."

Modernization theories enjoyed a vogue in the social sciences for about two decades following World War II, although they have been under a cloud ever since. The essence of modernization theory was that a combination of institutional changes (e.g., increases in urbanization, literacy, media penetration, industrialization) and psychological changes (increased individualism, optimism replacing fatalism, cosmopolitanism, secularism) would bring a society to a point where it crossed a threshold, or took off, or otherwise made the one-way leap from tradition to modernity. Drawing on the nineteenth-century dichotomies beloved of social science—mechanical solidarity/organic solidarity; feudal/capitalist mode of production; gemeinschaft/gesellschaft; agricultural/industrial; status/contract; enchanted/rationalized—modernization theory posited an either-or development model, whereby an individual or society either was modern or was not.

Beginning in the late 1960s, modernization theory came under withering attack from two sources: political and empirical. The political critique was that the theory was ethnocentric, that it assumed an eventual worldwide convergence toward a model from Western Europe and the United States, and that it assumed that all developing countries would follow the same steps as those taken by the West. Such thinking not only was arrogant but also, as attention focused on Japan, seemed plainly wrong. The empirical critique pointed out how the "traditional" and the "modern" were not separate stages or states, but interpenetrated one another to such an extent that it was foolish to talk about them as if they were discrete. And so the language in academic circles changed. Economists' talk turned to less-developed countries and development, sociologists talked about dimensions and rates of social change, political scientists talked about political institutions and participation, the liberal-to-left talked about the Third World, world systems theorists talked about the periphery, and everyone avoided the M-word.

Everyone, that is, but the people living in the less-developed countries, the places undergoing rapid social change, the polities moving (or not) toward democracy, the Third World, the periphery. Here people spoke and continue to speak without embarrassment about modernity as something different from their traditional way of life and, on the whole, desirable.

They refer to modern societies ("Nigeria will never be a modern country until we can attain political stability") and modern people ("My kids are very modern, growing up in Lagos; they don't even know how to speak Edo properly").

Nigerians like those involved with novels as writers, publishers, and/or readers—educated people of some affluence, what we might call the reading class—have a sense of living in two worlds: the modern world associated with cities and the traditional world associated with villages.[71] These worlds involve a separation of time and space; they include different people and activities; they often speak a different language. Both worlds are changing all the time, partly in response to one another, but although the city's influence on the village may be stronger than the reverse, the village persists as separate and distinct in the minds of Nigerians, even though it changes and, to varying extents, modernizes. Moreover, in part because of the frequent back-and-forth between city and village, "few people are committed to one or the other, so the urbanization of the countryside proceeds with the ruralization of the town."[72] Dual residences and occupations that necessitate going to and from the cities are two structural mechanisms that perpetuate, as well as reflect, the two-world orientation, as do the ties and claims of kinship.[73]

While village novels try to preserve the memory of a world that is passing, the city novel tries to capture the experience of moving between two worlds. *The World She Knew,* for example, is a pure city novel. Its characters work in the modern economic sector; Lagos represents opportunity, adventure, and sexuality; the dangerous excitements of the city is set against the boring security of the small town. Like *Things Fall Apart,* therefore, Nwoga's novel might be viewed as a story about an individual's experience of social change. Notice, however, that Vivien knows and leaves two "worlds." One is the nonurban world of her background, and it doesn't "fall apart" at all. It continues to exert claims on her. The other is the high-life world of nightclubs and businessmen keeping mistresses in lavish apartments. It doesn't fall apart either, and while she eventually moves out of this world, she doesn't reject it (or Mary), nor does the man she loves reject her because of it. The new couple will go on with their urban lives and with ties to their nonurban roots. They will continue to move between two worlds, just as Jagua, city woman, will continue to sail back and forth on the *Sweet Peace,* teaching each world the lessons learned in the other.

Nigerians are not the only people negotiating separate worlds, of course. In the phenomenological sense, everyone lives in a number of worlds, for example, that of the family, the workplace, the hometown, the friendship group. Everyone works at moving among, and balancing the claims of, their different worlds; the contemporary working mother juggling her household and workplace lives is a familiar example. In situations where one encounters an unfamiliar "world" in terms of its space, its symbols, its history, people will go to considerable effort to figure out such a world, or to construct a sphere of comfort within it; "learning your way around" and "nest building" may both be understood in this sense.

But the Nigerian situation is distinctive, although by no means unique, in one sense: that of the spatial and temporal disjunction between worlds. Such disjunction—a lack of connections or bridges—is one thing that characterizes rapid social change. For example, in a relatively stable society, when young people enter early adulthood, parents can advise them because the patterns of work, courtship and sexual behavior, educational institutions, city life, and so forth, are familiar to the parents. Parents try to steer and warn their children, because the situation is similar to what they faced when they were young. But under conditions of rapid change, the help they can give the young is limited not just because youth tend to reject it—this is probably universal—but because the experience of the elder generation is not relevant to what the younger one faces. This can be put in cultural terms. If culture is an inherited pattern of beliefs and dispositions by which people manage their lives, the culture into which the young people are socialized is less and less helpful.

Some Nigerian novels are about a single world: the village, the university community, the sophisticated city, the family. But most are about worlds in collision, as in romance novels where family collides with the individual on the choice of marital partner, or village novels where the glamorous city boy comes home to stir up trouble. One classic example of world disjunction, both experiential and literary, is the movement of youth from the country to the city. Thus the city novel is the purest version of the story of two worlds—sometimes parallel, more often on collision courses.

This is why the fifth step of the city plot, the visit to the village, is key. It is not enough that the protagonist move from one world to another; the two worlds must be shown parallel to one another, contending for the protagonist's soul. The strongest characters, like Jagua, are able to negotiate the back-and-forth movement to the benefit of both worlds, as well as themselves. Weaker (or more unfortunate) characters, like Gbola, are trapped in one world, caught like "bile in the dish," and succumb to it. The necessity to live simultaneously in parallel worlds highlights the roles of characters like Sonny and Prisca in *The World She Knew,* who operate as bridges between Vivien's city world and the world of town and family that she has exited but not really left. Structurally, Mary's role is the reverse of theirs; pure city, she must reenter the rural world to marry, and this reentry allows her to return to the even more cosmopolitan world of European cities.

The city novels make Lagos into a magic key that can unlock modernity without sacrificing tradition. Certain precolonial cities—Kano, Ife—were what urban historical Paul Wheatley has termed "cosmo-magical," in that they were symbolic centers as much as economic or political ones.[74] Through fiction Lagos has become a cosmo-magical city. And not just for Nigerians. From its winning the World's Least Livable City designation to the Federal Aviation Administration's warnings to traveling Americans that its airport is unsafe, Lagos has taken on symbolic dimensions to outsiders as well.

For most foreigners this city of the mind is a construction that holds only threat, whereas for Nigerians Lagos holds both threat and promise. True, the city is a tough place, no place for naive virgins, but virginity cannot be maintained if new productivity is to occur. This can be viewed as a violation—the village lost, something falling apart—or as an achievement, a welcome stage in maturation. "Dis Lagos, na waa." In the city, baboons chop. The novels suggest what Nigerians have come to believe: that if the monkeys-turned-baboons manage things properly, and if they are very lucky, they might be able to eat the sky.

WOMEN AND MEN

Favorite child of a distinguished father, Efuru marries a poor farmer named Adizua. A talented trader, she has "hands that make money," and the couple prospers, but after a while people begin to suspect that Efuru is barren. The local *dibia* (healer, diviner) assures her that she is fertile, although she doesn't have many children in her womb. Eventually Efuru gives birth to a daughter named Ogonim.

No more children appear. Adizua is away on an extended trip when Ogonim dies of convulsions. Efuru hears that Adizua is living with another woman and has no interest in returning to her. She decides to go back to her father's compound, thereby dissolving the marriage.

Soon Efuru is being courted by Eneberi/Gilbert, a childhood companion. Unlike Adizua, he pays the bride price promptly and everyone expects the marriage to succeed, but trouble develops when Gilbert blames Efuru for her failure to get pregnant. Even after Efuru dutifully finds a second and third wife for her husband, he treats her atrociously.

A *dibia* tells Efuru that she has been chosen as a follower of Uhamiri, the lady in the lake. Women favored by Uhamiri have few children, although they are usually wealthy and important nonetheless. Gilbert accuses Efuru of adultery. She is exonerated, but the experience leads her to conclude that marriage is not for her. Once again she returns to her father's compound.

When Efuru makes her decision, she dreams of Uhamiri—free, beautiful, wealthy, but childless. The last lines of the novel point out Uhamiri's (and

Efuru's) paradoxical position: "She had never experienced the joy of mother-hood. Why then did the women worship her?"

(Flora Nwapa, *Efuru*)

Appearing in 1966, Flora Nwapa's *Efuru* was the first novel written by a Nigerian woman and the first novel by any African women published in London.[75] Nwapa was an Igbo from Oguta in eastern Nigeria. She studied education at the University of Edinburgh in the 1950s, returning to hold a series of administrative and teaching positions in Calabar, Enugu, and the University of Lagos. Shortly after Chinua Achebe published *Efuru* in the African Writers Series, Nwapa returned to the east and spent the war years in Biafra. After the war she continued to write novels, short stories, and children's fiction. She founded her own publishing company in Enugu. Much honored in Nigeria and abroad, at the time of her death in 1993 she was "the materfamilias of Nigerian women's fiction."[76]

One might suppose that this first African Writer Series work by a woman would have been applauded, for breaking the sex barrier if nothing else, especially since it had been preceded by fully twenty-five books by men. In fact, *Efuru* created something of a scandal upon its publication. Western critics tended to be dismissive. West Africans were irritated at Nwapa's unflattering portrait of traditional Igbo sex roles from a woman's point of view and at her suggestion that a virtuous woman might find fulfillment despite being childless.[77] In the decades following *Efuru*, Nwapa struggled to define a place for herself and for Nigerian woman writers vis-à-vis both African patriarchy and a problematic Western feminist embrace.

Not just the first Nigerian novel written by a woman, *Efuru* was one of the first representatives of the genre that I call the women-and-men novel. These novels, which usually have a woman protagonist, focus on the relations between the sexes, on the enactment of and struggles over gendered roles in marriage, and on how gendered expectations intertwine with cross-generational conflicts. In the pages of women-and-men novels, gender becomes a Nigerian problem.

Efuru was not the first novel focusing on gender, for a year earlier a male author, Onuora Nzekwu, had published *Highlife for Lizards,* also in the African Writers Series.

Agom is a married woman who faces a series of problems: first, her infertility; second, her husband's bringing an unsatisfactory second wife into the household; third, British impositions on Onitsha, especially a new water system that the British ask residents to pay for.

The community thinks Odezue loves his wife Agom too much and is too subject to her influence. He attempts to exert his authority by withholding money from her, and then by taking a second wife, but he is always sexually bound to Agom and values her advice. The second wife, Nwadi, is a slattern;

she produces a daughter, but after Agom has a son, Odezue finally drives Nwadi from the house. Agom has more children and becomes a leader of the women, gaining respect even though the women's protest against the water system is overruled by the Obi.

Agom becomes a very successful palm oil trader and eventually a priestess in an ancestral cult, while Odezue also gains a title and becomes a leading elder. In the epilogue, on Agom's fiftieth birthday (1946), she advises girls in secondary school not to compete with men—both should stick to their traditional, natural roles. She goes on, much to Odezue's discomfort, to suggest that women are the ones with the real social power through their ability to influence men.

(Onuora Nzekwu, *Highlife for Lizards*)

These two early treatments of women and men in relation share much common ground. Both deal with problems brought about by infertility, polygamy, and the contradiction between women's economic power and their lack of social power. Both see women as first and foremost defined by their ability to bear children. But Nwapa takes a much more radical position. Umuahia really is both worshiped and childless, and Efuru both wonders about this puzzle and enacts it as she ends up a woman alone. Nzekwu's resolution of the women-and-men problems is far more conservative, for Agom does indeed produce sons, and her influence is the indirect one of using one's sexual and domestic influence to operate through men rather than independently. We see here the prototype of what would become a common pattern over the next four decades: female and male authors agreeing on a common, somewhat narrowly defined, set of gender issues but proposing different solutions.

The critical literature has addressed gender in the Nigerian novel in three ways. The most straightforward method is to focus on women writers and the stories they tell. This is the approach taken by Chikwenye Okonjo Ogunyemi in *Africa Wo/Man Palava: The Nigerian Novel by Women* (1996) and by the editors of *Nigerian Female Writers: A Critical Perspective* (1988) and of *Writing African Women: Gender, Popular Culture and Literature in West Africa* (1997), as well as by studies of individual woman authors. Such an approach would highlight Nwapa but would tend to give little attention to Nzekwu, thereby trading the advantages of comparison for those of a concentrated treatment of women's viewpoints.

A second starting position is to focus on works about but not necessarily by women, works whose central theme is women's experience. Here the comparative advantages are possible. Denise Coussy takes this approach in *Le Roman nigérian anglophone* (1988). In the chapter "Le Roman de la dependance sexuelle ou le monde des femmes," she discusses both Cyprian Ekwensi and Buchi Emecheta as authors who depict "la femme moderne."

The danger here is that "women" can become an autonomous classification rather than a relational one. In part, this is what Nigerians mean when they opt for the term *womanist* over *feminist;* they understand the latter as involving a rejection of men, rather than understanding women's experience.

Thus, the third way of dealing with the gender question is to consider works that focus not on women but on women and men in relation to one another. This is the approach of Florence Stratton in *Contemporary African Literature and the Politics of Gender* (1994). While organizing her discussion around individual authors (female and male), she looks at their consideration of gender broadly conceived, not just their treatment of women's experience and issues.[78] Here the danger is that women's concerns and issues may be downplayed unless they are clearly related to their relations with men.

Although there is some overlap between these approaches—*Efuru* would be a central text for all three—in some respects the third seems the broadest, for it allows a consideration of how authors of both sexes depict gender, sex roles, and relationships between men and women. It is the approach I am adopting; moreover, as I will try to show, it is the approach Nigerian writers themselves have adopted. In this section I will use some comparisons to show how male and female authors have conceptualized the problems associated with gender along somewhat different lines. This discussion does not include every novel with a woman protagonist. *Jagua Nana* is not primarily about gender or relationships, for example, but about making it in the big city, so it is a city novel and not a women-and-men novel according to my categorization. Nor does this third approach include every novel by a Nigerian woman, as would the first, for Nigerian women write about many things besides gender. Women-and-men novels, on the other hand, are firmly centered on issues involving gender.

One popular subcategory of the women-and-men novel is the romance. Based on the Western formula of the Harlequin/Mills and Boon variety, these stories treat a narrower set of issues by concentrating on courtship and love. Their authors usually regard such mass-culture stories about relationships—the formulaic romance novels—as craft more than art, but they can be as revealing as more ambitious works. I shall treat them separately in this chapter because they have a somewhat different publishing history and are intended for a somewhat different audience than the non-formulaic genres. Nevertheless, they share with all women-and-men novels a concern with changing relations between the sexes, and their manipulation of the Western formula is indicative of the gender-as-Nigerian-problem theme typical of the women-and-men novels more generally.

As with the village and city novels, the discussion of the women-and-men genre begins by analyzing the core narrative structure. Then follows a consideration of how this structure bears witness to the social changes Nigerian women in particular have experienced in the last half of the twentieth century, particularly those involving urbanization, influences from the West, and the lurching set of social dislocations loosely referred to as modernization. Next comes a look at the formulaic romance, showing how Nigerians reconstructed the Western pattern even as they were attempting to imitate it and considering what this reconstruction implies regarding sex roles and relations. Finally, I shall look at the costs of the women-and-men approach and consider the advantages of literary womanism versus literary feminism.

"Can Wealth Carry Firewood for You?": *The Women-and-Men Novel*

Born in Lagos to parents from Ibuza, both Aku-nna and her brother Nnanndo attend school. When she is thirteen, her father dies suddenly, and the family returns to Ibuza to live near Okonkwo, the father's brother. Aku-nna continues school and falls in love with the young teacher Chike, who loves her, too. But although his family is educated and prosperous, they are descended from slaves, a fact that makes marriage between Aku-nna and Chike unthinkable in the eyes of the village.

Okonkwo, who has married Aku-nna's mother, knows Aku-nna can fetch a large bride-price due to her education, and Okoboshi is the cruel but wealthy suitor he favors. Everyone, including her mother, warns Aku-nna against her love for Chike. When she is fifteen and starts menstruating, Okoboshi and his family kidnap her. She prevents him from deflowering her or wanting anything to do with her by claiming she has already slept with Chike.

She and Chike run off and begin a happy life in another town, calling their marriage bed "Joy." She teaches and he works for an oil company; Nna-nndo, whom they are helping finish school, also lives with them. Okonkwo curses her and refused to accept a bride-price from Chike's father, but the couple scoffs at the superstition that a woman whose bride-price is not paid will die in childbirth. Aku-nna becomes pregnant, and her pregnancy is difficult because she is anemic. She has a daughter by cesarean, and she asks that the baby's name be Joy. Aku-nna dies in Chike's arms. Her story is used to support the bride-price practice that they had opposed.

(Buchi Emecheta, *The Bride Price*)

Practices and beliefs relating to bride-price, virginity, romantic love, and education are all expressions of gender. Gender is the social inflection of biological sexual differences. If there were a world in which there was no social meaning to these differences, in which there was no sexual division of labor, no political or economic advantages enjoyed by either sex, no sex-based inequality of domestic power, no distinctions between girls and boys in their socialization or education, no stigma or privilege attached to same-sex versus cross-sex intimate relations, such a world would have sex but not gender. There is no such world, however. One of the most powerful and persistent messages that culture imposes upon human beings from the moment of their birth is that males and females are different, and that different things are expected from each.

Novels are not unique in their focus on the implications of gender, but from the era of *Pamela* and *Tom Jones* until the present day they have explored it more consistently than most cultural forms. Most novels, like most cultural forms in general, confirm the social order rather than challenge it. They train readers in what to take for granted, what is common sense. In most fiction, therefore, gender is implicit. Only when there is a violation of expectations associated with sexual differences does gender draw attention to itself. Such violations are at the heart of the women-and-men novels.

Authors weave the characteristic themes of the women-and-men novel through a structure where some form of gender deviance, some challenge to widely understood sex roles, produces a crisis of relationship. Sometimes the challenge is intentional, as in Aku-nna's wanting to marry for love and ignore bride-price, but usually it is unintended and often unwanted, as in stories about women who fail to bear children. Nevertheless, the deviants cannot help but be socially provocative, for they open to question some of the deepest principles of social organization.

Often the deviation is repeated several times, as in Efuru's leaving not one but two husbands, as if to underscore the provocation. Consider the structure of a rather slight novel by a third-generation writer.

> Tiena falls in love with Nzidi, but his parents object because she has no roots. She had been given to her family at birth in a hospital baby-switch when her birth mother and her (adoptive) mother's baby had both died. Her mother has brought her up strictly and loving God.
>
> When Tiena and Nzidi graduate from the university and want to marry, the truth of her parentage comes out. Nzidi goes away, leaving Tiena to uncover her roots, which she does to the satisfaction of all. He comes back and they marry.
>
> But they have only one girl, so soon his relatives pressure him to take another wife. He starts drinking heavily, and women begin to pursue him, as his relationship with Tiena grows tense. Then their daughter is in an accident and dies with her mother at her side, after the two discuss what heaven will be like. The tragedy brings Nzidi around, and he and Tiena rebuild their marriage. God rewards them with two sons and a daughter.
>
> (Oki Igbo, *Tiena*)

The novel's subtitle describes it as "the story of a girl who became victim of traditional fanaticism," but fanaticism seems too strong, for Nzidi's relatives are just acting conventionally. Tiena is caught in a web of conventions: people's social and biological backgrounds determine their marital suitability; families have the right to judge that suitability; boys are worth more than girls, and more children are better than fewer; men may marry multiple wives to produce children. She deviates from these twice. Both deviations—her own birth and her girl baby—are beyond her control; in both cases society, represented here by a rather passive boyfriend/ husband and his relations, steps in to correct things. Eventually her own efforts take care of the first problem, and God takes care of the second, leaving her with both a background and sons. The conventions themselves are left intact, just as Aku-nna's suffering actually reinforced bride-price in Emecheta's novel.

We have seen this pattern of deviance and social response repeatedly, in stories about traditional society (e.g., *Efuru*; *The Virgin*) and contemporary life (e.g., *Tiena*; *The Endless Search* discussed in Chapter 2). The basic structure of the women-and-men novel has five stages:

1. *Shared set of gendered roles and expectations:* Usually the protagonist begins by attempting to fulfill gender expectations. Girl and boy, or husband and wife, seem to agree regarding the nature of the relationship between the sexes, or at least regarding their own relationship. Typically the core relationship centers on marriage, although some novels feature intergenerational relationships. Efuru starts out marrying Adizua, for example. The marriage may have been unwise—her father is unimpressed, especially since Adizua cannot pay her bride-price—but it is a fact, and both partners are trying to fulfill their obligations. In *The Endless Search*, Nkoli and Chuma have had an egalitarian marriage in the United States, mutually supporting each other's educational aspirations while beginning their family. They have agreed upon a sequence: He will complete his American Ph.D., then she will return to her studies after they get back to Nigeria. At the start of both novels, as is true for most women-and-men novels, the women and men understand and intend to follow the social rules of gender as they have interpreted them in their particular relationship.

2. *The woman (or less often the man) deviates from expectations:* The pressure on the core relationship comes when one of the partners deviates from the conventional pattern. Efuru fails to produce the children that her husband and the community at large expect. This is not just a violation of norms but an affront to community values, where children are the only wealth that matters. "Can wealth carry firewood for you?" is the villagers' pointed questioning of Efuru's economic success.

Usually community values intrude on whatever arrangement of gender roles the couple has worked out. Thus the gender deviance may not be a new action but a new interpretation. In plots where an apparently egalitarian husband takes up patriarchal practices and attitudes, typically it is one of his relatives who precipitates the husband's change of heart whereby he comes to regard a previously satisfactory arrangement as an intolerable deviation from what is due to him. In *The Endless Search*, it is Chuma's mother and sister who remind him that a wife who has produced only daughters and is determined to get her degree is not fulfilling the Nigerian understanding of a woman's obligations, and that a husband who accepts such a wife is unmanly. Similarly, Nzidi seems unable to resist the pressure, and his drinking signals his weakening will. Relatives can exert their pressure regardless of resistance or acceptance, as when Okonkwo curses his stepdaughter and her husband.

Virtually always the deviation involves one of three things: fertility, fidelity, or women's achievements. These are often intertwined, as when villagers link Efuru's growing wealth with her barrenness, or when Chuma uses his desire for sons to justify his infidelity to Nkoli. Invariably the combination of a wife's aspirations and her failure to produce sons poisons the marriage.

Bearing a son for him does not guarantee a husband's faithfulness, however. Even if the community does not demand that a man take a second wife to ensure male offspring, polygyny remains an attractive and legitimate option for him. In Fakunle-Onadeko's *Chasing the Shadow*, the very traditional wife Grace has served as a helpmate to Dapo for twenty-four years, supporting the family by trading when Dapo was beginning his banking career, tolerating his infidelities, raising a successful son and daughter. This does not, however, prevent Dapo from announcing abruptly that he is marrying a younger woman.

The twist here is that Grace's enactment of traditional sex roles itself becomes a deviation, for Dapo has acquired new expectations about women, drawn from the sophisticated urban life that Grace made possible for him in the first place. Dapo's new wife, Kofi, offers a contrast to the devoted mother-and-helpmate model; she is glamorous, shines at restaurants and parties, and is more comfortable operating in Lagos high society than Grace ever can be. In such a story gender expectations are a moving target, and conformity to the old ones becomes deviation from the new ones.

3. Social pressure: Following the perception of deviation, kin or the entire community pressure the deviant party to conform. At the same time, they pressure the partner to break trust with the deviant. This is often connected with pointing out the social deviance in the first place, rendering a couple's private troubles as a community issue, as when a husband's relatives urge him to respond to his wife's infertility by taking a second wife.

Both parties to the conflict look for social supports. Aku-nna and Chike have her brother as well as a variety of friends who help them get established in their new home, while Okonkwo has all Ibuza on his side, even Aku-nna's own mother. In *The Endless Search,* Chuma is encouraged by his family to abandon his egalitarian understanding with Nkoli, while Nkoli's desire for a mutually supportive marriage is confirmed by Sally and Mike. Allies aside, the weight of community opinion is always against the deviant.

4. Crisis: Unable to resist the social pressure, usually either the deviant or the partner takes some action that precipitates a crisis in the relationship. For example, in her first crisis Tiena finds herself abandoned by Nzidi, and her hopes for their marriage will have to be abandoned unless she can solve the mystery of her parentage. Efuru manages two crises as well: her first husband abandons her for another woman, while her second accuses her of adultery. In *The Endless Search* it is Nkoli who leaves her husband, and their separation gives rise to a chain of events— his disastrous affair with Rose, her growing loneliness and embarrassing infatuation with Mike—that make them reevaluate their marriage. Sometimes the crisis is in the form of an accident or a child's death, but usually such an event follows an earlier crisis whereby the couple has become estranged. This is the case for Tiena's second crisis.

5. Gender roles are revised, one of the partners dies, or both: Never is a fully traditional relationship between men and women restored. Either some version of a more egalitarian relationship emerges, or permanent separation or death ends the core relationship. Efuru decides that marriage is not for her, thereby radically rejecting the socially prescribed role for women while embracing the new role of being Uhamiri's devotee. In the case of Chuma and Nkoli, after two crises, their separation, and then Chuma's accidental poisoning by his mother, they return to a companionable marriage. The relationship is egalitarian, although it also incorporates reconciliation with the elder generation when Nkoli nurses her mother-in-law back to health. This type of partial reconciliation whereby traditional gendered expectations (the dutiful daughter-in-law) coexist with a reformed relationship between the sexes (the aspiring wife and the egalitarian husband) is very common.

The five stages show the thematic structure of the women-and-men novel following the classic narrative form of disruption of social relations and then either their restoration in old or new form (e.g., comedy) or their continued breakdown (e.g., tragedy). Here the disruption is not presented as the individual torn between two worlds typical of the village and city novels, but as the relationship torn between two conceptions of gender. These competing conceptions generally involve bread-and-butter issues of everyday adult life: love and marriage, economic security, getting ahead, children.

Sometimes there is a distinctly feminist cast to the presentation of these issues, as in Buchi Emecheta's critique of "the joys of motherhood." Such openly critical novels are a minority, however. Most writers of the women-and-men novels are content to document difficulties between the sexes but then offer distinctly nonpolitical resolutions.

Themes

> Against the resistance of her parents, who favor a wealthier suitor, Chioma marries Chijioke, a fellow born-again Christian. Although enjoying a loving marriage for five years, they are grieved by the absence of children. Two friends, a minister and a nurse, offer comfort, and the four of them pray for God's eventual blessing.
>
> The larger community, however, is not willing to wait. Town elders try to get Chijioke to perform healing rites, which he angrily scorns as heathenish. Chioma's mother tries to get her to take herbal medicine from a juju woman, but she likewise refuses. When her nurse friend fixes her up with a gynecologist, he tries to seduce her. Another friend talks her own husband into sleeping with Chioma, who again must resist.
>
> Having undergone these trials, and sharing everything with each other, the couple is finally blessed with twins, and more children to follow.
>
> (Agwu Nwogo, *Destined to Be*)

Deviation from gender norms moves the action of women-and-men novels. This action plays out through a set of issue clusters —marriage and fertility are the most prominent—that set up sex-role expectations that generate conflict when they are violated. Male and female authors treat these issues rather differently.

One of the distinguishing characteristics of the women-and-men novels is that three-fifths of them are by women.[79] When we recall that only 15 percent of Nigerian novelists are women, the degree to which these women concentrate on gender seems remarkable. Moreover, five of the genre's fifteen female authors have written several such novels, while only one of the fifteen male authors has done so. Women like Flora Nwapa, Buchi Emecheta, and Funmilayo Fakunle specialize in novels that explore gender, while the men who have treated gender tend not to concentrate on it.

For the most part, authors of both sexes who write women-and-men novels do write about the same topics. Love and marriage, polygamy, and fertility are the three most common, each being a central focus for about half of the novels (often the same ones). The standard pattern is to have a happily married couple (stage 1 of the narrative structure discussed earlier) threatened by infertility (stage 2, deviation). Relatives urge the man to take a second wife (stage 3, social pressure), conflict occurs whether he does or does not (stage 4, crisis), and finally either the original couple is back together monogamously (and usually is rewarded with children) or, as in *Efuru*, the marriage ends (stage 5). Agwu Nwogo's *Destined to Be*, summarized previously, presents another story of infertility threatening an otherwise solid marriage. It engages in heavy-handed moralizing to make a case for egalitarian monogamy. Chioma and Chijioke must stave off their relatives, their friends, and public opinion, just as they must resist the temptation to blame each other for their plight. They are unusual in their steadfastness; more commonly the husband bows to social pressures and turns to polygamy or concubines in order to produce children.

Such social pressures are rooted in the belief that not just the institution of marriage but every individual marriage is a public concern. As in Adebowale's *The Virgin*, traditional marriages involve commitments between families and often between villages, not just or even primarily between individuals. While both rituals and contractual obligations vary widely, West African marital practices such as families arranging future spouses for very young children, bride-price payments to the girl's family, ceremonial visits and gift exchanges between the future in-laws, ritualized bride kidnapping, and public pronouncements on virginity all testify to the collective interests wrapped up in the union. And the collective defines its interests as lying in unions that support the social status quo, benefit the largest number of people, and produce multiple offspring, especially boys.

Yet although the Nigerian marriages depicted in the women-and-men fiction are public, open to the inspection of in-laws and neighbors, they are also hidden, intensely private, inducing claustrophobia, especially in women. According to Helen Chukwuma, "In this closed-in arena every married woman is to fight out her survival as an individual" (5).[80] And fight they do, from the squalid routine violence of Okpewho's *The Victims* to the sudden blows with which husbands or, less often, wives seek to redress grievances to the systematic beatings of a traditional patriarchy. It is not just physical violence that oppresses, but the closeness, the lack of privacy and room to breathe that city life and poverty exacerbate. In the polygamous marriage of *The Joys of Motherhood*, "Their room was choked with sleeping mats and utensils, and though they had acquired another bed for Nnu Ego [the senior wife], a wooden one which afforded her a little privacy, there was minimal space between the beds" (131). Separated only by a curtain, Nnu Ego listens in agony to her husband making love with his new wife.

The many novels that begin or end with a birth emphasize the fertility theme. For example, we saw earlier that Ojomo's village novel *The Young*

Brides begins with Agbeke's birth and ends with the birth of her daughter; moreover, a social balance is struck, as the second birth seems to compensate for Agbeke's forced marriage to a much older man. Kalu Okpi's *Love* begins with the birth of two babies, born at the same maternity clinic, who are destined to become the lovers. *Destined to Be* ends with the birth of twins. Fertility is both the problem and the solution to many plots, and its different impact on men and women structures gender relations in these novels.

Plots dealing with traditional life, or with couples who follow conservative Christian or Islamic practices, demonstrate the thematic emphasis on fertility, but so do plots involving modern, urban, secularized Nigerians. Here the novel may pose the conflict in terms of a rational, scientific approach to life on the one hand and a deeply rooted desire for offspring on the other. Ifeoma Okoye's *Behind the Clouds* sets this up through a contrast between Western medicine and faith healing, the latter being associated with polygamy as well.

Ije and Dozie, a middle-class Enugu couple (he's an architect, she's an accountant) are so close that they often think the same thoughts. The only problem with their five-year marriage is their childlessness. The story opens with Ije visiting yet another infertility doctor. In his waiting room she meets Beatrice, who vows to consult a faith healer if this doctor can't help. At home, Ije serenely orders her household; her servants dote on her, while she caters to Dozie by preparing his food with her own hands. Ije is a simple woman who just wants her husband's love and children. Her friend Ugo supports her throughout.

Dozie's mother has never liked Ije, so when Mama comes to visit, she urges Dozie to find another wife. Stifling her resentment, Ije waits on Mama attentively. Dozie resists Mama's interference, but without much conviction. Meanwhile, the new doctor produces no results. After running into a pregnant Beatrice, Ije agrees to see her faith healer, but when he suggests impregnating her himself, she leaves in disgust. Mama declares that Ije has bewitched Dozie into not wanting another wife.

One day a woman named Virginia shows up at the house claiming she is carrying Dozie's baby. Dozie admits to a stunned Ije that he had spent a drunken one-night stand with her. Virginia moves in and begins to take over the household, insulting Ije, driving the servants crazy, and wasting Dozie's money; he tolerates her because he desperately wants the baby. Devastated, Ije grows estranged from Dozie. Mama is delighted, but Ugo urges Ije to fight. When Virginia accuses Ije of poisoning their food and Dozie doesn't defend her, she moves out.

In a fight with Dozie, Virginia hints that the baby is not his. Distraught, Dozie makes a sudden trip to England. Upon returning, he throws Virginia out. Thereupon he tells Ije that the doctors have found the infertility caused by him, not her, and he begs her to return with him to England for an operation that will correct his problem. They both realize the Virginia episode was a blessing in disguise as their love is reborn.

(Ifeoma Okoye, *Behind the Clouds*)

For once, the husband accepts that the lack of children is not his wife's fault. Medical science, rationality, and egalitarian monogamy all fit neatly, triumphing over faith healing, polygamy, deceit, sexual promiscuity, and interfering relatives. The discovery of Dozie's infertility is a deus ex machina signaling a loss of nerve on Okoye's part, however, for at one stroke it solves the questions of Virginia's pregnancy, Virginia herself, and the couple's barrenness. Moreover, it gets Dozie off the hook in terms of his responsibility for his breaking faith and for his extraordinary passivity in the face of Virginia, as well as Mama. This is a prefeminist novel: it raises important issues of fidelity and fertility in the marriages of educated, modern African couples but then pushes them aside with a stroke of luck constituting a pseudoresolution.

The three main women-and-men themes—marriage, polygamy, and fertility—feature in novels by both men and women authors. Related themes of parenthood and of fidelity in marriage, analytically separate from the big three although often associated with them, are also treated by both. And, perhaps surprisingly, explicit feminism, rare though it is, is as likely to be found in a novel by a man as in one by a woman. The same cannot be said, however, for a group of themes involving women as independent actors, and for novels dealing with women's character. Here the author's sex seems to influence the treatment.

The first of these themes is that of women's independence. A number of women-and-men novels deal with money and with the different economic situations of men and women. As in *Efuru*, the plot often involves a woman's economic success and its relation to her overall happiness. Such novels are much more likely to be written by women. Both Flora Nwapa and Buchi Emecheta treat this theme repeatedly, as do less well-known women like C. A. Onwu. In contrast, fewer women-and-men novels by men feature women's economic activities and concerns, a notable exception being Chidi Ikonne's treatment of widow's property rights in *Our Land*.[81] Women authors are similarly more likely to treat women's aspirations for education and for career mobility than are men.

Buchi Emecheta's autobiographical novel *Second-Class Citizen* exemplifies the interweaving of women's economic and educational concerns.

Daughter of an Igbo railway man in Lagos, Adah dreams that education will empower her. So determined is she that she takes it upon herself to start schooling, even though her parents think education is not for girls. When her father dies, Adah's mother must marry her husband's brother. Allowed to continue schooling to increase her bride-price, Adah is treated like a servant by her new family. Finally, Adah steals two shillings from her family to pay the entrance examination fee for the elite Methodist high school.

After graduating, Adah wants more education, but she knows this will be possible only if she has a home and can study peacefully. Refusing to marry the elderly suitors her family presents and realizing she cannot live alone in the city, Adah marries Francis, a young accounting student, even though he cannot hope to pay the five hundred pounds set by Adah's family. The new-lyweds' first crisis comes when Adah lands a library job at the American consulate and earns more than Francis does. Then Adah's first child is a daughter, thus a disappointment, although she produces a boy soon after. She and Francis decide to go to England for further education and better jobs. Francis's father forbids Adah to go because the family needs her income; so, using her savings, Francis sails without her.

Undaunted by family disapproval, Adah saves her money and eventually joins Francis. Things in England consistently go wrong. Frustrated by his fail-ures, Francis grows surly and domineering. Adah works in a library to support the family, now grown to five children, and struggles to maintain a sense of self-worth. Francis starts beating her, making her life an emotional hell. To escape, Adah reads novels, especially by black writers such as Achebe, Nwapa, and James Baldwin.

Inspired by these authors, Adah writes a novel of her own. When an en-raged Francis burns the manuscript, Adah feels like he has murdered one of her children. She and the children move out, Francis pursues them, and a huge fight ensues. In court, Francis denies that she is his wife and disavows his chil-dren. Adah is finally free, but she has learned that as a black woman she is a second-class citizen.

(Buchi Emecheta, *Second-Class Citizen*)

Adah's troubles are far from over, as set out in *In the Ditch*, where she struggles as a single mother living in public housing while studying for a degree in sociology. Both books emphasize that woman understand the link between education and financial independence, and that the pursuit of either one is far more important and far more difficult for women. This is a subject dear to the hearts of women authors.

The link between education and gender concerns can be somewhat less direct. As described in Chapter 2, Nigeria is a country where boys are more likely than girls to get schooling in the first place, and where they go far-ther in their education. This makes any schooling and especially the pur-suit of more than the usual amount of education, a more radical step for girls than for boys. Along the same lines, recall how one of the ways Aku-nna and Chike asserted their independence was through supporting her brother's further schooling. Youthful rebellion and women's assertion both express themselves through education in a very non-Western pattern whereby the youth and the women demand more, and may sneak around behind their parents' or husbands' backs to get it.

As for women's economic aspirations, novels have always treated the subject of money much more directly than other literary genres have, perhaps because it was never a taboo topic in middle-class discourse. Nigerian novels are no exception. Money is significant to the plots of two-thirds of the Nigerian novels, and women and men are equally likely to write about it.[82] It is the narrower theme of women's financial independence—Efuru as a successful trader, Adah stealing money for school and later working in the library to support the family while Francis sulks—that is the particular domain of women writers.

West African women have always had considerable financial independence. They engage in petty trading, selling their farm products or prepared foods, and they keep the profits; married women are responsible for the day-to-day support of their own children. Yet one should not overstate women's economic power; the accent is on "petty" in women's farming and trade, for example, with men taking over the more profitable cash crop farming. The point is, however, that Nigerian women have not been dependent on their husbands. Such financial independence becomes a problem in two concrete settings: where it clashes with women's traditional roles as mothers, and where through education and opportunities women's economic achievements threaten to become no longer petty. This is where gender relations are strained, for the woman gains a certain freedom and, hence, power. It is no accident that African prostitutes are referred to as "free women."[83]

The image of the prostitute raises the question, Can a woman aspire to education, independence, and financial security for herself and her children while still retaining a good character? A second theme that women and men writers have developed differently is that of women's character.

Two types of character studies appear in women-and-men novels. One is the witch-bitch, the powerful female whose malevolence poisons the lives of those around her. This is not simply the meddling mother-in-law or the gold-digging other woman but a character whose essential evil moves the plot. For example, in Muda Atoyebi's *Countdown to Perdition,* a cautionary thriller about what can happen when you take a second wife, Awero is simply wicked.

Businessman Ajani and his first wife, Rolake, are childless. Both Ajani's family and Rolake herself urge him to take a second wife, so he marries Awero. Relations between the co-wives are friendly at first. Awero promptly gets pregnant but gives birth to a girl, while Rolake has a son, Folusho. Awero is jealous, hating mother and son even though she herself soon has two boys. When Rolake gets pregnant a second time, Awero gets some poison from a jujuman and kills her co-wife.

No one suspects Awero, who seems overcome with grief. Ajani is heartbroken and throws himself more and more into his work. Jealous of Rolake's memory, Awero nurtures her hatred of Folusho. She treats him badly while pampering her own three children, yet she fears him as well. Finally, she decides he must die.

In a series of poisonings and dealings with magicians and hired thugs, Awero schemes to kill Folusho. Each time something goes wrong and one of her own children dies instead. The house is filled with sorrow, but Ajani still suspects nothing. Finally, when her last child has been killed, Awero goes mad. She screams out the truth to Ajani, who grabs Folusho and escapes. Brandishing a dagger and howling like a dog, Awero rushes out to search the world for Folusho.

(Muda Atoyebi, Countdown to Perdition)

Sensationalism aside, we see the usual jealousy between spouses here, and the difficulty of reconciling a couple's Western lifestyle (the cover of the book shows their modern dress and housing) with the African pressure to produce sons. But such pressures cannot explain Awero's actions, which spring from sheer malevolence. Wicked women—usually in the witch-bitch combination of using magic against sexual rivals—make for great stories, of course, from Ilori's sluttish Bisi to Ovbiagele's scheming Chinwe to Akoji's maddened-by-love Onyeomowo, who kills her own child.[84] While a number of the women-and-men novels feature an irredeemably evil woman, who invariably gets her just desserts, male authors rely on these witch-bitch characters more than female authors do.[85]

On the other hand, women write about virtuous women while men do not. This is not to say that male-authored novels never feature decent female characters, but that novels that problematize woman's virtue, that consider the question of what is a "good women" independent of her maternal status, are exclusively by women.[86] Some novels, like Obong's *The Garden House*, suggest that women's spiritual ties imbue them with virtue and power independent of their social roles or their fertility. Other novels emphasize women's courage, patience, generosity of spirit, and endless capacity for hard work. All of these are character issues—in that sense comparable to the witch-bitch construction—and they contrast with the idea that women's virtue depends upon their fulfilling prescribed gender roles.

Zaynab Alkali's novel *The Virtuous Woman* offers an interesting example of how a reconsideration of female virtue can suggest a politically efficacious reconstruction, bridging cleavages beyond those of gender. To release her characters from sex roles, Alkali relies on the device of youth: her female characters are too young to have their fertility define or restrict them. Instead, the story of three girls' journey lays out a series of possible routes to virtue.

The time is the early 1960s. Nana Ai is a northern girl, lame and intelligent, who attends an elite secondary school in the south. Her late father was a doctor, but Nana fears she cannot follow his footsteps because of her sex; her herbalist grandfather encourages her to make her own choices. Two other local girls are entering the school, and Nana is escorting them south. One is Laila, an indifferent student and a flirt; the other is Hajjo, illegitimate and timid. As they leave, a village girl taunts Nana, saying that she will never marry.

At the bus stop Laila wants to accept a lift from two men, but Nana refuses. They travel to the district capital to go to the Secretariat, where they meet two young men who are also headed south, the exuberant Abubakar and Bello, whose handsome looks are described as feminine. Laila flirts openly; more reserved, Nana is drawn to Bello. The Secretary turns out to be one of the men who tried to pick the girls up, and he vengefully assigns a feeble old man as their escort.

The next stage of their journey takes place in a convoy of three southbound lorries, theirs named Hakuri, or "patience." Rain and mud delay their progress; Bello and Abubakar become heroes by obtaining food for the stranded travelers. A woman, the mother of twins and described as "masculine," becomes Nana's soul mate as she tells her the story of a man who ruined his life by wanting sons and not daughters. Watching Laila flirting, Nana concludes romance is not for her and consoles herself by cuddling the twins. When Nana is insulted and teased by Laila, Bello defends her. Nana begins to hope he might like her, but then remembers the Secretary's receptionist, who appeared to be Bello's girlfriend.

When the three lorries finally get on the road again, the heedless drivers of the front two cause a terrible accident. Abubakar, the twins' mother, and one of the twins are among the dead; Bello is wounded; Laila is hysterical; Nana is left tending the remaining twin. The lorry drives on, filled with the living and the dead; at the hospital Nana turns the baby over to his relatives and says good-bye to Bello.

After recovering, the three girls finally head south by train, Nana sadly recalling Bello while Laila flirts with an army officer. A sleeping, heavily bandaged man awakens, and he turns out to be Bello. He reveals that the Secretary's receptionist was his sister, much to Nana's relief; dozing, she dreams that her grandfather has blessed their love. They arrive at their destination, planning to meet at midterm. Laila is momentarily crushed to learn her officer is the father of a schoolmate and has no romantic interest in her, but she laughs it off, for "there are plenty more out there."

(Zaynab Alkali, *The Virtuous Woman*)

The Virtuous Woman is a political allegory as well as a parable about gender.[87] The three lorries are Nigeria's three regions, rushing headlong toward disaster in the early 1960s, while the women-and-men plot suggests a womanist healing of Nigerian divisions. Such healing depends on women's virtues, which are cast in terms of a wholesale reconstruction of gender. Crippled by polio, Nana is doubly disabled—she will not be able to fulfill the role of desired mate—just as Hajjo is disabled by her illegitimate birth and Laila by her daredevil sexuality. These will not be the virtuous wives, unblemished, sequestered, obediently delivering male babies, of conservative Islam. But their education—merging virtues of north and south, West and indigenous—may make them enabled, if disaster (or, in Laila's case, her own foolishness) does not intervene.

Such enabling will make them socially potent. Alkali makes clear that associating potency with masculinity is a mistake, as are the other dichotomies of gender. Bello's looks are feminine; the twins' mother is masculine and does indeed provide; cocky Abubakar is shy; Nana will never attract a husband through physical grace. The outmoded dichotomies are far more crippling than polio. Conceptions of virtuous women must be reconceived, and such conceptions will produce political virtue as well. This is a womanist theme, one written about exclusively by women.

Many Nigerian writers see a sharp distinction between feminism and womanism, the form of black feminism described by Alice Walker.[88] In their view feminism is Western, middle-class, and harsh, entailing a rejection of men. Womanism is non-Western, egalitarian, and strong but gentle; it embraces men and carries a vision of how woman's virtues enable both sexes to move ahead toward freedom. Flora Napa was particularly insistent on the womanist stance.

Other authors concerned with gender roles are more comfortable with the feminist label. Some are men: Tolu Ajayi writes directly on feminist themes and would not accept that race should influence an ethics of sexual equality; Chidi Ikkone sets African inheritance traditions and universalistic ideas about justice in opposition. The most unambiguously feminist writer is Buchi Emecheta.

Emecheta has had a brilliant career, being one of the most prolific Nigerian writers and perhaps the best-known member of the second generation.[89] Her fame in Europe and North America has come about even though her books have not appeared in the African Writers Series, which has usually been a requirement for African writers to get external recognition. Emecheta attracted the attention of British feminists in the 1970s with her two autobiographical accounts of an African mother in the United Kingdom struggling against racism, patriarchy, and poverty to improve her lot. The three novels that followed—*The Bride Price, The Slave Girl,* and especially *The Joys of Motherhood*—squarely opposed

Nigerian constructions of gender roles and drew enormous attention in the West.

Emecheta is not altogether comfortable with the Western embrace, even as she benefits from it in countless visits to academic forums for women's studies. She stresses the distinctiveness of the African woman's experience. But it is this very distinctiveness that makes her teeth so sharp, for she calls into question the fertility/fidelity combination that lies at the heart of Nigerian gender. *The Joys of Motherhood* poses the issue squarely.

Nnu Ego, devoted daughter of Ibuza chief Agbadi and his favorite mistress, is said to be the spirit of a slave woman sacrificed at the funeral of Agbadi's eldest wife. When married to a farmer, Nnu Ego "was failing everybody" by not getting pregnant. The husband takes a second wife, and Nnu Ego, agonized by her barrenness, suckles that wife's child. Beaten and shamed, she returns to Agbadi, and the marriage is over.

Her father sends Nnu Ego to Lagos to marry Nnaife, an Ibuza-born washerman for an English family. The ugly and servile Nnaife repels Nnu Ego, but since she fully accepts the idea that she is her husband's property, she tries to be a dutiful wife. She has a baby boy; when he dies suddenly, she is devastated and attempts suicide, only to be saved by some neighbors. Pregnant again, she dreams of finding a filthy child. The slave woman who is her *chi* (personal divinity) tells her, "Yes, take the dirty, chubby babies. You can have as many of those as you want." Nnu Ego is oblivious to the possible costs of such abundant maternity, and from this point on her fate—motherhood without joy—is sealed. Soon she has another son, Oshia.

With war breaking out, the English employers depart, leaving the family in desperate poverty. Nnaife gets work on a ship, while Nnu Ego, now with a second son, takes up trading black-market cigarettes. Nnaife returns and gets a job as a railroad grass cutter, making it possible for them to send Oshia to school. When his brother back in Ibuza dies, Nnaife marries the widow, Adaku, and brings her to Lagos. Nnu Ego resents her co-wife bitterly, and poverty injects continual tension into the household. As Nnu Ego has more children, nine altogether with seven surviving, she feels imprisoned and exhausted by the struggle to feed them.

Nnaife is conscripted into World War II, leaving his wretched household to survive as best it can. Nnu Ego goes to see her dying father in Ibuza. She is loath to return to her misery in Lagos, but her family admonishes her to be as good a wife as she has been a daughter. She goes back, and both she and Adaku are near starvation. Scorned because she has only daughters, Adaku finally leaves to become a prostitute. Things look up when Nnu Ego gets hold of some back pay of Nnaife's, allowing her to send her sons to school and to improve her business.

Nnaife returns, squandering most of his earnings in celebration and bringing in another wife, Okpo. Once again there are constant domestic battles.

The children are growing up now. Oshia goes to university in America, enraging his father, who thinks he should help support the family. When one of the daughters runs off to marry a Yoruba boy, Nnaife attacks the boy's family and is sent to prison.

Nnu Ego returns to Ibuza, brokenhearted because she never hears from Oshia or from her second son, now living in Canada. Nnaife gets released but refuses to live with her. Worn out in body and spirit, Nnu Ego grows vague and begins to wander the streets. When she dies alone in the street, her children return and organize a showy funeral. Afterward, Ibuza women who want to be fertile pray to Nnu Ego, but it is said that she never answers their prayers.

(Buchi Emecheta, *The Joys of Motherhood*)

Emecheta's ending inverts that of *Efuru*. Instead of worshiping a barren but powerful female principle as in Nwapa's novel, the Ibuza women pray to a fertile but embittered one who scorns their stupidity for believing, as she had, that motherhood would bring joy. Nnu Ego has not questioned Igbo gender ideology, which has told her that women, owned by their fathers and then by their husbands, exist to bear and raise children. Fertile beyond her dreams, Nnu Ego finds that fulfilling the socially prescribed roles —mother, daughter, senior wife—brings her no happiness. Her children disappoint her, her husband grows to hate her despite her years of support, her life is one of unremitting misery, her death is lonely, and no honor comes to her until after her death. Nnu Ego thus is a perfect mother, and this is one reason Ibuza women pray to her ancestral spirit for "increase." Nnu Ego's *chi* grants her the fulfillment of her dream, in terms that her culture respects, but denies her happiness in the achievement.[90]

Emecheta repeatedly emphasizes this critical view of motherhood, from the ironic title to the tragic end. "Her love and duty for her children were like her chain of slavery" (186). Not sacrificed at a single stroke like the slave women, Nnu Ego's entire life was a sacrifice. Emecheta's bitter joke is that such a life is supposed to be the source of joy.

If *The Joys of Motherhood* questions childbearing as the center of women's lives, seven years later *A Kind of Marriage* questioned marriage itself. The story is conventional, but the frame is not.

London-based Auntie Bintu, from a Yoruba Muslim family, returns to Nigeria for a visit; while staying with her brother in Lagos, she takes her sister-in-law, Amina, to a restaurant for lunch. Much is made of the daring nature of this outing: two women eating out together, unaccompanied by a man; the waiter and some men at the restaurant assume they are prostitutes, and the women must act imperiously to get any service at all. Auntie Bintu thinks it is good for Amina to get out of the house now and then, and Amina is both excited and shocked by her own boldness.

During the long lunch, Amina tells a story, interrupted by questions and comments from Bintu, about an Igbo man who married a second wife, and the tragedy that followed. The story itself is a typical one of a couple who marry in London and have a son, Osita, and a modern marriage; upon their return to Nigeria the husband's family pressures him into taking a second wife. Osita is a golden boy who studies medicine, while Afam, son of the second wife, is embittered and takes up with thieves. At the end Afam has killed Osita and been killed himself, the husband has committed suicide, and Osita's pregnant widow is left with her mother-in-law. The two women decide to constitute their own family and raise the twin boys who are soon born.

After Auntie Bintu and Amina have discussed this story, remarking how careers protect women from total dependence on men, the novel ends as Auntie Bintu says:

> "The two women have now got into a kind of marriage. May Allah help them with the twins, and may they be like their father Osita, but may they live long to see their great-grandchildren."
>
> "Amen, Amen, Amen," Amina sang with one hand uplifted to Allah. Then suddenly she asked, "Auntie, what do we need men for really?"
>
> "We need them to give us babies, and after that I don't know . . ."
>
> "And Auntie, do they not say that you can now have babies, without men, you know . . ."
>
> "Shush, Amina. That is not a nice thing to say." (120–21)

It may not be a nice thing to say, but it is the logical outcome of the story that has been told, framed as it is by one very independent woman and another just beginning to see the possibilities. Although Emecheta tries to have it both ways, presenting family and Islam (in its liberal version) in a positive, evenhanded way, the novel presents an interrogation of everything from restaurant norms to the relationship between conception and marriage. It is undeniably feminist. Emecheta is well aware, however, of the tension over the word itself. She poses the issue in *Double Yoke* when some women students at the University of Calabar are discussing beauty. Missy, an American (all the others are Nigerians) forces the issue by saying:

> "Suppose we all say, okay, I don't care. I want to look the way I am. I am fat, I remain fat, I don't care; I am skinny, I remain skinny. That I don't have to accept the dictates of society, what then?" Missy wanted to know.
>
> "And where will you find the courage? Here in Nigeria? If you do that, they'll say you are independent, that you are a feminist, then men will run away from you," Mrs Nwaizu said, knowingly.
>
> "But what is bad in being a feminist? My mother is a feminist. She is married; she had me, didn't she!" Missy declared.

"We are still a long way from that yet. Here feminism means everything the society says is bad in women. Independence, outspokenness, immorality, all the ills you can think of. So even the educated ones who are classically feminist and liberated in their attitudes and behaviour, will come round and say to you, 'but I am gentle and not the pushful type.'" (104)

This conversation takes place among women trying to prepare themselves to bear the "double yoke" of having education but living up to conventional expectations. "I want to have both worlds, I want to be an academician and I want to be a quiet nice and obedient wife, the type you want me to be," the heroine Nko tells her mother (94). Her mother cannot help her. She sees her choices starkly: "She must either have her degree and be a bad, loose, feminist, shameless, career woman who would have to fight men all her life; or do without her degree, and be a good loving wife and Christian woman to Ete Kamba and meanwhile reduce her family and herself to being beggars at Ete's table" (135). When Nko is forced to submit to a professor's advances, she makes the best of the situation by blackmailing him to give her passing grades, figuring she has to succeed academically since she is going to lose her fiancé anyway. She is right: when Ete Kamba discovers the affair, he rejects Nko as a "cheap whore" and reasserts his masculinity by beating up the professor. An openly feminist visiting professor urges him to reconsider, which he does, but his ultimate ability to accept Nko is left in doubt. His university friends tout the advantages of uneducated wives, virgins, and marriages arranged for procreation instead of love, and Nko herself is pregnant by the professor, so the cards seem stacked against the pair despite their reconciliation. For a young woman like Nko, Western-style feminism turns out to be ideologically available but practically useless, and she remains under the crushing weight of the double yoke.

While most authors of women-and-men novels do not go as far as Emecheta in posing gender issues in terms of feminism, they do display the gap between established sex roles and changing circumstances. The overall message is clear: Nigerian women's lives are changing, Nigerian men's expectations are not, and the increasing misfit—the necessary deviance that initiates the action in the narrative structure—produces conflict. Such conflict questions the core institutions—marriage, parenthood—through which gender is enacted.

One such institution, courtship, is the focus of the Nigerian romance.

"Love in the Battle Storm": The Formulaic Romance

Tokoni is an Ijaw secretary living in Lagos with her widowed mother. When she first informs her mother that she and Tolu, her Yoruba doctor boyfriend, are engaged, her mother snaps, "All these foreign romances you've been read-ing must have gone to your head." Sure enough, when Tolu had "slipped the ring on her finger . . . it was just as she had read in all those novels and seen in films." But in fact Tokoni is very traditional and wants parental consent. Her mother warns her, "The people from the majority areas still looked down on the people from the so-called minority areas. The Yoruba especially re-garded themselves as the first-class citizens, the builders of the nation. . . . They would not tolerate any child of theirs marrying a kobokobo [non-Yoruba]." But eventually her mother agrees to the union as long as Tolu's family goes along.

Tolu's family is violently opposed, however, and acts as nasty as possible, insulting Tokoni, calling her a tart, telling her mother they know she is just after the money. Tolu and Tokoni try to carry on and hope the parents come around; they have a very educated middle-class courtship, spending most dates going to plays and films. Finally the strain gets to Tolu, who becomes arrogant and treats Tokoni badly. Meanwhile, there is a gentlemanly Ijaw boy who loves Tokoni, but she declares that she will be faithful to Tolu no matter what.

Seeing that Tolu's parents remain adamant, Tokoni arranges for her com-pany to transfer her to Port Harcourt, where she lives with her grandmother and instructs her family not tell to Tolu where she has gone. Tolu is miserable without her, and Tokoni herself is unhappy but resolute. Tolu's parents are impressed by Tokoni's unwillingness to marry without their consent, so they finally relent. Before the two get together, Tolu is injured in a car accident, but Tokoni comes to his bedside and he soon recovers. At their marriage her grandfather gives her advice, including, "You are a stranger in your mother's house from today." Tokoni nods, whispers assent, and goes off with Tolu's people.

(Nyengi Koin, *All You Need Is Love*)

All's well that ends well, and although the reader is left with the impres-sion that Tokoni is going to have her hands full, *All You Need Is Love* ends with a marriage, as its title promises.[91] This is the romance formula: love strong enough to conquer all obstacles, even wavering on the part of the lovers themselves.

Formulaic novels are highly standardized treatments of themes that have widespread audience appeal. Courtship is one of these themes; the strug-gle between criminals and the forces of order is another.[92] Romances and crime novels (which I will examine in a later section) are the two largest categories of formulaic fiction. All formulaic novels are undemanding, have clear conventions, and come in formats that announce their formulaic sta-tus. Thus the romance is a standardized treatment of courtship that an-nounces its adherence to a set of conventions. While we find the same themes as in the women-and-men novels—marriage, polygamy versus monogamy, fertility, economic independence, character—in the Nigerian romance novels the vision is narrower, focusing on courtship and the protagonist's affective and sexual history.

Formulaic novels are relatively easy to write and to read. Nigerians read a lot of them, especially the ubiquitous Mills and Boons. They also write a lot. I have identified sixty-seven romances, as compared with only fifty non-formulaic women-and-men novels. And this understates the total, for many of the pamphlets that do not meet the sixty-page criterion for being "a novel" are, in fact, romances.

The Western formulaic romance—those paperbacks whose covers featuring embracing lovers and that come in lines named Harlequin Romance or Candlelight Ecstasy—constitutes the starting point for the comparison of Western models and Nigerian reconstruction of a single formula. North Americans refer to these books as Harlequin-type romances, after the Canadian publisher that developed and still dominates the industry, while British and Nigerian readers call the same formula the "Mills and Boon" books. The formulaic romance blends the long-standing interest in love and marriage that has been a staple of the novel since its inception with the formulaic packaging that is the product of the paperback revolution. Starting in the 1950s and accelerating from the 1970s until the mid-1980s, Britain, Canada, and the United States began mass-producing romance fiction in inexpensive paperback formats.[93] In 1957 the British publisher Mills and Boon, which had produced genre romances since the 1930s, began publishing romances exclusively. Harlequin Enterprises, a Toronto reprint house, had distributed the Mills and Boon line in North America since 1958. Harlequin dedicated itself to romances in 1964 and merged with Mills and Boon in 1971. Formulaic romances have enjoyed extraordinary market success.[94] Harlequin/Mills and Boon romances are distributed internationally, as a visit to a Nigerian bookstore makes abundantly clear.[95] The books published in Britain are still issued under the Mills and Boon imprint, while those published in Canada or the United States are Harlequins.

Western romance authors are usually middle-class women; male writers are rare, and the few who do exist write under women's names. Seldom has such a woman been a professional writer before turning her hand to romance writing. Typically, one day a reader tries her hand at writing an example of the formula she knows and likes, her efforts meet with success, and her career as a writer is launched. She joins an extensive network of romance writers and their readers, a network maintained by newsletters and professional associations. The typical romance author writes nothing but romances, and she is quite comfortable, even assertive, in describing her literary product as entertainment, the result of craft rather than inspiration.

She understands herself to be providing escape, a fantasy world attractive to women seeking diversion from the everyday.[96]

Romance readers in the West are virtually all women. The average reader is middle-class, has attended high school and often college, and is eighteen to forty-five years old; she is married and family-oriented, even though she probably works as well.[97] Less than 20 percent of women read romances, but many of those who do are apt to be heavy consumers, reading upward of twenty-five per month.[98]

While the success of the contemporary Western romance genre has brought considerable product differentiation, the fundamental formula has remained remarkably stable. In describing the formula, I am going beyond the typical plot outlines that I use to describe the other genres. Western romances are so highly standardized that it is instructive to see how their Nigerian counterparts do or do not adhere to the pattern. To do this I must examine features over and above the narrative structure. That formula has the following characteristics:

> *Theme:* Romance is central. As one set of editorial guidelines for authors expressed it, "The development of the romance should be the primary concern of the author, with other story elements integrated into the romance."[99] Both hero and heroine are obsessed with each other, much as they try to conceal their feelings, and the romance theme overwhelms all other plot elements.
>
> *Setting:* The settings of romances are usually middle class and familiar: homes, offices, hospitals, universities. Except for the missionary settings occasionally found in the "Christian" lines, virtually no action takes place in settings of poverty. Romance authors also pay a great deal of attention to describing the scenery and its emotional impact on the lovers, with both natural and man-made settings seen as contributing to and supportive of human emotions.
>
> *Point of view:* Although usually told in the third person, the story always conveys the woman's point of view.[100]
>
> *Characterization:* The heroine is described as "spirited," "spunky," and independent, as well as attractive. She is not seeking a man and is never an "adventuress" who uses romance as a means to social mobility.[101] The heroine is determined to preserve her independence in spite of her increasing obsession with her lover. Sometimes a heroine is sexually experienced, sometimes a virgin, but she is never promiscuous; instead, she is initially cautious about the developing sexual attraction between her and the hero. The hero is handsome, arrogant, and sure of himself; he is also usually wealthy, brilliant, or socially powerful.
>
> *Structure:* The plot involves the romance between one man and one woman. Heroine and hero are introduced early in the novel, and their

interaction organizes the novel until its conclusion. Other characters appear, but the focus remains on the primary pair. By the end of the first chapter, the experienced romance reader sees which man and woman will constitute the romantic couple, although initial circumstances may appear unpromising.

Plot: The romance plot proceeds linearly, beginning with the heroine's first encounter with the hero and ending with their mutual affirmation of love. The hero and heroine are strongly attracted to one another from their first meeting, but obstacles, past experiences, or misunderstandings make them hide their feelings. For most of the novel they express hostility, mockery, or indifference to each other, in spite of the fact that circumstances and their own urges keep drawing them together. Tension between the heroine's coexistent emotions of hostility and love is in evidence until the closing pages.

Ending: Eventually all the obstacles and misunderstandings are cleared up, and the two confess that they have loved each other all along. Since the novel is told from the woman's point of view, she has admitted her love for the hero to herself (and the reader) early on, but she is confused by his behavior and does not believe he really loves her. At the conclusion, he makes her understand that all of his indications of hostility were really signs of his love. He assumes a nurturing and supportive role, thereby indicating that he has become domesticated and can now both behave in ways typically seen as being feminine and retain his masculinity.[102] The hero and heroine end up together, married or about to be, all doubts and hesitations having been cleared away by their mutual revelation of love. Western romances without exception end upon this note of happy-ever-after.

Western romances of this type entered the Nigerian book market in quantity during the 1970s. Romances were not altogether a new phenomenon in Nigeria. In the 1950s the Onitsha market pamphlets had offered short romantic tales for the newly literate. Often these were didactic, offering either instruction on wooing (as in the pamphlets that told how to write a love letter) or warning about money-hungry girls and fast boys. A few British romances circulated as well, so in the early years of independence there already existed a market for this type of popular entertainment.

The social dislocations of the civil war were followed in the 1970s by relative political stability and oil-boom prosperity, both of which led to a vast educational expansion. Universal primary education became the goal, as the structures of schooling (the 6-3-3-4 plan, referring to how many years a student would spend at each level) were rationalized. The consequent increase in the number of literate young Nigerians with money to spend coincided with the enormous growth in production, and exports, of Western romances. New readers embraced the new formula.

Western romances continue to be popular with Nigerians, and widely available. In the mid-1980s bookstores were packed with Harlequins, Mills and Boon British romances, Candlelight Ecstasies, Sweet Inspirations, and the like, all selling for prices comparable to their Nigerian counterparts. More recently the Mills and Boon romances have gotten a lot more expensive, but they still are available and prized.

Another way Nigerians have had access to Western romances is via local publishers who repackage foreign novels under Nigerian covers. For example, Fagbamigbe's Eagle Romance series consists primarily of British-authored romances like Bertha M. Clay's *Love's Golden Reign*. The line features black beauties on the cover, but the stories within are lily-white British romances having no connection to Africa whatsoever.[103] The fact that Fagbamigbe produces dozens of these novels (some nineteen titles by Clay are on the Fagbamigbe list) indicates their popularity with Nigerian readers.

While Nigeria continues to offer a market for the romances written by Western authors, Nigerians began writing their own romances in the late 1970s. The number of locally written romances has steadily increased. Nigerian publishers have come out with specific romance lines, including Spectrum's Sunshine Romances, Fourth Dimension's Heart to Heart line, Paperback Publisher's Egret Romance and Thrillers, and Fagbamigbe's Eagle Romances (which include local as well as foreign works). The explicit packaging of cultural content that such lines provide is reinforced with covers that either follow the Western model of having embracing lovers or show a woman (or, less often, a man) undergoing one of love's torments described in the novel.

My analysis of contemporary Nigerian romance novels is based on sixty-seven romances. Nigerian producers of romance novels picked up and perpetuated the Western model to a remarkable degree. The Nigerian romances appear in cheap paperback formats, and they often replicate the Western covers, with a picture of a handsome man and beautiful woman embracing. Many announce their genre status as members of lines like Sunshine Romance. Some authors, such as Bisi Abejo, adhere to the Western formula so closely that their novels are virtually indistinguishable from the English and American genre except for location and the nationality of the protagonists. These facts, combined with the continuing popularity of Western-authored romances in Nigeria, indicate that the nonindigenous formula finds a ready market among the readers of Lagos and Ibadan.

Some characteristics of the Nigerian romance readership may be inferred. As we have seen, Western romance readers tend to be middle-class, young, and relatively well-educated women. In general, Nigerian readers are similarly educated and affluent; they also tend to be southern, Christian, urban, and "modern" in their attitudes. Although there is no direct evidence on romance readers in particular, it seems probable that they are also disproportionately female, since male Nigerian readers have traditionally favored self-help books, technical guides, and other forms of nonfiction over fiction, and since there are a number of romance magazines, like *Happy Romance and Ladies Digest,* aimed at women. In contrast to the Western romance series, however, none of the Nigerian series announce themselves as explicitly catering to a female audience, and it seems plausible that the readership of these novels is not as overwhelmingly female as in the West. Nigerian romance readers may be somewhat younger than their Western counterparts, for not only is literacy higher among youthful cohorts in Nigeria, but Nigerian romances take place in university settings more often than do the Western novels.

There are forty-eight Nigerian authors who have written at least one romance. Women do not dominate as they do in the West. On the contrary, thirty-three men, as opposed to fifteen women, have written a romance. Several women—Bisi Abejo, Helen Ovbiagele, Nyengi Koin—have specialized in the genre, as have some men, including Jide Oguntoye and Ike Ajogu.[104] Most Nigerian romance writers, whether men or women, have written other types of fiction as well, so there is not the same degree of craft specialization as among Mills and Boon or Harlequin writers. Nigerian romance authors are writers first and romance writers second; they are professionals of one sort or another earning a living—as teachers, editors, civil servants—rather than housewives trying their hands at a familiar formula.

Now I shall consider the seven characteristics of the Western formula as they have been reproduced or reconstructed in Nigerian romances.

THEME

By definition, Nigerian romances included here concentrate on romance. Love between the protagonist and one or more members of the opposite sex is key to the plot, determining most of the action, and marriage—its occurrence or failure to occur—is always of crucial significance. While other themes may be prominent—rural development (*True Love*), Christian forgiveness (*To Forgive Is Divine*) or hypocrisy (*The Flesh Is Weak*), conflicts between love and career (*Evbu My Love; Lift to the Stars*), civil war and its aftermath (*Love in the Battle Storm; The Cyclist*), or overcoming tribalism (*All You Need Is Love*)—romantic relationships dominate and structure the plot.

Joined by Love is a straightforward example of a standard Nigerian romance.

Jovi, a history student at the University of Ibadan, is home at Ase for the yam festival when he meets Dezi. He falls in love with her at once, and he is asked to escort her to Ibadan, where she will stay with her Aunt Chi Williams while she studies nursing. In Ibadan Jovi courts her, but he senses she is concealing something. Before going to Scotland for several months' study, Jovi tries again to learn what is bothering Dezi; she won't say but does tell him how she was hurt by her mother, who left the family fifteen years earlier and has not been in touch since. While Jovi is in Glasgow, Dezi meets Dr. Rukewe, an old friend. Years ago they had pledged love to each other, but he had not taken it seriously and is now married. Relieved, she writes to tell Jovi she is truly free.

Jovi returns, they confirm their love, and both are busy preparing for exams. One day a letter arrives from Dora in Glasgow, who informs Jovi she is pregnant by him; he knows this is impossible. When he tells Dezi, she feels abandoned once again. A friend of Jovi's in Glasgow writes to say that Dora has admitted to having lied about being pregnant. Jovi runs to show the letter to Dezi, but on the way he gets hit by a car.

Meanwhile, Dezi's mother has been teaching in Sierra Leone for years after her husband turned her out and forbade her to contact the family (he was bewitched). She returns to Ase and learns her husband had died after revealing that she was blameless in their breakup. She goes to Ibadan, finds Dezi, and explains the truth, and they are happily reunited. They go to the hospital, where Dr. Rukewe has operated on Jovi successfully. In front of her mother, Jovi proposes and Dezi accepts.

(Joy Ikede, *Joined by Love*)

Here we see the Western formula—love at first sight, misunderstandings, obstacles, coincidences, a final clearing up of all problems, and a declaration of lasting love leading to marriage. Ikede and Koin follow the formula closely, and the novels of Bisi Abejo reproduce it almost exactly.

SETTING

Nigerian romances are much more urban than their Western counterparts, for over 90 percent take place in cities.[105] All of the romances center on Africa, usually in a specific Nigerian location. Little by way of exotic locales or international adventures, which are featured in some Western lines, appears in the Nigerian novels; May Ellen Ezekiel's *Dream-Maker* is exceptional in that much of the action takes place in Wisconsin, although the story begins and ends in Lagos. Nigerian romances are virtually all contemporary, with only five taking place before independence, and there are no counterparts to the Western adventure-packed historical romances (known as "bodice rippers") that offer love on the high seas or in the wilderness.

The urban, contemporary settings allow the authors to describe consumer products in great detail, with much emphasis on luxury and brand names. The elaborate depiction of Arabella's interior decoration in *The Inconvenient Marriage,* the discussions of hairdos, clothing, and makeup in Abejo's novels, and the attention given to automobiles, usually specifying the make and model: by providing such lavish descriptions, the authors are assuming that readers share the characters' middle-class tastes and that they can gauge people's social status through their possessions and style. Not much in the way of scenic description is offered. The Western convention of depicting the natural surroundings as reflecting and reinforcing the characters' emotions is largely absent.

POINT OF VIEW

Unlike Western romances, Nigerian romances do not necessarily present the woman's point of view. The protagonist—and in a formulaic romance there is never a point of view other than that of the protagonist—is a man almost half the time. As might be expected, the protagonist's sex usually matches the author's, although male authors are more willing to feature female protagonists than the reverse.[106] Now and then the point of view switches. Lawrence Onyiuke's *Please Never Leave Me,* which is unusually long at 659 pages (and is only the first volume!), centers on Pauline for over half the book, then changes to Chris's point of view, switching from third to first person at the same time.

CHARACTERIZATION

Nigerian heroines resemble their Western counterparts: attractive, spirited, brave, independent, cautious with men but passionate, and faithful unless betrayed. Debola (*Love on the Rebounce*) is representative. When her boyfriend Ife inexplicably drops her, she goes to study in London and puts together a new life without him, attracting the attentions of Tony in the process. After a series of misadventures she is finally reunited with Ife, but she has spent the intervening years busy with personal and intellectual development, not passively awaiting Ife's return. Similarly Evbu, neglected by Jidi after she has gone to Lagos to be near him, pursues a secretarial career, after first supporting herself by working as a bargirl. Yinka (*Fools Rush In*), who fears she has destroyed her chances with her second lover because of her earlier involvement with her first, resolves to throw herself into her computer science studies while proudly scorning both men. A few women depart from the stereotype in one respect or another—Hannah (*Too Cold for Comfort*) is independent but frigid; Sisi (*Sisi*) is painfully shy, although she ultimately asserts her independence in love; Angy (*To Forgive Is Divine*) and Bintu (*The Undesirable Element*) get seduced by wealthy older men before returning to their true loves—but none represent a total departure from the model. Heroines who are passive or timid by nature, or who are not attractive, or who are too blatantly seeking a man are not found in Nigerian romances any more than in Western ones.

Although the heroines tend to reproduce the Western model, the heroes generally do not. This is the case regardless of whether the hero is the protagonist or the protagonist's love interest. While some male protagonists are successful and steadfast, more often they are, quite literally, losers. Obi (*The Wages of Sin*) loses Ojiji to the fast life and, eventually, suicide. Odigo (*The Cyclist*) loses his wife to another husband when he is off fighting for Biafra during the civil war, and he dies trying to get her back. Chris (a semi-protagonist in *Please Never Leave Me*) despairs of Pauline's ever marrying him and disappears into Lagos, leaving her pregnant and alone. Men who are loved by the protagonist are similarly feckless, faithless, incompetent, or so faintly drawn that their characters are imperceptible. Neither Ife's nor Tony's motivations are explained in *Love on the Rebounce*; Tade's (*The Hopeful Lovers*) and Jide's (*Evbu My Love*) recurring infidelities seem to run counter to their own interests; Kolade's behavior (*Too Cold for Comfort*) toward his lower-class mistress is reprehensible, but he is never made to take responsibility for his deeds or even acknowledge his guilt; and the men in *You Never Know* and *Love in the Battle Storm*, Peter and Mr. Joel in *The Marriage of Two Lovers*, and Joe in *The Hopeful Lovers* are so sketchily described that the reader has little insight into their characters or motivations. As we have seen, even Tolu in *All You Need Is Love* loses his nerve temporarily and starts taking it out on Tokoni.

If not merely unsuccessful in love, the heroes are downright vicious. In *A Changed Man*, Uzoma, the spoiled chief's son, uses medicine to kill his beloved rather than see her marry another man. The husband of *The Flesh Is Weak* is browbeaten by his family into taking a second wife after infecting the heroine, his first wife, with a venereal disease that renders her sterile. Raphael (*The Marriage of Two Lovers*) is a hardened criminal trying to hide his past in a middle-class marriage. The stereotypical hero along Western lines, the man who is strong, successful, sure of himself, and fundamentally loving, occasionally appears, for example, in Abejo's three novels. Most of the male love interests in most Nigerian romances, however, are an unending source of problems for the heroine.

Like their Western peers, most protagonists of Nigerian romances are adults in their twenties or thirties. The authors usually do not emphasize the protagonist's ethnicity, which either is not mentioned or is not problematic, since the lovers are members of the ethnic majority for the region. In a few novels, including *All You Need Is Love*, *Please Never Leave Me*, and *A House Divided*, a difference in ethnic backgrounds constitutes an obstacle to love. In others like *Sisi* and *Lift to the Stars,* on the contrary, every-one makes a point of the fact that the lovers' different ethnicity should not be considered a problem. Religion comes up more often, but it does not constitute a barrier to love.

Class is more of a problem, as in *All You Need Is Love,* for even though Tokoni and her widowed mother are comfortably middle-class, the mother worries about not fitting in with Tolu's wealthier family. Here class and ethnicity are intertwined. Another combination is that of class and urban versus rural background.

> Mabel, a middle-class Lagos girl studying pharmacology at the University of Lagos, falls in love with Yahaya, a medical student who comes from a village in Oyo State. Agnes, her mother, is furious with her for wanting to marry a "bushman," with tribal scars on his face yet. Family members get involved and take sides, while Conrad, Mabel's father, tries to restore peace without much success. Finally, Agnes's sister is hurt in an accident, and the young intern who saves her life turns out to be Yahaya.
>
> Meanwhile, Yahaya's parents start pressuring him to marry a local girl; they are disgusted that, at twenty-eight, he is still in school and not producing off-spring (and are especially incensed when he suggests that two children would be sufficient). When he takes Mabel home to meet his parents, his mother goes berserk, having already promised the local girl her son would marry her.
>
> Mabel begins her year of National Youth Service and gets posted to Oyo State. After the local girl gets pregnant and thus is conveniently out of the picture, Yahaya's mother gets sick. Mabel gets her to the hospital and oversees her treatment, the mother relents, and in the last paragraph Yahaya puts an engagement ring on Mabel's finger.
>
> (Ola Omiyale, *Ring Finger*)

In Omiyale's romance we see class twice: first in Agnes's horror at having a "bushman" as son-in-law (never mind the fact that he's a doctor), and later when Yahaya's mother does indeed stress traditional village norms by urging her son to stop educating himself and start producing offspring.

Like Mabel, most protagonists are from financially comfortable, middle-class families. This is especially likely if the hero is a woman. Men exhibit more social variation, as in the Mabel and Yahaya pattern. Tunde is a poor-but-ambitious barrow pusher in Bode Osanyin's *Shattered Dreams,* Obrata is poor and without prospects when he gets caught up by a religious cult where he meets his true love in Ike Ajogu's *Victim of Love,* Tokoni is from an elite family in *All You Need Is Love;* indeed, half of the male protagonists do not have middle-class backgrounds. The women usually do. It is a common pattern, regardless of which is the protagonist, for the woman to be from a higher-class background than the man. In Ayo Okuyemi's *Love at Stake* there is a parallel to *Ring Finger,* only in this case the rural mama has her way:

Kehinde, a young nurse, falls in love with Tosin. He is a socially ambitious insurance agent from a traditional village family in Oyo State, and is now going to Britain for further studies. To satisfy his mother's desire for grandchildren, he talks Kehinde into getting pregnant before he leaves, although they are not yet married. Her parents, who are middle-class people from Ibadan, are appalled and reject Kehinde and her twin babies.

Kehinde remains faithful, supporting her children by studying midwifery. At first Tosin writes regularly, but soon he takes up with an English girl, Dora. They marry and have two children. When Tosin finally brings his new family back to Nigeria, they live in Lagos and he makes no effort to contact Kehinde. Eventually he loses his job and begins drinking heavily; finally Dora goes back to Britain with their children.

Having given up on Tosin, Kehinde is being courted by Dr. Olagbaju, much to the delight of her parents. Tosin, his life in ruins, finally returns to his village, only to learn that Kehinde is about to marry. He goes to Ibadan to confront her, but she tells him it's over and serves him with court orders for child support. He returns to his parents, who are mystified by modern ways; they think he should just be able to claim his twins (even though he has never seen them and now they're seven!). Meanwhile Kehinde and Dr. Olagbaju marry and go to America for their honeymoon.

(Ayo Okuyemi, Love at Stake)

You can take the boy out of the village, but you can't take the village out of the boy. Tosin is unable to retain his grasp on an urban middle-class style of life, while Kehinde is drawn back to it after years of estrangement. Parental influence comes from both sides in this romance, and the older generation's expectations are class based: middle-class daughters *do not* have illegitimate babies, farmers' sons *do* produce offspring as soon as possible and *do not* allow others to claim them. The reversion to class backgrounds is common.

As we see in *Love at Stake*, and as is true in the vast majority of Western romances, most Nigerian romances start with a protagonist who has never been married. Most end with the protagonist married or about to be, although here there is considerably more variation. While women authors are more inclined to adhere to the Western formula than men in this regard, a quarter of the books by women end with the heroine unmarried, separated, or widowed, as do two-fifths of the books by men.[107] Ending up alone is unheard of in Western romances, but for Nigerians "shattered dreams," the title of two romances, are not uncommon.

Sex works very differently in Nigerian romances than in Western ones, not in terms of the explicitness of description, but in terms of sex's ability to indicate character. In Western romances, sexual encounters are symbolically important: sex reveals the fundamental character of the beloved, which he or she has attempted to conceal (the hero believes the heroine is cold but finds her to be passionate; the heroine finds the proud and overbearing man to be a gentle, considerate lover); sex sets standards for differentiating among characters (the hero's or heroine's previous lovers have been cold or greedy and superficial); sex is a measure of the progress of the central relationship (the heroine does not want to surrender to the sexual demands of the hero, whether in the form of a kiss or full intercourse, until they have established a relationship with some degree of trust and mutual knowledge); and sex marks significant turning points in the plot (once the hero and heroine have felt a sexual attraction, whether or not this culminates in intercourse, they have no further sexual relations with any other characters).

In the Nigerian romances, on the other hand, sex is just as powerful and potentially dangerous, but it does not carry the same symbolic weight. The assumptions are that the man will usually want sex before the woman does; that some degree of physical intimacy is inevitable in any relationship; that men almost certainly and women possibly will be attracted to others despite their primary love interest and regardless of whether they act on this attraction (both husband and wife carry on flirtations in *The Inconvenient Marriage,* although neither gets sexually involved with another; in *The Hopeful Lovers,* Tade loves and is engaged to Roseline but feels little compunction about conducting two other affairs); and that if there should be an estrangement between the two lovers, one or both will become sexually involved with another person. Sex often constitutes one of the obstacles between lovers (Tade's infidelity, Bintu's affair with a wealthy man in *The Undesirable Element,* Evbu's brief career as a bargirl), but it does not serve as a token of anything beyond itself. For example, the problem caused by the infidelities of Tade and Ojiji is simply that of infidelity, not some flaw in their essential characters as revealed by their behavior. In contrast, Kolade is unfaithful, which causes his wife much pain, but he is understood by himself and finally by her as having been justified, and his behavior in no way bars their eventual reconciliation.

STRUCTURES

The Western romance invariably follows the continuing, changing relationship between one woman and one man, here called the *continual pattern.* Woman and man meet, they don't like each other, they are attracted, they resist, obstacles develop, they overcome the obstacles, they confess their love, and they fall into each other's arms. The focus is on this pair from the first chapter to the end.

Fewer than half of the sixty-seven Nigerian romances exhibit the Western structure, with the plot following the developing relationship between

TABLE 3-4
Relationship Structures and Endings in Romance Novels

| | Relationship Structure | | | |
	Continual	Circular	Sequential	Total
Author				
Male	12	14	11	37
Female	16	3	6	25
Unknown	1	1	3	5
Total	29	18	20	67

| | Ending | | | | |
	Happy-ever-after	Ambiguous	Ruptured	Other	Total
Author					
Male	20	1	15	1	37
Female	18	2	5	—	25
Unknown	4	—	1	—	5
Total	42	3	21	1	67

one man and one woman (Table 3-4). Bisi Abejo's *Lift to the Stars* exemplifies this pattern. In the first chapter a handsome stranger kisses an ambitious secretary while the two are stuck on an elevator. The stranger turns out to be the secretary's new boss, and after many chapters of attraction vying with hostility, the two end up happily married. *Joined by Love,* as we have seen, follows this conventional pattern as well, as does *All You Need Is Love.*

The other romances are evenly divided between two patterns of love relationships, the circular and the sequential. In the *circular pattern* the protagonist and his or her lover are together at the beginning and end, but during most of the novel they are separated or estranged, with one or both being involved in other love relationships. In *Love on the Rebounce,* for example, Debola breaks up with her boyfriend Ife for obscure reasons (he declares he will never be good enough for her) on page 14 of the eighty-four-page novel. The rest of the novel tells of her studies in England, her affair with a medical student named Tony, her pregnancy, near marriage, miscarriage, breakup with Tony, and her return to Lagos. Not until the second-to-last page is she reunited with Ife, a surprise arranged by her sister. Despite the fact that he, too, has been involved with another partner, Ife declares that the two-year separation has made him love Debola more than ever, and the two get engaged that evening. In *The Second Chance,* Richard and Minda marry at the outset but are separated for years because of pressures from her overbearing parents, finally to be brought back together by their daughters. In *The Undesirable Element,* Bintu has been pledged to Faruk as a child, but she becomes another man's mistress and must be rescued by Faruk, now a lawyer. The circular pattern strays from the Western convention in two main respects: it involves the protagonist in love or sexual relationships outside the primary romance, and it separates the lovers so that their verbal byplay and the nuances of their sexual attraction are offstage for much of the novel.

The rest of the romances follow the *sequential pattern,* in which a single protagonist has a series of love relationships. This pattern occurs twice as often for female protagonists, while the other two patterns are evenly divided between male and female.[108] In the simplest version of the sequential pattern, the heroine is initially involved with a man who turns out to be unsuitable—usually because he is fickle, a womanizer, and negligent of her needs—and she eventually finds a more compatible mate. We saw this pattern in *Love at Stake,* where Kehinde replaces the faithless Tosin with the steadier Dr. Olagbaju. This also is the pattern of *Fools Rush In, True Love, Evbu My Love,* and *The Hopeful Lovers* (although in this last work the heroine does not end up with the second man either). More complex plots involve a series of three romances (*The Marriage of Two Lovers*), the loss of a perfectly satisfactory first love (*Love in the Battle Storm*), or the gradual death of what once had been a good relationship (*You Never Know*).

As Table 3-4 indicates, women authors favor the continual pattern, using it 64 percent of the time. Men are fairly evenly divided, with only a third presenting the continual pattern, the one that follows the romantic moral fantasy of one true love. The sequential pattern is more like the modern individual's experience of a series of romantic attractions, one (or more) of which eventually lead to marriage. And the circular plot allows the author to have it both ways: the protagonist can be shown having several romantic/sexual relationships, but the plot returns to the one-true-love convention. Women authors either perpetuate the conventional fantasy or present a more realistic story, while men seem inclined to have it both ways with the circular plot.

PLOT

As in Western romances, Nigerian romance plots are structured by a series of problems and misunderstandings that obstruct the protagonist from achieving his or her potential for happiness in love. The obstacles may be real (Tade's infidelity in *The Hopeful Lovers;* parental opposition to an interethnic marriage in *A House Divided*) or imaginary (Dele's assumption that Yinka is promiscuous in *Fools Rush In*). The narrative action, specifically the continuation of a particular love relationship, depends on whether the obstacles can be overcome.

The plot of *Time Changes Yesterday* exemplifies the obstacles/resolutions pattern. In this novel there are two problems for the lovers, which are solved in sequence: first, Kofo's reluctance to let herself fall in love, and second, the opposition of her lover's daughter.

> Kofo is a teacher raising a six-year-old son and still mourning her fiancé, who had died in a car crash a week before their wedding. Enitan, one of her students, tries to act as matchmaker for Kofo with Tayo, her widowed father. Tayo is immediately interested in Kofo, but she is reluctant to fall in love with him, having avoided men for years. Eventually Kofo is won over by Tayo's kindness and her own attraction toward him. Both families, as well as the families of the dead wife and the fiancé, are delighted with the proposed marriage. Now the problem is Joy, Tayo's teenage daughter, who resents anyone trying to replace her mother. For some time Kofo refuses to marry Tayo because of his daughter's opposition until Joy, seeing that her father is miserable, finally relents and the marriage takes place. Joy remains hostile to her stepmother, however, and her cold treatment of Kofo prevents the new family from being fully happy. Kofo quickly gets pregnant. She proves herself to be an understanding mother when Joy herself has a pregnancy scare, which turns out to be false, and Joy finally comes to love and accept her.
>
> (Nyengi Koin, *Time Changes Yesterday*)

Such obstacles and their resolutions reveal one notable difference between Nigerian romances and their Western counterparts: the extent to which the protagonist's romantic career is dependent on his or her social context. In the West, novels treating love and the choice of a marriage partner as the fundamental narrative problem arose when marital choice shifted from families to individuals in the eighteenth century. Western romances continue to be highly individualistic. The romantic pair work through their problems based on the strengths and vulnerabilities of their individual characters. They operate within a social context but are by no means dependent on it.

Nigerian romances are similarly individualistic. Their heroines and heroes frequently stress that they will choose their own marriage partners rather than allow their kin to make the selections; this corresponds to actual changes in marital practices among the more modernized, educated, and urban sectors of the society.[109] But sometimes the demands of their relatives overcome their desire to follow their hearts. And even when they do, in striking contrast to the Western novels, the Nigerian heroes and heroines are often unable to overcome the obstacles to their happiness without the intervention of a helper or facilitator. Sometimes, of course, the social context itself causes problems for the lovers; *A House Divided* is one clear case, and parental opposition strains the love relationship in many romances. Nevertheless, most of the romances emphasize that social differences of religion, class, ethnicity, or geographic background are unimportant; *Rich Girl, Poor Boy* exemplifies the triumph of love over parental snobbishness. The stories are constructed in such a way that the individual should—and usually does—resist family pressures of this sort; if not, "the flesh is weak."

But if the individuals can create their own problems, they cannot always create their own solutions. In most of the novels that end with the couple together, a friend or relative plays a key role in reconciling the lovers. In Abejo's very Westernized fiction, Yinka's friend Tunde is the "fool" who rushes in to put the lovers back on course when their pride has kept them apart and miserable. Aunt Chi provides moral and material support to the lovers of *Joined by Love*. Binda and Miatta get their parents back together in *The Second Chance*, just as Enitan brings about the marriage of her father and Kofo in *Time Changes Yesterday*; Hannah's mother straightens her out regarding her sexual responsibility to her husband in *Too Cold for Comfort*; Yetunde's daughter gets her to follow her heart in *You Never Know*; Debola's sister brings the long separated lovers together in *Love on the Rebounce*; Obi's friend Jimmy, who had earlier given him the helpful but unheeded advice to avoid involvement with Ojiji, arranges a temporary reconciliation between the two lovers in *The Wages of Sin*; Moses' father and his wives, won over by Arabella, encourage him to solve his marital problems in *The Inconvenient Marriage*.

The significance of helpers is underlined by the importance of same-sex relationships in these stories. Love between members of the same sex—for example, friends, sisters (never brothers), aunts—plays a significant role in seven out of ten Nigerian romances.[110] The same-sex bond and the helper role are usually female.

Explicit conflicts between traditional and modern ideas or practices—conflicts that the authors label as such—constitute a major obstacle in over half thirty-six of the Nigerian romances. Neither the sex of the author nor that of the protagonist influences the representation of this traditional-modern conflict. Strikingly, in no instance is the conflict resolved on the side of the traditional. Either the modern view prevails or the conflict is not resolved and leads to tragedy. The other half of the novels are strictly modern, with modernity as such not an issue.

As one would expect given the previous discussion of the women-and-men novels, a common source of problems that Nigerian romance protagonists have to resolve, one with no counterpart in Western romances, is fertility. Nigerian protagonists usually have no children at the story's beginning, and more often than not they have become parents by the end. Strikingly, in close to half of the novels fertility issues of one type or another constitute a serious problem for the protagonist.[111] The most common type of problem is where the woman partner in a relationship is unable to conceive children, to bear a son, or to raise children who survive infancy. A variety of other fertility-related problems occur, including false pregnancy claims (e.g., *Joined by Love*), in-laws who criticize a modern mother's desire to limit fertility (e.g., *Broken Promises*), illegitimate pregnancies (*Sisi; Time Changes Yesterday; The Undesirable Element*), hidden pregnancies (*Please Never Leave Me*), and pregnancies in relationships where one of the lovers dies (*Silhouette*).

A formulaic romance about how true love overcomes class barriers, *Rich Girl, Poor Boy* illustrates how fertility issues impinge on romantic fortunes.

> As a child, rich girl Tokumba befriends a poor boy named Lai, earning the disapproval of her family, especially her paternal grandmother. When she grows up and attends the university, Tokumba again meets Lai, now involved in radical student politics, and they fall in love.
>
> Tokumba becomes pregnant. Lai's family had promised Lai to Adeota years earlier, but he drops her for Tokumba; the grief-stricken Adeota, also pregnant, had a miscarriage. Tokumba's family continues to oppose the match, so Lai and Tokumba secretly marry and set up house in a poor area.
>
> Lai leads a student demonstration. At home, Tokumba is attacked by Adeota, who tells her that her father was actually a poor orphan adopted by her barren grandmother. Seriously injured, Tokumba loses her baby and undergoes a hysterectomy. Lai and Tokumba's family, now reconciled, keep this a secret from Tokumba; recovering in the hospital, she assures Lai she will soon be pregnant again. As he comforts her, police come to question him about a demonstration; he promises her he will soon be back, and that he loves her.
>
> (Bode Osanyin, *Rich Girl, Poor Boy*)

As this summary shows, issues related to fertility appear repeatedly in the plot of this romance—two pregnancies, two miscarriages, infertility in the past, hysterectomy in the present, an illusion of future pregnancy—each time constituting a potential barrier to the couple's happiness.

ENDING

Just as Western romances end with the hero and heroine in each other's arms, planning their future together, over half of the Nigerian romances have such happy-ever-after endings (see Table 3-4). The close of *True Love*, for example, could have come straight out of any Western romance:

> As she reached the car, a beloved figure got out and, seeing her flying towards him, held out his arms in welcome. She flew to them as a bird flies into its nest.

> ... Once more she heard Koye's voice whispering those words that she thought she must have dreamt, all those weeks ago, "Oh my darling, my darling." But this time his voice was vibrant with happiness, and then their two souls met at last, in a kiss of perfect love. (140–41)

But things don't always work out so well for the Nigerian lovers. *Rich Girl, Poor Boy* ends with a husband in the hands of the police and a lie—the secret of Tokumba's hysterectomy—at the heart of the marriage. *The Cyclist* ends with Odigo dead and his beloved Celina driven mad. Chuma is murdered on the morning of his wedding in *A House Divided*. In *The Hopeful Lovers*, not only does Roseline's first love prove unworthy of her, but also her second suitor is ultimately repelled by her newfound religious fanaticism. *Broken Promises* ends with the couple's twenty-year marriage in ruins. *Shattered Dreams* and *A Changed Man* both conclude with the man's weakness resulting in the death of his lover. In *Love in the Battle Storm,* one of Ifeoma's sweethearts disappears at the front and a second is killed, leaving her a single mother in a land devastated by war. In *The Wages of Sin*, Ojiji commits suicide without ever reconciling with Obi. A surprising twist on the Western formula comes at the end of *You Never Know*: as the two lovers embrace, the man is planning their future together while the woman is silently vowing to hang on to her independence. And while other novels do have the happily-ever-after endings, the heroine is often not paired with her initial lover (the sequential pattern) and in a few cases (Steve in *Evbu My Love* and Mr. Joel in *The Marriage of Two Lovers*) the man whom the heroine will ultimately marry enters the novel very late as a deus ex machina.

These atypical endings are of two sorts: the ambiguous, where the protagonist is left facing an unknown romantic future, and the ruptured, where the principal or final love relationship is ended by death or permanent estrangement. Ruptured endings are associated with, though not restricted to, male protagonists, and on the whole female authors favor happy-ever-after endings.[112]

A Final Observation

Lolade, daughter of a wealthy businessman, is a hardworking university student. She has a boyfriend whom her family likes, but he's a playboy who treats her with little respect. She begins taking guitar lessons from a blind accounting student, Leke, and soon they fall in love. She admires how he copes with his disability, and his efforts to rise from a humble background. Needless to say, her parents oppose the match because of Leke's class and his disability. Lolade gets support from her medical student brother, but their parents are determined to break up the lovers.

Events come to a climax when Lolade gets pregnant. They had planned to wait before marrying, but now Leke goes to Lolade's parents to ask for their blessing. They agree, but only if he goes to Europe for an operation to restore his sight. Lolade opposes her parents' interference, but Leke is willing if following their wishes will bring peace. During the surgery, he has a reaction to the anesthetic and dies. Lolade vows to be strong for the baby's sake.

(Bunmi Oyinsan, *Silhouette*)

Lolade, even more than her blind lover, is totally modern in this ruptured romance, for she is willing to ignore parental objections to her lover and does not want to go along with her parents' last-ditch demands. In the women-and-men novels, and in the romances, it is typical for the man to be most influenced by family and other traditional pressures and obligations, and for the woman to be most willing to cast them aside, perhaps because they hold greater advantages for him than for her.

"The modern individual was first and foremost a woman."[113] In her influential study of gender politics and the novel, Nancy Armstrong argues that through the eighteenth- and nineteenth-century novel, the assessment of a person's worth based on an intricate, kinship-based status system gave way to an assessment based on individual subjectivity, qualities of mind and personality. This change took place first of all for women, through the cultural project that created the domestic woman as the desirable ideal, but by the mid–nineteenth century men also had come to be so evaluated.

While the replacement of kinship and traditional forms of status by individualism has not taken place in Nigeria to the degree that it had in Britain by the end of the eighteenth century, two things are clear. First, the bundle of social changes that constitute modernization impinge with particular urgency on women—simply put, their lives change more drastically than do those of men, if they change at all—and these changes have to do with a release from the obligations of a kinship-status form of stratification. Second, such changes are both encouraged and represented through the quintessentially modern genre, the novel.

The big themes of the women-and-men novels—fertility, polygamy, women's financial independence, the possibility of individual romantic love in a social order organized around kinship obligations—are the big themes of Nigerian gender politics. These issues even intrude upon the formulaic romance. By and large, male characters are lined up with the sex roles of patriarchal convention, while women navigate the uncharted waters of more egalitarian gender relations. This may be why the male characters in romances are so feckless: they represent a fairly predictable set of problems for women, rather than being full-drawn individuals. In the Nigerian women-and-men novel, men are in the harbor, while women are at sea.

PEN AND SWORD

An orphan boy tells how an eccentric teacher comes to the village and turns life upside down. Didi arrives one day loaded with books, sets himself up in an isolated area, and begins teaching at the local university. He fascinates everyone with his odd ways (e.g., he's a vegetarian), his learning, and his kindness. Soon he has befriended the lonely young narrator, as well as a girl servant named Nkechi, a crippled outcast named Oputa, and a flock of students. But he also makes enemies of the local chiefs. One chief lusts after Nkechi; another is trying to force his rebellious daughter to marry; Didi supports the defiance of both. He also saves a starving old woman after she is treated cruelly by a chief's wife. The local elite, invested in the status quo, feels threatened by the new ways Didi brings to the community.

Despite his saintly behavior, Didi has a violent past. He had been imprisoned in England for ten years for having killed six men in an outburst of rage. This episode is never clearly explained, although Didi calls it his "redemption," suggesting a rediscovery of individual or racial pride.

The chiefs attack Didi repeatedly. He is fired from the university. His students are threatened. When these acts don't drive him away, his house is torched. Didi is inside, and Oputa crawls in and saves him, though he pays with his life. Terribly burned, Didi gives the narrator a manuscript that describes what happened in England. He finds a sponsor to pay for the boy's education, allowing him to realize his dream of becoming a writer. Nkechi turns to prostitution to escape marrying the old chief; she, too, has found some kind of freedom through Didi's inspiration. After Didi dies, the narrator vows to write a book about him.

(Obi Egbuna, *The Madness of Didi*)

Obi Egbuna's 1980 novel has many loose ends. Didi's experience in England is never clear. Nkechi's love for him is left dangling—on his deathbed Didi pays little attention to her—as is her future. The book is overwritten and longer than necessary. Egbuna comes off as an imaginative writer but not a very disciplined one. Yet in spite of its shortcomings, the novel captures the essential opposition between intellectuals and the socially powerful. This opposition structures a group of Nigerian books that I am calling the intellectual novels. Even more fundamentally, it structures the way Nigerian intellectuals think of themselves as social actors.

Nigerian critic Adewale Maja-Pearce claims that Nigerian novels as a whole "are less interesting as literature than as a record of the *dilemma* of the Nigerian intellectual in the modern world."[114] Maja-Pearce takes a dim view of most of these novels, and his acerbic opinions are controversial, but his sense of Nigerian fiction as centering on the dilemmas of intellectuals may be more on target than he realizes. A literary critic deals only with novels aspiring to some literary value, aspirations that, according to Maja-Pearce, are largely not met (his favorite adjective seems to be *disastrous*). In a country like Nigeria, where only thin slivers of the population read fiction, attend universities, or write anything, however, Nigerian writers and readers—those whom I have called the reading class—can all be regarded as intellectuals. And in their writing and their reading, they represent and enact their fundamental dilemma.

People identify intellectuals either by what they have or by what they do. What they *have* may be a position—on a faculty or in the media, for example—but more typically what they have is education. The key credential that separates "intellectuals" from everyone else is a certain level of schooling. The level itself varies—the Chinese apply the term *zhishifensi* (intellectuals) to all those having any postsecondary education at all, while Americans usually reserve the term for those possessing a Ph.D.—but all societies recognize certain people as being more highly educated than the norm and, hence, different.[115] In West Africa, attendance at a university qualifies one to be considered an intellectual, even if one fails to complete a degree, and such people have particular glamour if their post-secondary education has taken place in Europe or America.[116]

What intellectuals *do*, the second defining characteristic, is work with ideas, manipulating and disseminating them via words or images. Not just any ideas, however, for there is an implication of modernity in the way most people use the term. In Nigeria a magician, however wise, is not seen as being an intellectual, while a young freelance journalist, however foolish, is. The distinction refers to the specialization and rationalization that are associated with modern, as opposed to traditional, forms of knowledge.

Thus to be an intellectual in the strict sense of the term implies some combination of credential, institutional affiliation, and rationalized practice. A particular individual may not meet all these criteria. A prominent poet may lack formal education, and a tenured professor may lack new ideas, yet both would be considered intellectuals. The category as a whole possesses some scholarly credentials, is associated with institutions of communication or pedagogy, and engages in activities involving the accumulation, expansion, and dissemination of knowledge and ideas. To be an intellectual is to be a particular social type, and in Nigeria that type has had a significant, though possibly oppositional, encounter with foreign learning.[117]

Nigerian novelists are intellectuals whether one applies the broader or narrower definition of the term. As described in Chapter 2, in Nigeria only about 3 percent of young adults go on past secondary education, yet over 71 percent of novelists have completed a university degree, and almost half have done graduate work. Over half work in education, the media, or one of the professions. Moreover, they are public intellectuals, aspiring to public influence, convinced that they have a responsibility to bear witness to social problems.

The entire Nigerian reading class can be considered intellectuals, in that they are far more educated than average and they do something—read novels—that is highly unusual. Only about a fifth of Nigeria's youth attend secondary school. Of those who attend, not all graduate. And of those who graduate, fewer than 30 percent can pass the English portion of the West African School Certificate exam or similar exams.[118] We must assume that regular fiction readers, even those who read only the formulaic love-and-crime novels, must have at least this degree of competence, so we can see that the reading class draws from only 6 percent of the population. In such a context, their practice makes them intellectuals.

This section examines how Nigerian writers depict the place intellectuals occupy in contemporary Nigeria. It looks at their lives and their writing about their lives, particularly those novels involving artists, university life, or other intellectual milieus. It will concentrate on three themes—intellectuals and their callings; the culture of disappointment; and the response of intellectuals to the Nigerian civil war—all of which have been sources of acute frustration for Nigerian writers. This section will explore the literary representation of this frustration.

The Intellectual Novel: Structure

Okolo, recently out of school ("too much book," say the people in Amatu), is searching for meaning, which he refers to as *it*, and Chief Izongo, profiting from the changing times, wants him to stop. Okolo finds shelter with Tuere, known as a witch, telling her that in these rootless times, "I am the voice from the locked-up insides." The chief and Abadi, his educated second in command, order Okolo to leave Amatu. When a friend warns Okolo that "this thing you are doing is too heavy for you," Okolo declares: "Our fathers' insides always contained things straight. Our insides were also clean and we did the straight things until the new time came. We can still sweep the dirt out of our houses every morning." Tuere says that Okolo constitutes a threat to the chief because he has been to school.

Okolo takes the canoe to the city of Sologa (i.e., Lagos). During a storm, he shelters a sleeping girl; later her fiancé's mother accuses him of molesting her. Passengers argue over what really happened. Meanwhile, back in Amatu, Izongo and his cronies decide that Okolo will never be allowed to return. Her crippled assistant, Ukule, reports this to Tuere, who declares that he will return because his umbilical cord is buried there.

In Sologa a mysterious voice warns Okolo not to try to get to the bottom of things and leads him to a room full of human bones. Okolo tells a constable, who informs him that a Big One, whom the law protects, owns the house.

A restaurant owner feeds him and urges that he end his search; a white man says he's crazy; and Okolo is tempted to follow the no-nothing/care-nothing path. But, persisting in his search for meaning, Okolo decides to go back to Amuta to speak to the people themselves. Meanwhile, the relatives of the girl on the canoe hold a hearing on whether Okolo touched her. Okolo swears his innocence, but the groom's mother is skeptical, and he is warned that he will be sent to a madhouse if he ever comes back to the city.

Two Amuta men discussing Okolo begin to suspect Izongo's money is evil. Hearing this, Tuere thinks Okolo's words may have taken root. The elders meet and, after praising themselves, plan a celebration of the town's release from Okolo's influence. Heading home, Okolo muses how every life must have a purpose; he vows to keep his purpose clean "as a virgin sheet of white paper."

He gets back to Amatu on the day of the celebration and tells Tuere and Ukule he wants to face the people. When he asks the elders if they know *it*, the celebration falls apart. In a council meeting Abadi, who is beginning to have doubts about the whole matter, urges restraint, but a rival encourages Izongo to carry out his threatened punishment. Tuere vows to go with Okolo, and she asks Ukule to "tell our story and tend our spoken words." The next day a canoe carrying Okolo and Tuere, bound to the seats, drifts down the river and is swallowed up in a whirlpool.

(Gabriel Okara, *The Voice*)

There is a strong resemblance between Okara's novel *The Voice* (1964) and *The Madness of Didi*, published sixteen years and a civil war and oil boom later. Another intellectual fighting the powerful, another defeat, another outcast left to tell the tale. This pattern appears over and over in the intellectual novels.

Actually, there are three types of novels about intellectuals: novels depicting the conflict between intellectuals and the powers, such as *The Voice* or *The Madness of Didi*, satires on academic life; and popular love or crime novels that take place in universities or schools. These types have different impacts on their readers—the first is largely tragic, the second usually comic, and the third may be either—and are aimed at somewhat different readerships as well.

At the same time, the three types of intellectual-life novels share a number of features. Teachers, professors, artists, and other intellectuals are both respected for their learning and despised for their impotence. People associated with academic institutions are often pompous, competitive, small-minded, and sexually rapacious, while those portrayed as independent intellectuals—often the protagonists—are more sympathetic. A standard figure is the lone intellectual or artist fighting against his or her social context, which is characterized by corrupt institutions and venal people in power, by heeding "the voice" or orienting himself according to "the landscapes within."[119] Students must compete for the favor of their teachers and mentors, and they often are exploited. Whether they maintain their integrity or are corrupt, intellectuals aspire to change the system—organizational, political, or social—but rarely succeed.

The following structure applies most clearly to the first of the three types, the intellectuals-versus-the-powers novels, but elements from it shape some of the satires and popular works as well.

1. *The disturbing intellectual:* An intellectual comes to oppose, or at least unsettle, the socially powerful. The intellectual is honest, kind, and ineffectual, while the powerful are corrupt, sexually predatory, vindictive, and effective. Didi comes from England. Okolo returns from school. In another aptly titled work, the intellectual is the man who comes "from the back of beyond."

2. *The intellectual versus the powerful:* The intellectual and the powerful oppose each other. Usually their struggle is over a principle or a woman, often both. Even though his house is set well apart from the village and he minds his own business, Didi upsets the status quo by his very presence. His kindness draws the weak and the lonely, and he can not help but cast the cruel, selfish chiefs and their wives in an unfavorable light. Thus his existence constitutes a threat to their power. Similarly, the elders recognize that Okolo, with his "too much book," means trouble even before he starts searching for *it.*

3. *Skirmishes and standoff:* There are a series of skirmishes between the opposing forces, with neither side gaining the upper hand. The chiefs try to drive Didi out, while his ragtag band of supporters tries to protect him. In the case of Okolo, the elders actually succeed, temporarily, in getting him out of town.

4. *Precipitating action:* The intellectual makes some decision or takes some action that will put him at the mercy of his enemies. In Didi's case it is his unwillingness to abandon his house even after he has been fired and his continued support of Nkechi and of the radical students that provokes the chiefs to the ultimate act of violence, burning his house with him in it. For Okolo it is his insistence on returning to Amuta that leads to the climax.

5. *Death of the intellectual:* The intellectual is killed or utterly defeated by the powerful. He may or may not have been successful in defending the woman or principle at stake. Didi has successfully saved the narrator and has made it possible for the wretched Oputa to die a hero; the radical students will probably make it as well, but Nkechi's fate is more uncertain. As for Okolo, he may indeed have planted a seed—the messen-

gers, Abadi, Ukule all seem ready to question the powers that have killed him—but it is not clear whether anything will change.

6. *The witness:* Someone, a bystander or a minor participant in the action of the novel, remains to tell the story. Works like *Didi* and *The Voice* put the "bearing witness" theme very directly: the intellectual may die, but his story will be told, and as long as this happens he has not been totally defeated.

I have used masculine pronouns in the preceding discussion, and for good reason. Intellectual novels are extraordinarily masculine. Only two books in this genre are by women. The intellectual-in-society appears to be a problem men are thinking about far more than women. Of the forty intellectual novels, only six have female protagonists. Two of these are university-girl-goes bad, and one, Ike's *The Chicken Chasers*, is a satire of academic politics where the protagonist, "Baby Face," is an older version of university-girl-goes-bad. In the other three the heroine herself is an intellectual: a writer (Ike's *To My Husband from Iowa*), a university graduate in French doing youth service and headed for a career in public administration (Bamisaiye's *Service to the Fatherland*), and a bad-girl-turned-social-worker-and-writer (Jidenma's *Kasie*). Kasie is especially interesting because we see some of the struggles with sexual predators that also occur in the women-and-men novels.

> The story opens when Kasie, formerly a brilliant student, is moping back at her family's village home, considering suicide because she has failed her law exams at the university. Her sister, boyfriend Ikenna, and friends make great efforts to cheer her up, and eventually they succeed. It is revealed that her failure is due to the wicked Professor Imo, who had tried to seduce her when she first came to the university and now is having his revenge for her rejection. Her own uncle, Dr. Uche, is another professor who spreads rumors about Kasie's promiscuous behavior, but her immediate family refuses to believe him.
>
> Once she has decided to go on living, Kasie chooses to follow her altruistic bent and study social work at a different university. She does so successfully. Later she learns that Dr. Uche has been fired for trying to fail Ikenna. Kasie and Ikenna marry, and the novel ends with their honeymoon, as Kasie thinks of writing a book about her experiences. An epilogue says she has won the Nobel Prize for literature and justice.
>
> (Iji Jidenma, *Kasie*)

This is a lightweight effort and another case of young people against the odds, but the emphasis is on Kasie's desire for education, not on her love life. Her deviation is being brilliant as well as beautiful, the powerful are the university professors, and she is stymied but with the help of family and friends is able to pursue her degree through other means. Here the intellectual does not die, she gets married—and wins the Nobel Prize to boot. Most intellectuals don't end up so well.

Models from the first generation of authors have been influential for a number of genres. The earlier discussion of the village novels emphasized how Achebe's *Things Fall Apart* set the pattern for subsequent writers. The same thing may have happened with Wole Soyinka's novel *The Interpreters* (1965), a complex portrait of a set of intellectuals, all of whom have studied abroad, several years after independence.

The "interpreters" include Egbo, a foreign service officer, ambivalent about his heritage in the ruling lineage of a creek-dwelling tribe; Sagoe, a journalist; Kola, an artist who is painting a pantheon in which people he knows are portrayed as traditional gods; and Sekoni, a sculptor and engineer who goes mad when his project for generating cheap electricity is squelched by the politicians and who is reduced to stammering mysticism. Surrounding this group are memorable characters like Faseyi, the sycophant lecturer who frets over the behavior of his English wife, Monica; Joe Golder, a homosexual American, one-quarter Negro and desperately seeking African roots; and the outspoken Mama Faseyi, who (atypically) defends her daughter-in-law.

The story moves between Lagos and Ibadan, just as it moves between farce and tragedy. Part 1 begins in a Lagos nightclub, where the group drinks in the rain as Egbo contemplates his "apostasy" toward his heritage. Later, at a reception, Kola is an embarrassed witness to Faseyi's mortification at Monica not wearing gloves. Scenes between the intellectuals and their women reveal both their desires and their limits: Egbo's sexual initiation with the prostitute Simi; Sagoe telling his girlfriend how he got his newspaper job in return for keeping a secret about a Big Man; Egbo meeting a mysterious student and making love by the river. At a funeral Sagoe sees a young thief saved from lynching by Lazarus, an albino preacher. Later he comes to Ibadan from Lagos and goes to a stultifying academic party where Monica again disgraces her husband.

In Part 2 Sekoni, still disoriented, dies in an accident. All mourn his wasted talents as they plan an exhibit of his sculpture. Sagoe develops his philosophy of "voidancy" (everything is shit), as relationships and understandings start to come unglued. The group visits Lazarus's church in the swamp, where Noah is baptized and worshiped, but imprisoned as well. Kola is now hopelessly in love with Monica. Simi comes looking for Egbo, having learned about the student-lover. Noah flees from Lazarus in the swamp, and later they hear he has died falling from Joe Golder's window when Joe made a pass at him. The last scene is at the exhibit of Sekoni's sculpture and Kola's pantheon; Joe Golder sings a requiem for Sekoni, as the academics gossip.

(Wole Soyinka, *The Interpreters*)

Here Sekoni is the disturbing intellectual who is crushed—first mentally and then physically—by the powers that be, with hapless Joe Golder the unlikely witness and praise singer. Golder's marginality is national, racial, and sexual, thereby offering a caricature of the marginality that all the intellectual-interpreters share. In the early 1960s, when he wrote *The Interpreters*, Soyinka seemed to think that Nigeria's challenge would be to develop an educated vanguard free from the vacuity, anomie, and ineffectuality that had characterized West African intellectuals of the late colonial period. With hindsight, one can see how drastically he underestimated the corrosive effects of tribalism, militarism, and sheer greed; *The Interpreters* is a view from the academy, and it has something of an ivory-tower naïveté about power. (After being imprisoned during the civil war and being forced into exile under the Abacha regime, Soyinka no doubt lost whatever naïveté he may have had.) Nevertheless, Soyinka's novel established the standard portrait of the intellectual who, despite being lost, foolish, and destroyed, still serves to record the social dislocations of his time. This has been the fundamental story told about, and by, Nigerian intellectuals ever since.

One characteristic of the intellectual novel is that the protagonist is called to his (or, very rarely, her) vocation. He cannot help but be a writer, artist, or freethinker. Therefore, when he comes into a new social context, many of his problems arise from his inability to adapt to whatever system of social power is in place. Didi could not help but try to save Nkechi, lift up the spirits of Oputa and the narrator, assist the old woman, just as he could not help but cart his library around with him. Kola can not help but paint, Sagoe can not help but write, Sekoni can not help but try to engineer solutions to everyday problems. All such compulsions are socially disruptive, for they bear witness to the way things are, thereby making strange and noticeable that which otherwise would be taken as inevitable.

As presented in such novels, the calling to the intellectual life can come to anyone. Labo Yari's *Man of the Moment* (1992) combines the village-boy-comes-to-Lagos theme with that of the undeniable vocation, in this case toward being a writer.

Amadu is an aspiring poet who comes from a family of leatherworkers. After an expatriate high school teacher strongly encourages his interest in literature, Amadu leaves his village and comes to Lagos to pursue a literary career. Like many young migrants, he meets discouragement at every turn. Unable to earn anything from his writing, he stays with a series of friends, for he cannot afford his own housing.

He meets a woman, Anyanwu, with whom he lives for a time. Amadu and Anyanwu have endless conversations about literature versus art, all of which are lavishly sprinkled with names of European (and a few African) artists and intellectuals.

Finally, when neither the relationship nor Amadu's career seems to be going anywhere, Anyanwu leaves Amadu, thereby forcing him to move in with yet another friend. Shaken by his loss, Amadu vows to turn his life around—it's not clear how—and to cease worrying about success, reputation, or material comforts. Suddenly, out of the blue, he gets a letter from a publisher accepting his latest manuscript, *Ode on a Traffic Jam*. Crowning his triumph, he hears from Anyanwu, who says she is coming back to him.

(Labo Yari, *Man of the Moment*)

Yari's Künstlerroman is not much of a novel. Its episodes are melodramatic and unconnected, the ending a deus ex machina, and the long, artsy conversations sound like undergraduate name-dropping. Be that as it may, *Man of the Moment* reveals a number of assumptions about intellectuals that are more obscured, although still present, in more skillfully written novels.

First, Amadu feels a calling to be a writer. He is coming to Lagos not in search of just any opportunity but in search of a specific career as a man of letters. He cannot be content with a future as a leatherworker, any more than Egbo could have simply carried on his elite family's traditions. Being an intellectual seems to be something of a compulsion, if not a curse.

Second, Yari presents a highly individualistic view of artistic achievement. For example, Anyanwu assures Amadu that his poetry will survive him if only he can get it published, but "great artists must suffer rejection of their works at the beginning" (81). One of his later poems is called "Epic of Transcendental Ego," suggesting the romantic image of individual art rising above its social context.

The social context of the would-be writer is far from insignificant, however. Amadu's unpublished early works include "Epic of Peasant Life," "Epic of Go-Slow," and "Epic of Noise," all written when he first comes to Lagos. So the third point is that despite their individualistic conception of the writer, Amadu and Anyanwu are both bearing witness to collective experience, particularly that of the change from rural to urban life. At one point, when they are discussing Descartes (spelled "Desecrate") and his "I think therefore I am" philosophy, Anyanwu argues that people in Lagos must not be living because "in Lagos the only way you can survive is to live without thinking" (48). Later she talks about the anxiety felt not by ordinary Nigerians but by "so-called modern Nigerians . . . especially the Lagos motorists" (54). Amadu represents this anxiety; he thinks about what he is experiencing, responds to it emotionally, and writes.

He writes, he can not help but write, but is he a writer? When conducting oral interviews with Nigerian authors, I often posed questions using a phrase like, "How does a writer like yourself see . . ." or "As a writer, what do you think your responsibilities are toward . . ." Many interviewees corrected me with a flat statement: "I am not a writer." At first I was puzzled

by this response, which was unnerving given that I was interviewing subjects for a book on Nigerian writers. After I had encountered it several
times, I began to probe a bit to determine what they meant. The authors
would explain that they were not "really" writers because writing did not
generate a sufficient income; "real" writers, in their view, were people like
Frederick Forsyth (the author most frequently mentioned), who could earn
a living by writing alone. Nigerian novelists had the impression that most
Western writers were able to write for a living, while for them this was impossible.

While the former belief is unfounded, the latter is certainly true. Only a
handful of novelists—Achebe, Soyinka, Emecheta, Okri—earn their livings
from their literary activities. Two other implications of this response are
notable. The first is the novelists' inflated sense of the prosperity of Western writers, whom they assume are living, and living well, off of their royalties. The truth is quite different, of course, but Nigerian authors measure
themselves by this image of the man of letters supporting himself by his
pen. The second implication is the linking of the term *writer* not to the intellectual's "calling" but to his moneymaking capacity. This is a partial reverse of the Western pattern, where the "vocation" of writer is something
sensed, often at an early age and independent of actual production; "unpublished" or obscure writers may be the object of amusement, but they
are still considered to be writers, especially by themselves.[120]

Not so in Nigeria. There is considerable public skepticism about who can
claim to be a writer, and the writers themselves seem to have the strongest
doubts. At the same time, Nigerians believe in a writer's, artist's, or intellectual's calling. Thus, there exists a self-defeating system of thought where
people are compelled to do something that, by definition, most will not
succeed at doing. Amadu cannot help but be a writer, yet he will never be
a writer according to the Frederick Forsyth standard.

It may be that the impossible standard itself has given rise to a clutch of
academic satires. Best known is Chukwuemeka Ike, himself a high-level educational administrator for many years, whose early novels like *The Naked
Gods* and *The Chicken Chasers* poked fun at professorial rivalry, self-important lecturers, meddling foreigners, and the rarefied bitchiness of university gossip. Later Ike was to take a more serious turn, although without
ever losing his satirical touch. In *The Bottled Leopard,* he describes comic
scenes of schoolboy life in the 1940s while narrating the dilemma of
Amobi, a brilliant student at the elite British Government College who discovers he has the powers of a leopard-man and can inhabit a leopard's body
(the leopard spirit runs in the family). Amobi recognizes that this would
be unacceptable to his colonial schoolmasters, so he decides to keep these
two parts of his life strictly separate, like the Africans who use chewing
sticks at home but toothbrushes when they are around Englishmen. Some-

day he will pursue the mysteries of African science, but for the time being Amobi will keep his leopard bottled up tight.

Sometimes the line between academic satire and political satire is blurred, as in *Kolera Kolej,* by playwright Femi Osofisan. When a cholera epidemic strikes a prominent university, the prime minister convenes his cabinet, drawing it away from such duties as inspecting brothels or securing some of the nation's wealth in Switzerland. The ministers propose various steps—the education minister thinks the epidemic can best be fought by restoring Latin to the curriculum—but finally decide to get rid of the problem by granting the university total independence. So Kolera Kolej becomes its own nation, dedicated, in the words of the vice-chancellor, to "fat, felicity, and fecundity." With the stakes higher, academic infighting transforms into coups and assassinations, and the ending is far from comic. The hand of the satirist is still evident, however, as when the vice-chancellor unwittingly avoids assassination by refusing to see his would-be killers because they don't have an appointment, or when he sets up a committee, chaired by his brother-in-law, to purge the new nation of nepotism.

Satires of intellectual life oscillate between the strictly entertaining and the more serious. Popular fiction, while far from profound, has captured some of the same themes. For example, two slight novels deal with the contention between tradition and modernity, drawing the opposite conclusions. In *Tears of the Fathers,* M. A. C. Odu offers Kalu, a traditionalist student leader who defends the ways of the ancestors against the campus progressives. Kalu, heartened by richly robed elders who visit campus to support his attempts to turn university youth back to the ways of the fathers, wins most of his battles, but at the end, despondent over a setback, he hangs himself. His wife follows suit; upon finding the bodies, so does the leader of the progressive opposition. In *Dying on Tradition,* on the other hand, Onuma E. Onuma offers Azu, a Nigerian studying in the United States who rejects all traditions, be they Igbo, modern Nigerian, or American. When all sides disapprove of his marrying an American girl, Azu vows never to marry. In this case tradition seems to refer less to processions of elders and more to the status quo; the most spirited critique comes from Azu's difficulties in getting a visa. While neither novel can claim much literary merit, it is notable that both the pro-tradition and the antitradition heroes—both more absolutist than Amobi and his bottled leopard—meet defeat.

Another form of defeat much beloved by popular writers is that of the university student who squanders his or her chances. Some, like Bayo Adeleke's *Web of Love,* describe the university-girl-gone-bad.

> Tola, an undergraduate, has a boyfriend, Tayo, and the story opens with scenes of their neglecting their studies in favor of lovemaking. Tola is hungry

for experience and determined to live her university years to the fullest, so when the lecturer Dr. Chinua propositions her, she consents. The same day a banker, the Alhaji, offers her material goods in return for sex, and she consents to him, too. She juggles three lovers, expecting good grades from the lecturer, getting money from the banker, but loving the unsuspecting Tayo. Two girlfriends encourage her promiscuity, but a third (Anita) warns that she is headed for trouble.

For a while Tola manages to keep the three men unaware of one another, but eventually the Alhaji finds an incriminating note and throws her out. Then Dr. Chinua gives her a failing grade, explaining that he too has discovered her double-dealing (it turns out that he and the Alhaji are old friends). To make matters worse, she finds she's pregnant. She has a botched abortion and from her hospital bed writes to Tayo confessing all, with Anita as the go-between. The brokenhearted Tayo sends her back a poem of farewell. Tola dies as her mother and younger sister, who has been eagerly anticipating going to the university some day, look on.

(Bayo Adeleke, Web of Love)

A melodrama with the usual double standard, the story of Tola's downfall follows the structure of the intellectual novel. Both Tola's sexual promiscuity and her willingness to deceive Big Men (as well as little ones like Tayo) upset the established system of power at the university, where powerful men don't sleep with each other's mistresses. The witness role is split here between Tayo, hurt into poetry so to speak, and the little sister who sees what happens to girls who break the rules. The point is not that the life at the university is any different for women's freedom, but that it is not.

The theme of university tramps is the counterpart to the vicious attacks on Acadas that appears now and then. Although it's a women-and-men novel rather than an intellectual novel, Funmilayo Fukunle-Onadeko's *The Sacrificial Child* dramatically illustrates how men, and indeed everyone else, criticizes the overeducated woman.

Nike meets Sina when she is returning home from the University of Ibadan for a weekend. He gives her a ride, teasing her for being an Acada (pejorative term for educated woman) when he sees her reading a novel. Sina, a student at Lagos from an elite but loveless Ondo family, begins courting Nike and seems to agree with her feminism. They fall in love and plan to marry. Sina's relatives object because Nike is from Ibadan, not Ondo, and because she is an Acada.

The first cloud on their love appears after both have taken finals and Nike gets the better degree; thereupon Sina goes around disparaging her results, finally accusing her of sleeping with her professors. Nike is confused by Sina's contradictions, his loving side and his jealous, hateful side, but he manages to behave well enough until their marriage.

Once married, Sina drops all the loving words and treats Nike poorly, insulting her and belittling all Acadas. Nike tries to build trust, but her in-laws, especially Sina's sister Ronke and stepmother Olori, make their low opinion of her known. When Sina demands her subservience, she refuses, and their marriage seems to be falling apart. She sees that Sina can put on a modern front when he is with educated people, but with his friends and relatives he drops this and espouses old beliefs about witchcraft and the evils of educated women. Soon he begins beating Nike, increasing her contempt for him.

At Ronke's instigation Sina threatens to get a second wife and throw her out. Nike begins to study business, planning on getting a higher-paying job to support her and the baby after its birth. Sina's hatred approaches madness, and he becomes convinced she is trying to poison him. Nike is miserable but also pities her husband.

The baby is born and named Tola. At first Sina is delighted by his fatherhood, but his relatives mock him because the baby is a girl, and he responds by ridiculing Nike. Since Nike must soon return to work, Olori is brought in to tend the baby. Nike receives her business diploma and wants to get a better job, but she is afraid to tell Sina, who opposes her efforts at further study or self-improvement. Tola gets sick. Behind Nike's back but with Sina's concurrence, Olori makes her a traditional medicine of leaves, but one of the leaves is poisonous, and Tola dies. Sina feels guilty, but he throws Olori out and resolves to save his marriage.

For the next few days Nike is beside herself with grief and ignores Sina's tentative efforts to comfort her. Her parents come for a visit, and she surprises everyone by announcing she is ending her marriage and becoming a nun. His relatives tell Sina to let her go and good riddance, but he musters his gumption to tell them off. Nike's own parents assure her they will still love her whatever she decides. Hearing this, Sina tells her he has never known what family love can be and begs her to give him another chance. She agrees, although feeling in her heart that a happy marriage was not worth the sacrifice of Tola.

(Funmilayo Fukunle-Onadeko, *The Sacrificial Child*)

The novel repeatedly pits ignorance and supersitition against education. The gender inflection of the anti-intellectualism is intense; merely being an educated woman and having aspirations for further intellectual growth makes Nike the object of scorn. And while the novel is melodramatic, gibes against Acadas are common (the term is the Nigerian equivalent of *bluestocking*), so it seems reasonable to conclude that the stereotype of university-girl-as-slut is a form of cultural revenge.

Bad girls have been good subjects for Nigerian popular fiction since the days of Mabel-the-Sweet-Honey, but boys can similarly waste their chances and break the hearts of those who have supported their educational opportunities. These stories often take the form of the student who studies abroad, which is invariably described as seeking to "bring back the golden fleece," only to return a failure. Sam Adewoye's *The Betrayer*, with the usual moral message of the Pacesetters, is the cautionary tale of one such student.

> A cherished only child, Olayemi does well in school and gets engaged to Bimpe. Borrowing money from her family, he goes to study in London, where he promptly forgets Bimpe and his family, runs with a fast, free-spending crowd, and gets roped into marriage by Rita, whose two children he now must support. Leaving school, he takes a menial job as a hospital orderly. Meanwhile, his parents die heartbroken. Bimpe recovers from her disappointment and marries a doctor; they go to America, she gets a master's in education, and they return to Nigeria with three children.
>
> Eventually Olayemi wakes up, divorces the greedy Rita, finishes his degree, and returns to Nigeria. He conducts a proper funeral for his parents, praying for their forgiveness. Then he gets a teaching job—and the principal turns out to be Bimpe. He is overwhelmed by the shame of this ironic turn of events.
>
> (Sam Adewoye, *The Betrayer*)

This theme of the ungrateful student who dashes his relatives' hopes and wastes their money is a common one. In Aliyu Abdullahi Jibia's *The Hunt Begins*, it takes a particularly melodramatic form. Saidu's uncle and aunt have literally starved themselves to pay his university fees, but their ungrateful nephew is too busy debating Rastafarianism and questions of the intellectual's role in society even to bother returning for his uncle's funeral. His aunt, reduced to penury, loses two of her children to an accident when she is out begging, and she promptly goes mad. Saidu, unmoved by what he has set in motion, goes on to a life of utter corruption. So much for campus idealists.

Youth, especially educated youth, betray their elders, but the intellectual novels also report how elders have betrayed the youth. Once again Chukwuemeka Ike, who has had a finger on some of the most serious issues involving Nigerian education for thirty years, writes the most dramatic account of the generation's mutual betrayal in the searing *Our Children Are Coming*. A presidential commission holds hearings involving a series of parents who testify about the bad things done by their teenage children: prostitution, selling the family car to pay for college in England, laziness, and various types of immoral and/or illegal behavior. (The commissioners themselves are promiscuous, corrupt, and primarily interested in their upcoming foreign junket.) The students set up their own tribunal, in which a parade of young people testifies regarding the avarice, hypocrisy, and prejudice of their parents. Ike leaves little doubt where his sympathies lie, and his witnesses—a retired university administrator and a political science professor who are discussing the events—applaud the eventual victory of the young people in pressing their demands. As in *The Bottled Leopard*, Ike takes an unusually hopeful view of such conflicts. Most writers are far more pessimistic about the ability of the educated to change things, even for themselves.

The Culture of Disappointment

Educated Nigerians hold to a Western model of the successful life, one of individual achievement based on merit. The young person gets the needed credentials, finds a job, works hard, avoids temptation, and rises to the top, winning respect and prosperity. This model does not necessitate a rejection of African ways—the young person may retain the bottled leopards of African spiritual power, may find his initial opportunity or opening through kin, hometown, or tribal networks, and may feel a strong sense of obligation to share his good fortune with his extended family—but it does emphasize the connection between character, effort, education, and advancement. This connection has been a standard theme of the English novel.

In sharp contrast is the specifically Nigerian theme of the Disappointed Young Man who has education but no future, who cannot succeed despite his individual efforts, or who is unable to resist the temptations that will derail him. Early versions of this story, like *No Longer at Ease*, Achebe's 1960 sequel to *Things Fall Apart*, emphasized colonialism and its aftermath as the root of the problem. *No Longer at Ease* tells the story of Obi Okonkwo, grandson of Okonkwo in the earlier novel, son of the Christian convert whom Okonkwo had rejected, and a classic torn-between-two-worlds figure of the late colonial period.

> Obi has been educated in England, thanks to support from his hometown of Umuofia, and he returns to Lagos to take a prestigious civil service position with the scholarship board. He is idealistic and is convinced that merit, not nepotism or bribery, should rule, and he resists early attempts to offer him financial and sexual favors. He is also in love with Clara, a fellow Igbo whom he had met on the trip back from England.
>
> But problems mount. Clara is *osu*, and his family back in Umuofia is violently against their marriage. Money problems are severe: Obi is expected to pay back his debt to the Umuofia Progressive Union, assist his relatives, and maintain an urban lifestyle. And his supervisor at work has nothing but contempt for educated Africans.
>
> Most of the novel deals with the mounting pressure Obi faces. Estranged from Clara, he finally succumbs to accepting bribes, both monetary and sexual. At the end, he has been arrested, is on trial for corruption, and is brought to tears when the judge says, "I cannot understand how a young man of your education and brilliant promise could have done this." The novel constitutes an extended answer to the judge's question.
>
> (Chinua Achebe, *No Longer at Ease*)

Achebe's second novel is not an intellectual novel, for Obi is no intellectual himself, and he doesn't unsettle anything. It is his own lack of a center of gravity, Western or African, that contributes to his downfall. But he is the prototype of the Disappointed Young Men who, unlike the Horatio Alger types of the Onitsha market novels, do not find the success they had anticipated.

Subsequent versions of this theme, especially in the years during and after the oil boom, have turned away from colonialism to stress the particularly Nigerian nature of the problem. The view seems to be that merit is actively discouraged, and that the nation suffers as a consequence. For example, in Dibia Humphrey's crime novel *End of Dark Street*, Abba Bello is a young, intelligent civil servant distinguished by his integrity. His venal boss, irritated by Bello's incorruptibility (and by his ill-disguised contempt), arranges to have him fired despite his superior work. As he leaves the office for the last time, his fellow workers comment on the sad turn of events:

> "How can any sane person retire a man like Mr. Bello?" asked a third man.
>
> "He is the only one among the 'ogas' [bosses] who kept his head while the entire Board went berserk over money," said a fourth man.
>
> "I can swear for Oga Bello. That man was almost a saint."
>
> "While the others kept their eyes and their hands on the till, he alone spared any time for actual work." . . .
>
> At that moment, Bello stepped out of the office building, a handsome figure, face as unlined as that of a child. The third man ventured.
>
> "Ah, look, he is so young. This country had better be careful how it treats its intelligent young men." (30)

The message found over and over in crime novels and city novels, as well as in novels about intellectuals, is that Nigeria has not treated its intelligent young men well at all.

The Disappointed Young Man haunts Nigerian fiction. He gives way to crime and corruption, he is killed or commits suicide, or he remains a defeated witness to the society that ensured his defeat. Uzoatu's 1989 novel *Satan's Story* offers a good example of the frustrations-of-an-educated-young-man tale.

> Masta is a university student whose passing involvement in radical student politics gets him thrown out of school. He dreads returning to his village a failure, especially disappointing his peasant father. Nor is his love life going well; he is Igbo, and his girlfriend, Anu, is the daughter of a wealthy Muslim Yoruba, so her family opposes the match. Meanwhile, Satan, his double and nemesis, shadows him.
>
> With nothing to go back for, Masta knocks around in various cities—Lagos, Ibadan, Onitsha—getting and losing a teaching job, hearing that one of his

student friends died in a campus riot, learning Anu is pregnant, and observing corruption and misery all around. Finally, Anu is found dead from a
botched abortion, and Satan accuses Masta. He is arrested, is beaten by the
police, briefly escapes, is caught, and is buried alive by the villagers.

(Uzor Maxim Uzoatu, *Satan's Story*)

The device of Satan is not well integrated with the rest of the story, but
Uzoatu may have been trying to express the idea of a destiny that one cannot escape, even by going to the university. One painful episode suggests
the futility that intellectuals face. Masta is teaching in a secondary school
where teachers have been paid no salaries for months. He longs to read
Uncle Tom's Cabin, which sits on the shelf of a local bookstore, and he reflects that "perhaps books are written to adorn the shelves of the rich or,
much more cruelly, to gather dust in bookshops while tempting the poor"
(54). Eventually he tries to steal the book; he gets caught and has to flee
the school. This is a world where intellectuals are marginal in multiple ways;
they don't get paid, they can't read, they can't teach. Those who have believed in the achievement-through-education model become thoroughly
disillusioned and embittered in such a world.

Intellectuals everywhere fancy themselves as outsiders, misunderstood
and unappreciated, but the Nigerian variant is unusual because it penetrates
the popular culture as well. Over and above the postcolonial disillusionment with the high hopes of the late colonial period, a number of specifically Nigerian factors lay behind this culture of disappointment. These include an elite class with an unusually large gap between the intellectuals
and the powerful; a generational divide marked by the oil boom and subsequent bust that shattered the hopes of the postindependence generation;
and, perhaps most of all, the experience of the civil war. Altogether these
made optimism, especially confidence in the life of the mind and the ability of the learned and the clever to succeed, seem the utmost illusion.

The position of Nigerian novelists can be understood in terms of a mul-
tiply split elite. Kristen Mann has described the consolidation of the elite
in colonial Lagos. For this group, many of whom descended from American slaves repatriated to Sierra Leone (Saros), endogamy and common participation in economic, ritual, and educational institutions created tight social networks among families. Such people were a circle of highly educated
professionals, colonial civil servants, and merchants who shared and perpetuated their capital and human resources. Their lifestyles included Western education, in England if possible, the practice of Christianity and
church marriage, and a close relationship with the colonial administration.
This elite's sense of social superiority vis-à-vis the indigenous Yoruba was
to be shaken by the increasing racial exclusion of the later colonial period,
but its sense of constituting a definable group of the good Lagos families

persisted. Later a similar status group emerged among the Western-educated Igbo. The Hausa-Fulani case was quite different, for there the elite was tied to a traditional Islamic aristocracy distinguished by its very distance from Western education and practices.

As described in Chapter 2, Nigerian novelists come from precisely this former type of educated, Westernized background. Both the Yoruba of the southwest and the Igbo of the southeast feel a powerful sense of loss. For example, Mann describes how the descendants of the early twentieth-century Lagos elite believe they have "lost control of the city that their ancestors built."[121] Their alienation is not simply the sense of separation intellectuals tend to have anywhere but the specific loss of status of a Westernized elite. This took different forms for the Yoruba and the Igbo, but the result was the same: a bitter sense of the lost status of the educated southern families. To put this in class terms, what Nigeria has is a split in its bourgeois class between those who have the money and power, on the one hand, and those who constitute the holders of the cultural capital, on the other.[122] The educated old elites, and the writers who are their direct and spiritual heirs, still mourn their loss.[123]

And this is only the first loss. One might have expected that, with sufficient cultural capital, the sons and daughters of the old elite might be able to trade their cultural advantages for economic and social ones, just as Bourdieu has suggested. But here comes the particular historical conjunction of oil boom/oil bust with the generations of Nigerian writers. The first generation was able to maintain the ideals of the old elites, although mourning their decline. The second anticipated a revival of fortunes through the market opportunities that would enable them to cash in their cultural capital. Yet these hopes were dashed after only a decade or so. And the third generation never had the same degree of confidence that cultural production was to be the key to success and the good life, much as they hoped it might.

Outside of literature, writers express the bitterness of these two losses in different ways. Some of the older writers claim that things were better under the British. The younger ones talk vaguely about the need for social discipline. In their writing, they are united by a concern for social reform, reform of some sort. From the point of view of paradise either lost or never quite attained, any reform, any change, has got to be for the better.

Solidifying the first loss—the power of the less educated, less Westernized northerners—and preceding the third loss of the oil bust was a second loss that was sudden, dramatic, and a bloody metaphor for the disappointment of the reading class. This was the defeat of Biafra in the Nigerian civil war. War novels are a genre in and of themselves and will be treated as such, but they also contain the essence of the disillusion and disappointment that have marked the Nigerian intellectuals from independence to the present day.

Loss and Memory

Five weeks after the founding of the Darban Republic (Biafra), fourteen-year-old Ayota is shaken out of normality when the war closes his school. He returns to his hometown to find his father, Nkem, has lost most of his wealth fleeing the township, and his house is now filled with refugees. Ayota resents being sent off to stay in the village with his grandmother, but Nkem describes the disaster, and he realizes everything has changed.

Ayota becomes a conductor on one of his father's trucks and starts trading in cigarettes and other goods procured by risky trips through the war zone. He witnesses typical wartime incidents: accusations of sabotage; refugees returning to occupied homes; the execution of a deserter. Such scenes lead Ayota to reflect that war was "not what Darbans bargained for." Theft by prominent Christians and the death of a dear cousin in an air raid increase his disillusionment with the war, as increased shelling makes his trading more hazardous.

Ayota and his father begin to learn traditional Igbo ways. In one incident a bee "gives a message" to Ayota, whereupon a soldier returns Nkem's stolen truck. The chief priest explains that Idemile [a local spirit protecting the village] had harassed soldiers to return the truck. Nkem makes a thanksgiving sacrifice of a small goat and promptly gets bitten by a scorpion, whereupon he decides that Idemile requires a bigger sacrifice.

Ayota mourns the death of a palm wine tapper, formerly a successful businessman in the north who had lost everything. One despairing old woman says things were better under colonial rule. Shaman shelling comes close to the village, and the residents prepare to flee, some destroying their livestock, but the final attack never comes. Ayota starts trading palm oil, doing well until bombing destroys his inventory, once again shattering his hopes. He tends his sick grandmother, then he himself sickens; a *dibia* says he is *ogbanje*, but rituals save him.

The Shamans break through, and Darba surrenders. Everyone fears the soldiers, but most treat the Darbans kindly. Ayota goes to a large town where he sees piles of corpses, but also the market full of food. School reopens, with the buildings damaged, the white missionaries gone, and many teachers dead. The boys share their war experiences, as Ayota concludes that "the story of the aspirations and tragedies of Darba and her people would never fully be told."

(Joseph Ugochukwu Ogbuefi, *The Time Between*)

Joseph Ugochukwu Ogbuefi's *The Time Between*, published in Enugu in 1985, is one of twenty-nine war novels I have identified. The book's cover shows the rising sun of Biafra tracked with footprints that grow larger—the boy grows to manhood during the civil war. We recognize that this typical Nigerian civil war novel parallels the structure of the intellectual novel: from education to disruption by powers beyond one's control to disillusionment to the role of the witness. War novels are not the same as intellectual novels, but they share the themes of loss and disappointment.

To understand this genre, it is important to recall Nigeria's colonial and postindependence history of regional conflict and the civil war itself. With the coming of independence in 1960, Nigeria's three regions competed for economic and political advantages. One ethnic group dominated each region: the Hausa in the north, the Yoruba in the west, and the Igbo in the east. The three main regions differed dramatically in development. The east, particularly the Igbo, was the most modernized and Westernized, was largely Christian, and had high levels of education; the Islamic north was least developed economically and had low levels of education; and the west, having Lagos as the country's economic powerhouse and capital, fell in between. Politics in the First Republic quickly degenerated into the struggle among national leaders to win benefits for their particular regions, and popular disgust with the government was widespread.

In January 1966 a group of mostly Igbo army majors attempted a military coup against the government of Sir Abubakar Tafawa Balewa, who was a Hausa and the federal prime minister since independence. Failing in their overall objective of seizing control of the government, they did succeed in killing Balewa and many regional political leaders. Into the vacuum stepped the military under Major-General John Aguiyi-Ironsi, the supreme commander of the armed forces and an Igbo who had not been involved in the conspiracy. The military takeover was met with rejoicing among a population tired of the rampant corruption of the former Big Men. But Ironsi proved to be an inept politician; for example, his slowness in bringing the conspirators to trial encouraged suspicions of Igbo favoritism. In May he announced two "unification decrees" aimed at abolishing the federation of three regions in favor of a more centralized government (republic), complete with a national rather than regionally based civil service. Northerners regarded these decrees as a straightforward Igbo power grab. Outbreaks of violence led to the massacre of hundreds of Igbos, who had been living in the north for years, working as traders, civil servants, and in technologically advanced sectors. Igbos began to trickle back into the east. Ironsi refused to back down, despite the protests of the northern emirs and their governor, Hassan Katsina.

In a July coup, northern officers kidnapped and killed Ironsi, although his death was not confirmed for some months, and commenced on a bloody purge of Igbos in the military. Northerners under Lieutenant Colonel Yakuba Gowon (himself an Angas, one of the northern minority tribes) took over the government. The political issue confronting the new government was still that of federation versus separation. For years the Northern Region had argued for separation (especially through the influential Araba movement), fearing its continued disadvantage vis-à-vis the more developed southern regions. But during the Ad Hoc Constitutional Conference held in August, the north—once again on top—sharply reversed its policy and came out in favor of federation and strong central authority.

In September and October a pogrom broke out in the north, bringing the slaughter of thousands of Igbos and the seizure of their property.[124] Igbo refugees flooded into the Eastern Region, already the most densely populated part of the country, and their relocation put new strains on the regional government. Now it was the east that argued for the weakest of federations, hoping to avoid more violence and continued northern domination. At the Aburi Conference of the regional governors held in January 1967, which had been called to determine the future political relationship among the regions, Chukwuemeka Ojukwu, governor of the Eastern Region, managed to get passed a set of declarations favoring minimal ties among the regions. Gowon, whose advisers quickly pointed out that the Aburi Declarations essentially meant the end of Nigeria, decided he had been taken in at Aburi and simply ignored the declarations to which he had just agreed. In May, attempting to defuse the regional tensions, Gowon proclaimed that Nigeria would henceforth consist of twelve states, only one of which would be predominantly Igbo. The former Eastern Region promptly and predictably seceded; on May 30, 1967, Ojukwu declared the independence of the Republic of Biafra.

After a five-week hesitation, Nigeria attacked Biafra. The Nigerian (federal) theme of the war was unity. "To keep Nigeria one / Is a task that must be done" was a popular slogan, as was the phrase, "Go On with One Nigeria," which yields the acronym GOWON. The Biafran theme was freedom, with a subtheme of vigilance, indicating the new republic's anxiety over internal conspiracy and sabotage. The Nigerian civil war, with its technologically advanced weaponry, aerial bombings, and sophisticated external and internal propaganda, was the first modern war fought in Africa. Nigeria was armed and strongly backed by Britain and to some extent the Soviets; Biafra was supported to a limited extent by the French (who, however, never accorded the republic diplomatic recognition).

Biafrans had extraordinary enthusiasm, fueled by their sense that the Igbo faced genocide if the secession failed, and they developed a capacity for production of war materials and other goods that was impressive, if never sufficient. Nigeria had the advantages of size as well as external support, and the early months of the war saw swift federal victories. Biafran forces made one dramatic excursion into the midwest, even threatening Lagos briefly, but the attack bogged down and they were eventually repulsed. Nigeria imposed an effective blockade on goods coming into Biafra, and in the densely populated area that had never produced enough food to feed itself, starvation and disease, especially kwashiorkor (malnutrition caused by protein deficiency) among children, were the result. Despite international humanitarian relief efforts, Biafra reached its low point in 1968; the next year Biafra recovered some territory, and the war dragged on in a military stalemate, accompanied by an increasing arousal of world opinion to stop the dying. Biafra finally surrendered in January 1970 and disappeared in fact if not in memory.

The first war novel, Sebastian Mezu's *Behind the Rising Sun*, was published the following year, brought out by Heinemann's African Writers Series. It is awkwardly constructed, with abrupt shifts in tone, telling of the war as seen through the eyes of Freddy, a young historian for the Biafran Historical Research Center working in Paris.

> Freddy observes attempts by Biafran diplomats to procure arms from European merchants; plans fall through repeatedly, due to unscrupulous arms dealers and pilots, and to corrupt and incompetent Biafrans. Freddy is appalled by the diplomats' high living in France as contrasted with the suffering at home. Feeling he must get back, Freddy travels to Biafra by a circuitous route, picking up Titi, a young student worryied about her parents, en route. They finally arrive shortly after the fall of Port Harcourt.
>
> From this point on the book gives a moving account of the misery of the refugees in the late days of the war. Freddy and Titi go behind enemy lines to engage in sabotage. Nigerians take Owerri, but Biafrans recapture the city, inspired by a priest at Our Lady of Mount Carmel. Love grows between Freddy, whose former sweetheart has become promiscuous with officers, and Titi.
>
> The final chapter is a switch: Freddy organizes a miserable village of refugees into a communal paradise (no mention of the end of the war or outside events). At the close, joyful villagers celebrate Freddy and Titi's wedding, while everyone vows to tell Biafra's story to the world.
>
> (Sebastian Mezu, *Behind the Rising Sun*)

The contrast between the artificiality of the ending and the realistic scenes of suffering that preceded it is stark. It is as if one illusion—gallant little Biafra with its clever people and can-do spirit—has been replaced with another, an egalitarian neverland that still manages to bear witness to Biafra's rise and fall. Subsequent war novels—and there have been at least twenty-eight since *Behind the Rising Sun*, record the disillusion without offering a replacement.

The novels have been published in western Nigeria, the center of most Nigerian publishing activity, in the east, and in London. The war genre constitutes over 5 percent of Nigeria's novels published since the war. Of the twenty-nine novels, three-quarters are by Igbo authors.

Maxwell Nkem Nwagboso's *The Road to Damnation*, a work far superior to most war novels, illustrates the depths of the Igbo disappointment, and how it is the intellectuals' disappointment as well.

In the Biafra town of Owerri, an Igbo writer named Herbie and a magazine editor named Edna are about to get married when Nigerian forces shell the town. In the first of many flashbacks, Herbie recalls growing up nearby with his sister Mary, who sexually tempts him. "Papa" (James Obioma) discovers them and hauls Herbie off to Father Uche, who reveals that Herbie was abandoned and raised by Obioma, and thus is not Mary's brother at all. Herbie lives for five years with Father Uche, who gives him both education and an understanding of Nigerian problems but then abruptly tries to seduce him. Back to the present: the marriage ceremony takes place, with only Father Uche and James Obioma in attendance. Afterward Herbie tells Edna that he feels no bitterness toward either man.

Returning to their new house, the couple learns that Edna's brother Ben, an officer in the Biafran army, has been wounded and hospitalized. They make plans to leave if Owerri is evacuated, but at same time they want to carry on normal life, for example, worrying about how to get paper for Edna's magazine, *African Womanhood*. In another flashback, Herbie recalls fleeing Father Uche's house after the attempted seduction, getting drunk, meeting an American friend, going to play Ping-Pong at a recreation club, and meeting Edna there for the first time.

The shelling of Owerri resumes the next day. Herbie and Edna go to see Ben in the hospital, which is in chaos, before Ben has surgery. They picnic in a nearby forest and make love. Afterward, Herbie reads Edna a story he has written about a village dancing contest for the hand of the chief's daughter. The girl prefers an older widower to a boastful young man; the older man, mourning his first wife, first refuses to dance but then does and wins the contest. Herbie says his theme is that life goes on. The older man's generosity to his rival seems to echo Herbie's forgiveness of Father Uche and James Obioma.

The couple heads back to the hospital and is harassed by a group of soldiers at a checkpoint. As they reach the outskirts of Owerri, Nigerian planes bomb the town. Edna is hit and dies in Herbie's arms. With a stranger's help, Herbie buries her on the spot. Going on to the hospital, he finds Ben dead of infection.

Mad with grief, Herbie almost hangs himself, but concludes that his death would constitute too easy a victory for the enemy. He sees a stream of evacuees from Owerri. Returning to their house, he recalls first meeting Edna, their initial courtship, her reading his story about a butcher's struggle to get education for his son, their long lovers' conversations. At one point after lovemaking they talked of the possibility of peace in the world and the interconnections among all people. All this goes through Herbie's mind as he surveys the empty house.

The next morning, Herbie walks through the town, now occupied by Nigerian troops. He is taken to Owerri Government College, once a fine school but now a detention center. From there he witnesses an unsuccessful Biafran counterattack on the town. Later he sees a group of soldiers building a fire of books in order to roast a goat; the dead goat seems to smile.

Herbie is locked in a cell with other prisoners, including a young boy named Emeka and his grandfather. Before long Emeka and Herbie become cooks for other prisoners. One day, while out looking for provisions, they encounter Emeka's mother, who tells them she had been raped by one of the soldiers guarding them. Emeka blindly attacks the soldier, who kills him on the spot. Herbie reports the incident to the center commander, who does nothing. Back in the cell, Herbie tells the boy's grandfather that Emeka is being held in another place; the old man remarks that he hopes they let the boy have some books there.

A Hausa officer gets Herbie released and takes him to visit Mary, who has become the officer's mistress. Herbie first assumes she has stayed behind as a Biafran guerrilla, but instead finds that she is involved in the "attack trade," the exchange of goods between enemy lines that went on throughout the war. Mary tries to talk him into staying in the "liberated zone" and trading, since Biafra's coming defeat is inevitable, but Herbie sets off for the Biafra lines. He feels a vague sense of pride and even tranquillity, despite his awareness that Biafra is on "the road to damnation."

(Maxwell Nkem Nwagboso, *The Road to Damnation*)

The first thing to notice is how this plot follows the basic structure of the intellectual novel. Both Herbie and Edna are writers, both modern, rational communicators. Their very existence—putting out magazines, telling stories—is an affront to a world in which might rules. Even after burying Edna, Herbie refuses to give in to the war, to lose his faith, to turn to hatred, to follow Mary into profiteering, to end his own life in despair, or to stay in the safe zone of the powerful. Over and over he takes the path of the rational man who believes in order in the face of chaos. He writes and will go on writing in a world that burns its books and kills its readers.

Second, if one were to identify the most prominent theme or message presented in the Nigerian civil war novels, it would be that of the utter meaninglessness of the war. Both Igbo and non-Igbo authors render the war experience as being ultimately pointless, with lofty ideals undercut by cynicism, determined efforts negated by random destruction, patriotism and collective purpose undone by external meddling and internal corruption. And yet Nwagboso presents Herbie as finding meaning, and even peace, in and among the damned.

The Road to Damnation is a complex novel, with things seldom being what they seem: a sister is not a sister, a father not a father; a kindly priest is a depraved seducer who then turns back into being a kindly priest; a school is a prison; an enemy officer can produce both corruption and freedom. Nwagboso portrays the inability of the various philosophies presented in the novel—Herbie's Christian forbearance, Edna's love and affirmation of life, their shared recognition of the interconnections between people, Herbie's faith in the power of the written word (early in the novel, Herbie's love for words is contrasted with Father Uche's suspicion)—to respond adequately to, or account for, what has happened. Herbie's final sense of resolve in the face of disaster seems unwarranted, another illusion and one specific to intellectuals. Herbie will write about what has happened, but books have been shown to be fragile and vulnerable, fuel for roasting meat, reading material for the already dead. The novel's lasting image is the smile of the slaughtered goat, a terrible emptiness.

Like the other genres, many war novels share a mythic structure that organizes their presentation of the civil war experience. *Echoes in the Dark*, a much simpler novel than *The Road to Damnation*, reveals this structure clearly.

> The wealthy owner of an Enugu construction firm, Iheneme has a fleet of trucks, money in the bank, four children, and an altogether good life. The novel opens with the evacuation of Enugu. One of Iheneme's sons, a second-year law student, is a soldier. The family evacuates to Iheneme's home village, where there seems to be both safety and plenty of food.
>
> Soon the war comes to the village, and things turn dark. A series of ups and downs marks the family's experience: profiteers making money off the suffering of their countrymen; the marriage of Iheneme's daughter to a soldier; hunger and kwashiorkor; soldiers singing war songs to whip up flagging war fever; and the death of Iheneme's student son. The family ends up in a refugee center, hungry and stripped of everything. At the end of the war everyone congratulates one another for surviving, and a penniless Iheneme starts over.
>
> (Sun Chi Okereke, *Echoes in the Dark*)

Like the intellectual novels, war novels like this show the movement from hope to disillusion, and from a principled involvement to a struggle for survival on any terms. Also like the intellectual novel, war novels end with witnesses. The overall structure has six stages:

1. Confidence and high hopes: The novel may begin with young soldiers marching and singing war songs (*Sozaboy*), schoolchildren released from school (*The Time Between*), or a couple preparing to marry (*The Road to Damnation*). Spirits are high as everyone gets caught up in the dawn of a new day. Biafra, formerly the Eastern Region, has the rising sun as its symbol, and often the novels emphasize this dawning of hopes.

2. Intimations that all might not go well: It quickly becomes apparent that the early war fever, often cast in terms of a self-confident Biafra convinced that it will prosper through sheer will and brains, was wildly off the mark. Freddy sees that the Biafran diplomats don't know what they are doing. Herbie and Edna see death all around them. Ayota starts to realize that war was "not what Darbans bargained for." The dawn may be a false one.

3. *Ups and downs of wartime:* Plots vary, but they usually involve the growing suspicion of various internal enemies: saboteurs, profiteers, officers enjoying themselves while soldiers suffer, and women engaging in the "attack trade" or giving themselves to enemy officers to survive. The civilian viewpoint is the most common here, although sometimes the naive soldier is the observer.

4. *Increasing despair, chaos, death, and horror:* Bombs fall, towns are lost, and starvation threatens. War novels catalog the increasing horrors of war, as people find themselves unable to escape its devastation. Often the horror involves a great betrayal, as with Pastor Barika and Chief Birabee, the village notables in *Sozaboy.*

5. *The death of someone who is educated, wise, or otherwise highly valued:* Iheneme does not give way to total despair until he loses his law-student son in *Echoes in the Dark.* Such a loss represents the loss of hope, a hope based on the powers of education and rationality. A similar moment comes in *The Road to Damnation* when Emeka, the boy who loves books, dies for defending his mother. The smile of the goat on a burning pile of books, or the dead teachers in *The Time Between* capture such losses.

6. *Survival plus disillusionment:* The war ends, the bombs stop falling, and people greet one another with "Happy survival," an indication of how their hopes have shrunken. As they prepare to put their lives back together, some witnesses take on the task of telling the story, even while recognizing, as *The Time Between* put it, that "the story of the aspirations and tragedies of [Biafra] and her people would never fully be told."

War novels tend to fall in one of three forms. Some use allegory representing a homologous "moment of madness" to universalize the phenomenon of civil war. This is done through allegorical places and names (e.g., "Darba," or Ken Saro-Wiwa's *Sozaboy* for "soldier boy") and through direct universalization of the war-is-hell theme. One extended allegory, Kole Omotoso's *The Combat,* has two former friends fall out and prepare for a duel to decide who will get to keep an injured boy that one of them may have fathered. As the day of the duel nears, local and foreign advisers encourage each man, and each defends his position on principle to the press. Neither has the chance to question "what paranoic wrath drove us this far." So caught up are they in the coming combat that neither they nor anyone else notices that the boy himself has died.

A second means of representing the war is through a microscope. These novels, including *The Road to Damnation,* look at the war by concentrating on a single individual coping with the adversities of the time. Teresa E. Meniru's *The Last Card* is another example, in which a modern, urban Igbo mother, separated from her husband following the fall of Port Harcourt, must take refuge in her husband's village and cope with getting food and shelter for her children while being mistreated continually by a jealous mother-in-law. Over half of the war novels are focused at this micro, local level.

The war novels contain strikingly few references to the north or to the regional, ethnic, and religious conflicts that were the root of the war. The enemy is not characterized or personalized beyond the term *vandal.* Virtually no attempt at structural analysis of the conflict is made in most war novels. The few modest exceptions are notable because of their very reticence, as when characters in Eddie Iroh's *Sirens in the Night* discuss the conflict between "tribalism" and "patriotism" (i.e., Nigerian nationalism) without referring to specific ethnic conflicts such as those between Igbo and Hausa. Only three novels engage in extensive structural analysis, and their approaches differ sharply. Festus Iyayi's *Heroes* is a straight Marxian account, suggesting that class conflict lies at the source of the war. Buchi Emecheta's *Destination Biafra* emphasizes the manipulations of the British and their impact on Nigerian political structure. Only Cyprian Ekwensi's *Divided We Stand* attempts to offer a full account of the regional, ethnic, and religious tensions that operated at the levels of both politics and popular sentiment and that led to the war.

Two themes appear which I call displacement devices, in that in their analysis of the problems leading to the war or its consequences, they set up certain problems that displace structural problems as causal factors. The first of these displacement strategies is an emphasis on foreign involvement and interference in the war, coupled with almost no consideration of the local bases for conflict. Eddie Iroh's *Forty-eight Guns for the General,* the story of an idealistic young Biafran officer fighting the enemy, is the most extreme example. In this case the enemy is, however, not the federal forces but a motley group of white mercenaries (led by a Frenchman and including a South African, a Briton, a German, etc.) who are bent on robbing and cheating Biafra while ostensibly in her service.

In the second displacement device, many of the war novels depict internal corruption, often with a sexual component. Corruption is a concern of both Igbo and non-Igbo authors, and both Biafra and Nigeria are depicted as riddled with greed and hypocrisy. A number of novels depict corrupt relief officials and military officers who use their positions for personal gain. Typical are Peter (in S. M. O. Aka's *Midday Darkness*), who sheds his idealism, accepts bribes, and finally sets up an elaborate scheme to steal the pay intended for soldiers at the front, and Major (in T. Uzodinma Nwala's *Justice on Trial*), who trades in "liberated" goods, property from Biafran territory retaken by federal troops. Other novels depict the "girls of war,"[125] young Igbo women like Nwagboso's Mary who sold themselves sexually to army officers and war profiteers. Such "girls" are usually presented quite sympathetically; they were just trading what they had in order to survive, and after all the Igbo are a trading people. The real villains (as in the title of Iroh's second war novel) are the "toads of war," the profiteers and armchair officers who can afford the girls' favors.

I have already referred to the overrepresentation of Igbo among Nigerian authors in general. The writers of the war novels are even more disproportionately Igbo. Of the twenty-nine novels in the genre, we know the authors' ethnicity for twenty-six; twenty-two (85 percent) are Igbo. In fiction, the story of the Nigerian civil war is being told by its losers.[126]

Consider now the position of Igbo intellectuals during war. Igbo lecturers at the University of Ibadan had drawn up a blueprint for secession in April 1966, even before the northern pogrom or the breakup of the regions into twelve states. The early return of intellectuals to the east in July 1966 allowed them to play prominent roles in advising the Eastern Region and later Biafran government. Cyprian Ekwensi, the former director of the Federal Information Service, became director of the Biafran Information Service. Chinua Achebe, former head of Nigerian external broadcasting services, also worked for the Biafran Information Service and was a member of the Political Orientation Committee. This was a group of intellectuals working on the future organization of Biafran society; their influence was seen in Ojukwu's Ahiara Declaration of June 1969, which envisioned the New Biafran Social Order as utopian, socialist, and Christian. V. C. Ike was chancellor of the University of Biafra. Pius Okigbo was Biafran minister of finance; his brother Christopher, a poet and one of the prewar Biafran intellectual core, was killed in the early days of the war and became a popular martyr. For Biafra, the war was an intellectual's war, and most of the Igbo war novelists had been involved in the production of propaganda or other war-related activities.

They were involved in other ways as well. Since the war was fought on Biafran soil, and since air raids and starvation affected all social groups, few Igbo writers were spared personal losses. V. C. Ike, when responding to the question on the author survey about his wartime experiences, wrote, "My wife and I lost our entire library at Nsukka . . . and virtually all our material possessions, starting life anew in January 1970. We also lost our second son (in 1968)." His reply was not unusual for easterners. The Nigerian civil war was, to an extraordinary extent, fought and lost by intellectuals.

Ghosts and Illusions

Sozaboy (soldier boy), a primary school graduate, is a driver in Dukana when he hears rumors of war. He meets Agnes, who fled Lagos when the killings started; Agnes says she wants a strong man to defend her. Old men like Zaza, who once fought "Hitla" in Burma, encourage war fever. Entranced by these stories and by Agnes's promise of marriage, Sozaboy decides to join the army. As the war is beginning, Sozaboy marries Agnes and enlists, still having no idea what he is getting into.

At the battlefront, the educated Bullet takes Sozaboy under his wing. An enemy soldier shares cigarettes with them; they nickname him Manmuswak (from "man must work so man can chop [eat]"). Sozaboy remembers seeing the soldier in a local bar before the war, so apparently he has switched sides. After Manmuswak tells them their captain is hoarding liquor, the soldiers find it, get drunk, and are beaten when discovered; Bullet is humiliated by being made to drink urine. Later, on patrol, Bullet shoots their sadistic captain. An enemy plane bombs the soldiers, killing Bullet, and Sozaboy flees into the bush.

Sozaboy awakens in an enemy hospital, being nursed by Manmuswak. He is imprisoned and threatened with death for lying when he says he doesn't know how to shoot, but is saved when he tells them he can drive; he becomes driver for Manmuswak, who is busy looting and trading in stolen goods.

Worried about Agnes and his mother, Sozaboy runs away to Dukana, which he finds bombed and deserted. He begins a tour of hellish refugee camps, seeing people dying of kwashiorkor, stripped of possessions and hope. The chief and the pastor, who had supported the war, are now hoarding food. When Sozaboy exposes them, the chief charges him with being a saboteur, and he is imprisoned. His guard is Manmuswak, who has switched sides again. Manmuswak takes out a group of prisoners to shoot, but he runs out of bullets and Sozaboy escapes.

He returns to the devastated Dukana, where the survivors, now dying of cholera, shun him. A cripple finally tells him Agnes and his mother died in the bombing. The villagers, thinking Sozaboy is a ghost who has brought disease to them, want to kill him. Totally disillusioned, he leaves Dukana for an unknown future.

(Ken Saro-Wiwa, *Sozaboy*)

Written in "rotten English," a mixture of pidgin and standard English, Ken Saro-Wiwa's *Sozaboy* is an allegory of naïveté being replaced by bitter experience. Zaza will fight the wrong war, the chief will betray his people, Agnes will seek a protector in vain, Manmuswak will profit no matter what. Sozaboy's war experience is one of progressive disillusion: his certainties evaporate, his trust in political and religious leaders, in love, and in his own abilities is shattered; and he ends up a witness wandering into the unknown. This was the war experience for Biafran intellectuals.

When history produces patriots of a nation that no longer exists (or never did), as when a secession has failed or as the result of a diaspora, various cultural responses are possible. One, directed externally as well as internally, is a defiant preservation of the flame, with the avowed intention of some-day trying again (ethnic separatist movements such as the Basque or Quebecois, or the Palestinians' quest for their lost homeland). A second is perpetuation of a sense of another, a "real," home (Israel for the Jewish Diaspora, Ethiopia for Jamaican Rastafarians). A third possibility is a turning inward, a cultural withdrawal into localism (regarded outside as "sullen," licking local wounds—the American South during the late nineteenth and early twentieth centuries). A fourth is assimilation, resigned or with a certain enthusiasm, maintaining a handful of cultural distinctions but essentially undifferentiated from the rest (despite pockets of cultural and even political resistance, Scotland and Wales fit this pattern). A fifth is embracing a position of marginality, taking the cultural role of "the stranger" who is *in* the larger society but never *of* that society.

The first and second of these responses were not available to the former patriots of Biafra. As for the third, while all Nigerian ethnic groups practice some degree of cultural localism, the Igbo do not seem to celebrate their traditions more then anyone else. Indeed, they often call themselves "the Jews of Nigeria" because of their being so scattered in the late colonial period, when they willingly left their homeland in the east to get education, to follow trading opportunities, or to staff the colonial civil service. This is why the *sabon gari* (strangers' quarters) of northern cities were full of Igbos and thus vulnerable to genocidal riots. It might be said that pre-civil war Igbo were implicitly headed for the fourth route of assimilation in most respects. The Biafra years dramatized their group distinctiveness in blood, yet even in the 1970s there was a widely shared image of the New Nigerian—cosmopolitan, educated, traveled, modern—for whom tribalism consisted only of a cultural remnant, cherished but not significant in everyday life. With their Westernization and education, the Igbo may have been particularly susceptible to this image. Most Nigerians see the Igbo, like everyone else, attempting to preserve the local and traditional while also amalgamating into the larger society, the goal being federation and co-operation, without the loss of particular distinctiveness.

Yet the New Nigerian, the sophisticate who had moved beyond the tribe, was a fragile creature of the oil-boom years, who disappeared in the wave of particularism that came with the hard times of the 1980s. The case can be made that culturally the Igbo are in fact following the fifth response outlined here, preserving a culturally marginal position, the "strangers" of Nigeria. They are keeping alive a critical stance toward Nigerian society, comparing it always to the lost ideal (not just the golden age, but Biafra, land of the rising sun) and finding it wanting.

Paradoxically, they are able to preserve this marginal position because they are so culturally strong. As noted earlier, the Igbo are overrepresented among Nigerian authors and vastly overrepresented among war novelists. The tales they tell, to a disproportionate extent, become the tales of Nigeria. It is not an exaggeration to say that the Igbo have organized the literary experience of the reading class.

The position of the Igbo, their response to the war and to their defeat, is the position of Nigerian intellectuals as a group. This is the case partly because so many of the latter are themselves Igbo and partly because the Igbo experience is a metaphor for the disillusion felt by those who had cast their lot with rational, secularized, Western learning. The experience of the Igbo as rendered in the war novels is the experience of Nigerian intellectuals as a whole: conflict with "the powers," disillusion, temptation into compromise and corruption, defeat, marginality. Like the Igbo after the war, the intellectuals make do—*manmuswak,* after all—but with a sense of disappointment, waste, and almost futility.

Almost, but not quite, for writers are storytellers, and readers want stories to help make sense of their lives. The Nigerian intellectuals in general, the writing and reading class, are the ghosts that return to tell the tale. They are the orphan boy in *The Madness of Didi,* the schoolchildren of *The Time Between,* all the Disappointed Young Men who have witnessed the ongoing defeat of the educated by the powerful, and who are compelled to tell what happened. Nigerian intellectuals are walking through the ruins, the land of bombed-out schools and burned books, looking to collar other members of the reading class with their stories.

CRIME AND POLITICS

Setting out on a business trip, Joe Offaro encounters a hit-and-run victim. Joe drives the bleeding man to the hospital, but before he can get a doctor's attention, the man dies. Intending to go to the police, Joe first returns home to wash off the blood. There he finds his wife, Naomi, in bed with Dayo, an old boyfriend visiting from the United States. The two men fight, with Dayo getting the worst of it. When Joe finally goes to report the hit-and-run accident, the police seem to suspect him of murdering the unidentified man. Disgusted with life, Joe heads for an old friend's house to drown his troubles.

A few days later the police arrest Joe for murder. He and the contrite Naomi, both hoping to downplay the Dayo episode, give incomplete accounts of what happened. When a lawyer named Itav takes Joe's case, he explains that the circumstantial evidence is overwhelming: blood in Joe's car and on his clothes, his bruised face, his delay in reporting the death to the police, and his apparent hiding out afterward. The only one who can corroborate the story about the fight is Dayo, but he has since gone back to the United States.

As the case comes to court, Itav tries desperately to find Dayo. He succeeds finally and brings the witness back to testify. But Dayo is out for revenge because the beating has made him impotent, so he swears that the story Joe and Naomi have told about the tryst and fight is a lie. The court convicts Joe of murder, his appeal is denied, and he is hanged.

(Tony Marinho, *The Victim*)

The Victim is a crime story but an ambiguous one, for it may be that no crime has been committed; it may be that the novel is about a crimeless victim. While somewhat implausible—the dead man is never identified, for example, and no one suggests a motive for Joe killing him—*The Victim* holds the reader's interest with its Kafkaesque account of an innocent man trapped by circumstances and by a legal system impervious to the truth. The real victim is not the man struck down on the street but Joe, the middle-class businessman who is victimized privately by his wife having an affair and publicly by the police pinning a crime on him. His two forms of victimization eventually merge, and the reader recognizes that the dying man has been Joe all along.

The multiple ambiguities of *The Victim* tell a story over and above the plot itself: They tell the treacherous nature of contemporary Nigerian public life. The very institutions that should ensure law and order—the police and the courts —destroy Joe. He is the victim not so much of a cheating wife or a vengeful Dayo as of a system uninterested in distinguishing between innocence and guilt. This Nigerian Everyman-of-the-modern-sector is done in by institutions that fail him at every turn: the hospital fails to provide emergency care, the police fail to provide protection, and the courts fail to provide justice. Far from securing order, the public institutions create disorder. Instead of pursuing the truth, the system first creates a fiction, a story with Joe as the villain, and then relentlessly enacts its consequences.

The tension between order and disorder in the public sphere is depicted in two closely related genres of Nigerian fiction: the crime novel and the political novel. Like the romance novels considered previously, the Nigerian crime novel is a form of popular entertainment that is a direct offspring of formulaic Western fiction. Political novels are less formulaic and purport to be more serious, yet they cover much the same ground, depicting the Manichaean battle between order and chaos in contemporary Nigeria. This section will show how, together, these two types of novel bear witness to Nigerian institutional failure, anomie, and rationality overwhelmed by power.

Why Crime and Politics Are Not the Same Thing

Chief Balogun, a respected government official (formerly head of the Department of Works), is actually the leader of a criminal gang, aided and abetted by various policemen on the take. One of his new recruits is Jimmy, who had come to Lagos as an orphan after his uncle had stolen the land that was his inheritance. Unable to find work, Jimmy joins Balogun's thugs and becomes a vicious thief and killer. Although he pursues women and the fast life, Jimmy often regrets not having had a wife and children.

After the gang robs a bank, Balogun double-crosses the others. In the ensuing battle the gang members shoot one another until only Jimmy, who himself kills Balogun, is left. Jimmy gets away with the loot, the police hot on his trail. Before they can capture him, he turns his gun on himself. As he pulls the trigger he prays, "God, I'm coming home." He seems to see his mother, "smiling a welcome to him. They ran to each other and embraced. It was wonderful" (155).

(Abu Aremu, *Kill Me Gently*)

Thus ends Abu Aremu's *Kill Me Gently,* with sentimentality vying with pathos. The contrast in this crime thriller is not between good and bad, for all of the leading characters are criminals, but between evil opportunist and malleable victim. Chief Balogun, himself from a poor background, has seized the main chance for political and economic mobility. He has enriched himself first through corruption in the Department of Works and later through smuggling, drugs, and robbery. He is a Big Man, both in the government and in the criminal underworld.

Jimmy, on the other hand, seems more a victim than a born predator. Orphaned as a youth, cheated by his uncle, unable to make a living by farming, he has fled to Lagos. Like so many Johnny-Just-Comes, he seeks opportunity in the city and, like so many, fails to find it. It is not until after he has searched for employment with mounting desperation, and has learned that his school certificate is worthless without influential connections, that he takes to crime. Although he kills half a dozen people along the way, Jimmy has a tender side: he regrets not settling down with a family, and he experiences his own death as going home to mother's arms— kill me gently, indeed. Jimmy is far more sympathetic than Balogun, the police, or anyone else in the novel.

Aremu's story is about power: the Baloguns, police, and uncles of the world have it, while the Jimmys don't. It is also about corruption, specifically the abuse of public office. It might be considered a political novel, but its title, its plot, and its dialogue ("Yes, you're dying, right now. This day, this moment, you dirty pig") clearly mark it as a crime novel. How different, then, are these two types of novels?

When I first began to study Nigerian novels, I saw no difference at all. During a visit to Lagos and Ibadan, I spoke with about forty authors and publishers. Showing each interviewee the list of genres I had developed after reading some two hundred novels, I would say something like, "It seems to me that most Nigerian novels fall roughly into seven groups: city novels, village novels, novels about relations between women and men, novels about the civil war, novels about intellectuals or academic life, romances, and crime novels. Do these categories sound right to you?" By and large my respondents agreed that these were the basic categories; usually they even, with some qualification, accepted my categorization of their own works. There was one exception, however: a number of them asked me, "What about politics?"

True enough, I had no separate category for political novels. My reason was straightforward: since the political novels were invariably about corruption, since the big men of crime novels were sometimes political figures and sometimes private businessmen, and since they (like their real-life counterparts) moved readily between the public and private spheres, I had simply categorized all of them as crime novels. Nigerian authors and readers, however, saw a significant difference. They pointed out that although theft and misuse of power might be rampant in both the public and private spheres, the abuse of public office constituted a specific type of social problem and not just another case of robbery and violence, and they thought my categories ought to reflect this. At first I found it hard to see much difference, aside from the fact that in political novels some of the crooks held office, but gradually I came to see that the distinction was not so much one of deed as of implication. While crime (and crime fiction) suggest that someone is violating the rules of the system, political corruption (and political fiction) suggest that there is something wrong with the system itself.

So I established a separate category for political novels. Doing this allowed me to replicate the distinction made by the Nigerian writers and readers themselves and to identify more precisely some novels that would otherwise be categorized as "Other," such as Achebe's *Anthills of the Savannah*. More important, making the separation between crime and political novels allowed me to compare the two genres, and this comparison tells its own story.

At the most basic level, both crime and political novels are about people trying to figure out their social world. Characters try to answer questions or solve problems so they can get on with their private agendas. These novels are narratives of adversity. In telling stories about social problems, in effect they explain them, and they offer scenarios of what happens to people—the Jimmys, and the Baloguns as well—who participate in the problematic social complex that is Nigeria. Through such fictions, members of the reading class exchange ideas about coping with contemporary Nigerian life. The novels, therefore, are not only *about* people addressing problems. They *are* people addressing problems.

We can get a perspective on this by looking at a completely different type of writing, the obituary. In the many death notices in Nigerian newspapers, people use print to figure something out, specifically to suggest a story that makes sense of the intrusion of disorder into the orderly lives of the rich or prominent.[127] Paid for by relatives or clients, these obituaries may fill an entire page with photos and detailed information about the achievements of the deceased and his or her family. Such obituaries frequently point the finger of suspicion toward enemies of the deceased, hinting of murder. For example, after recounting the distinguished accomplishments of a dead chief, one obituary suggests that those unspecified enemies who have brought him down will "reap the whirlwind." Such a statement implies that someone may have had a hand in the chief's death without really saying so. Like *The Victim*, it suggests that a crime may have taken place, but it places no hope in institutional investigation, instead leaving justice in the hands of providence. An obituary like this, which might be viewed as an attempt to comprehend the biggest puzzle of all,[128] is another discursive means by which Nigerians try to figure things out, attribute agency, and redress wrongs where institutional means are inadequate. It is another story that makes sense of the senseless.

Crime novels and political novels do the same thing. They tell a story of rationality and its limitations. When told by men and women as committed to modern rationality as is the Nigerian educated elite, such a story is profoundly pessimistic because it describes a public sphere that is ultimately irrational.

As I have repeatedly argued, novels are stories for the reading class. This class reads for entertainment and instruction. All novels, even the most lightweight entertainment, offer some instruction in how the world works (just as all novels, even the most didactic, must entertain or they will not be read). Such stories of entertainment and instruction do not just wash over readers and drench them with meaning. They treat issues of interest to the reading class, and readers of fiction, like the readers of obituaries, make use of the textual suggestions to draw their own conclusions about their society—which, as we have seen, is just what the writers want them to do.

To show this, I shall first look at the Nigerian crime novels and their variation on the Western formula. Authors of crime novels see themselves as bearing witness to social dislocations, and I shall show how they structure this witness. Crime novels and political novels are cast in similar forms, so I shall look at some of what they have in common and at how they differ. With respect to political fiction, we shall consider what it means to tell a story about politics in a context where "the generals don't read." Finally, we shall assess what I call the glamour of impotence, the situation of writers telling stories about public life to a helpless or indifferent public.

Cops and Robbers

Police at a roadblock shake down Lagos motorists. Facto's gang pays them off, then rob a wealthy couple, who get no help from the police. The scene switches to the affluent Ikoyi area, where an accountant named Iphrian and his wife, Mercy, are starting their day. As Iphrian drives to work, a military vehicle plows into his car; the driver, Captain Ikabo, berates Iphrian and demands payment. The police haul Iphrian off. Although he has faith that reason and justice will prevail, he is thrown into jail.

Late that night, Mercy hears what has happened and goes to the police station, only to be told to come back in the morning. As she returns home, Facto's gang seizes her, and one of them rapes her; they steal her Volvo and leave her in shock. Neighborhood vigilantes attack the gang (recalling an earlier account of vigilantism by traders) and kill the rapist.

Upon his release, Iphrian learns what has happened, and he tells a sympathetic police commissioner. The latter assigns an honest cop named Edu to bring Facto to book. Edu plants Achike, another officer, in the gang. Time passes: Mercy is no better, the police don't seem to be coming up with much, and Iphrian is thoroughly disillusioned by the corruption and chaos of "another side of Lagos" that he now sees. He decides to pay off Ikabo, who has been hounding him, and take justice into his own hands.

The gang plans a truck robbery, using Iphrian's stolen Volvo. Achike has to go along and doesn't have a chance to alert Edu. Iphrian has been trailing the gang. At the scene of the robbery, he manages to kill them all except Achike, who hasn't seen him and cannot figure out what happened.

Edu and Achike visit Iphrian, who is packing up to move his family to his home village near Calabar. The policemen are suspicious, but they can't believe this quiet accountant could have wiped out the criminal gang. The two policemen become heroes, Captain Ikabo gets promoted, and Iphrian and family find a peaceful life far from Lagos.

(Philip Phil-Ebosie, *Dead of Night*)

Robbers infest the night, preying on women and on people lucky enough to own Volvos. Police blame the victim. A mild-mannered accountant must deliver his own justice. Philip Phil-Ebosie's *Dead of Night* offers a damning portrait of Lagos, of military arrogance, and of most police. Such a portrait is typical of Nigerian crime fiction.

It is important to tease out what is specifically Nigerian here, of course, for criminal gangs, shoot-outs, and citizen-avengers are staples of crime fiction everywhere. Crime stories seem universal, and they proliferate to meet the demands of the newly literate. Early twentieth-century Shanghai, for example, saw a rapid growth of the reading public, and of magazines that published fiction for this public. An editor of one such magazine, after analyzing the sales of his own publication, reported that issues with detective stories sold best.[129] Similarly, the rise of crime and detective fiction in England and the United States was associated with the mid-nineteenth-century expansion of the reading public. Nigeria follows the same pattern: in the late colonial period, new readers who wanted lively and not-too-demanding reading created a market for crime stories that has lasted to this day. Crime novels are members of a larger set of Nigerian reading materials that includes sensational newspaper accounts of crimes, detective magazines, and many of the Onitsha market pamphlets.

Of the eight genres discussed in the present study, the crime novel is by far the largest, constituting close to a quarter of all Nigerian novels (see Table 3-1). Nigerian readers enjoy British and, to a lesser extent, American crime fiction as well. Nigerian writers openly imitate the style of popular authors like James Hadley Chase and Ian Fleming. Despite such use of Western models, however, Nigerian crime writing has some distinctly Nigerian characteristics. As I did with the romances, I shall first look at the Western model for the crime novels. Then I can consider the changes that Nigerians have made.

Western crime novels are built around a puzzle—"Who did it?"—and the eventual solution to the puzzle constitutes the moral fantasy of a rational universe, a world of specific causes for specific effects that satisfies the scientific cast of modern Western thought.[130] If crime is necessary and functional because it gives a society occasion to reaffirm its norms, as Émile Durkheim argued, then crime novels are similarly functional. They explore these norms and socialize readers with respect to them, especially norms involving the powers of rational thinking and the inevitability of retribution following deviation.[131]

English crime literature goes back at least as far as the cony-catching pamphlets of the Elizabethan age that told of thieves and tricksters meeting their just desserts. While the eighteenth century produced romantic portraits of criminals and their pursuers, like William Godwin's *Adventures of Caleb Williams* and the Gothic horror fantasies of Anne Radcliffe and Monk Lewis, it was the nineteenth century that saw the proliferation of popular, affordable, and often formulaic crime fiction. Such popular entertainment was a product of the Industrial Revolution and its urbanization, expanded literacy, and increased leisure time of the middle and working classes. Early in the century the high price of novels kept them out of the reach of the lower middle class, but a subliterature of broadsheets and pamphlets, blue books (abridgments of Gothic novels) and penny dreadfuls (books sold in weekly parts, begun by Edward Lloyd in 1841) catered to the demand for the cheap and the sensational. By the 1850s, private subscription libraries such as Mudie's, and later public libraries, as well as cheap editions (yellowback "railway novels"), appeared to meet the increasing demand for fiction.

Detective fiction more specifically arose with the establishment of urban police forces, with the Metropolitan Police Act of 1829 setting up the London police.[132] The early London force was understaffed and undistinguished, but it gradually improved, and the urban middle class came to regard the police in general, and the detective in particular, as the protectors of social order. Charles Dickens expressed his admiration for the police in *Household Words,* thereby helping to create a climate of public esteem that the British police have enjoyed ever since. The detective began to replace the criminal as the hero in crime fiction. Contemporary police procedurals (mysteries that give a detailed picture of police operations) directly represent this legacy, while stories involving private detectives combine the procedural with the gentleman-sleuth tradition begun in the United States by Edgar Allen Poe but associated especially with British writers such as Arthur Conan Doyle and Agatha Christie. The less gentlemanly private eyes of American writers like Raymond Chandler and Dashiell Hammett followed, and today these tough but basically decent investigators have female counterparts in the books of Sara Paretsky, Sue Grafton, and other women writers.

Crime fiction continues to be immensely popular in the West. Bookstores invariably, and libraries usually, shelve "mysteries" separately from other fiction, both catering to the demand of many readers for just this type of book and suggesting a certain distance between crime novels and real literature. Crime writing represents the largest single category of fiction published, amounting to about one-quarter of the titles published annually.[133] It is reviewed separately in major reviewing outlines, and —like other formulaic fiction—it sustains an elaborate apparatus of organizations and awards.

As for the content of this hugely successful category of writing, the typical Western crime novel, be it police procedural, murder-in-the-parsonage, or spy thriller, moves from order to disorder to reestablished order. A crime is committed, unsettling social relations. The detection of and pursuit of the perpetrator follow. When the latter is caught, justice prevails and order returns. Crime novels confirm the powers of the rational intellect to figure things out—the world makes sense once you follow the clues and analyze the evidence correctly—and thus confirm the fundamental order underlying social relations.

To a considerable extent the Nigerian crime novel resembles its Victorian English predecessors. Like them, it (1) is a product of a rapid expansion of literacy, (2) is aimed at an urban market and urban concerns, and (3) was preceded by a pamphlet literature that made sensational stories available to the semiliterate of limited means.[134] Drawing inspiration from more contemporary police procedurals, James Bond thrillers, and the James Hadley Chase sex-and-sadism school, many Nigerian crime authors have followed the Western model closely. A simple example is found in *Labulabu Mask*.

> A criminal mastermind named Wilson concocts an intricate plot to steal a venerable mask from State Art Museum in Lagos. He and his three henchmen succeed in making off with the mask. Arogundade, an ambitious police inspector, uses forensic lab work and various paid informants to crack the case. Trapped, the criminals end up killing one another. Dying, Wilson points the finger at the museum manager as the person who actually orchestrated the theft.
>
> (Adetokunbo Abiola, *Labulabu Mask*)

Such a novel exhibits the classic Western structure: (1) the move from order to disorder following a criminal act; (2) the detection and pursuit of those responsible for the crime; and (3) the determination of guilt, the capture or death of criminals, and the reestablishment of order. *Labulabu Mask* has a certain antiestablishment tone—the museum director is a senior civil servant, and, as a crook points out, "businessmen are not to be trusted"—but the crooked organization head is a familiar figure in Western crime fiction as well. Some Nigerian local color is present. The novel is sprinkled with references to Yoruba institutions, the police chief thinks the population will be against him "all because he wasn't an indigene of this God-forsaken town," and a Yoruba priest goes on television to curse the thieves. Such localisms notwithstanding, by and large the plot adheres to the Western model, especially in its movement from order to disorder to order.

There are some differences, however, some particularly Nigerian characteristics of this and most other Nigerian crime novels. First of all, the crime is robbery, not murder. Killings often take place in the course of the action, but theft, rather than hatred, revenge, or madness, is invariably the primary motivation. Facto's gang in *Dead of Night* and Wilson in *Labulabu Mask* are first and foremost robbers; killing and rape are chance events, unplanned and ultimately destructive to the criminals' operations. In this respect Nigerian crime novels are quite different from their Western counterparts, where the focus is on murder, and where any number of motives—revenge, hatred, madness, sexual obsession, as well as financial gain—may lie behind the killing.

Second, action rather than detection moves the plot. We never see anything like the classic Western detective story, where the detective's accomplishments are a matter of brainpower, as with Sherlock Holmes or Hercule Poirot. Instead, Nigerian heroes like Arogundade or Iphrian spend little time in reflection. They are constantly on the move, running down leads, interviewing people, threatening smaller crooks to get to the bigger ones, and carrying out daring schemes to catch the criminals. Such heroes are brave, determined, and individualistic, and they place confidence in their energy and courage, not in their powers of deduction.

Third, most Nigerian crime novels are of the hard-boiled type, featuring rather humorless male protagonists and much violence. They rarely include any whimsy or eccentric characters of the sort found in murder-at-the-vicarage mysteries. Not just the criminals, but the detectives or heroes—the good guys—ignore legal and moral restraints. Some, like Iphrian, simply kill criminals; some they vent their frustrations by roughing up citizens. In *Labulabu Mask,* detective inspector Arogundade is chasing the thieves when he hits another car. He drags the driver out, gives him "two hot slaps," and screams, " 'Do you know what you've done? You've prevented me from arresting some armed robbers!' He glared at the man. 'You're one of them! I know you!'" And he proceeds to handcuff him. Although his chief later frets that the mistreated citizen might sue, Arogundade never stops to consider, let alone regret, his action.

Fourth, the novels portray a deep mistrust of official institutions, especially those purported to ensure law and order. Neither the police nor the courts can be counted on to provide justice. Typically the protagonist is an individual acting alone, outside of any organization. Although this type of vigilantism is not unknown in Western novels, it occurs much more frequently in Nigerian ones; *Dead of Night,* for instance, has three separate and unconnected episodes of vigilante action. *Labulabu Mask* does not follow the vigilante pattern, but it does present a case of an official institution—the museum administration—that is rotten at its core.

While most Nigerian crime novels share these four features, their structures vary, and they often do not follow the order-disorder-order structure. In spite of what might be charitably regarded as the excessive zeal of the police, *Labulabu Mask* does exhibit the basic restoration-of-order format characteristic of the Western model. In *Dead of Night,* however, Iphrian and his family must create their own order, first by his killing the robbers, then by leaving the city. Moving further from the model, a great many Nigerian crime novels are like *The Victim* in that they end in disorder, not order. Joe is hung, and nothing can ever restore the previous state of affairs. Another example is Nwokolo's *Dangerous Inheritance,* a routine thriller about a cheating businessman and a corrupt senator conniving to possess some rich uranium fields, which has an investigative journalist tracking down the crooks. After a series of violent encounters, the novel ends with a bomb explosion. It is not clear who is left alive and who is not, and the final image is one of utter chaos.

So while the order-disorder-order format can be found, a different progression structures many Nigerian crime novels. As described earlier, the city novel has the following plot pattern: (1) urban migration, (2) hardship and disappointment, (3) opportunity, (4) success, (5) visit to the village, (6) turn of fortune, and (7) destruction or restoration. Crime novels generally proceed on parallel tracks, and they often present the lured-by-the-bright-lights-of-Lagos theme as well. The crime novel, though almost always set in a city, may or may not involve an urban migration, the opportunity stage entails committing a crime, and the migration and return to the village pattern may not appear, although the village occasionally serves as a moral referent.

Thus the crime plot looks like this:

1. *Hardship experienced by a basically decent person:* Joe and Iphrian are both unjustly accused of crimes; Joe's first hardship occurs when he is forced to interrupt his trip to be a Good Samaritan in the first place. Jimmy's uncle robs him of his inheritance, and his education doesn't help him land a job. Such people start out as victims, either of malicious individuals or of a harsh, uncaring world.

2. *Crime offers an opportunity to overcome hardship:* In the simplest version, a Jimmy turns to crime for money and power. In the vigilante stories, an Iphrian turns to crime to restore his good name or secure justice. There are variations—Joe's beating of Dayo, though an act of great violence, is hardly premeditated—but more typically the person knows he is choosing to do something illegal and/or immoral.

3. *Temporary success:* The person achieves the money, power, sex, or revenge that has motivated the criminal action. Sometimes this takes place only in the minds of the observers, as when the police in *The Victim* assume that Joe has gotten away with murder.

4. *Turn of fortune:* The police, a fellow crook, a scorned lover, or a virtuous hero uncovers the criminal secrets and gets on the trail of the criminal. Even in *Dead of Night*, Edu and Achike finally figure out that Iphrian has been the vigilante, although then they can not believe their own finding.

5. *Destruction or restoration:* If the protagonist is a hardened criminal, he or she usually dies or goes to prison. If the protagonist is a more or less innocent victim, restoration is possible, as in Iphrian's move to Calabar. More often, the victim is destroyed, either because events have been set in motion that cannot be stopped (e.g., Joe) or because he or she has gotten involved in crime too deeply to get out (e.g., Jimmy). The ending of *Kill Me Gently* is unusually satisfying because Jimmy's dying vision of his mother's arms merges his destruction and his restoration.

Plots often end in disorder, which may take several forms. In one, the protagonist is a criminal or somehow in the wrong, has a change of heart and attempts to do the right thing, but is somehow prevented from doing so. For example, Dan Fulani has written a series of thrillers about the sins of multinational corporations; one of these, *The Fight for Life,* deals with the export of powdered infant formula into poor countries.

> The product is Tiger's Milk, produced by an amoral American conglomerate and touted in Nigeria by Tiger, a none-too-bright boxer manipulated by the company. Amina, an educated northern girl rebelling against her conservative family, gets a job promoting this stuff and even pushes it on her reluctant sister.
>
> The denouement comes when Amina goes to Lagos to be crowned Tiger Milk Queen after Tiger triumphs in a rigged fight. Before the fight, a secretary warns Amina that Tiger's Milk does more harm than good, and she learns that her sister's baby has died. Amina goes to the fight prepared to make a speech telling the truth. She never gets to deliver it, however, because the whistle-blowers have gotten the other boxer to fight for real. Tiger is beaten, pandemonium ensues, and Tiger Milk's image is shot.
>
> (Dan Fulani, The Fight for Life)

Amina ultimately lacks agency—her change of heart does not affect the outcome—and the story ends in a riot. At least some sort of order is restored, nevertheless, in the sense that the reader trusts Nigerian babies are off Tiger's Milk and back to the breast. A more complex situation exists when the reader, not the protagonist, is fooled.

> Khaleel is managing director of a charter airline owned by his wealthy but nasty wife, Maryam. One day Bilkisu, Khaleel's lost love, walks into his office; divorced, she wants to marry Khaleel, as their Islamic religion permits. Khaleel leaps at the chance for happiness, but Maryam will have nothing to do with the idea of a second wife. A short time later Maryam is found strangled, and Khaleel is accused.
>
> A courtroom drama ensues as Gana, Maryam's greedy uncle and the company's second in command, tries to pin the blame on Khaleel, while Khaleel's lawyer argues that it was Gana who committed the murder. Despite considerable evidence against Gana, in a surprise ending Khaleel admits to Bilkisu that he, driven crazy by his love for her and by Maryam's scorn, had indeed killed his wife. Summoning family and friends to hear his confession, Khaleel swallows cyanide just before they arrive.
>
> (Mohmed Tukur Garba, Forgive Me Maryam)

In *Forgive Me Maryam,* the ending comes as an unpleasant shock: Garba has portrayed Khaleel as an honorable and sensitive man, so the reader is dismayed to learn he is a murderer. This revelation barely registers before Khaleel undercuts what dignity he has left, for instead of carrying through with his public confession, which would give him a certain tragic stature, he kills himself. The reader is left thinking Khaleel was both a murderer and a liar, even lying to the woman he loved.

Both Khaleel and Amina exemplify the pattern of initially decent but weak people who get drawn into evil. Khaleel's passion and Amina's naïveté (or, for that matter, Tiger's stupidity) make them somewhat more sympathetic than the heroes who turn to crime strictly for financial gain, as in Okereke's *The Other Side*. Here is a case of sheer greed. Ibe, diploma in hand, comes to Lagos and gets a job, but he wants a more luxurious life than he can afford on his clerk's salary; luxury means women, but also very specific material goods—a new rug, a new fan, a TV. So Ibe starts passing information to a gang of robbers and eventually gets caught, convicted, and executed. No noble motivations here, and the reader's sympathy is minimal. Whether or not the hero raises our sympathy, all such stories begin with someone who succumbs to temptation. Even when the careers of such figures end with the discovery of their corruption and their death, there is little sense of justice having been done. Gana is still a nasty piece of work even if he didn't kill Maryam; Lagos is still a hollow dream for village boys like Ibe; there is no restoration of a moral order in these stories.

We have seen many works like *The Other Side* that present the frustrations of the ambitious young man. This is a major theme—indeed, the primary theme—of contemporary Nigerian fiction. Whether or not the youth in question succumbs to a criminal career, over and over again Nigerian authors tell the story of young men (or, much more rarely, women) who get an education but are unable to succeed in urban Nigeria. Talent and honesty are blocked repeatedly by corruption, stupidity, ethnic favoritism, and nepotism. Dibia Humphrey's thriller *The End of Dark Street* (1992) offers a poignant example of the Disappointed Young Man.

> Bello—educated, principled, a good Muslim, and a devoted husband—works as a civil servant for the Import License Board. Following a military coup, Bello argues with Salami, his corrupt boss (who spends his working days having sex with his secretary), over whether the change in government will mean progress. Bello's earnestness irritates Salami, who uses the coup as a chance to get the young man fired.
>
> Devastated, Bello wanders the city and finally ends up living in a hovel on "Dark Street." He goes to work for a crime syndicate headed by his old secondary school teacher, another educated man who couldn't succeed by staying within the law. Bello turns out to be a successful criminal and falls for a crime queen, Czarina. On their honeymoon in Tahiti, he hears on the radio that another military coup has taken place. Shortly thereafter, his bride, whose first loyalty is to the syndicate, kills him. Bello's dying prayer is for his first wife's forgiveness.
>
> (Dibia Humphrey, *The End of Dark Street*)

Nothing profound here, but *Dark Street* presents a competently told tale of a talented man's fall into corruption. Although this is a crime novel, it has some of the same characteristics as a novel about intellectuals. Bello is nicknamed "the Brain," and he has the educated-but-jobless-young-man role when he is fired. The novel also takes oblique aim at military government, for one of its casualties has been the decimation of the civil service.

Over and over, crime writers tell the story of the decent young man's loss of employment, desperation, and descent into crime. Jide Oguntoye's *Harvest of Tricksters* tells the tale of Kunle, retrenched from his job as hotel cashier, now "looking for a job in spite of the fact that he had only the [primary] school certificate in a country where university graduates were unemployed in their thousands, the secondary school leavers and middle-class trained professional in their millions." (61) Of course he is unsuccessful, and of course he turns to crime. Oguntoye's story is familiar, remarkable only for the scene in which a car filled with bank robbers on their way to a holdup gets stuck in a go-slow! "They were at a bottleneck before a fly over now. Kunle and his men were tense and angry. . . . They were wondering: would there never be a final solution to [the] traffic problem in Lagos?" (Or the crime problem?)

Nigerian crime fiction strikes the reader as unusually masculine, not just in its violence but even more in its focus on masculine problems: getting a job, attracting women, supporting a family, maintaining one's integrity in public life. The combination of work, love, and honor can be rendered in feminine terms, of course, as in the formulaic romances, but in crime fiction it is inflected along distinctly male lines. Crime novels have an extraordinarily high rate of male protagonists and authors in comparison with other genres. Of the 104 crime novels, men have written 100.[135] The masculinity of the genre is equally striking when one looks at the sex of the protagonists. Overall, Nigerian novels have a higher rate of female protagonists (26 percent) than of female authors (15 percent), since male authors write about female protagonists more than women write about men. Only 6 percent of the crime novel protagonists are female, slightly higher than the percentage of women crime authors, but insignificant nevertheless. And the three crime novels by women all have male protagonists.

Let's look at one of the rare crime novels written by a woman. Jumoke Serrano's *The Last Don Out* offers an interesting variation on the relentless tough-guy viewpoint, even though it has a tough-guy protagonist. Except for the twist at the end, this is an utterly routine crime thriller about Don, a Mafia-connected drug lord, casino operator, gang leader, and bank robber in Lagos. The plot is a string of episodes about the various robberies and other operations of his gang, with the usual rounds of sex, violence, and action. What is unusual is Don's relationship with his mistress, Christy. At the beginning, during what appears to be just another steamy sex scene, he and Christy talk about marriage, and he says, "I'd be lost without you." His need for her is a continuing motif throughout the novel, despite his occasional outbursts of calling her a bitch and hitting her, for which he is always (very atypically) remorseful. At the end, the police having destroyed Don's Lagos headquarters and shot him in the leg, he and Christy hole up (literally) in an underground hideaway in rural Ifo, as she tenderly nurses his wound. Then, after some more torrid sex, she shoots him dead. Totally mad, she talks animatedly to the corpse for a few days, then heads for Lagos, where the police catch her.

Christy's toughness is not unusual, but Don's tenderness is, and the focus on their relationship—which brings to mind films like *Duel in the Sun* or *Bonnie and Clyde,* which similarly present the passion and tenderness between outlaws—is unique. There are other criminal couples, such as the poor but ambitious Miki and the half-Arab sexpot Jordana who go into the smuggling business together in Dibia Humphrey's earlier novel *A Drop of Mercy,* but such relationships are presented as combinations of greed and lust, having nothing of the complex intensity Serrano depicts. A few other crime novels have partnerships between the good characters, most notably Victor Thorpe's attractive journalist-lawyer couple and Kalu Okpi's journalist-policewoman pair; both pairs appear in several Pacesetters, and both share a bantering, generally egalitarian relationship. Such books are rare exceptions to the typical depiction of women as sexpots and the protagonist's usual love-'em-and-leave-'em pattern.

Even more striking than the masculinity and misogyny of the crime novels is their relentless distrust of institutions, especially of the police. Even when cops are the good guys, they tend to be savages. Dimeji Popoola's *Near the Rainbow* features a sadistic Dirty Harry type of policemen: "Not the typical police officer . . . Ben Karim was a killer, ruthless and unforgiving [whose] brutality bordered on criminality" (9). He is fairly typical of the good (i.e., effective, not totally corrupt) police in such thrillers; recall those two hot slaps in *Labulabu Mask.* Such behavior might be forgiven as a way of getting the job done, but it hardly improves community relations.

A partial explanation for the dim view of the police in Nigerian crime novels may come from the relationship between urbanization and the establishment of the police force. Detective fiction in England emerged shortly after the founding of the London police. The urban middle class had experienced unchecked crime in cities, saw the establishment of the police as the solution to the problem of maintaining social order, and therefore romanticized and extravagantly admired policemen. But in Nigeria the police force was in place in colonial times, well in advance of the massive urbanization of recent decades. When rural immigrants to Lagos or other large cities encounter the crime and anomie of urban life, without the social controls of the village, they see the police as an ineffective, if not hostile, presence. Such people have no reason to admire the police, for they are associated with the problem of crime, not its solution.

On their side, Nigerian police tend to feel aggrieved by their low pay and low prestige relative to the military. Their bullying tactics and shakedowns may be partially a result. Starved for resources, ineffectual as well as corrupt, and hugely unpopular: such police are hardly likely to emerge as heroes in Nigerian crime fiction. And, indeed, they have not.

The mistrust of institutions goes deeper than a distaste for the police, however, for the novels show all institutions—government, private, educational, medical (recall those uninterested doctors in *The Victim*)—to be similarly indifferent to public welfare. Officials and organizations are sometimes the core of the problem, sometimes merely useless, but they never inspire trust. Protagonists must step outside of institutions to get what they want. The journalist who takes a leave from his paper to ferret out the story, the vigilante who takes justice into his own hands, and the criminal who pursues his ambitions on the wrong side of the law are all taking parallel actions to succeed.

Crime fiction in Nigeria, especially depictions of the mistrust of institutions and the tendency toward disorder, essentially is an elaboration on the familiar theme of disappointment and frustration. Young people come to the city, meet with frustration of their high expectations, and are overwhelmed. Middle-class people try to live middle-class lives, meet with frustration of their aspirations toward a predictable existence, and are overwhelmed. In crime fiction this frustration is presented in a particular key—violent, masculine—but it is the same story.

One reason that official institutions are suspect is because the line between the public and the private, between the good guy and bad guy categories, is blurred for Nigerians daily. Travelers coming through Murtala Muhammed Airport in Lagos, for example, encounter a bewildering array of men in uniform. It is hard to figure out who's who—who are customs officials, who are airport security, who are military, who are police—but everyone seems to be asking, "Have you got something for me?" Outside, the line is even harder to draw. Police just outside the airport constantly stop Nigerians leaving in private cars (a sign of wealth). The charge is obscure, something about taillights perhaps, but the solution is straightforward, and money changes hands. One can become matter-of-fact about such transactions, but the thought recurs: if the police, the defenders of public safety, are the robbers, then to whom does the private citizen turn for relief from other criminals?

It is not an idle question. In contemporary Nigeria the lines between public and private, between state moneys and private wealth, between politics and crime, between loyalty and corruption, have eroded. The collapse of the public-private distinction has been exacerbated by the oil economy, where a single source of revenue coming into the federal government perpetuates the "debilitating political economy of corruption that has immobilized state operations in Nigeria."[136] Corruption is endemic, even by Third World standards. In 1996, when Transparency International, an anticorruption pressure group founded by a former World Bank official, put out a list of nations ranked according to the prevalence of bribery in business dealings, Nigeria had the dubious distinction of topping the list.[137] Some nations in the top ten were rapidly developing economies like China (number 5) and Indonesia (10), while others were relatively developed economies that had stagnated or were slipping backward, like Venezuela and Russia (7 and 8). Nigeria's economy was neither developing nor developed, but forever, tantalizingly, promising. Now, of course, this is the view from outside—foreign businessmen and World Bank types who would rather do deals in squeaky-clean places like New Zealand and Denmark, where bribery is all but unknown—but Nigerians themselves endlessly decry the corruption of the public and private sectors.

And then there's the necessary preoccupation with security. In present-day Lagos, residents have taken to erecting gates at the entrance to their streets to keep out armed robbers, or to prevent those who do get in from escaping the rough justice meted out by the community.[138] One or more gates, locked or unlocked at specified periods during the day, impede ready access to a residential area, and some people now think it risky to live in streets lacking such gates. Proponents claim the street gates are especially effective at reducing car thefts. Critics see the gates as inconvenient, however, locking out residents more than robbers. And the police decry the gates as examples of vigilantism —which they are, of course—and claim that the illegal structures are counterproductive because they prevent police officers from patrolling neighborhoods effectively. Lagosians scoff at the idea of the police protecting them from robbery, gates or no gates, and continue taking protection into their own hands.

The gates typify the general pattern. At virtually all levels of the political system, of the economy, and of daily life, private gain has pushed out public responsibility, institutions are ineffectual, and therefore private action is the most rational response. Security is something only the wealthy can afford, and even they need luck. The response of middle-class Nigerians has been less one of outrage than of bewilderment. Where do you turn for justice? What does a decent person do in a corrupt system? Whom can we trust?

As moral fantasies, crime novels should offer solutions to these problems, and they do, but these are not the solutions of triumphant rationality found in the Western model. Rationality doesn't usually triumph in the Nigerian crime novel, for that particular fantasy would be simple incredible. Instead, the rock of vigilante action (*Dead of Night*) and the hard place of being destroyed by the system (*The Victim*) are the alternatives, bleak but believable, to which the crime novels bear witness.

Political Fictions

Benjamin Oke, a high-ranking civil servant, hears unsettling news about the execution of a man he vaguely remembers. Later, on his way to a funeral, his VIP escort hits a car, then beats the hapless driver to death. At the funeral Oke remembers how he and his deceased friend quarreled after the civil war over Oke's profiteering. The next day Oke gets stuck in a "go-slow" for hours. While killing time, Oke reads in the newspaper that the executed man was an educated youth who turned to crime after being rejected for a job for which he was well qualified in favor of another who hadn't even bothered to show up for the interview. Oke ponders on this, and when they finally get going, he has a heart attack.

Some months letter, Oke is dying. He writes to his children confessing his corrupt practices over the years: war profiteering, schemes for buying foreign pharmaceuticals, siphoning off government funds, keeping a mistress and three illegitimate children, and giving his eldest son a job ahead of a more qualified candidate, the executed man. Now Oke wants to make amends. He leaves modest bequests to his children, a substantial amount to his mistress, Ondalia, to support their children, and the rest, a fortune, to the federal and Anambra state governments, Oke's way of returning the wealth he had stolen. Barrister Chimaluze will execute the will, and Oke requests a simple funeral.

The final section opens as Ondalia reads the newspaper about Oke's death and the lavish funeral planned for later that month. Currently fending off another sugar daddy whom she abhors, she is frantic to know if Oke has provided for her as he had promised. She goes to the funeral and hears the eldest son castigate whoever produced a fake will; guessing the truth, Ondalia faints. Barrister Chimaluze sends an angry letter to the son and siblings, defying their efforts to discredit Oke's will. The case is headed for court. Two months later, Ondalia learns that Barrister Chimaluze has been shot dead. She waits with resignation for her sugar daddy.

(Lawrence Nwokora, *The Legacy*)

Oke's funeral symbolizes the corruption of the Nigerian elite. When a wealthy Nigerian dies, the family often keeps the body in cold storage for a considerable time while they make elaborate and costly funeral arrangements—an example of the conspicuous consumption practiced by Oke's social class. For many people it is money from corruption that makes such consumption possible.

The Legacy is a political novel that suggests how difficult it is to reestablish the boundary between the public and the private purse, even with the best of intentions. The irony of Oke's intended legacy versus his real one is clear. Although it could use some editing, Nwokora's book shows in detail how corruption corrodes all social institutions: the family, the law, business, and public life. If vigilantism and annihilation are the alternatives presented in the crime novel, the political novels are altogether bleaker in outlook, for they present no viable alternatives whatsoever. When the public and private have been merged, the damage cannot be undone; no basis exists for order to emerge from disorder; no social precipitate can organize the chaotic Nigerian mixture. This is the starkly pessimistic picture.

But what exactly is being corrupted? Earlier I have noted that the state of Nigeria itself is the biggest political fiction. Officially it is the Federal Republic of Nigeria, but it is hardly federal, for virtually all power comes from the center. It is hardly a republic, either, not when thirty of the past thirty-nine years have been military governments. As for the name Nigeria, this Latin word dreamed up by a colonial governor's sweetheart represents no group's sense of nationhood. Moreover, the Nigerian state has never really taken root. The search for a stable system of federal democracy has dominated Nigerian politics since at least the early 1950s, but no such system has been found. (At the time of this writing, in 1999, yet another transition to democratic government has taken place; it remains to be seen how long it lasts.) Competitive civilian politics based on ethnicity and region, the political hegemony of the military elite, perverse distributive pressures inherent in the oil-based economy, and disagreements over the design of federal institutions have so far prevented the achievement of a stable democratic federation.[139] Federal Republic of Nigeria, indeed!

If Nigerians, whose increasing political cynicism is rooted in bitter experience, do not share any clear sense of some ideal Federal Republic of Nigeria that is being corrupted, it becomes hard to identify the paradise in the paradise-lost story told by political novels. It isn't the village, for political novels rarely pay much attention to traditional rural life. Nor is it some specific point in Nigerian history; there are occasional references to the can-do optimism of early Biafra or to the sense of possibility excited by Murtala Muhammed's reforms, but both regimes were too brief to have engendered substantial loyalties of the collective memory. Instead, what seems to have been lost is what might be called the Nigerian Dream.

The Nigerian Dream, articulated in the 1970s, was a product of the oil-boom affluence and of the astonishingly smooth reintegration of the country following the civil war. The postwar genocide feared by the Igbo and by Nigerian progressives of all ethnicities did not take place. The torrent of petro-naira was going to wash away poverty and underdevelopment. Optimism was high. The Nigerian Dream, born in this heady atmosphere, has three essential components:

1. *The New Nigerian:* He or she was a cosmopolitan and affluent African individual, unbound by ethnic or religious background, moving easily among different groups. New Nigerians were to be relatively egal-

itarian in terms of gender, and were to reward education and achievement rather than social background or demographic characteristics. Such New Nigerians would be dynamic, suave, and sexy as well.

2. *The Giant of Africa:* Nigeria, and specifically the Nigerian state, was the powerhouse of the black world, leading the fight against apartheid, showing less fortunate African and diaspora blacks what a fully developed and politically powerful black nation could look like. This was the basis for Nigerian demands to be given a seat on the United Nations Security Council. It was also at the heart of FESTAC '77, the celebration of pan-Africanism whereby Nigeria sought "to neutralize the paradoxes of state wealth and power in a universalizing black nationalist ideology."[140]

3. *The Best of Both Worlds:* Nigerians would preserve the most valuable elements of their traditions, especially communalism, family obligations, respect for elders, oral wisdom showing how the world works, and folk knowledge about spiritual life and about specific remedies such as herbal medicines. At the same time they would appropriate Western science and technology, as well as cultural forms ranging from Christianity to fashion to popular music, all of which could be rendered in distinctly Nigerian idioms. Such a view made the tradition-versus-modernity dichotomy obsolete.

Not even during the 1970s, when the Giant of Africa could at least lay plausible claim to some bragging rights, did the Nigerian Dream come close to realization. Writers and intellectuals during the oil-boom years gave a number of reasons—greed, corruption, individual malfeasance, external meddling in Nigerian affairs, indiscipline, colonialist leftovers, the lingering aftermath of the war's dislocations—but these were seen as glitches, temporary obstacles that could and would be surmounted as Nigeria moved inevitably toward her destiny.[141] All of this sounds very much like the American Dream, and it had the same Achilles' heel: it depended on continuing affluence. The Nigerian Dream was especially vulnerable because it depended on an unpredictable global market for a single commodity and because Nigeria's unrestrained population growth put relentless pressure on its infrastructure and institutions, but for a while it seemed to capture a future order that was both feasible and desirable.

All such dreaming ended with the oil bust. From the early 1980s until the present, Nigerians have had ever-decreasing confidence in their country's capacity to produce cosmopolitan men and women, command respect as the military and moral heavyweight of Africa, or create a good life for its citizens drawing on Western and African intellectual resources. Ethnic and religious differences continue to draw blood and to determine life chances regardless of qualifications. Anyone foolish enough to be a nontribal, non-regional, nonsectarian New Nigerian will miss out on the patronage flows. Actually, there are such New Nigerians, but they live in Toronto, Houston, or Stockholm, not in Kano or Ibadan.

The Giant of Africa has been seen to be increasingly powerless. Locally Nigerians see the inability of the Nigerian-led Economic Community of West African States (ECOWAS) forces to bring stability to Liberia or, for that matter, the inability of the state to control crime in Lagos. Continentally the new giant that Africans look to is postapartheid South Africa. And globally, Western nations occasionally castigate Nigeria for its failure to maintain democracy, control its drug trade, or operate a safe international airport, but most of the world simply ignores it.

And instead of the best of both worlds, Nigerians seem to be getting the worst. Just as traditional rural institutions continue their unstoppable decay and traditional wisdom is lost to memory, so too does Western knowledge become less accessible than ever before. The proliferating yet crumbling universities, the neglected primary schools, the lag in electronic communications, the prohibitive cost of books, the decreased ability of educated Nigerians to travel outside the country, the increased censorship within—all have prevented Nigerians from keeping pace with the growth of new knowledge.

The reading class is painfully aware of how its hopes have been dashed. Novelists have represented this erosion of confidence, especially as the first and second generations give way to the third. Corruption has gone from being *a* theme to being *the* theme of the Nigerian novel, regardless of the writer's literary talents or aspirations. Achebe took corruption as one characteristic of a culture that had been wrenched from its moorings, most notably in *No Longer at Ease*, but it was only one among many. By the time he wrote *Anthills of the Savannah*, the thoroughgoing corruption of institutions and interactions all but overwhelms individual efforts to maintain integrity. Similarly, but at a more popular level, Ogali A. Ogali expressed pure enthusiasm for all things Western—including material advance, technology, Christianity, and social success in modern cities—in his early Onitsha market pamphlets. His post–civil war writings questioned these early enthusiasms, now attacking cultural imperialism and defending traditional ways. But by the late 1970s publication of *Coal City*, one critic noted that Ogali was responding to the full implications of the new social order that has in fact replaced the traditional one. And his response, as he "opens up a vista of corruption so vast, so pervasive, so comprehensive, that the possibility of honest and constructive social action is effectively ruled out," was one of cynicism and despair.[142]

Ogali and Achebe's increasing preoccupation with corruption is typical and is borne out statistically as well. If we take the end of the seventies as a break point, we find that 38 percent of Nigerian novels published by that date featured corruption as a central theme, but this rose to half of the novels published in 1980 or after.[143]

Political novels chart this loss of confidence. Unlike crime novels, they rarely begin with order, for the Nigerian Dream was never realized. As in *The Legacy,* political novels have ominous indicators, if not actual social chaos, in their opening chapters. They do resemble the crime novels in their representation of social breakdown and rampant thievery, and in their accounts of how decent people—the educated young people with hope and ideals— get drawn into corruption. They offer some feeble hope for a restoration or reconstruction of order, the realization of the Nigerian Dream, but it almost never comes to pass: justice is not done, social disorganization continues, the legacy of greed and corruption is more of the same. As Table 3-5 shows, the political novels resemble the crime variant where the moral fantasy is a move not toward order but toward greater disorder.

An early political novel that foretold how difficult it would be to maintain political order is Aluko's *Chief the Honourable Minister* (1970), which provides a bleak portrait of corruption in a newly independent African state.

TABLE 3-5
Crimes and Political Plots

	Plots		
Stages of the plot	*Western crime novel formula*	*Nigerian crime novel variant*	*Nigerian political novel*
Opening	Order	Order	[Previous or potential order assumed but rarely depicted]
Initiating action	Disruption of order by crime: disorder	Disruption of order by crime: disorder	Disruption of order by corruption: disorder
Protagonist's involvement	Protagonist seeks to restore order	Protagonist drawn into disorder	Protagonist drawn into disorder
Action	Detection and pursuit	Detection and pursuit	Detection and pursuit; hopes for restoration of order
Ending	Justice prevails; restoration of order	Justice prevails; restoration of order *or* Failure of justice; continued disorder	Failure of justice; continued disorder
Examples	*Labulabu Mask; The Writer*	*The Victim*	*The Legacy; Anthills of the Savannah*

Alade Moses, a school headmaster, unexpectedly gets appointed minister of works in the new government. Moses has more integrity than most of his fellow ministers and political operatives, but, after some agonizing, he starts going along with dubious and then outright corrupt practices. Fiddling with contracts, dirty tricks against the opposition party, election frauds—for all these, Moses is the initially appalled onlooker who eventually is sucked in to the system. Ministers, expatriates, and party operatives like the memorable Gorgeous Gregory are all one in their cynicism and greed. Finally, a rigged election in his hometown ("Newtown") triggers violence between party thugs, and many politicians are killed, including Moses. The military takes over, vowing to restore order.

(T. M. Aluko, *Chief the Honourable Minister*)

Alade Moses is one of Aluko's passive protagonists infected by the political disease around him. He squanders his chance for leadership on a wider scale, wasting his dream of becoming schoolmaster to the nation. Like that of the idealistic young teacher in Achebe's *A Man of the People,* published four years earlier and quite similar to Aluko's book, Moses' initial integrity wilts once he is given opportunities to amass personal power and wealth. This Moses will lead his people nowhere.

Yet the ending of *Chief the Honourable Minister* is faintly optimistic: Military discipline may prove a corrective to the Gorgeous Gregorys of the new state. In the ensuing years greater experience with reformist regimes, both civilian and military, gives rise to a greater sense of hopelessness. Areo's *Paradise for the Masses* (1985), for example, ends with a lonely radical trying mightily to preserve a reformist movement, despite the corruption of its founder.

A thirty-year-old university graduate, Dita founds the Gerania Youth Movement to overturn the corrupt regime. He is joined by a radical professor named Ife and by the illegitimate daughter of the Minister of Finance. The movement's first campaign is a city clean-up accompanied by attacks on police, fire, and government offices. Its early success terrifies the ruling party, which tries to co-opt Dita, first by giving jobs to his relatives, then with threats. Finally, the party sends Agnes, an old friend who has slept her way to a glamorous job as a television news reporter, to seduce him. She succeeds. Dita joins the party, becomes minister of youth, and marries Agnes. Ife, bitterly disappointed by Dita's betrayal, urges Geranian youth to continue the struggle.

(Agbo Areo, *Paradise for the Masses*)

Here the novel begins with a repressive regime and ends with the same regime, somewhat destabilized. The basic structure of most political novels is the movement from order (both an ideal version—the not-yet-realized Nigerian Dream —and the actual reality, a state of oligarchy, domination, and corruption) to disorder through the experiences of a protagonist who starts out as a decent person but is compromised or destroyed by the powers that be. The plot structure moves through the following stages:

1. *An ideal of political order:* Political novels always have some character who believes that a just political order is possible. If the ideal has not yet been achieved in Nigeria, this is due to corrupt leadership or lack of discipline, but it is not impossible. Aluko's and Achebe's novels begin from the dream shared by African nationalists of the 1940s and 1950s: a postcolonial African state whose democratic institutions reflect the will of the people. Areo's Dita holds a more radical and egalitarian ideal, similarly not yet achieved. Oke's futile attempt to make amends is cast in light of an ideal of public service that he has betrayed.

2. *Corruption:* Greed, lust, and the perquisites of power have distorted the movement of political life toward the ideal order. Big Men within the nation and cynical foreign interests are derailing progress. Institutions like the police and fire departments—targets for the Gerania Youth Movement's wrath—are corrupt and consequentially ineffective, if not oppressive.

3. *An initially honorable protagonist gets seduced by power, wealth, and/or sex:* Heroes start honest but weak, and they are unable to resist temptation. These temptations are often sexual—the pattern here was set as early as Achebe's *No Longer at Ease*—but the issue is a more general ethical meltdown. Opportunities like war profiteering or being cozy with His Excellency are more than the protagonists can resist. They often rationalize their co-optation, but their excuses become less persuasive, even to themselves.

4. *Feeble hopes for reform:* Oke tries to leave a legacy that will atone for his sins, Moses initially fights the system, and Ife urges that the struggle continue even after its leader has defected. This theme of feeble hopes may come at the end of the book or may precede the ultimate seduction of the protagonist. It is never very convincing. Who listens to Ife's haranguing, Areo implicitly asks, and how could the outcome be different this time?

5. *Apocalypse and/or impotence:* Moses ends up dead. So does Oke and his lawyer, with Oke's will, in both senses, overturned. Dita is bought off and married to a whore. In this novel Ife, who retains his political ideals, seems just one more intellectual out of touch with reality; it is the Agneses of Nigeria who understand how things work. Just as seduction works as a metaphor for the corruption of ideals, so does impotence or a more general failure of issue represent the inability of political ideals to give birth to a lasting order.

As the 1980s gave way to the 1990s, the faint hopes represented by an Ife grew feebler, and the endings more catastrophic. An over-the-top example is Adebayo Williams's *The Remains of the Last Emperor* (1994), a hallucinatory combination of political allegory, the book of Revelation, and magical realism.

> A story within a story: An editor named John, busy editing a general's manuscript, is fascinated by an old homeless man who tells him he knows the true story of what happened twenty years earlier when the first military coup took place, the emperor was killed, and the Liberation Building was destroyed. He gives the editor a mysterious manuscript that keeps disappearing, and several days later he tells the story to the editor.
>
> The old man had been a famous musician who went mad. In the madhouse outside the city on the lagoon he joins "the leader," Brother Jerry, and the other madmen. Each of the madmen has a story, all intertwined with the political life of the nation under the tyrannical, increasingly paranoid emperor. The inmates experiment with democracy (the election of the leader), communalism, and something called the Laboratory of Peace.
>
> As the nation collapses into anarchy while the emperor retreats further into his isolation, the separation between the asylum and the outside collapses. Refugees flood the madhouse, while its inmates decide to make a last stand for justice. They storm the city and take over the Liberation Building, which falls to ruins because it has no foundation. Only the musician survives, whom Brother Jerry has instructed to tell the story. The musician witnesses the fall of the emperor's palace; the emperor is eaten by a boa constrictor, which is then killed and eaten by soldiers in a military coup. All of this the musician explains to the young editor, who publishes the manuscript as *The Remains of the Last Emperor*.
>
> (Adebayo Williams, *The Remains of the Last Emperor*)

There is a playing with narratives here—the interior story, the manuscript, becomes the exterior, the book—and each story has others layered within. Very much a modernist in style, Williams peppers his novel with literary, biblical, and political allusions. While *The Remains* is somewhat undisciplined, Williams displays a vivid allegorical imagination. But it is an allegory of despair, a nation that reproduces its tyranny by eating itself. Only the story remains, bearing witness to what has happened.

Observing the political novels and their increasing tone of despair, I formulated two hypotheses. First, since women have been minimally involved in Nigerian political life, I expected the political novels to be like the crime novels: overwhelmingly masculine. Second, since the failure of the Second Republic meant that the inevitable transition to democracy was more and more questionable, the political future more and more urgent, I expected the production of political novels to increase after 1983.

TABLE 3-6
Political Novels by Date of Publication

Date Published	Political novels	Other novels	Total
1952–83	13	227	240
	(30%)	(53%)	(50%)
1984–Present	31	205	236
	(70%)	(47%)	(50%)
Total	44	432	476

Both hypotheses were borne out. Political novels are even more masculine than crime novels, for every one is written by a man.[144] And, as Table 3-6 shows, political novels have increased since the fall of the Second Republic. In spite of the military government's capacity's for censorship, the concerns of the reading classes have turned more and more to politics, especially in the aftermath of Nigeria's second failure to maintain a democratic civilian government, and the novelists are representing and responding to these concerns.

Nigerian writers are remarkably unconcerned with censorship. When I asked them about it, many replied with breezy assurance that "the generals don't read." Others talked about how easy it is to avoid direct criticism. They seemed to think that libel or direct criticism of the current regime were the only things to worry about, and thus it was easy enough to give political messages some perfunctory disguise, which was all that was necessary. The Abacha regime, which routinely imprisoned editors and executed Ken Saro-Wiwa, may have cut into this authorial complaisance, but it had survived previous bouts of repression, including the 1986 letter-bomb assassination of outspoken newspaper editor Dele Giwa, a murder many assume to have been carried out by, or at least with the tacit encouragement of, the regime. Writers of fiction have felt they were immune to the threats journalists face.

An example of this political insouciance comes from Ohiaeri's *Behind the Iron Curtain*. During the last decade of the colonial period, a young student who wins a scholarship to study medicine in East Germany is harassed repeatedly by the colonial office for being a communist. When he finally returns to Lagos ten years later, on the eve of Nigerian independence, a police officer interrogates him one last time about whether he intends to overthrow the government. The exasperated doctor responds:

> All these things are a bunch of lies framed up by the colonial office. . . . Now, I wish to assure you that I'm a Nigerian and I've no intention of overthrowing any government. But one thing is clear: whether a government will be over-

thrown or not depends on the performance of that government. . . . Nigeria will soon be independent and it can only be a stable country when it provides jobs for the teeming jobless masses and enough houses for the homeless people and good health services. From what I have seen in the few days since I arrived, Nigeria has been divided into three regions. There's no national feeling; rather people are region-inclined. There's a lot of tribal feelings among the people. There's also a lot of unhealthy political rivalry and it seems to me that the powerful politicians who have not got enough political experience will soon take over the mantle of the government of this country. If care is not taken, they'll hit the rocks soon after independence. If they grind to a halt, are you going to lay the blame on me? Not at all, I shall not be responsible for that. (137)

Such a speech is a Cold War defense of socialism in the face of capitalism. The overall plot is more simply anticolonialist. Most of the book takes place in London, where British administrators are knocking themselves out trying to prevent the student from traveling to East Germany; the student and his compatriots are incensed that with Nigerian independence looming, the British government is still meddling in the movements of a private Nigerian citizen. But in 1985, the date of *Behind the Iron Curtain*'s publication, neither socialism nor colonialism was pressing political issues in Nigeria. Inequalities, oligarchy ("a government controlled by a few rich men"), regionalism, and tribalism were. Ohiari's readers could easily update the radical political message here, but its placement in the mouth of a young doctor more than a quarter century earlier would seem to be enough to protect the author—especially from generals who don't read.

Unlike most political novels, which are published in Nigeria, the most devastating was first published outside. The more affluent members of the reading class have read it, however, along with expatriates and scholars. Chinua Achebe's *Anthills of the Savannah,* with its blend of apocalyptic despair and dogged hope, characterizes the somewhat schizophrenic political thinking of this group.

"First Witness—Christopher Oriko": Chris is PR man for His Excellency (HE) military ruler of Kagan and an old friend. A demonstration infuriates HE, who is told by secret police chief Ossai that the demonstrators are from the drought-ridden Abazom. Sycophants warn that Chris and Ikem, a newspaper editor, are stirring up trouble. Chris dutifully asks Ikem to send a photographer to cover the "goodwill delegation," and Ikem is furious at being asked to participate in such a distortion of the truth. He composes a "Hymn to the Sun" about the terrible drought that drove starving farmers to Abazom years ago. The image is used of "anthills surviving to tell the new grass of the savannah about last year's brushfires."

"Second Witness—Ikem Osodi": Ikem argues with Elewa, his illiterate girlfriend. After she leaves, he takes a shower, praising its inventor and all such beneficial cultural mixes. Planning more crusading editorials, he worries that Chris, who formerly edited the paper, now regards such writing as asking for trouble. Ikem thinks that HE could be saved if he and Chris could reach him.

Chris's voice: Chris drinks with Mad Medico, an English expatriate, and they discuss Kagan's "strange and poisonous" politics. Later Chris tells his girlfriend, Beatrice, about the early days when Ikem, Sam (later "His Excellency"), and he were school friends, young and full of promise.

Beatrice's voice: HE invites her to a dinner at his palatial retreat to give "the woman's angle" to an American reporter; the evening is a fiasco, as the reporter tries to seduce HE. Later Beatrice reflects on women, including her fervent evangelical maid Agatha and her own sheltered life. She thinks about her long friendship with Ikem, going back to London university days; they have seen each other less recently due to the increasing coolness between Ikem and Chris. Recalling a story of Idemili, daughter of God, Beatrice worries that she doesn't know the stories of her own people. She warns Chris of coming danger to Ikem and to them all. Chris says he is unwilling to fight or to quit, and he can't help Ikem.

Ikem goes to meet with the dignified old man heading the Abazom delegation, who gives an eloquent account of their plight. Afterward he is harassed by a police officer. Two taxi drivers praise Ikem yet implicitly criticize him for not living luxuriously like other Big Men.

HE orders Chris to suspend Ikem for consorting with Abazom troublemakers. Chris and Beatrice advise Ikem to lay low, but instead he gives a radical speech to students and is accused of advocating regicide. Ossai, who has gotten Mad Medico deported, has Ikem arrested. The radio reports that the police have uncovered a plot, led by Ikem, to overturn the government, and that Ikem has been fatally wounded while trying to escape.

Chris goes into hiding, after first giving a statement to the students that the official account of what happened to Ikem was patently false. Pregnant, Elewa moves in with Beatrice. The police search Beatrice's house; one captain seems sympathetic and later warns her that Chris must move again. Chris is passed around, helped by taxi drivers and students. After a final night with Beatrice, he takes a bus to the north (Abazom), accompanied by Emmanuel, the student leader, and Braimoh, the helpful taxi driver. Suddenly soldiers celebrating a coup and HE's assassination stop the bus. In the confusion a sergeant tries to rape a schoolgirl. When Chris intervenes, the sergeant shoots him dead.

Some months later, Beatrice hosts a naming ceremony for Elewa's baby. Emmanuel, Braimoh, the girl who was almost raped, and the captain gather, but Beatrice remains depressed. The captain reports a rumor that Ossai has been killed. They name the baby girl Amaechina ("May the path never close"—a boy's name). Murmuring "beautiful," Beatrice finally seems to break through her mourning and return to the life around her.

(Chinua Achebe, *Anthills of the Savannah*)

The path may never close, but all three representatives of the nation's leadership class—the soldier, the journalist, and the communicator—lie dead at the end of the day. With the principal witnesses gone, is Achebe suggesting that only the anthills remain to tell the story? He seems to have a more hopeful ending in mind. At one point Ikem tells Beatrice that all future hope is in the hands of women, and indeed the network of women, students, and working-class people had been effective, hiding Chris and remaining together in the face of catastrophe. So there are witnesses other than anthills, but they are weak. Indeed, the basis for any political optimism seems shaky. Giving the baby girl a boy's name suggests that a reconfiguration of gender may set into motion a reconfiguration of social possibilities more generally. Although this development in Achebe's thinking is surely welcome when compared with the gendered assumptions of his earlier fiction, the connection between gender politics and national politics is far from clear.[145] Like the political novels in general, only far better written, *Anthills of the Savannah*'s analysis of the problems is brilliant, but the proposed solution is opaque. Of course, witnesses aren't supposed to solve problems, just testify about what they have seen.

The Glamour of Impotence

On October 31, 1995, Ken Saro-Wiwa and eight other members of the Movement for the Survival of the Ogoni People (MOSOP) were convicted of causing the death of the four Ogoni leaders in May 1994. They had been charged under the Civil Disturbances (Special Tribunal) Decree 2 of 1987, which holds that the accused may be found guilty if he has encouraged the act of murder, even if he were not directly responsible. As leader of the more militant wing of MOSOP and lately the organization's president, Sara-Wiwa was said to have encouraged the deaths by organizing rallies for the purpose of instigating a riot in which the four conservative Ogoni leaders, who had advocated working with the government, were killed. Such tortured reasoning and far-fetched attributions of responsibility are typical of Nigeria's military governments. Saro-Wiwa, who was nowhere near the area where the men had been killed, said he was not surprised by the verdict.

Unfazed, though apparently surprised, by the mounting national outcry, the Provisional Ruling Council (PRC) confirmed the verdict. A summit meeting of Commonwealth leaders in Auckland debated what action to take over the death sentences. South Africa's Archbishop Desmond Tutu and Saro-Wiwa's son Ken Wiwa, urged that sanctions be imposed on Nigeria to ensure that the nine men were not executed, but others, notably South African President Nelson Mandela, argued in favor of "quiet diplomacy." On November 10 all nine men were hung. As his executioners repeatedly botched the attempt to hang him, Saro-Wiwa, exasperated as ever by "'dis nigeria" and its confusion, blurted out, "What type of country is this?"

Mandela changed his tune and called for Nigeria's expulsion from the Commonwealth. A statement endorsed by all Commonwealth members except The Gambia suspended Nigeria's membership in the body, declaring the country would be expelled permanently if Nigeria did not return to democratic rule in two years. A number of countries, including the United States, Britain, and South Africa, recalled their ambassadors; the European Union imposed an arms embargo; but the oil embargo advocated by Ken Wiwa and others did not happen. The PRC, accusing outsiders of interfering in its affairs, remained defiant. By early 1996 the ambassadors had trickled back.

Nigerian novelists take seriously their self-appointed roles as nation builders and social critics. Achebe has pointed out that the "running battle between the Emperor and the Poet in Africa" is nothing new, for it goes back to the ancestral poets and griots, who were not always unambiguously praise-singers."[146] We have seen how contemporary writers by and large adhere to a social aesthetic, seeing the writer's role as one of focusing on specific social problems rather than more universal human concerns. While discouraged by the slowness of Nigeria to develop a reading culture, they are basically optimists. More to the point, they are modernists. The believe in public debate leading to rational decision making; they believe democracy is not only preferable to other forms of government but also somehow inevitable; they believe in the development of the public sphere, based on the reading public; they believe that intellectuals should serve as guides for the less educated or less aware. They see themselves as bearing witness to present problems and future possibilities.

Their tragedy, dramatically enacted in Ken Saro-Wiwa's grotesque execution, is that they are modern men and women in a nonmodern context. None of the things they believe in—rational public discourse, democratic political institutions, a reading public that looks to intellectuals for leadership—have come to pass in Nigeria, and perhaps they never will. But if they have not, then the reading class, the Nigerian writers, publishers, booksellers, and readers who live by these values, is superfluous and impotent at home.

Nigerian writers don't believe this for a moment. As Saro-Wiwa wrote in a letter he smuggled out of prison, "There's no doubt that my idea will succeed in time, but I'll have to bear the pain of the moment. . . . The most important thing for me is that I've used my talents as a writer to enable the Ogoni people to confront their tormentors. I was not able to do it as a politician or a businessman. My writing did it. And it sure makes me feel good." The letter was addressed to William Boyd, a British author who had written a book with the now haunting title *A Good Man in Africa*. Boyd quoted it in an article that appeared in the *New Yorker* several weeks after Saro-Wiwa's execution. The writer bears witness to other writers.

In this letter Saro-Wiwa was engaging in that most modern of practices, self-fashioning, presenting himself to a certain audience for a certain effect. To non-Nigerians, especially to the British and Americans who read interpretations by people like Boyd, Saro-Wiwa was a writer. To the left and the green, he was an environmentalist. To many others he was a human rights activist. But to Nigerians he was an Ogoni first, a public figure second. The Nigerian response to his execution was muted; Saro-Wiwa was one more crusader for democracy undone by the generals, one more ethnic politician fighting for his own group's rights. Most Nigerians, not being Ogoni, were not surprised; what did he expect? It was the outside world, for whom the categories of writer, environmentalist, and human rights (or minority rights) activist were more compelling than that of Ogoni, that was—for a time—appalled.

In his writing, and in his self-fashioning as a writer, Saro-Wiwa was performing a role characterized by the glamour of impotence. He was writing and living scripts: the Disappointed Young Man now grown up, the bemused social critic, the passionate patriot, the martyr. Virtually all Nigerian writers enact these scripts as they bear witness, although most assume their martyrdom to be symbolic rather than actual. Committed to social aesthetics at home in Nigeria, they are most successful at precisely what they do not want to succeed in doing: impressing outside audiences with their universal human concerns. A most significant contradiction exists in the tension between the rationality and optimism of the crime novel and the irrationality and pessimism of the political novel: as writers and modernists they are committed to the former, but as Nigerians they are impressed by the latter. "What type of country is this?" indeed. The crime and political novels suggest that the reading class of Nigeria may have had it all wrong.

Chapter 4

CAPTURING THE PAST AND INVENTING THE FUTURE

FRUSTRATED CHARACTERS haunt Nigerian novels: the Disappointed Young Man, the wife aghast at her husband's heartlessness, the crime victim who gets no help from the police, the Johnny-Just-Comes and Village Girls done in by the big city, the barren couple desperate for children, the working girl whose parents prevent her from following her heart, the village elder unable to preserve the traditional ways that are falling apart, the mourning war victim, the brilliant-but-despised Acada, the commuter stuck in a go-slow. All such characters have had a sense of how their lives should be working out, and all are finding that they have been mistaken. Education, a loving and loyal heart, rationality, ambition, community stature—none of these offer protection against the vicissitudes of life in Nigeria. Characters in the novels, and the novelists themselves, bear witness to this fact and register their frustration.

One might draw an analogy between the frustrations represented in Nigerian fiction and the notorious go-slows in Lagos. The city's rampant growth and its many bridges over which all traffic must funnel produce routine traffic jams of gargantuan proportions. The futuristic expressways with their soaring flyovers look dramatic but cannot begin to accommodate the traffic. Congestion is the rule, punctuated by the go-slows, which are really dead halts. Cars and buses can sit for literally hours until the congestion clears. Drivers often abandon their cars to pursue their business on foot. Hawkers swarm around potential buyers, who are immobilized and might just be bored enough or hungry enough to buy a newspaper, loaf of bread, bag of cough drops, garden hose, bottle of Fanta, or whatever the venders are offering that day. Exasperation mounts, and outbursts of violence are common. So are horns beeping incessantly, a pointless venting of frustration. Eventually, mysteriously, the go-slow clears up a bit, the hawkers retreat, and the cars move on.

If Nigeria is a go-slow, Nigerian novelists regard themselves as traffic cops. They want to straighten things out, to help get things moving, to direct people toward social improvement. The transition to a modern, democratic, prosperous society has become bogged down somehow, and writers give themselves the heroic task of unscrambling the mess. They can do so by telling stories.

Novelists take this self-assigned role of storyteller-as-hero very seriously. When I ask whether they would rather write a world classic, write a novel that would make them and their families wealthy, or write a novel that would contribute to social improvement, two-thirds opt for social improvement. Over and over they speak of documenting, representing, bearing witness to social problems. Writers of bloody crime novels or lightweight romances see themselves as shedding light on social problems just as do the writers of the more traditional problem novels about urban poverty, the conflicts between women and men, or political corruption.

These novelists are willfully oblivious to the irony of their position. In 1991 I attended the annual meeting of the Association of Nigerian Authors. The meeting, whose theme was "Literature and Nation Building," was being held in Minna, hometown of then military ruler Ibrahim Babangida, which meant, among other things, that it had a disproportionately large airport, crawling with security personnel. I used the opportunity to interview both established and new novelists, and I asked them about censorship. Over and over they presented the image of the fearless writer documenting social and political pathologies. They undercut this bold image a bit by telling me that "the generals don't read," this in spite of the fact that a representative of the military governor in full uniform opened the conference, thereby giving the generals' blessing. Over and over, the speakers on the program lectured about the constructive contribution writers could make to national development. No one saw any contradiction. The president of ANA who chaired the meeting was Ken Saro-Wiwa. He and his fellow writers deeply believed in "literature and nation building." Writers could make a difference. The generals don't read, but the reading class does, and someday—after the current, inexplicable go-slow—surely they will help build the nation by providing the blueprints.

This is a glorious image for writers to have of themselves: the witness as hero, turning things around with the power of his testimony. It is a self-image born in a modernist belief in open public discourse, the self-evident power of rationality, and democratic decision making by enlightened minds. The models are Léopold Senghor, Thomas Jefferson, Winston Churchill—all men of letters who were also leaders, nation builders, and preservers. And Nigeria has its own models: Achebe excoriating tribalism, Soyinka hounded into exile and mustering world opinion against tyranny, Saro-Wiwa dying for his advocacy. Such an image can motivate writers to get up at dawn and turn out the pages, never expecting financial gain or world recognition, only the satisfaction of having made a difference to society through their words.

Ken Saro-Wiwa spoke for all the heroic writer-witnesses: "My writing did it. And it sure makes me feel good." And his death, like any martyrdom, only adds to the sacredness of the heroic conception. Intellectuals like Didi burned alive among his books, Ikem framed and shot by the rotten regime he had tried to save, or Okolo, he with "too much book," going down in the whirlpool—or Saro-Wiwa, murdered by the generals who don't read—become part of the myth. No sacrifice is too great for those who believe that the power of ideas, ideas put into writing, will prevail.

Nigerian readers do not always see their reading as somehow participating in social improvement, nation building, or the heroism of literary endeavor. They read to pass the time, to learn about other ways of life, to show how modern they are, to attract the interest of similarly educated mates, to improve their own writing, or to hone their appreciation of fine literature. They know they are out of touch with the centers of political and economic power, but they take what satisfactions they can, from fiction and elsewhere. They read for pleasure and instruction, not primarily for documentation of social problems. They don't need to read novels about crime or tribalism or corruption or traffic jams in order to recognize these as problems. Everyone knows about them already.

At the same time, they share the view of the writers, publishers, and booksellers that Nigeria will eventually develop a reading culture. They never question that this reading culture is both inevitable and a good thing. They resonate with the frustrations of the characters in the novels, and they accept without question the premise that educated people, readers like themselves, have the tools to cut through the frustrations if they ever get access to the levers of power. They may not quite see the writers as traffic cops, but they do see the reading class as the group to get the traffic moving. And they accept the idea that Nigeria is undergoing a transition, and that they and their educated counterparts will be key to it.

Nigerian writers and readers see themselves as bearing witness to a transition, actually, to a number of them: transitions to modernity, to democracy, to the Giant of Africa taking her place on the world scene, to social justice, to abundance, to the New Nigerian, to an industrialized economy, to a reading culture. The idea of transition is used to suggest that a seemingly chaotic state is actually part of a pattern. Like the chrysalis, like the liminal period of a ritual, like the woman in labor, transition exists between a known before and a known after. Transition is a conceptual way of comprehending and thereby taming change.

This idea of transition is very hard to give up. It defends against anomie by suggesting a set of rules that are only temporarily suspended in a social go-slow and will return when things get back to normal. This is why Nigeria's military regimes have set up countless "transition programs": regardless of how many times the promised transition fails to materialize, the word itself reassures people that things will not always be the way they are now. Or, as signs on the buses remind everyone, "No condition is permanent."

Abandoning the attractive but empirically unsupported idea of transition does not mean accepting the idea of society as perpetual chaos. Chaos is actually quite rare. It is flux, not chaos, that characterizes Nigeria. Flux means patterns that are unstable, that dissolve into other patterns. Like adherents of one religious sect after another or like the political parties that are formed, then banned, then re-formed, the component parts recombine into new patterns. Like the crowds that turn out to welcome a new regime, without assuming it will last any longer than the previous one, most Nigerians simply cope with the arrangements of power and necessity that are in place at the moment.

But where does the novel fit into this? Novels are about transitions, about protagonists making the move from one state to another. Politicians, businesspeople, and street hawkers can master social flux and surf the web of contemporary culture, but can novels? What is the point of being a witness if your evidence does not contribute to a just outcome?

It may be that the heroic model was never the right one. Writers aren't traffic cops clearing up the go-slow; they are people caught in it themselves, and taking notes. Their readers are stuck, too. They are reading the notes not as a way of getting moving again but as a way of passing the time. Moreover, life does not stop moving until someone straightens things out. Hawkers trade, lovers quarrel, businessmen make calls, passengers take naps, drivers stretch their legs. People watch their fellows, observing and commenting on their behavior.

Instead of being gloriously heroic, a more accurate description is that writers and readers are weak witnesses. Recall how many of the fictional witnesses left to tell the tale are themselves socially powerless. An orphan outcast will tell Didi's story. Sozaboy is similarly outcast, a ghost to his own people. Preparing to die with Okolo, Tuere asks her crippled servant to "tell our story and tend our spoken words." The manuscript of "The Remains of the Last Emporer" is in the hands of an ancient musician and a young editor struggling with madness. Only the anthills remain to tell what happened to Abazom.

These seem like weak witnesses indeed, shaky foundations for nation building, especially in comparison to the heroic man of letters, but they are survivors. And mere survival—"Happy survival," as they said at the end of the war—can itself be a form of heroism. Recall Jagua and her three Lagos lovers: the intellectual (Freddie), the politician (Uncle Taiwo), the criminal (Dennis). All three die. She alone survives, picking herself up after her men and her baby have died, heading off to try her luck in Onitsha. She is the intimate observer who survives to bear witness to corruption and ruined lives. Socially weak but personally tough, Jagua is a different type of witness, resilient, no hero but also no martyr.

The writer-as-hero comes from a particular stage in the history of the novel. The early novels were private, domestic. Their eighteenth-century authors were first and foremost representing individual experience, not addressing social problems. It was not until the middle of the nineteenth century that writers like Dickens and Zola and Norris—and schools of novelists like the realists, the naturalists, the muckrakers—suggested the novelist-as-hero.

This heroic model may have run its course. An artifact of high modernism, its assumptions about the public sphere and the reading culture do not fit Nigeria. (For that matter, they do not fit much of the rest of the contemporary world either.) What we may be seeing in Nigeria is a return, on the part of some writers, especially the increasing proportion of women writers, to a more private witnessing. The readers have been private all along. A baby is christened "May the path never close." And since "no condition is permanent," such private moments may produce unexpected blessings under some future set of conditions. Meanwhile, the weak witnesses cope, make do, writing and reading their novels on the margins of social power.

As Chris catches his bus to escape to the north in *Anthills of the Savannah*, he is bemused by how the sign writers who were supposed to just paint "BUS" on the vehicle couldn't resist adding more, just like

> that unknown monk working away soberly by candle-light copying out the Lord's Prayer as he must have done scores of times before and then, seized by a sudden and unprecedented impulse of adoration, proceeded to end the prayer on a new fantastic flourish of his own: *For thine is the kingdom, the power and the glory, for ever and ever, Amen!*
>
> The sign-writers of Kangan did not work in dark and holy seclusions of monasteries but in free-for-all market-places under the fiery eye of the sun. And yet in ways not unlike the monk's they sought in their work to capture the past as well as invent a future. (186)

The Nigerian reading class seeks to do the same. In a place where day-to-day life is as difficult as in Nigeria, mustering the time and energy to write or read a novel is a fantastic flourish. The acts themselves bear witness not to a set of social problems but to the irrepressible creativity of the human mind. Here is where the heroism lies, and here also lies the possibility of inventing a future.

Appendix A

NIGERIAN NOVELS

(1) These are the 476 Nigerian novels that I was able to locate, read, and analyze for this study.

1. Abani, Christopher. 1985. *Masters of the Board*. Enugu: Delta.
2. Abdul-Ganiyu, Adebayo O. O. 1988. *Love in the Pot-Pouri*. Nigeria [no city]: Tropical.
3. Abdulkadir, Masud. 1991. *The Rise and Fall of General Musa Smith*. Akure: Trudon.
4. Abejo, Bisi. 1982. *Fools Rush In*. Ibadan: Spectrum.
5. Abejo, Bisi. 1982. *Lift to the Stars*. Ibadan: Spectrum.
6. Abejo, Bisi. 1983. *True Love*. Ibadan: Spectrum.
7. Abejo, Bisi. 1986. *Love at First Flight*. Ibadan: Spectrum.
8. Abio', Rufus O. 1977. *Angels of Double Faces*. Hicksville, N.Y.: Exposition Press.
9. Abiola, Adetokunbo. 1986. *Labulabu Mask*. Lagos: Macmillan Nigeria.
10. Abwa, Moses. 1988. *The Homogeneous Republic*. New York: Vantage Press.
11. Achebe, Chinua. 1958. *Things Fall Apart*. London: Heinemann.
12. Achebe, Chinua. 1960. *No Longer at Ease*. London: Heinemann.
13. Achebe, Chinua. 1964. *Arrow of God*. London: Heinemann.
14. Achebe, Chinua. 1966. *A Man of the People*. London: Heinemann.
15. Achebe, Chinua. 1987. *Anthills of the Savannah*. London: Heinemann.
16. Adebanjo, Olalekan. 1986. *Don't Attend My Wedding*. Ibadan: Abiprint.
17. Adebanjo, Segun. 1987. *The Birthday Party*. Ibadan: Paperback Publishers.
18. Adebayo, Augustus. 1991. *I Am Directed*. Ibadan: Spectrum.
19. Adebiyi, T. A. (Bayo). 1980. *The Brothers*. Akure: Fagbamigbe.
20. Adebomi, Sunday D. 1982. *Symphony of Destruction*. London: Macmillan.
21. Adebowale, Bayo. 1985. *The Virgin*. Lagos: Paperback Publishers.
22. Adebowale, Bayo. 1987. *Out of His Mind*. Ibadan: Spectrum.
23. Adeleke, Bayo. 1987. *Web of Love*. Ibadan: Abiprint.
24. Adeniran, Tunde. 1984. *The Flag Bearer*. Ibadan: Onibonoje.
25. Adenle, Tola. 1979. *Love on the Rebounce*. Ibadan: Onibinoje.
26. Adewoye, Sam. 1979. *The Betrayer*. London: Macmillan.
27. Adewoye, Sam. 1987. *Glittering Fragments*. Ilorin: Ilorin University Press.
28. Adeyemi, 'Tunji. 1992. *Adorable at Sight*. Ibadan: Mabamdu.
29. Adibe, Jideofor. 1984. *Fool's Paradise*. Enugu: Fourth Dimension.
30. Adinde, Celsus A. 1986. *Village Girl*. Ibadan: Abiprint.
31. Agburum, Ezenwa. 1986. *Broken Graduate*. Orlu, Imo: Culson Publication.
32. Agienoji, Monday K. 1989. *The Irony of Our Time*. Benin City: Supreme Ideal.
33. Agu, Paul. 1989. *Victims of Love*. Ibadan: Fagbamigbe.

34. Agunwa, Clement. 1967. *More Than Once.* London: Longmans, Green.
35. Ajayi, Jare. 1990. *Bile in the Dish.* Ibadan: Creative Publishers.
36. Ajayi, Tola. 1983. *The Year.* London: Macmillan.
37. Ajayi, Tola. 1985. *The Lesson.* Lagos: Granny Fatima.
38. Ajayi, Tola. 1990. *The Ghost of a Millionaire.* Ibadan: Heinemann.
39. Ajiboye, Goke. 1982. *Abiku.* New York: Vantage Press.
40. Ajogu, Ike. 1982. *Victim of Love.* Enugu: Fourth Dimension.
41. Ajogu, Ike. 1984. *It's You or Never.* Enugu: Fourth Dimension.
42. Ajogu, Ike. 1985. *Love Trials of Edga.* Enugu: Fourth Dimension.
43. Aka, S. M. O. 1973. *Mid-day Darkness.* Ibadan: Onibonoje.
44. Aka, S. M. O. 1979. *Cheer Up, Brother.* Benin City: Aka.
45. Aka, S. M. O. 1980. *The Weeping Undergraduate.* Benin City: Aka.
46. Aka, S. M. O. 1982. *Medicine for Money.* Benin City: Aka.
47. Akadiri, Oladele. 1990. *A Sin in the Convent.* Ibadan: Heinemann.
48. Akaduh, Etim. 1983. *The Ancestor.* Oron (Akwa Ibom): Manson.
49. Akintola, A. O. 1974. *The Marriage of Two Lovers.* London: Akintola.
50. Akoji, Richard. 1984. *Teardrops at Sunset.* London: Macmillan.
51. Akpan, Ntieyong Udo. 1965. *The Wooden Gong.* London: Longman.
52. Akwanya, Amechi. 1991. *Orimili.* Oxford: Heinemann.
53. Ali, Hauwa. 1988. *Destiny.* Enugu: Delta.
54. Ali, Hauwa. 1989. *Victory.* Enugu: Delta.
55. Alily, Valentine. 1980. *Mark of the Cobra.* London: Macmillan.
56. Alkali, Zaynab. 1984. *The Stillborn.* Harlow: Longman.
57. Alkali, Zaynab. 1987. *The Virtuous Woman.* Ikeja: Longman Nigeria.
58. Aluko, T. M. 1959. *One Man, One Wife.* Lagos: Nigerian Printing and Publishing.
59. Aluko, T. M. 1964. *One Man, One Machet.* London: Heinemann.
60. Aluko, T. M. 1966. *Kinsman and Foreman.* London: Heinemann.
61. Aluko, T. M. 1970. *Chief the Honourable Minister.* London: Heinemann.
62. Aluko, T. M. 1973. *His Worshipful Majesty.* London: Heinemann.
63. Aluko, T. M. 1982. *Wrong Ones in the Dock.* London: Heinemann.
64. Aluko, T. M. 1986. *A State of Our Own.* London: Macmillan.
65. Amadi, Elechi. 1966. *The Concubine.* London: Heinemann.
66. Amadi, Elechi. 1969. *The Great Ponds.* London: Heinemann.
67. Amadi, Elechi. 1978. *The Slave.* London: Heinemann.
68. Amadi, Elechi. 1986. *Estrangement.* London: Heinemann.
69. Andrew, Chire Nongu. 1987. *Devil at the Wheel.* Ikeja: Longman Nigeria.
70. Aniebo, I. N. C. 1974. *The Anonymity of Sacrifice.* London: Heinemann.
71. Aniebo, I. N. C. 1978. *The Journey Within.* London: Heinemann.
72. Anieke, Richard. 1985. *Shameful Sacrifice.* London: Macmillan.
73. Anigbedu, Laide. 1986. *Hero's Welcome* (also published as *The Triumph*). Yaba, Lagos. Writers' Fraternity. [Laide Anigbedu is a pen name used by Ola Omiyale for this book.]
74. Anionwo, Clement. 1988. *The Deep Glimpse.* Enugu: Anionwo.
75. Anyebe, A. P. 1984. *Agony of a Patriot.* Enugu: Fourth Dimension.
76. Are, Lekan. 1976. *Always a Loser.* New York: Vantage Press.
77. Are, Lekan. 1977. *Challenge of the Barons.* New York: Vantage Press.

78. Aremu, Abu. 1982. *Kill Me Gently*. Akure: Fagbamigbe.
79. Areo, Agbo. 1977. *Director!* London: Macmillan.
80. Areo, Agbo. 1979. *The Hopeful Lovers*. London: Macmillan.
81. Areo, Agbo. 1985. *A Paradise for the Masses*. Lagos: Paperback.
82. Asemota, Mac Morgan. 1982. *Who's to Blame*. Lagos: Citadel.
83. Atoyebe, Muda. 1990. *Countdown to Perdition*. Lagos: Macmillan Nigeria.
84. Avee-Rai'noy, Kezi. 1985. *Can't Stop My Bed Creakin'!* Lagos: Newruby Brothers.
85. Ayoola, Hansen. 1985. *She Died Yesterday*. Enugu: Delta.
86. Azikiwe, Okafor. 1977. *Gifts for Mother*. Benin City: Bendel Newspapers.
87. Babalola, Mary Adeola. 1982. *The Flesh Is Weak*. Akure: Fagbamigbe.
88. Babarinsa, Akinbolu. 1985. *Anything for Money*. London: Macmillan.
89. Bamisaiye, Remi. 1985. *Service of the Fatherland*. Yaba, Lagos: Macmillan Nigeria.
90. Bandele-Thomas, Biyi. 1991. *The Man Who Came in from the Back of Beyond*. London: Bellew.
91. Bandele-Thomas, Biyi. 1991. *The Sympathetic Undertaker*. London: Bellew.
92. Bedford, Simi. 1991. *Yoruba Girl Dancing*. London: Heinemann.
93. Bialonwu, Uche. 1988. *Long Claws of Fate*. Ikeja: Longman Nigeria.
94. Bishak, Al. 1988. *Mrs. President*. Enugu: Delta.
95. Bisi-Williams, Kowus. 1987. *The Black Godfather*. Ibadan: Abiprint. [Bisi-Williams is a pen name used by Bisi Ojediran for this book.]
96. Borisade, Omobola. 1988. *Sweeter Than Honey*. Ibadan: University Press.
97. Boyo, Temple Omare. 1981. *Somolu Blues*. Akure: Fagbamigbe.
98. Chukwu, John. 1992. *Destined to Live*. Ibadan: Spectrum.
99. Dangana, Yahaya S. 1986. *Corpse as a Bridegroom*. Kaduna: New Nigerian.
100. Dangana, Yahaya S. 1989. *Blow of Fate*. Lagos: Writers' Fraternity.
101. Dauda, Bola. 1982. *The Will to Succeed*. Ibadan: Macmillan Nigeria.
102. Denga, Daniel I. 1991. *The Healing Memories*. Calabar: Rapid Educational Publishers.
103. Echewa, T. Obinkaram. 1976. *The Land's Lord*. London: Heinemann.
104. Echewa, T. Obinkaram. 1986. *The Crippled Dancer*. London: Heinemann.
105. Echewa, T. Obinkaram. 1992. *I Saw the Sky Catch Fire*. New York: Dutton.
106. Egbuna, Obi. 1974. *Elina (Wind vs. Polygamy)*. London: Faber and Faber.
107. Egbuna, Obi. 1975. *The Minister's Daughter*. Glasgow: Fontana.
108. Egbuna, Obi. 1980. *The Madness of Didi*. Glasgow: Fontana.
109. Egbuna, Obi. 1980. *The Rape of Lysistrata*. Enugu: Fourth Dimension.
110. Egejuru, Phanuel. 1993. *The Seed Yams Have Been Eaten*. Ibadan: Heinemann (Nigeria).
111. Egharevba, Chris. 1989. *Canopy of Thunder*. Ikeja: Longman Nigeria.
112. Ekezie, Ngozi. 1988. *Nothing Need Change*. Lagos: Macmillan Nigeria.
113. Ekineh, Aliyi. 1989. *No Condition Is Permanent*. London: Galago Publishers.
114. Ekwensi, Cyprian. 1954. *People of the City*. London: Andrew Dakers.
115. Ekwensi, Cyprian. 1961. *Jagua Nana*. London: Hutchinson.
116. Ekwensi, Cyprian. 1962. *Burning Grass*. London: Heinemann.
117. Ekwensi, Cyprian. 1963. *Beautiful Feathers*. London: Hutchinson.
118. Ekwensi, Cyprian. 1966. *Iska*. London: Hutchinson.

119. Ekwensi, Cyprian. 1976. *Survive the Peace*. London: Heinemann.
120. Ekwensi, Cyprian. 1980. *Divided We Stand*. Enugu: Fourth Dimension.
121. Ekwensi, Cyprian. 1986. *For a Roll of Parchment*. Ibadan: Heinemann.
122. Ekwensi, Cyprian. 1986. *Jagua Nana's Daughter*. Ibadan: Spectrum.
123. Ekwuru, Andrew. 1979. *Songs of Steel*. London: Rex Collings.
124. Ekwuru, Andrew. 1980. *Going to Storm*. Walton-on-Thames: Nelson.
125. Emecheta, Buchi. 1972. *In the Ditch*. London: Barrie and Jenkins.
126. Emecheta, Buchi. 1974. *Second-Class Citizen*. London: Allison and Busby.
127. Emecheta, Buchi. 1976. *The Bride Price*. London: Allison and Busby.
128. Emecheta, Buchi. 1977. *The Slave Girl*. London: Allison and Busby.
129. Emecheta, Buchi. 1979. *The Joys of Motherhood*. London: Allison and Busby.
130. Emecheta, Buchi. 1982. *Destination Biafra*. London: Allison and Busby.
131. Emecheta, Buchi. 1982. *Double Yoke*. London: Ogwugwu Afor Company.
132. Emecheta, Buchi. 1982. *Naira Power*. London: Macmillan.
133. Emecheta, Buchi. 1983. *The Rape of Shavi*. London ("& Nigeria"): Ogwugwu Afor Company.
134. Emecheta, Buchi. 1986. *A Kind of Marriage*. London: Macmillan.
135. Emecheta, Buchi. 1989. *Gwendolen* (In the U.S. it was entitled *The Family*). London: William Collins.
136. Emecheta, Buchi. 1994. *Kehinde*. London: Heinemann.
137. Eneh, Peter. 1989. *Darkness in Malata*. Ikeja: Longman Nigeria.
138. Enekwe, Ossie Onuora. 1984. *Come Thunder*. Enugu: Fourth Dimension.
139. Essien, Jimmy. 1985. *Giant of the Cemetery*. Enugu: Delta.
140. Essien, J. E. 1985. *Nerissa: The Story of Love*. Enugu: Fourth Dimension.
141. Ezekiel, May Ellen. 1988. *Dream-Maker*. Lagos: MEE.
142. Ezekiel, May Ellen. 1989. *Centerspread*. Lagos: MEE.
143. Ezeokpube, G. 1988. *The Last Laugh*. Onitsha: Jet.
144. Ezifeh, Ifeanyi. 1985. *The Year of the Locusts*. Onitsha: Leadway Books.
145. Fagbola, Patrick Kayode. 1987. *Kaduna Mafia*. Ibadan: Heinemann.
146. Fajenyo, Ezekiel. 1990. *Night of the Godmothers*. Minna: Afrolink Business Communications.
147. Fakunle(-Onadeko), F. 1978. *The Sacrificial Child*. Oshogbo: Fakunle.
148. Fakunle, Funmilayo. 1980. *Chasing the Shadow*. Oshogbo: Fakunle.
149. Fakunle, F. 1983. *Chance or Destiny?* Oshogbo: Fakunle.
150. Fakunle, Victor. 1984. *Tentacles of the Gods*. Oshogbo: Fakunle.
151. Falemara, Francis Ola. 1982. *The Last Chance*. Lagos: Fally.
152. Falemara, Francis Ola. 1991. *Reward of Nature*. Lagos: Fally.
153. Faux, J. C., and G. Koko. 1970. *A Son of Iroko: Being a Story in a West African Setting*. London: Curson.
154. Fulani, Dan. 1979. *The Hijack*. Lagos: Nelson Africa.
155. Fulani, Dan. 1981. *God's Case: No Appeal*. London: Hodder and Stoughton.
156. Fulani, Dan. 1981. *No Condition Is Permanent*. Ibadan: Spectrum.
157. Fulani, Dan. 1981. *The Price of Liberty*. London: Hodder and Stoughton.
158. Fulani, Dan. 1982. *No Telephone to Heaven*. Ibadan: Spectrum.
159. Fulani, Dan. 1982. *The Fight for Life*. London: Hodder and Stoughton.
160. Fulani, Dan. 1983. *Flight 800*. Ibadan: Spectrum.
161. Fulani, Dan. 1983. *The Power of Corruption*. Ibadan: Spectrum.

162. Gagu, Gideon I. 1988. *Patience, Boy, Patience.* Lagos: Macmillan Nigeria.
163. Garba, Mohmed Tukur. 1981. *The Black Temple.* London: Macmillan.
164. Garba, Mohmed Tukur. 1983. *Stop Press: Murder!* London: Macmillan.
165. Garba, Mohmed Tukur. 1986. *Forgive Me Maryam.* London: Macmillan.
166. Gbulie, Ben. 1978. *Figments and Nothing.* Enugu: Fourth Dimension.
167. Gimba, Abubakar. 1985. *Trail of Sacrifice.* Enugu: Delta.
168. Gimba, Abubakar. 1986. *Witnesses to Tears.* Enugu: Delta.
169. Gimba, Abubakar. 1988. *Innocent Victims.* Enugu: Delta.
170. Gimba, Abubaker. 1991. *Sunset for a Mandarin.* Ilupeju: West African Books.
171. Giwa, Amina Abdul-Malik. 1995. *Painful Surrender.* Enugu: Delta.
172. Hume-Sotoni, Tanya. 1991. *The General's Wife.* Ibadan: Spectrum.
173. Humphrey, Dibia. 1987. *A Drop of Mercy.* Ikeja: Longman Nigeria. [Dibia Humphrey is a pen name used by Umunna Humphrey Orjiako.]
174. Humphrey, Dibia. 1992. *The End of Dark Street.* Ikeja: Longman Nigeria. [Dibia Humphrey is a pen name used by Umunna Humphrey Orjiako.]
175. Ibizugbe, Uyi. 1979. *Mysterious Ebony Carver.* Benin City: Ethiope.
176. Ibukun, Olu. 1970. *The Return.* Nairobi: East Africa Publishing House.
177. Ifejika, Samuel U. 1973. *The New Religion.* London: Rex Collings.
178. Igbo, Oli. 1993. *Tiena.* Enugu: Inselberg (Nigeria).
179. Igbozurike, M. Uzo. 1977. *Across the Gap.* Ibadan: Onibonoje.
180. Igbuku-Otu. 1989. *The Thirteenth Coup.* Lagos: African Network.
181. Igbuku-Otu. 1989. *Voodoo Republic.* Lagos: African Network.
182. Igbuku-Otu. 1991. *Lamentations of a Nigger.* Lagos: African Network.
183. Igbuku-Otu. 1994. *The Cult.* Ikeja: African Network Communications.
184. Ighavini, Dickson. 1980. *Bloodbath at Lobster Close.* London: Macmillan.
185. Ighavini, Dickson. 1981. *Death Is a Woman.* London: Macmillan.
186. Ighavini, Dickson. 1982. *Thief of State.* Zaria: Northern Nigerian Publishing.
187. Ijeh, Chuks. 1985. *State of Chaos.* Enugu: Delta.
188. Ike, Vincent Chukwuemeka. 1965. *Toads for Supper.* London: Harvill Press.
189. Ike, Vincent Chukwuemeka. 1970. *The Naked Gods.* London: Harvill Press.
190. Ike, Vincent Chukwuemeka. 1973. *The Potter's Wheel.* London: Harvill Press.
191. Ike, Vincent Chukwuemeka. 1976. *Sunset at Dawn.* London: Fontana.
192. Ike, Vincent Chukwuemeka. 1980. *The Chicken Chasers.* Glasgow: Fontana.
193. Ike, Vincent Chukwuemeka. 1980. *Expo '77.* Glasgow: Fontana.
194. Ike, Vincent Chukwuemeka. 1985. *The Bottled Leopard.* Ibadan: University Press.
195. Ike, Vincent Chukwuemeka. 1990. *Our Children Are Coming.* Ibadan: Spectrum.
196. Ike, Vincent Chukwuemeka. 1991. *The Search.* Ibadan: Heinemann.
197. Ike, Vincent Chukwuemeka. 1996. *To My Husband from Iowa.* Lagos: Malthouse.
198. Ikede, Joy. 1985. *Joined by Love.* Ibadan: Paperback Publishers.
199. Ikejiani, Okechukwu. 1975. *Nkemdilim.* New York: Vantage Press.
200. Ikonne, Chidi. 1980. *Born Twin.* Nairobi: Kenya Literature Bureau.
201. Ikonne, Chidi. 1987. *Unborn Child.* Owerri: KayBeeCee.
202. Ikonne, Chidi. 1992. *Our Land.* Ibadan: Heinemann.
203. Ikpenwa, Ude. 1988. *When Men Were Men.* Enugu: Chiecs Publishers.

204. Ikpenwa, Ude. 1993. *Hunting the Hunters.* Enugu: Budiks.
205. Ikujenyo, Modupeola. 1989. *Return from World Beyond.* Lagos: M. Abinibi Business Enterprises.
206. Ikwue, Kaija. 1982. *Inconvenient Marriage.* Akure: Fagbamigbe.
207. Ilori, Remi. 1993. *Bisi.* Lagos: Nigerian Publicity Agency.
208. Ilouno, Chukwuemeka. 1985. *Up from Polygamy.* Enugu: Bema Press.
209. Iroh, Eddie. 1976. *Forty-eight Guns for the General.* London: Heinemann.
210. Iroh, Eddie. 1979. *Toads of War.* London: Heinemann.
211. Iroh, Eddie. 1982. *The Siren in the Night.* London: Heinemann.
212. Iyayi, Festus. 1979. *Violence.* London: Longman.
213. Iyayi, Festus. 1982. *The Contract.* Harlow: Longman.
214. Iyayi, Festus. 1986. *Heroes.* Harlow: Longman.
215. James, Ademola. 1983. *A Man of Conscience.* Zaria: Northern Nigerian.
216. Jibia, Aliyu Abdullahi. 1982. *The Hunt Begins.* Kano: Triumph.
217. Jidenma, Iji. 1992. *Kasie.* Onitsha: University Publishing.
218. Johnson, Louis Omotayo. 1980. *No Man's Land.* Akure: Fagbamigbe.
219. Johnson, Louis Omotayo. 1981. *Black Maria.* Ibadan: Spectrum.
220. Johnson, Louis Omotayo. 1981. *Murder at Dawn.* Ibadan: Spectrum.
221. Johnson, Louis Omotayo. 1981. *Rest in Pieces.* Akure: Fagbamigbe.
222. Johnson, Louis Omotayo. 1983. *Oil Pirates.* Ibadan: Spectrum.
223. Johnson, Rotimi. 1986. *Too Young to Love.* Ibadan: Fagbamigbe.
224. Kachikwu, Ibe. 1986. *Cocaine Connection.* Ibadan: Spectrum.
225. Koin, Nyengi. 1982. *Time Changes Yesterday.* Lagos: Macmillan Nigeria.
226. Koin, Nyengi. 1986. *The Second Chance.* Ibadan: Paperback Publishers.
227. Koin, Nyengi. 1987. *All You Need Is Love.* Lagos: Macmillan Nigeria.
228. Komolafe, Omotoso. 1992. *Tough! Tough!! Lagos Here I Come.* Lagos: Omo-Kay Media.
229. Launko, Okinba. 1989. *Cordelia.* Lagos: Malthouse. [Okinba Launko is a pen name used by Femi Osofisan for this book.]
230. Lawal, Ayo. 1980. *A Nigerian Story in Share.* Ilorin: Lawal.
231. Madu, Adaeze. 1986. *Broken Promise.* Ibadan: Paperback Publishers. [Adaeze Madu is a pen name used by Rosina Umelo for this book.]
232. Mangut, Joseph. 1982. *The Blackmailers.* London: Macmillan.
233. Mangut, Joseph. 1982. *Have Mercy.* London: Macmillan.
234. Mangut, Joseph. 1984. *Women for Sale.* London: Macmillan.
235. Mansim, Okafor. 1985. *Chinelo.* Enugu: Fourth Dimension.
236. Marinho, Tony. 1984. *The Victim.* Ibadan: Onibonoje.
237. Marinho, Tony. 1987. *Deadly Cargo!* Ibadan: Spectrum.
238. Meniru, Teresa E. 1987. *The Last Card.* Yaba, Lagos: Macmillan Nigeria.
239. Mezu, S. Okechukwu. 1971. *Behind the Rising Sun.* London: Heinemann.
240. Munonye, John. 1966. *The Only Son.* London: Heinemann.
241. Munonye, John. 1969. *Obi.* London: Heinemann.
242. Munonye, John. 1971. *Oil Man of Obange.* London: Heinemann.
243. Munonye, John. 1973. *A Wreath for the Maidens.* London: Heinemann.
244. Munonye, John. 1974. *A Dancer of Fortune.* London: Heinemann.
245. Munonye, John. 1978. *Bridge to a Wedding.* London: Heinemann.
246. Njoku, Charles. 1973. *The New Breed.* London: Longman.

247. Njoku, Charles. 1978. *Race to the Navel*. London: Bell.
248. Njoku, Jerry N. 1985. *To Forgive Is Divine*. Enugu: Fourth Dimension.
249. Njoku, Jerry N. 1985. *Vengeance Is Sweet*. Enugu: Fourth Dimension.
250. Njoku, John E. Eberegbulam. 1976. *Refund My Brideprice*. New York: Vantage.
251. Njoku, John E. Eberegbulam. 1977. *The Dawn of African Women*. Hicksville, N.Y.: Exposition Press.
252. Nkala, Nathan Okonkwo. 1988. *Bridal Kidnap*. Onitsha: Leadway Books.
253. Nwachukwu-Agbada, J. Obi J. 1980. *No Need to Cry*. Akure: Fagbamigbe.
254. Nwachukwu-Agbada, J. Obi J. 1981. *A Taste of Honey*. Akure: Fagbamigbe.
255. Nwachukwu-Agbada, J. Obi J. 1987. *God's Big Toe*. Ikeja: Longman Nigeria.
256. Nwagboso, Maxwell. 1982. *The Road to Damnation*. Ibadan: African Universities Press.
257. Nwagboso, Maxwell. 1991. *A Message from the Madhouse*. London and Port Harcourt: Saros International.
258. Nwakoby, Martina. 1985. *A House Divided*. Enugu: Fourth Dimension.
259. Nwala, T. Uzodinma. 1973. *Justice on Trial*. Ibadan: Onibonoje.
260. Nwankwo, Nkem. 1964. *Danda*. London: Andre Deutsch.
261. Nwankwo, Nkem. 1975. *My Mercedes Is Bigger Than Yours*. London: Andre Deutsch.
262. Nwankwo, Nkem. 1984. *The Scapegoat*. Enugu: Fourth Dimension.
263. Nwankwo, Peter. 1989. *Devil's Playground*. Ikeja: Longman Nigeria.
264. Nwankwo, Peter. 1992. *Dance of the Vultures*. Lagos: Pelin's.
265. Nwankwo, Victor. 1985. *The Road to Udima*. Enugu: Fourth Dimension.
266. Nwapa, Flora. 1966. *Efuru*. London: Heinemann.
267. Nwapa, Flora. 1970. *Idu*. London: Heinemann.
268. Nwapa, Flora. 1975. *Never Again*. Enugu: Nwamife.
269. Nwapa, Flora. 1981. *One Is Enough*. Enugu: Tana Press.
270. Nwapa, Flora. 1986. *Women Are Different*. Enugu: Tana Press.
271. Nwikwu, Mezie. 1993. *In the Heart of the Hereafter*. Enugu: Delta.
272. Nwoga, Chinyere. 1993. *The World She Knew*. Enugu: Fourth Dimension.
273. Nwogo, Agwu. 1985. *Destined to Be*. Owerri: New Africa.
274. Nwokolo, Chuma, Jr. 1983. *The Extortionist*. London: Macmillan.
275. Nwokolo, Chuma, Jr. 1988. *Dangerous Inheritance*. London: Macmillan.
276. Nwokora, Lawrence N. 1990. *The Legacy*. Onitsha: Jet Publishers.
277. Nwoye, May Ifeoma. 1993. *Endless Search*. Ibadan: Kraft.
278. Nzekwe, Amaechi. 1985. *A Killer on the Loose*. Enugu: Fourth Dimension.
279. Nzekwu, Onuora. 1961. *Wand of Noble Wood*. London: Hutchinson.
280. Nzekwu, Onuora. 1962. *Blade among the Boys*. London: Hutchinson.
281. Nzekwu, Onuora. 1965. *Highlife for Lizards*. London: Hutchinson.
282. Nzeribe, Grace Nnenna. 1972. *Love in the Battle Storm*: Enugu: Reveille.
283. Obiakor, Anyi. 1981. *Justice under the Sun*. New York: Vantage Press.
284. Obodumu, Kris. 1997. *Die a Little*. Lagos: Malthouse.
285. Obong, Eno. 1988. *Garden House*. Ibadan: New Horn.
286. Odu, M. A. C. 1982. *Tears of the Fathers*. Lagos: Cross Continent.
287. Odugbemi, Sina. 1988. *The Chief's Granddaughter*. Ibadan: Spectrum.
288. Odunwo, Thelma. 1988. *Hands of Destiny*. Ibadan: Evans.

289. Ogali, Ogali Agu. 1977. *Coal City*. Enugu: Fourth Dimension.
290. Ogali, Ogali Agu. 1978. *The Juju Priest*. Enugu: Fourth Dimension.
291. Ogbobine, Rufus. 1984. *Death in the Triangle*. Benin City/Warri: Ruf-Bine.
292. Ogbobine, Rufus. 1985. *No Bail for the Permanent Secretary*. Benin City: Ruf-Bine.
293. Ogbobine, Rufus. 1986. *The Policeman's Dilemma*. Warri: Ruf-Bine.
294. Ogbobine, Rufus. 1987. *A Post in the Military Government*. Benin City: Ruf-Bine.
295. Ogbor, Wisdom Onyi. 1985. *King Zugo's Clan: A Novel about Domination and Fear*. Dallas, Tex.: Ashiedu Publications.
296. Ogbuefi, Joseph Ugochukwu. 1985. *The Time Between*. Enugu: CECTA.
297. Oguine, Priscilla Ngozi. 1987. *In Search of My Home*. Jos: National Museum Press.
298. Ogundaisi, Yinka. [1990 or later; no date indicated]. *The Charmed Lock*. Nigeria. No publisher indicated.
299. Oguntoye, Jide. 1980. *Too Cold for Comfort*. London: Macmillan.
300. Oguntoye, Jide. 1987. *Come Home My Love*. Ibadan: Paperback Publishers.
301. Oguntoye, Jide. 1988. *Harvest of Tricksters*. Ibadan: Onibonoje.
302. Oguntuase, Femi. 1987. *Scoundrels in Uniform*. Ikeja: Longman Nigeria.
303. Ogunyele, George Obasa. 1982. *Wives and Lovers*. Akure: Fagbamigbe.
304. Ogunyele, George Obasa. 1983. *Confessions of a Black Vagabond*. Nairobi: Kenya Literature Bureau.
305. Ogunyemi, M. A. 1987. *The D.O.* Ibadan: University Press.
306. Ogwu, Sulu. 1975. *The Gods Are Silent*. Ibadan: Onibonoje.
307. Ohiaeri, A. E. 1984. *Nwaulari: A Human Tragedy*. Enugu: Fourth Dimension.
308. Ohiaeri, A. E. 1985. *Behind the Iron Curtain*. Enugu: Fourth Dimension.
309. Ohuka, Chukwuemeka. 1980. *The Return of Ikenga*. Lagos: Macmillan Nigeria.
310. Ohuka, Chukwuemeka. 1985. *The Intruder*. Ibadan: Paperback Publishers.
311. Ohuka, Chukwuemeka. 1987. *A Bride for the Brave*. Onitsha: L. O. Ekwem.
312. Ohunta, M. O. B. 1981. *Web of Avarice*. Onitsha: University Publishers.
313. Ojo-Ade, Femi. 1987. *Home, Sweet, Sweet Home*. Ibadan: University Press.
314. Ojomo, Olatunde. 1982. *The Young Brides*. Lagos: Macmillan Nigeria.
315. Okara, G. Imomotimi G. 1964. *The Voice*. London: Andre Deutsch.
316. Okediran, Wale. 1987. *Rainbows Are for Lovers*. Ibadan: Spectrum.
317. Okediran, Wale. 1991. *The Boys at the Border*. Ibadan: Spectrum.
318. Okediran, Wale. 1991. *Storms of Passion*. Ibadan: Evans.
319. Okereke, Sun Chi. 1990. *Echoes in the Dark*. Benin City: Idodo Umeh.
320. Okereke, Sun Chi. 1990. *The Other Side*. Benin City: Idodo Umeh.
321. Oko, Atabo. 1988. *The Secret of the Sheik*. Ibadan: Heinemann Nigeria.
322. Okoba, Chinye. 1990. *Aura of Divinity*. Benin City: Idodo Umeh.
323. Okogba, Andrew Danbri. 1987. *When a Child Is Motherless*. Benin City: Idodo Umeh.
324. Okolo, Emmanuel C. 1979. *The Blood of Zimbabwe*. Enugu: Fourth Dimension.
325. Okolo, Emmanuel C. 1985. *No Easier Road*. Enugu: Fourth Dimension.

326. Okolo, Emmanuel C. 1985. *The Scorpion*. Enugu: Delta.
327. Okorie, Uchegbulem. 1992. *Date with Destiny*. Ibadan: University Press PLC.
328. Okoro, Anezi. 1974. *Dr. Amadi's Postings*. Benin City: Ethiope.
329. Okoye, Ifeoma. 1982. *Behind the Clouds*. Harlow: Longman.
330. Okoye, Ifeoma. 1984. *Men without Ears*. Harlow: Longman.
331. Okoye, Ifeoma. 1992. *Chimere*. Ikeja: Longman Nigeria.
332. Okoye, Prince Ifeanyi. 1987. *Mammy Water Daughter Married*. Lagos: Prifiko.
333. Okpalaeze, Inno-Pat Chuba. 1987. *Oriental Passion*. Onitsha: Allied Communications.
334. Okpewho, Isidore. 1970. *The Victims*. London. Longman.
335. Okpewho, Isidore. 1976. *The Last Duty*. Harlow: Longman.
336. Okpi, Kalu. 1977. *The Smugglers*. London: Macmillan.
337. Okpi, Kalu. 1980. *On the Road*. London: Macmillan
338. Okpi, Kalu. 1982. *Biafra Testament*. London: Macmillan.
339. Okpi, Kalu. 1982. *Coup!* London: Macmillan.
340. Okpi, Kalu. 1982. *Cross-Fire*. London: Macmillan.
341. Okpi, Kalu. 1982. *South African Affair*. London: Macmillan.
342. Okpi, Kalu. 1983. *The Politician*. London: Macmillan.
343. Okpi, Kalu. 1991. *Love*. London: Macmillan.
344. Okri, Benjamin. 1980. *Flowers and Shadows*. London: Longman.
345. Okri, Benjamin. 1981. *The Landscapes Within*. Harlow: Longman.
346. Okri, Benjamin. 1991. *The Famished Road*. London: Jonathan Cape.
347. Okri, Benjamin. 1993. *Songs of Enchantment*. London: Jonathan Cape.
348. Okri, Benjamin. 1996. *Dangerous Love*. London: Phoenix House.
349. Okuboh, Ervine S. 1982. *Rome Summit*. Akure: Fagbamigbe.
350. Okunoren, Segun. 1991. *A Gift to the Troubled Tribe*. Ibadan: Spectrum.
351. Okuofu, Charles O. 1986. *Death Contractor*. Ibadan: Abiprint.
352. Okuyemi, Ayo. 1987. *Love at Stake*. Ibadan: Abiprint.
353. Okwechime, Ireneus. 1987. *The Sacrifice*. Benin City: Idodo Umeh.
354. Olafioye, Tayo. 1984. *The Saga of Sego: An African*. Martinez, Calif.: PCA Enterprises.
355. Ologbosere, N. A. 1961. *Eloghosa*. London: African Tribune.
356. Olowa, Yemi. 1983. *On the Run*. Ilorin: Woye Press and Book.
357. Oloyede, Sola. 1981. *I Profess This Crime*. Akure: Fagbamigbe.
358. Oloyede, Sola. 1982. *A Gift of Death*. Akure: Fagbamigbe.
359. Oloyede, Sola. 1983. *Memory of a Silence*. Ibadan: Soorg Books.
360. Olugbile, Femi. 1991. *Leader!* Lagos: Royal Image.
361. Olugbile, Femi. 1995. *Batolica!* Lagos: Malthouse.
362. Olumhense, Sonala. 1982. *No Second Chance*. Ikeja: Longman Nigeria.
363. Omiyale, Ola. 1988. *Ring Finger*. Lagos: Writers' Fraternity.
364. Omiyale, Ola. 1988. *Second Dream*. Lagos: Writers' Fraternity.
365. Omiyale, Ola. 1988. *Sins and Sinners* (also published as *Return Journey*). Lagos: Writers' Fraternity.
366. Omiyale, Ola (Anigbedu). 1992. *Last Laugh*. Lagos: Writers' Fraternity.
367. Omotoso, Kole. 1971. *The Edifice*. London: Heinemann.

368. Omotoso, Kole. 1972. *The Combat*. London: Heinemann.
369. Omotoso, Kole. 1974. *Fella's Choice*. Benin City: Ethiope.
370. Omotoso, Kole. 1974. *Sacrifice*. Ibadan: Onibonoje.
371. Omotoso, Kole. 1976. *The Scales*. Ibadan: Onibonoje.
372. Omotoso, Kole. 1978. *To Borrow a Wandering Leaf*. Akure: Fagbamigbe.
373. Onugha, Chukwudim. 1988. *The Money Collectors*. Uruowulu-Obosi: Pacific.
374. Onuigbo, Ifeanyi. 1991. *Shattered Dream*. Minna: Afrolink Business Communications.
375. Onuma, Onuma E. 1982. *Dying on Tradition*. New York: Vantage.
376. Onwu, Charry Ada. 1982. *One Bad Turn*. Akure: Fagbamigbe.
377. Onwu, C. A. 1982. *Catastrophe*. Akure: Fagbamigbe.
378. Onyeama, Dillibe. 1976. *Sex Is a Nigger's Game*. Isleworth, U.K.: Satellite.
379. Onyeama, Dillibe. 1977. *Juju*. London: Satellite.
380. Onyeama, Dillibe. 1978. *Secret Society*. London: Satellite.
381. Onyeama, Dillibe. 1979. *Female Target*. London. Satellite.
382. Onyeama, Dillibe. 1980. *Revenge of the Medicine Man*. London: Sphere.
383. Onyeama, Dillibe. 1982. *Night Demon*. London: Sphere.
384. Onyeama, Dillibe. 1985. *Godfathers of Voodoo*. Enugu: Delta.
385. Onyekwelu, Fidel Chidi. 1979. *The Sawabas*. Lagos: Daily Times.
386. Onyekwelu, Menankiti. 1988. *The Maids Are Not to Blame*. Enugu: Hillys Press.
387. Onyeneke, Onyewuotu. 1970. *I Will Kill You and Get Away with It*. Lagos: Lukab.
388. Onyenorah, Edith. 1987. *The Gorgeous Black Prince*. Elms Court: Stockwell.
389. Onyiuke, Chuks. 1985. *Please Don't Say No*. Enugu: Fourth Dimension.
390. Onyiuke, Prince Lawrence. 1992. *Please Never Leave Me*. Vol. 1. Lagos: Onyiuke International Publishers.
391. Oparandu, Ibe. 1980. *The Wages of Sin*. London: Macmillan.
392. Orewa, G. Oka. 1982. *The Unknown Tomorrow*. Yaba, Lagos: Macmillan Nigeria.
393. Oricha, John M. 1991. *The Missing File*. Lagos: Bornitz Books.
394. Osahon, Naiwu. 1971. *Sex Is a Nigger*. Apapa, Lagos: DiNigro Press.
395. Osanyin, Bode. 1984. *Rich Girl, Poor Boy*. London: Macmillan.
396. Osanyin, Bode. 1985. *Shattered Dreams*. Lagos: Paperback Publishers.
397. Osi-Momoh, A. 1978. *The Ignoble End*. Sapele: Central Printing.
398. Osifo, Gracy Nma. 1985. *Dizzy Angel*. Ibadan: University Press.
399. Osikemuwe, Obogai Basil. 1993. *Beyond Resistance*. Benin City: Jodah Nigeria.
400. Osofisan, Femi. 1975. *Kolera Kolej*. Ibadan: New Horn Press.
401. Ossai, Anji. 1979. *Tolulope*. Sunbury-on-Thames: Nelson Africa.
402. Osuji, Chuks. 1987. *The Ugly Citizen*. Owerri: Opinion Research.
403. Otuokpaikhian, J. U. 1982. *The Tree Must Go Down*. Lagos: Macmillan Nigeria
404. Ovbiagele, Helen. 1980. *Evbu My Love*. London: Macmillan.
405. Ovbiagele, Helen. 1982. *A Fresh Start*. London: Macmillan.
406. Ovbiagele, Helen. 1982. *You Never Know*. London: Macmillan.
407. Ovbiagele, Helen. 1985. *Forever Yours*. London: Macmillan.

408. Ovbiagele, Helen. 1986. *Who Really Cares?* London: Macmillan.
409. Ovbiagele, Helen. 1991. *The Schemers.* London: Macmillan.
410. Oyajobi, Akintunde. 1988. *Nostalgia.* Enugu: Delta.
411. Oyegoke, Lekan. 1982. *Cowrie Tears.* Harlow: Longman.
412. Oyegoke, Lekan. 1984. *Laughing Shadows.* Harlow: Longman.
413. Oyinsan, Bunmi. 1991. *Silhouette.* Ibadan: Spectrum.
414. Phil-Ebosie, Philip. 1982. *The Cyclist.* London: Macmillan.
415. Phil-Ebosie, Philip. 1983. *Dead of Night.* London: Macmillan.
416. Popoola, Dimeji. 1987. *A Matter of Upbringing.* Ibadan: University Press.
417. Popoola, Dimeji. 1989. *Near the Rainbow.* Ikeja: Longman Nigeria.
418. Salihu, Mohammed A. 1983. *Pretoria's Assault.* Zaria: Northern Nigeria.
419. Sanni, Agboola. 1978. *The Choice.* Ilesa, Oyo State: Ilesanmi Press.
420. Saro-Wiwa, Ken. 1985. *Sozaboy—A Novel in Rotten English.* Port Harcourt: Saros International.
421. Saro-Wiwa, Ken. 1987. *Basi and Company: A Modern African Folk Tale.* Port Harcourt: Saros International.
422. Saro-Wiwa, Ken. 1988. *Prisoners of Jebs.* Port Harcourt: Saros International.
423. Saro-Wiwa, Ken. 1991. *Pita Dumbrok's Prison.* Port Harcourt: Saros International.
424. Segun, Omowunmi. 1992. *The Third Dimple.* Ibadan: Heinemann.
425. Serrano, Jumoke. 1986. *The Last Don Out.* Ibadan: Abiprint.
426. Sikuade, Yemi. 1981. *Sisi.* London: Macmillan.
427. Sowande, Bode. 1981. *Our Man the President.* Ibadan: Spectrum.
428. Sowande, Bode. 1982. *Without a Home.* Harlow: Longman.
429. Soyinka, Wole. 1965. *The Interpreters.* London: Andre Deutsch.
430. Soyinka, Wole. 1973. *Season of Anomy.* London: Rex Collings.
431. Sule, Mohammed. 1977. *The Undesirable Element.* London: Macmillan.
432. Sule, Mohammed. 1979. *The Delinquent.* London: Macmillan.
433. Sule, Mohammed. 1982. *Infamous Act.* London: Macmillan.
434. Sule, Mohammed. 1988. *The Devil's Seat.* Derby, U.K.: Sphinx.
435. Sule, Muritala. 1987. *Shadows of Hunger.* Ikeja: Longman.
436. Tahir, Ibrahim. 1984. *The Last Imam.* London: Routledge and Kegan Paul.
437. Taju, Hammid. 1980. *From Fadama with Cane Sugar.* Ilorin: Matanmi and Sons.
438. Thorpe, Victor. 1979. *The Worshippers.* London: Macmillan.
439. Thorpe, Victor. 1980. *The Instrument.* London: Macmillan.
440. Thorpe, Victor. 1981. *Stone of Vengeance.* London: Macmillan.
441. Thorpe, Victor. 1983. *Blind Bartimaeus.* London: Macmillan.
442. Thorpe, Victor. 1987. *The Exterminators.* London: Macmillan.
443. Tutuola, Amos. 1952. *The Palm-Wine Drinkard.* London: Faber and Faber.
444. Tutuola, Amos. 1954. *My Life in the Bush of Ghosts.* London: Faber and Faber.
445. Tutuola, Amos. 1955. *Simbi and the Satyr of the Dark Jungle.* London: Faber and Faber.
446. Tutuola, Amos. 1958. *The Brave African Huntress.* London: Faber and Faber.
447. Tutuola, Amos. 1962. *Feather Woman of the Jungle.* London: Faber and Faber.

448. Tutuola, Amos. 1967. *Ajaiyi and His Inherited Poverty*. London: Faber and Faber.
449. Tutuola, Amos. 1981. *The Witch-Herbalist of the Remote Town*. London: Faber and Faber.
450. Tutuola, Amos. 1987. *Pauper, Brawler and Slanderer*. London: Faber and Faber.
451. Ugah, Ada. 1985. *Hanini's Paradise*. Sherbrooke, Quebec: Éditions Naaman.
452. Ugwu, T. Chijioke. 1985. *A Changed Man*. Enugu: Fourth Dimension.
453. Uhiara, Albert O., and Kalu Uka. 1970. *The Fugitives*. Enugu: Fourth Dimension.
454. Uka, Kalu. 1981. *A Consummation of Fire*. Enugu: Nwamife.
455. Uka, Kalu. 1985. *Colonel Ben Brim*. Enugu: Fourth Dimension.
456. Ukoli, Neville. 1987. *Blood on the Tide*. Lagos: Macmillan Nigeria.
457. Ulasi, Adaora Lily. 1970. *Many Thing You No Understand*. London: Michael Joseph.
458. Ulasi, Adaora Lily. 1971. *Many Thing Begin for Change*. London: Michael Joseph.
459. Ulasi, Adaora Lily. 1974. *The Night Harry Died*. Nigeria: Educational Research Institute.
460. Ulasi, Adaora Lily. 1978. *The Man from Sagamu*. Glasgow: Fontana.
461. Ulasi, Adaora Lily. 1978. *Who Is Jonah?* Ibadan: Onibonoje.
462. Ulojiofor, Victor. 1982. *Sweet Revenge*. London: Macmillan.
463. Ulojiofor, Victor. 1990. *Struggle for the Throne*. Enugu: Liz Press Services.
464. Umeasiegbu, Rems Nna. 1986. *End of the Road*. Enugu: CECTA.
465. Umelo, Rosina. 1978. *Felicia*. London: Macmillan.
466. Umelo, Rosina. 1984. *Finger of Suspicion*. London: Macmillan.
467. Umelo, Rosina. 1986. *Something to Hide*. London: Macmillan.
468. Uzoatu, Uzor Maxim. 1989. *Satan's Story*. Lagos: Pen Publishers.
469. Uzodinma, Edmund Chukuemeka Chieke, (E. C. C.). 1967. *Our Dead Speak*. London: Longman.
470. Williams, Adebayo. 1989. *The Year of the Locusts*. Ikeja: Longman Nigeria.
471. Williams, Adebayo. 1994. *The Remains of the Last Emperor*. Ibadan: Spectrum.
472. Yari, Labo. 1978. *The Climate of Corruption*. Enugu: Fourth Dimension.
473. Yari, Labo. 1992. *Man of the Moment*. Enugu: Fourth Dimension.
474. Yewande, Emmanuel Oluwole. 1979. *This Man Is Poison*. Ibadan: Onibonoje.
475. Yusuf, Ahmed Beita. 1978. *The Reckless Climber*. Ibadan: Onibonoje.
476. Zubair, Usman. 1988. *In That Glitter*. Kano: Triumph.

(2) Following are novels that I located too late to include in the analysis.

Obi, Ubaka. *The SSG vs. the Tigers*.
Obi, Ubaka. *The Unfaithful Wife*.
Omotoso, Kole. *Memories of Our Recent Boom*.

(3) These are titles I was unable to locate. Some may have never been published; for example, some titles came from publishers' lists, which may have included forth-

coming works that never actually appeared. Some of the ones that were published may not be novels; Edia Apolo's titles may be pornographic pamphlets, for example. Some undoubtedly are novels that should have and would have been included in my data set if I had managed to obtain a copy. The small print runs of many Nigerian novels make many books difficult to find just a few years after publication; T. C. Nwosu's novels, for example, were self-published in the 1970s, and Nwosu himself was unable to locate copies in the early 1990s.

Achuzia, Gona H. *Hamza: Our Man in London*
Adebayo, Augustus. *Sound and Fury.*
Adewoye, Sam. *A New Order.*
Ajiboye, J. *Yetunde.*
Akinyele, J. I. *The Spoilt Child.*
Anieke, Richard. *The Survival Game.*
Apolo, E. *Love-Pot Festival.*
Apolo, E. *Mr. Sugar Daddy.*
Apolo, E. *Rituals of a Sweet Mama.*
Apolo, E. *One Hole Too Many.*
Egbuna, Ben. *Guerillas in Lagos.*
Egudu, Romanus. *Spine of Darkness.*
Fenuku, A. *A Fatal Choice.*
Horne, Etim Brian. *The Diplomat's Daughter.*
Laleye, Dapo. *Love Betrayed.*
Maxwell, Gerard. *The Takers.*
Menkiti, F. L. O. *The End of the Road.*
Mutai, B. B. *A Second Chance.*
Nwosu, T. C. *Born to Raise Hell.*
Nwosu, T. C. *Hot Road.*
Nwosu, T. C. *A Ride on the Back.*
Obatala, J. K. *An Undesirable Guest.*
Ogali, Agu Ogali. *Talisman for Love.*
Ogwu, Sulu. *For a Better Tomorrow.*
Okoro, Nathaniel. *The Warriors.*
Oloyede, Sola. *The Suicide Brokers.*
Oloyede, Sola. *The Warehouse Gang.*
Oloyede, Sola. *A Woman's As Old.*
Onuma, E. *The Marriage.*
Onuma, E. *Solo Vendetta.*
Orubu, Dumo. *Tears to Remember.*
Osahon, Naiwu. *A Life for Others.*
Sowande, Bode. *Dangerous Games.*

Appendix B

NIGERIAN AUTHORS

Following are the 261 authors of the Nigerian novels. Where authors have used a pen name, I have listed it under their real name and put the pen name in parentheses (see Appendix A). In the case of J. C. Faux and G. Koko, who collaborated on one novel, I am counting them as a single author. I have no information on them except that Faux is "a European" and Koko "an African," presumably a Nigerian, although his name sounds Ghanaian, so I am in effect combining them into a single, second-generation author of one novel.

1. Abani, Christopher
2. Abdul-Ganiyu, Adebayo O. O.
3. Abdulkadir, Masud
4. Abejo, Bisi
5. Abio', Rufus O.
6. Abiola, Adetokunbo
7. Abwa, Moses
8. Achebe, Chinua
9. Adebanjo, Olalekan
10. Adebanjo, Segun
11. Adebayo, Augustus
12. Adebiyi, T. A. (Bayo)
13. Adebomi, Sunday D.
14. Adebowale, Bayo
15. Adeleke, Bayo
16. Adeniran, Tunde
17. Adenle, Tola
18. Adewoye, Sam
19. Adeyemi, 'Tunji
20. Adibe, Jideofor
21. Adinde, Celsus A.
22. Agburum, Ezenwa
23. Agienoji, Monday K.
24. Agu, Paul
25. Agunwa, Clement
26. Ajayi, Jare
27. Ajayi, Tola
28. Ajiboye, Goke
29. Ajogu, Ike
30. Aka, S. M. O.
31. Akadiri, Oladele
32. Akaduh, Etim
33. Akintola, A. O.
34. Akoji, Richard
35. Akpan, Ntieyong Udo
36. Akwanya, Amechi
37. Ali, Hauwa
38. Alily, Valentine
39. Alkali, Zaynab
40. Aluko, T. M. (Timothy Mofolorunso)
41. Amadi, Elechi
42. Andrew, Chire Nongu
43. Aniebo, I. N. C.
44. Anieke, Richard
45. Anionwo, Clement
46. Anyebe, A. P.
47. Are, Lekan
48. Aremu, Abu
49. Areo, Agbo
50. Asemota, Mac Morgan
51. Atoyebe, Muda
52. Avee-Rai'noy, Kezi
53. Ayoola, Hansen
54. Azikiwe, Okafor
55. Babalola, Mary Adeola
56. Babarinsa, Akinbolu
57. Bamisaiye, Remi
58. Bandele-Thomas, Biyi
59. Bedford, Simi
60. Bialonwu, Uche
61. Bishak, Al
62. Borisade, Omobola
63. Boyo, Temple Omare

64. Chukwu, John
65. Dangana, Yahaya S.
66. Dauda, Bola
67. Denga, Daniel I.
68. Echewa, T. Obinkaram
69. Egbuna, Obi
70. Egejuru, Phanuel Akubueze
71. Egharevba, Chris
72. Ekezie, Ngozi
73. Ekineh, Aliyi
74. Ekwensi, Cyprian
75. Ekwuru, Andrew
76. Emecheta, Buchi
77. Eneh, Peter
78. Enekwe, Ossie Onuora
79. Essien, Jimmy
80. Ezekiel, May Ellen
81. Ezeokpube, G.
82. Ezifeh, Ifeanyi
83. Fagbola, Patrick Kayode
84. Fajenyo, Ezekiel
85. Fakunle, Funmilayo
86. Fakunle, Victor
87. Falemara, Francis Ola
88. Faux, J. C., and G. Koko
89. Fulani, Dan
90. Gagu, Gideon I.
91. Garba, Mohmed Tukur
92. Gbulie, Ben
93. Gimba, Abubakar
94. Giwa, Amina Abdul-Malik
95. Hume-Sotoni, Tanya
96. Ibizugbe, Uyi
97. Ibukun, Olu
98. Ifejika, Samuel U.
99. Igbo, Oli
100. Igbozurike, M. Uzo
101. Igbuku-Otu
102. Ighavini, Dickson
103. Ijeh, Chuks
104. Ike, Vincent Chukwuemeka
105. Ikede, Joy
106. Ikejiani, Okechukwu
107. Ikonne, Chidi
108. Ikpenwa, Ude
109. Ikujenyo, Modupeola
110. Ikwue, Kaija
111. Ilori, Remi
112. Ilouno, Chukwuemeka
113. Iroh, Eddie
114. Iyayi, Festus
115. James, Ademola
116. Jibia, Aliyu Abdullahi
117. Jidenma, Iji
118. Johnson, Louis Omotayo
119. Johnson, Rotimi
120. Kachikwu, Ibe
121. Koin, Nyengi
122. Komolafe, Omotoso
123. Lawal, Ayo
124. Mangut, Joseph
125. Mansim, Okafor
126. Marinho, Tony
127. Meniru, Teresa E.
128. Mezu, S. Okechukwu
129. Munonye, John
130. Njoku, Charles
131. Njoku, Jerry N.
132. Njoku, John E. Eberegbulam
133. Nkala, Nathan Okonkwo
134. Nwachukwu-Agbada, J. Obi J.
135. Nwagboso, Maxwell
136. Nwakoby, Martina
137. Nwala, T. Uzodinma
138. Nwankwo, Nkem
139. Nwankwo, Peter
140. Nwankwo, Victor
141. Nwapa, Flora
142. Nwikwu, Mezie
143. Nwoga, Chinyere
144. Nwogo, Agwu
145. Nwokolo, Chuma, Jr.
146. Nwokora, Lawrence N.
147. Nwoye, May Ifeoma
148. Nzekwe, Amaechi
149. Nzekwu, Onuora
150. Nzeribe, Grace Nnenna
151. Obiakor, Anyi
152. Obodumu, Kris
153. Obong, Eno
154. Odu, M. A. C.
155. Odugbemi, Sina
156. Odunwo, Thelma
157. Ogali, Ogali Agu

158. Ogbobine, Rufus
159. Ogbor, Wisdom Onyi
160. Ogbuefi, Joseph Ugochukwu
161. Oguine, Priscilla Ngozi
162. Ogundaisi, Yinka
163. Oguntoye, Jide
164. Oguntuase, Femi
165. Ogunyele, George Obasa
166. Ogunyemi, M. A.
167. Ogwu, Sulu
168. Ohiaeri, A. E.
169. Ohuka, Chukwuemeka
170. Ohunta, M. O. B.
171. Ojediran, Bisi
172. Ojo-Ade, Femi
173. Ojomo, Olatunde
174. Okara, G. Imomotimi G.
175. Okediran, Wale
176. Okereke, Sun Chi
177. Oko, Atabo
178. Okoba, Chinye
179. Okogba, Andrew Danbri
180. Okolo, Emmanuel C.
181. Okorie, Uchegbulem
182. Okoro, Anezi
183. Okoro, Nathaniel
184. Okoye, Ifeoma
185. Okoye, Prince Ifeanyi
186. Okpalaeze, Inno-Pat Chuba
187. Okpewho, Isidore
188. Okpi, Kalu
189. Okri, Benjamin
190. Okuboh, Ervine S.
191. Okunoren, Segun
192. Okuofu, Charles O.
193. Okuyemi, Ayo
194. Okwechime, Ireneus
195. Olafioye, Tayo
196. Ologbosere, N. A.
197. Olowa, Yemi
198. Oloyede, Sola
199. Olugbile, Femi
200. Olumhense, Sonala
201. Omiyale, Ola (Laide Anigbedu)
202. Omotoso, Kole
203. Onugha, Chukwudim
204. Onuigbo, Ifeanyi

205. Onuma, Onuma E.
206. Onwu, Charry Ada
207. Onyeama, Dillibe
208. Onyekwelu, Fidel Chidi
209. Onyekwelu, Menankiti
210. Onyeneke, Onyewuotu
211. Onyenorah, Edith
212. Onyiuke, Chuks (Prince Lawrence Onyiuke)
213. Oparandu, Ibe
214. Orewa, G. Oka
215. Oricha, John M.
216. Orjiako, Umunna Humphrey (Dibia Humphrey)
217. Osahon, Naiwu
218. Osanyin, Bode
219. Osi-Momoh, A.
220. Osifo, Gracy Nma
221. Osikemuwe, Obogai Basil
222. Osofisan, Femi (Okinba Launko)
223. Ossai, Anji
224. Osuji, Chuks
225. Otuokpaikhian, J. U.
226. Ovbiagele, Helen
227. Oyajobi, Akintunde
228. Oyegoke, Lekan
229. Oyinsan, Bunmi
230. Phil-Ebosie, Philip
231. Popoola, Dimeji
232. Salihu, Mohammed A.
233. Sanni, Agboola
234. Saro-Wiwa, Ken
235. Segun, Omowunmi
236. Serrano, Jumoke
237. Sikuade, Yemi
238. Sowande, Bode
239. Soyinka, Wole
240. Sule, Mohammed
241. Sule, Muritala
242. Tahir, Ibrahim
243. Taju, Hammid
244. Thorpe, Victor
245. Tutuola, Amos
246. Ugah, Ada
247. Ugwu, T. Chijioke
248. Uhiara, Albert O.
249. Uka, Kalu

Appendix C

CODING FORMS

NIGERIAN NOVELS

Author

Title

Publishing information

Source

Unless otherwise indicated, 8 = other [should be specified] and 9 = unknown

AUTHSEX   Sex of author: 1 = male; 2 = female

SETTING

SETMAC   Setting of main action: 1 = city; 2 = village; 3 = wilderness

LOCMAC   Location of main action: 1 = Africa; 3 = England; 4 = other Europe; 5 = United States

TIME   Time in which story is set: 1 = precolonial; 2 = colonial; 3 = independence to present; 4 = future; 5 = combination

PROTAGONIST [name]

SEX   Sex of protagonist: 1 = male; 2 = female

AGE   Age of protagonist: 1 = child; 2 = adolescent; 3 = young man/woman (twenties or thirties); 4 = middle-aged; 5 = elderly; 6 = entire life; 8 = combination

ETHNIC   Ethnicity of protagonist: 3 = Hausa; 4 = Yoruba; 5 = Igbo

PROREL   Religion of protagonist: 1 = indigenous, animist; 2 = Muslim; 3 = Christian

SOCBACK   Protagonist's social background: 1 = peasant; 2 = rural elite; 3 = urban poor; 4 = urban middle class; 5 = urban elite

SOCMOB   Does protagonist experience social mobility? 1 = no; 2 = yes, upward; 3 = yes, downward; 4 = up then down; 5 = down then up

TRAVIN   Does protagonist travel within the country? 1 = no; 2 = rural to urban; 3 = urban to rural; 4 = rural to rural; 5 = urban to urban

TRAVOUT   Does protagonist travel outside country? 1 = no; 2 = yes; to

U.K.; 3 = yes, to Europe other than U.K.; 4 = yes, to U.S.; 5 = yes, some other country; 8 = combination or other

MARBEGIN   Protagonist's marital status at beginning of novel: 1 = never married; 2 = married and living with spouse; 3 = married, not living with spouse; 4 = divorced or separated; 5 = widowed; 6 = engaged

MAREND   Protagonist's marital status at end of novel: 1 = never married; 2 = married and living with spouse; 3 = married, not living with spouse; 4 = divorced or separated; 5 = widowed; 6 = engaged

MARIMP   Marriage important to the plot? 1 = no; 2 = yes

MARPROB   Problem of marriage between different groups important to plot? 1 = no; 2 = yes; religion; 3 = yes, race; 4 = yes, class; 5 = yes, tribe or ethnicity

LOVOPP   Is love between protagonist and nonrelated member(s) of opposite sex important to plot? 1 = no; 2 = part of plot but not key; 3 = of key significance

LOVSAME   Is love or friendship between protagonist and nonrelated member(s) of same sex important to plot? 1 = no; 2 = part of plot but not key; 3 = of key significance

PARBEGIN   Does protagonist have children at beginning of novel? 1 = no; 2 = yes

FERTILE   Is protagonist's fertility or parental status important to plot? 1 = no; 2 = yes, wants children but infertile or children die; 3 = yes, wants children of particular sex; 4 = yes, has too many children

PAREND   Does protagonist have children at end of novel? 1 = no; 2 = yes

PARCHILD   Are parent-child emotional relationships important to plot? 1 = no; 2 = yes, protagonist and his or her parents; 3 = yes, protagonist and his or her children; 4 = yes, both 2 and 3

OCC   Occupation of protagonist: 1 = homemaker; 2 = peasant, small farmer; 3 = petty trader, small business; 4 = student, teacher, intellectual; 5 = professional (doctor, lawyer, civil servant); 6 = artist; 7 = servant

GET JOB   Is protagonist's search for work important to plot? 1 = no; 2 = yes

PRODIE   Does protagonist die? 1 = no; 2 = yes

PLOT   (for all of the questions in this section, 1 = no; 2 = yes)

MONEY   Is money important to plot?

RELIG   Is religion or the supernatural important to plot?

TRIBE   Is tribal or ethnic conflict important to plot?

COLONIAL Is conflict between a colonial power (England) and colonized important to the plot?

INTERNAT Are international relations (e.g., economic dependency, cultural influence of West) important to plot?

ARTIST Does the plot involve the responsibility of the artist?

INTELL Does the plot involve the responsibility of the intellectual?

EDUCAT Is education important to the plot?

POLITICS Is politics—local or national—important to plot?

INDEP Is the move for independence important to plot?

ELECT Does the plot involve elections?

CORRUPT Does the plot involve corruption among politicians or civil servants?

MILITARY Does the plot involve the military or war?

CENTRAL CONFLICT [specify]

CONFLSOR Source of the central conflict? 1 = from society, social forces; 2 = from nature; 3 = from one or more individual antagonist; 4 = from protagonist's own personality, weakness

CONFLRES Resolution of central conflict? 1 = from society, social forces; 2 = from nature; 3 = from one or more individual helper; 4 = from protagonist's own personality, strength, effort; 5 = not resolved

TRADMOD Was the conflict between traditional and modern ways important to plot? [If the answer is 2 (yes), specify how and how resolved.]

WRITING STYLE

REALISM Would you call this novel realistic? 1 = no, involved fantasy, supernatural intervention; 2 = no, events not fully or realistically depicted; 3 = yes, plot autobiographical or based on actual events; 4 = yes, plot sounds plausible, could have happened

HUMOR Did the novel seem intentionally humorous? 1 = no; 2 = yes [If the answer is 2 (yes), give example.]

PUBLISHING AND GENRE

PLACEPUB Place of first publication: 1 = Nigeria; 3 = England, U.K.; 4 = other Europe; 5 = U.S.

GENRE Which genre, if any, does the novel fit into? 1 = city; 2 = village; 3 = intellectual life; 4 = civil war; 5 = women-and-men; 6 = romance; 7 = crime; 8 = other; 9 = political

SIZE Length of novel: 1 = short; under 50,000 words; 2 = medium; 3 = long, over 100,000 words

FIRSTNOV   Was this the first novel by the author? 1 = first; 2 = second; 3 = third, etc.

ROMANCE NOVELS ONLY

RELSTRUC   What was the relationship structure? 1 = continuous; 2 = circular; 3 = sequential

ENDING   What was the ending? 1 = happy-ever-after; 2 = ambiguous; 3 = ruptured

NIGERIAN AUTHORS

Unless otherwise indicated, 8 = other [should be specified] and 9 = unknown

DATSRC   Author information comes from? 1 = survey; 2 = survey plus interview; 3 = interview only; 4 = secondary sources only (back of novel; Zell et al.; etc. [specify])

SEX   Sex of author: 1 = male; 2 = female

PLACBRTH   Place of author's birth: 1 = west (Oyo, Ogun, Ondo, Lagos); 2 = midwest (Bendel); 3 = east (Rivers, Akwa Ibom, Imo, Anambra, Cross Rivers); 4 = north (Niger, Kano, Katsina, Kaduna, Sokoto, Bauchi, Borno); 5 = middle belt (Kwara, Benue, Plateau, Gongola, Federal Capital Territory)

CLASSBKG   Class background of author, estimated from parents' occupations or author's own statements: 1 = peasant, farmer; 2 = rural middle-class or elite; 3 = urban working-class or poor; 4 = urban middle-class or elite

ETHBKG   Ethnicity: 1 = Yoruba; 2 = Igbo; 3 = Hausa-Fulani

RELBKG   Religion practiced by family of origin: 1 = Christian (Protestant); 2 = Christian (Roman Catholic); 3 = Christian (denomination unknown); 4 = Islam; 5 = indigenous religion, animism; 6 = none

EDUC   Highest level of schooling: 1 = primary; 2 = secondary; 3 = some university or other postsecondary; 4 = university degree; 5 = some postgraduate study; 6 = advanced degree (M.A., M.D., Ph.D., etc.)

TRAVEL   Travel outside Nigeria: 1 = none; 2 = to U.K.; 3 = to Europe other than U.K.; 4 = to U.S.; 5 = Europe (including U.K.) and U.S.

OCCUP   Field of primary occupation: 1 = education, teaching; 2 = media, journalism, broadcasting; 3 = civil service; 4 = business, private enterprise, trade; 5 = profession (law, medicine, clergy); 6 = none, still a student; 7 = writing only

CIVWAR Involvement in Nigerian civil war: 1 = none; 2 = little involvement, living in west; 3 = little involvement, living in east or midwest; 4 = little involvement, living in north; 5 = active involvement, living in west; 6 = active involvement, living in east or midwest; 7 = active involvement, living in north

NOVELS How many novels has author written (use exact number)

OTHWRTG What other writing has author published? 1 = children's books; 2 = poetry; 3 = plays, screenplays; 4 = short stories; 5 = combination, including nonfiction; 6 = nonfiction only

HA/SA Answer to survey question about writer's primary obligation: 1 = serve society; 2 = be the best writer possible

POSSBLTS Answer to survey question about which would choose? 1 = write a literary classic; 2 = become wealthy from writing; 3 = inspire social improvement through writing

MARRIED Has author ever been married? 1 = yes; 2 = no

CHILDREN Does author have children? 1 = yes; 2 = no

RELNOW What religion does author currently practice? 1 = Christian (Protestant); 2 = Christian (Roman Catholic); 3 = Christian (denomination unknown); 4 = Islam; 5 = indigenous religion, animism; 6 = none

GENERTN Which generation does the author belong to: 1 = first, published first novel by 1970; 2 = second, published first novel between 1971 and 1983; 3 = third, published first novel 1984 or later

NOTES

CHAPTER I
TO UNDERSTAND THE NOVEL IN NIGERIA

1. Hannerz (1992) offers the metaphor of a global swirl of cultural elements, which he contrasts both to the image of cultural homogenization and to the idea of a mosaic whereby different cultural components retain their distinctive qualities.

2. The Noma Award for Publishing in Africa.

3. Brewer (1997).

4. This ideological construction of the autonomous author is discussed in Bürger (1984) and Foucault (1977).

5. Directional terms can be confusing when writing about Nigeria, where internal regions like "the north" have official meanings sometimes and popular meanings always. This confusion can be compounded in the case of "the west" or "the West," so I shall adopt the following conventions: throughout this book the "West" and "Western" refer to that combination of North American and Western European countries that has had such overwhelming political, economic, and cultural influence in the nineteenth and twentieth centuries. When I refer to Nigerian geography, I shall use the lowercase form, as in "The Igbo are dominant in the east and the Yoruba in the west." When referring to formal administrative regions from the late 1940s through the 1960s, I shall use the full names, such as "Western Nigeria" or the "Western Region."

6. See also my list of abbreviations.

7. Anderson ([1983] 1991).

8. See Laitin (1986) and Apter (1992) for the history of this imposed stabilization.

9. Most Nigerians regarded this issue as having been settled once and for all by the civil war that ended Biafra's attempt at secession. Recent political developments outside Nigeria and inside—Eritrea's success at finally gaining independence, the likelihood of post-Mobutu Zaire/Republic of Congo breaking up, and sharp Yoruba disappointment at having Moshood Abiola's 1993 election victory stolen from him by the military—have revived the possiblity in the minds of some. Obasanjo's election quieted such talk for the time being, although paradoxically some of his own Yoruba people, under the banner of the Odudua Peoples' Congress, have continued to campaign—sometimes violently—for a separate country. Many Yoruba deeply mistrust Obasanjo because of his close links to the northern military elite, especially to Ibrahim Babangida.

10. Saro-Wiwa (1985): 44.

11. My discussing the literature of a single African country is not unique; see, for example, Bjornson (1991) on Cameroonian writing, Coussy (1988) on Nigerian novels, or the large body of work treating South African writers.

12. The first definition is from Beckson and Ganz (1989): 180–81, the second from Abrams (1988): 117. The entry goes on to point out that some critics use "prose romance" to refer to extraordinary tales of isolated individuals pursuing a quest, while reserving the "novel proper" designation for more realistic, everyday

stories. The "recognizable characters" quotation comes from Radway (1988); on this point of readers' expectations of familiar characters, see also Long (1992).

13. Novels had been written in a number of cultures, including classical Greece and China, but these experimental writings did not give rise to a lasting popular genre as did the eighteenth-century English novel.

14. For example, Michael McKeon (1987) argues that the novel did not so much grow out of the romance as become distinguished from it slowly as the two genres interacted and dialectically defined one another.

15. Hunter (1990). Hunter disagrees with Watt's historical account more than with his definition of the genre. He contends that there was a two-generation gap between the "rise" of the middle class and the "rise" of the novel, so the former could not have "caused" the latter in any immediate way. Instead, other forms of writing such as newspapers catered to the tastes of the newly literate and increasingly urban middle classes of late seventeenth-century England during the decades "before novels."

16. Chinweizu, Jemie, and Madubuike (1983): 163.

17. Ibid., 156.

18. Ngũgĩ wa Thiong'o (1986): 27. Many African writers respond by arguing that English and French *are* African languages by now.

19. More surprisingly, Wole Soyinka himself put in a good word for Swahili at a pan-African language during FESTAC '77 (Apter 1996).

20. See especially Amuta (1986). Amuta also rejected a great deal in Marx and Engels as being inappropriate for contemporary Africa.

21. "Cultural object" refers to shared significance embodied in form (Griswold 1987). The object may be tangible, audible, visible, or capable of being articulated. A religious doctrine, a style of dress, a song, or a novel would all be cultural objects in this sense. Of course, with respect to the flows of cultural objects between developed and developing countries, the transfers go both ways; for example, African art had more influence on European modernism than the other way around.

22. Classic texts of modernization theory include Parsons (1951), Lerner (1958), and Inkeles and Smith (1974). These writers envisioned societies "taking off" as they made the leap into modernity, a leap that amounted to a one-way transformation into a new way of life. Contrasts between traditional and modern ways constituted the dichotomy at the heart of the model. Parsons, for example, suggested that modernizing societies come to emphasize individual achievement more than ascriptive characteristics as the basis for social rewards. For most people, Nigerians included, modernization remains the commonsense theory of cultural change despite its diminished persuasiveness for those who study political or economic development.

23. This theme has been discussed in Little (1973).

24. A typical domination argument maintains, for example, that exported Western television programs dominate the market for televised entertainment in Third World countries, with locally produced programs unable to compete. See, for example, Tunstall (1977), Smith (1980); for a critique, see Thompson (1990). The designation of countries as "Third World," although never very precise, seems to be outliving the bipolar postwar era, perhaps because other contenders like "South" have not been widely adopted.

25. Cultural centers and peripheries are discussed in Shils (1975). The idea of center and periphery has also been used in political analysis (as in the work of Norwegian political scientist Stein Rokkan) and in economic analysis (as in dependency theories whereby peripheral nations are locked in relationships of economic dependency with respect to advanced industrial nations at the center of world trade).

26. For a thoughtful discussion of the coexistence of dominant (hegemonic), alternative (resisting), and residual cultural elements, see Williams (1980). For exemplary studies of resistance, see Scott (1990) and Comaroff and Comaroff (1991).

27. Some African cultural producers themselves advocate the self-conscious artistic perpetuation of indigenous styles of thought (e.g., Achebe 1975), although others have suggested a certain artificiality of such efforts, which can be a case of "the invention of tradition" (Hobsbawm and Ranger 1983).

28. An example of this type of research would be Ashcroft, Griffiths, and Tiffin's (1995) examination of the linguistic competition between English (standard, dominant) versus english (postcolonial, reconstructed) that is going on in former British colonies.

29. See Peterson (1978) for a discussion of how the organization of production influences content, and Whiteside (1980) for an account of how this mass production, which he calls the "blockbuster complex," works to the detriment of literature.

30. While the reading of novels is usually private and solitary, their interpretation is more subject to collective action. See, for examples, Radway's (1984) discussion of how romance novel readers collectively evaluate their favorites and Long's (1992) discussion of the interpretive activity of reading groups.

31. The standard discussions of the impact of literacy and print may be found, respectively, in Goody (1977) and Eisenstein (1979); the novel form in particular is discussed in Watt ([1957] 1974).

32. One of the classics of modernization theory is *The Homeless Mind* (1973), by Berger, Berger, and Kellner.

33. They are crude because they take cultural objects as undifferentiated indicators of social processes—modernization, domination, the colonial encounter, markets, genre imperatives—rather than as creations of specific historical conjunctions. They are inadequate because they regard the human beings who write and read novels as "cultural dopes" (Harold Garfinkle's memorable put-down of functionalist reasoning) instead of active and thinking people participating in the construction of their own lives and meanings.

34. Anthropologist Clifford Geertz has made this point repeatedly (e.g., 1983).

35. For a fuller discussion and an argument that cultural analysis requires methods drawn from both the humanities and the social sciences, see Griswold (1987).

36. Although this series of procedures is straightforward, it is neither theoretically nor methodologically neutral. Theoretically, I take a position of realism and proceed with what I call "provisional, provincial positivism." *Positivism* is, of course, a fighting word. It is my sense that a great deal of work in contemporary cultural studies involves taking a critical stance toward mainstream research practices without offering much to replace them. I urge, and try to practice, a systematic form of analysis that, while trying to avoid the narrowness and untenable as-

sumptions associated with strict positivism, aims at the rigor that the term implies. In other words, I believe that one explanation of a phenomenon is, based on current evidence, better than another. I try to gather and analyze data in order to come up with better explanations for a cultural object's characteristics and impact.

37. Griswold and Bastian (1990).

38. For example, although Desmond Ohaegbulam's *Adventures of Api* is 228 pages long and has no illustrations or study questions, it is without question a children's book. It tells about a thirteen-year-old rebel who, with his more conventional pal, Sunday, outrages the village by getting into scrapes of one sort of another. The chapters are mostly self-contained—"Api and the Dog," "Api Loses His Shirt"—and the adventures involve youthful themes: playing tricks on parents, trouble at school, sports, getting stranded on an island. Such a book is clearly intended for readers who are about the same age as Api and his cronies.

39. Schmidt (1965) used a similar cutoff, considering anything under sixty pages to fall into the chapbook category. The *American Book Publishing Record* (1994) follows the UNESCO definition of a book—(1) forty-nine pages or more excluding covers and (2) nonperiodical publication—but reserves the right to include some shorter works if they are of sufficient importance. My sixty-page limit is somewhat more restrictive than UNESCO's definition, although I do reserve the right to make the odd exception. The Onitsha pamphlets will be treated in Chapter 2.

40. Reader-response criticism has alerted us to the fact that any interpretation of a literary work is, at least to some extent, a projection of the interests and expectations of the reader. While I acknowledge this methodological problem that researchers face when summarizing literary works or discussing aspects of their meanings, I do not think these attempts should be forgone by sociologists of literature; being methodologically self-conscious should not require eschewing analytic techniques. In the case of Nigerian novels, I have tried to deal with the problem by comparing my own summaries to those in Zell, Bundy, and Coulon (1983), and by discussing my understanding of the novels with their authors when possible. No doubt my readings have biases, as well as areas of blindness or misunderstanding; at least these will be consistent throughout the data, since I am the only interpreter.

CHAPTER II
THE NIGERIAN FICTION COMPLEX

1. See Simmel ([1918] 1971), "The Conflict in Modern Culture." Homi Bhabha (1985) contends that the colonial response to the colonizers' efforts toward cultural domination, represented most forcefully in cultural objects like "the English book," is one of parody, mimicry that foregrounds difference and rejects the colonialist assumptions; this strategic rejection constitutes a new cultural formation of mutation or "hybridity." See also Ashcroft, Griffiths, and Tiffin (1995): part VI.

2. Geertz (1973): 448. We see this steady-state imagery in Geertz's very definition of culture as a "historically transmitted pattern of meanings embodied in symbols, a system of inherited conceptions expressed in symbolic forms by means of which men communicate, perpetuate, and develop their knowledge about and attitudes toward life" (89).

3. I am enough of a believer in facts and data to be convinced that understanding a literary topic requires that all three be addressed. At the same time, posing such questions incorporates a number of assumptions of which we should be aware. Most baldly, I am introducing the assumptions that there are such people as "authors" and such a thing as "literature." These two assumptions are mutually reinforcing: "literature" implies "author," even if collective or unknown (as Foucault [1979] put it, contracts and letters may be written by someone, but they don't have authors). Peter Bürger (1984) has persuasively delineated the "institution" of literature—the commonly held idea that literature, like all art, constitutes an autonomous field, separate and distinct from other forms of communication—which he regards as a relatively recent product of bourgeois thinking. For my purposes the important thing about Bürger's point is not the artificiality of the distinctive status of literature, but its incorporation into the common sense of modernity, whether that common sense is on the part of a Nigerian or a European. And those who write what we call literature, as opposed to contracts and letters, are what we call authors. Foucault has argued that this "author" concept depends upon and encourages presuppositions about individual agency and the stability of persons. The concept is also functional: "the author" classifies texts, establishes relationships between and among texts, and neutralizes contradictions. But no matter how functional they are for us, we should bear in mind that "the author" and "literature" are not natural categories but rather are ideological constructs.

4. Becker (1982): 34–35.

5. The concept of "world culture" is discussed in Meyer et al. (1997).

6. Cancel (1993) discusses the *ajami* writing.

7. Mann (1985) describes the world of the turn-of-the-century Lagos Yoruba elite.

8. Cancel (1993).

9. In 1994 Dapo Adeniyi, reviews editor of the *Daily Times of Nigeria,* translated and published Fagunwa's third novel, *Irinkerindo Ninu Igbo Elegbeje,* translated as *Expedition to the Mount of Thought.* The book was published by Obafemi Awolowo Press in Ile-Ife.

10. See Piłaszewicz (1985). Malam Bello Kagara's *Gandoki* followed the adventures—based partly on concrete history, partly on sheer imagination—of its eponymous hero, who took part in both the Fulani jihad in the early nineteenth century and the British colonial conquest of 1901, and at the same time managed to defend the Muslim faith in the land of the spirits. *Shaihu Umar,* written by Abubakar Tafawa Balewa, who would later become the first prime minister of independent Nigeria, is another adventure tale, this time about life in the villages and courts of nineteenth-century Hausaland, with the characteristic emphasis on Islamic virtues. The third prize winner, *Jiki Magayi,* translates as "You will pay for the injustice you caused"; this is a largely realistic story of love, hate, and multiple revenge ("largely" realistic in that it includes an episode involving a magic wood that resembles Fagunwa's forest of a thousand demons). Alhaji Abubakar Imam, a brother of Kagara's, won a prize for his *Ruwan Bagaja;* another quest tale, this book tells about a cunning man who travels the spirit world seeking the healing waters to cure the son of his town's ruler. Of particular interest is the opposition between the hero (named after the author), whom Pilaszewicz describes as a "shrewd crook," and a

corrupt *malam* or Islamic scholar-teacher; with typical Nigerian pragmatism, the two finally make peace and swear their fidelity on the Koran. Rounding out the five is Muhammadu Gwarzo's *Idom Matambayi,* or "The eye of the enquirer," which, like *Ruwan Bagaja,* draws heavily on traditional folktales and fables.

11. For discussion of later work in these languages, see Babalola (1985) and Piłaszewicz (1985).

12. Linguist Kay Williamson (1993), who has assembled an inventory of Nigerian writing in minority languages (i.e., languages other than Yoruba, Hausa, Igbo, or English), finds 117 such languages having some writing. Some of these have nothing beyond parts of the Bible, while others have textbooks, religious texts, and traditional literature such as collections of proverbs. Very few have modern literary forms, and only two—Efik and Idoma Central—include a novel.

13. UNESCO (1991): Table 7.4 "Book production: number of titles by language of publication."

14. Okara (1991) sees writers as having one of three common attitudes toward the use of English: "neo-metropolitans" regard English as a tool in the hands of Africans just like anyone else; "rejectionists" demand that writers employ some indigenous African language; and "evolutionists/experimenters" like Achebe manipulate and reshape English in order "to express the totality of the message of African culture" (16).

15. In other accounts he said it took him three or five days; see Lindfors (1975): 276.

16. Ibid., 283.

17. See Lindfors (1975) for a full discussion of Tutuola's use of standard West African folktales.

18. Libraries initially cataloged it under English fiction, and so it remains.

19. For example, in his interview with Tutuola, Dimeji Popoola refers to the book as "the first novel in English by any Nigerian" without further qualification (1988a: 16).

20. Lindfors (1975): 286.

21. Palmer (1979): 31.

22. Zell, Bundy, and Coulon (1983): 383.

23. I have only included figures through 1993 because my collection of novels has been less complete for the later 1990s. The general pattern of decreased production is confirmed by figures published in the *African Book Publishing Record,* as well as by the drop in titles put out by series such as Pacesetters.

24. For example, the United States, with nearly five times the population of the United Kingdom, publishes only 50 to 70 percent as many titles of full-length fiction (Greenfield 1989: 28).

25. Information about and quotations from individual authors like Dr. Ajayi come from personal interviews and from the author surveys. I have used published sources for some demographic and career information when no author survey was available. Quotations from published sources are so indicated.

26. Unlike epic poetry, drama, or lyric, the novel is always a written genre. Theoretically an illiterate person could create and dictate a novel, but the effort of memory would be prodigious, given the prose form (long epic poetry uses verse and repetition as mnemonic devices [Lord 1960]). Moreover, neither the reciter nor

the receiver would be likely to recognize the result as a "novel." The novel not only is written but is also a print genre; if not in print, some modifier is added, as in "unpublished novel."

27. Of the 261 novelists, I know the sex of 246. Of these, 210 (85 percent) are male and 36 (15 percent) are female. If we count by novels rather than by authors, we get roughly the same result. I know the author's sex for 459 novels; of these, 383 (83 percent) were written by men, 76 (17 percent) by women.

28. For those authors for whom both sex and ethnicity are known, women constituted 13 percent of the Yoruba authors, 16 percent of the Igbo, and 20 percent of the Hausa-Fulani (since there were so few Hausa-Fulani authors, this higher percentage is not meaningful).

29. The number of male-authored novels (383) divided by male authors (210) = 1.823; female-authored novels (76) divided by female authors (36) = 2.111.

30. Tuchman (1989).

31. The 1985 Survey of Public Participation in the Arts asked respondents if they had worked on "any creative writings, such as stories, poems, plays, and the like" during the past year. About 6 percent of adults had done so; of these, 63 percent were women, 37 percent men (Zill and Winglee 1990: Table 1, p. 13). The study does not ask about writing novels, however, so I don't know the sex breakdown of would-be novelists.

32. In a sample of 163 novels taken from the *American Book Publishing Record* for 1987 for which the author's sex was known, there were 99 male and 64 female authors (Griswold and Hull 1998).

33. I know the religion practiced by 107 authors. Eighty-seven of these, or 81 percent, were Christian; these seemed to be about evenly divided between Protestant and Catholic, although I did not know the denomination for over a third. Fifteen (14 percent) were Muslim, three were followers of traditional animism only (Christians and Muslims often practice traditional religion to some degree as well), and two followed some other religion such as Hindu.

34. UNESCO: "Participation in education. Gross enrollment ratio and Net enrollment ratio. Third level." Broken down by sex, we find that 5.8 percent of the young Nigerian men and 2.2 percent of the young women were enrolled in tertiary education. (An American like myself is tempted to say "in college," but in Nigeria "college" usually refers to secondary school, as in Queen's College.) This is in line with much of sub-Saharan Africa; note that South Africa has far higher tertiary enrollment of 17.3 percent. The United States has 47 percent enrollment (taken from UNESCO Web site http://unescostat.org//indicator/).

35. Of the 177 authors whose educations are known, 1 had only primary education, 6 had only secondary, 43 had some tertiary but had not yet attained a degree, 41 had a BA or its equivalent, 22 had education beyond the BA, and 64 had a postgraduate degree.

36. Enoh (1994): 39. Nigeria had five universities at independence; by 1994 it had 24 Federal Universities and 12 state universities. The production of qualified teachers and prepared students has not kept pace with this tertiary-level expansion.

37. Federal Ministry of Education and Youth Development (1993): Table 4, p. 22.

38. Yakubu (1996): Table 12, p. 43.

39. Ibid., Table 5, p. 35.

40. Bonham-Carter (1984): 163

41. Mann (1982): 25; emphasis in original. Only a system with high levels of government patronage, such as that of Norway, can routinely allow authors to earn their livings from their writing. Private philanthropy such as the Guggenheim Foundation or the MacArthur Foundation can temporarily free an author from the need to pursue other sources of income, but these provide support for only a limited period of time.

42. Occupations were known for 175 novelists. Of these, 46 were teachers or school administrators, and another 43 worked in the media; 25 were in the professions, 18 in business, 14 in civil service; 7 were still students, while 21 had some other occupation. I considered only one—Buchi Emecheta—to have been a full-time writer for most of her career; lately Ben Okri would be another. Achebe and Soyinka have both been teachers for much of their adult lives, with Achebe also having an early career in radio.

43. All quotations are from the author surveys unless otherwise indicated.

44. Achebe's own position is more complicated than those who simply take up the title of *Things Fall Apart* and its ironic ending often seem to recognize. Neither writer sees traditional Igbo life as a golden age for all concerned.

45. *Newsline*, September 9, 1990, 6.

46. The oil boom ended in the middle of 1981, but for some time Nigerians believed that this was just a temporary interruption in their prosperity. Furthermore, many novels were well along in the publishing process by that time, although they did not actually get published until a year or two later. This lag, coupled with the fact that the military took over the government, ending the Second Republic, on December 31, 1983, makes me choose 1984 as the beginning of a new era for writers, as for Nigeria as a whole. This is what led me to use this date to mark the appearance of the third generation.

47. "A Little Something," in May-Ifeoma Nwoye, 1994. *Tides of Life* (Lagos: UTO Publications, 1994).

48. A point stressed by Amuta (1986).

49. When I asked them to "choose among three possibilities: (a) writing a novel that would be regarded throughout the world as a literary classic; (b) writing a novel that would sell so many books that you and your family would become wealthy; or (c) writing a novel that would inspire some major improvements in Nigerian society," 17 (22 percent) out of 78 chose a literary classic, 7 (9 percent) chose wealth, 48 (62 percent) chose social improvement, and 6 (8 percent) chose "other," usually indicating some combination of the first three choices.

50. When asked which authors he most admires, Dr. Ajayi mentions T. M. Aluko, Robert Bloch, Heinrich Böll, A. J. Cronin, Anton Chekov, Cyprian Ekwensi, D. O. Fagunwa, Ernest Hemingway, Henrik Ibsen, Hans Helmut Kirst, W. Somerset Maugham, and Émile Zola. He likes to read novels that have "captured the international reading public's imagination," as well as biographies and histories of the many countries he has visited.

51. This discussion of early publishing draws on Rea (1975) and Hill (1980).

52. These fifteen authors are Achebe (I), Aluko (Y), Amadi (Other), Aniebo (I), Echewa (I), Ekwensi (I), Iroh (I), Mezu (I), Munonye (I), Nwankwo (I), Nwapa (I), Nzekwu (I), Okara (Other), Omotoso (Y), and Soyinka (Y).

53. She has edited an international anthology entitled *Daughters of Africa* (Lena Williams, "Celebrating Literary Women with Roots in Africa," *New York Times,* October 16, 1997).

54. Paren (1978).

55. Ibid., 17. She notes that "the expansion of the list of the 'African Writers Series' must be aided by the fact that some of the titles are prescribed reading in schools all over Africa." The implication is that this was somehow unfair, although presumably Heinemann's success in having its books required in the schools was largely a result of its having cornered the market for African writers of literary merit, not because the publisher was twisting African arms in the ministries of education.

56. Letter from Pauline Tait to the author, June 15, 1989.

57. From the 1982 quiz.

58. In the Eastern Region, Fourth Dimension, which has continued to be an important publisher of fiction, somehow managed to bring out Desmond Ohaegbulam's *The Adventures of Api,* a novel for children, during the civil war itself and was ready with Albert Uhiara's *The Fugitives* as soon as the war ended.

59. The standard discussion of the Onitsha pamphlets is Obiechina (1972), on which the following account draws.

60. The examples are from Obiechina (1972).

61. On the back of *The Country Is Hard,* Oniororo refers to his works as "booklets." Some titles include *Persevere Dear Brother, Problems of Moba People, Lagos Is a Wicked Place,* and *No More a Minister.* Most are short, but *The Country Is Hard* has eighty-seven pages. Because of its length and the absence of authorial interjections, it could be viewed as a novel. I have not included it, since Oniororo does not distinguish it from his other pamphlets, nor do Zell, Bundy, and Coulon (1983) consider it a novel, but it is on the border between market pamphlets and novels proper.

62. Offering up to a dozen new titles a year, the Pacesetters—along with the closely associated small line of M-Novels, which were intended to be somewhat more demanding reading—kept the proportion of Nigerian novels published in Britain artificially high through the early eighties. This is a bit misleading in that, unlike other British publishers, Macmillan marketed its Pacesetters and M-Novels almost exclusively in Africa.

63. These problems are of particular concern in the case of Nigerian children's books, for young children are often attracted to books in the first place because of their pictures and other physical qualities (Osiobe, Osiobe, and Okah 1989).

64. See Akinfolarin (1989–90).

65. They disappeared from library shelves as well. Akinfolarin (1989–90) describes how desperate students, unable to afford the textbooks they need, sharply increased the rate of book theft and mutilation from the already beleaguered university and school libraries.

66. I am grateful to Bernth Lindfors, who was in Nigeria at the time, for providing these 1992 figures.

67. The "sharp decline in fiction publishing" since the early 1980s has been experienced throughout Africa, with the situation in West Africa being especially acute (Bgoya 1996: 169).

68. Adebowale (1990): 10.

69. UNESCO (1991); Figure 2, "Distribution of book production (in numbers of titles) by continents and major areas," reported that in 1985, 53.9 percent of the titles published came from Europe and the USSR, 23.3 percent from Asia, 13 percent from North America, 6.3 percent from Latin America and the Caribbean, 1.5 percent from Oceana, 1.3 percent from Africa, and 0.8 percent from the Arab States.

70. See Bgoya (1996) for comparative discussion.

71. From a study made by Cameroon on publications in Africa presented to the OAU information ministers' conference, Addis Ababa, January 1988; reported in *Books* 1, no. 2 (April 1988): 47.

72. Popoola (1988b).

73. Bgoya (1996) sees three groups of countries: (1) those he calls "adequate capacity countries" with efficient infrastructures "where private-sector printing, publishing, and distribution operate efficiently and where quality books are available at reasonable prices"; (2) "adequate capacity, raw material constrained countries," which have "basically the same well-developed infrastructure but due mostly to political reasons are unable to meet their book needs"; and (3) "low-capacity countries" with rudimentary infrastructures where "books are expensive, poor in quality, and erratically produced." He sees South Africa, Zimbabwe, and Kenya as falling into the first category, and Nigeria as the sole member of the second.

74. Of 281 novels published in Nigeria, 41 percent were short (under fifty thousand words) and 10 percent were long (over one hundred thousand words); of 195 novels published in Britain or the United States, 27 percent were short and 20 percent long.

75. The first line is from 'Tunji Adeyemi's novel *Adorable at Sight (or Africaman's Love)* (Ibadan: Mabamdu, 1992); the second is from Ike Ajogu's *Victim of Love* (Enugu: Fourth Dimension, 1982).

76. Odugbemi (1995): 682.

77. This discussion is based on visits to the Bestseller on May 15 and 17, 1995.

78. Marabel Morgan's *The Total Woman,* which instructs wives on how to be sexy for their husbands while maintaining a conservative Christian understanding of women's and men's roles, was something of a sensation in the United States when it first came out in 1973.

79. The exchange rate at the time—May 1995—was eighty naira to the dollar.

80. Based on a visit to the CSS Bookstore May 16, 1995.

81. *New Creation,* vol. 3, no. 1. The article, written by Dolapo Kwapowe, came to no conclusion about God's political intentions, but it was unambiguous about those of the Nigerian voters: "The Presidential mandate has been given to Abiola by the electorate but the government in power has consistently resisted it by the use of all at their disposal" (21).

82. See *Books* 1, no. 2, p. 43.

83. Some 130,000 people out of Baltimore's total population of 740,000 are functionally illiterate ("Inner Cities: Battling Schmoke," *The Economist,* September 10, 1994, 27–28).

84. This is not an idle boast; one study showed that 94 percent of adult Americans had read books, magazines, or newspapers during the previous six months, and over half (55 percent) had read a book (Cole and Gold 1979).

85. See discussion of literacy as a human right in Oxenham (1980).

86. Forgacs (1990): Table 1.2, p. 19.

87. A National Endowment for the Arts survey for 1985 found that 86 percent of the adult population had read some form of book or magazine during the past twelve months (Zill and Winglee 1990: Table 1, p. 13).

88. In the United Kingdom, for example, 45 percent of adults said yes to the survey question "Are you reading a book currently?" (Euromonitor 1980: Table 2.1). Other European countries have comparable figures: 40 percent in West Germany in 1980, 41 percent in Denmark (1976), 45 percent in Switzerland (1980), 36 percent in Spain (1978) (Curwen 1986: 175). In the United States, 37 percent of those polled in 1991 said yes when asked, "Do you happen to be reading any books or novels at the present time?" (Gallup 1992: 50).

89. Gallup (1987): 104; Gallup (1992): 49–50

90. In the previously mentioned 1985 NEA survey that found 86 percent of adults had read a book or magazine during the previuos year, 65 percent (or 56 percent of all adults) had read "literature," defined as novels, short stories, poetry, and/or plays (Zill and Winglee 1990: Table 1, p. 13). While 36 percent of the adult population had some college education, 42 percent of the readers and 49 percent of the readers of literature did; likewise, 25 percent of the population had less than a high school education, but only 20 percent of the readers and 14 percent of the readers of literature did. See also Selsky (1989).

91. While young people are believed to be heavy readers, this may be overrated. One study in Britain suggested that well over a third of fourteen-year-olds never read books for pleasure (Mann 1982: 157).

92. Cole and Gold (1979) did not find a significant rural-metropolitan difference.

93. Ibid.

94. See Nell (1988). Sociologist Richard A. Peterson (1992) has shown that while working-class people participate in a narrow range of cultural activities, middle-class people tend to participate in all kinds of culture, both popular and highbrow. He calls these individuals who like both opera and country music "cultural omnivores." (Likewise, Cole and Gold's study [1979] shows that book readers tend to participate in leisure-time activities more than non–book readers.) In the same sense, serious readers are "literary omnivores," for they almost always read mysteries, romances, or other forms of popular fiction as well as more demanding literature. From the 1960s to the late 1980s, according to a Gallup survey, reading books seems to have risen together with reading magazines and watching television (but not newspaper reading, which has declined), perhaps suggesting that more people are becoming culturally omnivorous due to higher rates of education (Selsky 1989).

95. Oxenham (1980): 1.

96. As in most non-Western societies, a push for literacy has been encouraged by African governments and applauded by outside agencies. "There is . . . a clear belief that the skills of literacy have much to do with transforming a person—to use the phraseology of current fashion—from a passive object of history to an autonomous subject aware of the nature of his society and able to assist in changing it" (Oxenham 1980: 12).

97. See Malmquist (1992). Islamic fundamentalism, as in the Taliban movement in Afghanistan, offers instances of women's increasing rates of education being reversed; when the Taliban revolutionaries seized power, one of their first acts was to close schools for girls.

98. UNESCO (1991): Table 1.3; I have rounded off these percentages. Illiteracy is not defined by UNESCO, which says that the rates are taken "from the latest census or survey held since 1970," so there may be variation from one country to another in terms of just what is being measured.

99. One notes that such illiteracy is rare in the Western Hemisphere, even in developing countries. Mexico, for example, has only 13 percent adult illiteracy, and Jamaica a mere 1.6 percent. Only Haiti (47 percent illiterate) and Guatemala (45 percent) approach the Nigerian rate (UNESCO 1991: Table 1.3).

100. Yet schooling in Nigeria is far from universal. In 1989 only 70 percent of primary school-age children were in fact going to school—77 percent of the boys, 63 percent of the girls (UNESCO 1991: Table 3.2, "Enrolment [sic] ratios for the first, second, and third levels of education").

101. The four most widely read magazines in Nigeria were *Drum* (read by 28 percent of urban and 7 percent rural respondents), *Trust* (20 and 4 percent), *Spear* (19 and 4 percent), and *Newsweek* (16 and 2 percent) (*Index to International Public Opinion, 1982–1983,* 294).

102. Popoola, Adesanya, and Adamolekun (1988): 5.

103. Amuta (1986): 80, 81.

104. Schmidt (1965): 99.

105. Ibid., 95.

106. UNESCO (1991): Table 3.2.

107. I made this calculation as follows: UNESCO (1991): Table 1.2 estimates that in 1990 out of a total sub-Saharan African population of 476,656,000, there were 50,711,000 in the fifteen to nineteen age-group and another 42,396,000 in the twenty to twenty-four age-group. This means that roughly 20 percent of Africans were young adults. If the Nigerian population at the time was somewhere around 90 million, there were perhaps 18 million young adults, and if 20 percent of them can read sufficiently to read a novel, the potential young-adult market for a novel was 3.6 million readers.

108. M. H. Panman, head of Readers Services, National Library. Quoted by Kenneth Tadaferua in "Wanted: Reading Culture to Check Decline in Education Standard," *Sunday Mail,* July 19, 1987. See also Nweke (1987) for a description of the campaign, along with the usual lament about Nigerians being slow to embrace the reading habit.

109. I am using the term *reading culture* as virtually synonymous with *novel-reading culture.* Although it is perhaps true, as Hunter (1990) claims, that early modern England had a reading culture "before novels," now that the genre has been established it seems that every culture that attains popular literacy along with the widespread use of print media produces and consumes novels. Link (1981) offers a good example of this tight association of print, literacy, and popular fiction in early twentieth-century China.

110. The habit of parents reading to young children is particularly important in this regard, and the link between parents who read to their children and chil-

dren's academic achievement is well established (see Heath 1983; Zill and Winglee 1990).

111. In this respect reading for pleasure is like other pleasures in that the novice has to learn, through social interaction, how to do it and how to enjoy it. Howard Becker's (1953) classic interactionist study of how people become marijuana users showed that for the habit to become established, people had to learn how to smoke, what to expect when smoking, and that the expected sensations are considered enjoyable. Reading is not all that different; the pleasures of fiction are not simply inherent in the physical presence of the text but are a learned skill.

112. Starker (1990).

113. See discussions in Crowder (1978) and Isichei (1983).

114. Isichei (1983): 330–31.

115. *Europa Yearbook 1988,* 2029–32.

116. One socialist magazine, *The Analyst,* claimed to publish in English, Igbo, Hausa, and Yoruba.

117. Sanders (1994) has suggested that there is a universal pattern whereby children are introduced into orality through their mothers and that such oral culture is in the vernacular, whereas participation in literate culture comes through fathers and male-dominated institutions. This may be an exaggeration, for in the primary grades most children learn their first functional literacy from women. Nevertheless, it is certainly the case in Nigeria that men direct and staff those institutions most associated with advanced literacy in English, including especially secondary and tertiary education as well as the Christian church/mission complexes historically. Koranic schools, which are also nonvernacular, are male preserves as well.

118. Even in large cities like Lagos or Ibadan, Nigerian Electric Power Authority (NEPA) is said to "take the light" frequently, often for hours at a time. Wealthy people cope by having private generators, but most people have candles and lanterns at the ready, or simply go without light until the inscrutable NEPA "gives it back."

119. Cole and Gold (1979).

120. Nigeria has a population density of 117 people per square kilometer. This is high even by African standards; Ghana's density is 63 per square kilometer, Kenya's is 43, South Africa's is 29, which is roughly the same as the United States. While a few small African countries like Rwanda are even more densely populated than Nigeria, none of the large ones are anywhere near as crowded; Egypt, second to Nigeria in population, has 53 people per square kilometer; Ethiopia, third in size, has 40. Unlike many African countries, especially those with large deserts, Nigeria has no large areas devoid of settlement, although the population is considerably more dense in the south than in the north. Of course, population density alone does not preclude a reading culture; France is almost as crowded as Nigeria, and the United Kingdom, with 234 people per square kilometer, is twice as crowded. See UNESCO (1993): Table 11.

121. Newa (1990).

122. UNESCO (1991): Table 7.1.

123. The information on the library comes from Director Andrew Thomas, Librarian Sylvester Ogwara, the "Library and Information Services in Nigeria" pamphlet put out by the British Council, and from my two visits to the Lagos branch in May 1995.

124. *Igbo Traditional Verse,* compiled and translated by Romanus Egudu and Donatus Nwoga (London, Heinemann, 1973); Albert S. Gerard, *African Language Literatures: An Introduction to the Literary History of Sub-Saharan Africa* (Washington, D.C.: Three Continents, 1981); Kofi Awoonor, *The Breast of the Earth: A Survey of the History, Culture, and Literature of Africa South of the Sahara* (Garden City, N.Y.: Anchor Press, 1975).

125. From field notes made on October 27, 1991. Airports and airline flights offer a good context for observing natural reading practices, for the observer and the observed are in close proximity for an extended period of time in circumstances conducive to reading. A similar technique whereby the researchers distinguished readers from nonreaders by observing subjects at an airport (readers were those who read for at least ten consecutive minutes) was used in West, Stanovich, and Mitchell (1993).

126. On domestic flights in the United States I have often counted readers; typically about half of the passengers on a flight is reading. On international flights I have observed that about half of American, Asian, or European passengers are reading at any particular time except during meals or a film, and perhaps two-thirds read at some time during the course of the flight.

127. When the Euromonitor survey asked those 45 percent of all adults who said they were currently reading a book to describe the book, just under two-thirds (or some 30 percent of all adults) said it was a work of fiction (Euromonitor 1980: Table 2.2). If the survey had excluded job-related reading, the percentage of fiction would likely be somewhat higher. The NEA survey (reported in Zill and Winglee 1990) found that 40 percent of adult Americans claimed to have read a novel during the past year, although one-quarter of these are questionable (either the respondent could not remember the novel's name or author, or the respondent named a book that was not, in fact, a novel), so 30 percent may be a more accurate figure.

128. Nell (1988):19.

129. Ibid., 25. Similarly, the Euromonitor survey showed that while fiction was the largest single category of books published in Britain during the 1970s, it accounted for only 10 to 12 percent of the total. Education and school textbooks were next, with 7 to 9 percent, closely followed by children's books and political science. There is a large category of "Other" (36 to 39 percent), which may account for why the Euromonitor fiction percentages are lower than Nell's, since some of these titles may be fiction (Euromonitor 1980: Table 4.17).

130. The two most popular categories in the Euromonitor survey were romances and crime/thriller, each being named by 14 percent of the book readers; historical fiction was next, at 12 percent. By contrast, only 6 percent of the book readers claimed to be reading a "modern novel," and only 3 percent a "classic" (Euromonitor 1980: Table 2.2). Similarly in the United States, while perhaps 30 percent of all adults have read a novel in the past year, only a third of these (11 percent of the total respondents) have read a work of "literary merit" (data from John Robinson et al., *Americans' Participation in the Arts,* as reported in Zill and Winglee 1990: Table 4).

131. The overall reading rate—the number of actual readings out of a total of the potential readings if every one of the 292 respondents had read all twenty nov-

els—was less than 1 percent, and only 12 respondents had read more than one of the books (Mann 1982: 172–74).

132. Newa (1990) reports that when peasants in rural Madagascar were asked why they wanted to learn to read, their priorities were, first, to be able to read family letters and, second, to gain access to "books in general and agricultural brochures in particular" (82).

133. Cole and Gold (1979): 58–59.

134. Schmidt (1965): 95. Although scarcely remembered today, Marie Corelli, a pseudonym for Mary Mackay (1855–1924), was an immensely popular British author. She wrote over thirty novels, one of which, *The Sorrows of Satan* (1895), was praised by Queen Victoria and had gone through sixty printings by the time of the author's death. Her works were romances with a strong streak of spiritualism, conveyed in "fiction that is vulgar in the fullest sense, clichéd, melodramatic, uninformed; yet with an imaginative flair, theatricality, and self-conviction that ultimately defies criticism" (James 1994). Corelli was very popular in colonial Nigeria, and both authors and readers report having been entranced by her novels in their youth.

135. Schmidt (1965): Table I, p. 129.

136. Ibid., 72.

137. Osiobe, Osiobe, and Okah (1989).

138. Mann (1982): 175; cf. Radway (1984).

139. Long (1992); Radway (1988).

140. Samuels (1989).

141. Mann (1982): 158.

142. Okedara (1981). Page numbers in the text come from Okedara's collection.

143. Radway (1984).

144. Harris (1989).

145. This may be a cultural analogue to the late-development effect. Dore (1973) has suggested that countries like Japan, which industrialized late, came up with technologies and organizational patterns that were more advanced, more suited to current conditions, than were those of the early industrializers. Similarly, Nigeria's emerging multiplicity of cultural options, with a reading culture being just one, may prefigure the future for all of us.

CHAPTER III
NIGERIAN NOVELS

1. It is this emphasis on similarities and differences, as perceived by people who interact with cultural objects (write them, read them, analyze them) that gives rise to provisional generic classifications. Genres are not ontologically given, but result from decisions made by people in contact with cultural objects; see Griswold (1987) for further discussions of the methodological implications of sorting cultural objects into genres.

2. Other classifications are possible, depending on the interests of the classifier. For example, concerned with the role of literature in advancing or obstructing socialism, Amuta (1986) dismisses many novels of the popular sort as commodities

not worthy of attention. He sees the remainder as divided into four types, roughly sequential in Nigerian literary history: works of cultural reaffirmation, identity crisis, postcolonial disenchantment, and ideological commitment (African socialist realism).

Coussy (1988) presents six categories in her analysis: Tutuola's mythic works; the experimental novels of Okara and Soyinka; and novels of social change, which she subdivides into the works of Achebe, writings about women, novels about the man of two worlds (e.g., Munonye), and war novels. While Coussy does not disdain all popular fiction, her categorization has a somewhat academic quality, most notably in the fact that she does not include a separate category for crime novels.

A bookseller, with different "interests," might place the Spectrum books together, making an implicit genre classification that draws a line between "Spectrums" and "everything else" simply because the publisher has provided him with materials to set up a display devoted to its books. This was the case in the CSS Bookstore discussed in Chapter 2. In all these instances, people are making generic distinctions based on how they see the world of cultural objects, how they expect or intend others to see it, and their own interests or convenience.

3. Parts of this and the following section appeared in Griswold (1992).

4. Interview with Bayo Adebowale in Lagos, Nigeria, September 1990.

5. Northrop Frye (1957) has described the romance, one of his four core literary archetypes, as characterized by "its extraordinarily persistent nostalgia, its search for some kind of imaginative golden age in time or space" (186).

6. Achebe, *Things Fall Apart*, 4.

7. See Zabus (1991), who suggests that Achebe's adroit use of proverbs constitutes only a temporary remission of their cultural decline. "Transposing proverbs from the oral to the written medium is . . . disabling and foreshadows the death of a species, for proverbs are generally collected in writing when about to die. . . . Thus isolated and cut off from their original context, proverbs fall prey to a textual glottophagia whereby Igbo proverbs are 'eaten up' by the English words of the European narrative" (26).

8. A traditionalist to the end, Okonkwo has followed the Igbo script that encourages murderers to restore harmony by hanging themselves. See discussion in Uchendu (1965): 43–43.

9. Turner (1991) points out that the novel's tragedy is precipitated by two social systems in conflict, not by Okonkwo's bullheadedness, and that the ending is an overthrow of the former order, not its restoration. Thus a reader feels no tragic catharsis, nor did Achebe intend one.

10. When I give talks on this research, I often ask those attending—usually they are groups of social scientists and other academicians interested in culture who are not, for the most part, specialists on Africa—if they have read any Nigerian novels and, if so, which ones. The typical response will be that one-quarter to one-third of those present will have read a Nigerian novel. All of these, almost without exception, will have read *Things Fall Apart*. A few will also have read another Nigerian novel, sometimes one by Buchi Emecheta or the recent Booker Prize winner, Ben Okri's *The Famished Road*, sometimes another novel by Achebe.

11. Coquery-Vidrovitch (1988): 118.

12. For a discussion of transparency in Igbo villages, see Uchendu (1965).

13. Anderson ([1983] 1991): xx.

14. See discussion in Coquery-Vidrovitch (1988).

15. Examples include Tonnies's *gemeinschaft* and *gesellschaft,* Durkheim's mechanical and organic solidarity, Marx's precapitalist and capitalist social formations, and Weber's distinction between the highly rationalized and disenchanted world of modernity and its predecessors. Although these theorists varied in their emphases, all stressed the division of labor and the coming of industrial capitalism as producing the shift from the earlier form of social relations to the later.

16. Gusfield (1975) argued that "community," especially insofar as social and spatial relationships were conflated, has always been more a metaphor than a social fact. Wellman (1979) suggested that sociologists replace their "community lost" versus "community saved" paradigm with a "community liberated" model of network ties; in this approach "community," especially for urban dwellers, is not geographically based and is more a matter of weak ties than of solidarity.

17. The contemporary realization of the community ideal is highly circumscribed in "defended neighborhoods" or "communities of limited liability," but even urbanites construct their lives so that they manage "to dwell among friends," thus approximating the lost ideal (Suttles 1972; Janowitz 1952; Fischer 1982). Sociologists readily acknowledge that some communities are more imaginary than others. Hummon (1990) shows how suburbanites have a hard time getting a symbolic fix on their residential locales; others suggest that in brute social reality, community is being replaced by lifestyle enclaves (Bellah et al. 1984), is an illusion put together by boosters and developers (Logan and Molotch 1987; Suttles 1990), or has mutated into Disneyland (Baudrillard 1988). Furthermore, different types of residents imagine the same community differently—Elijah Anderson (1990), for example, demonstrates that "the Village" is a different place for whites than for blacks—but they all agree that they are living in a particular community. Such research attests to the continued power of the community ideal, despite its seeming lack of empirical grounding.

18. Cf. the archetypal Joe Gorman in *Habits of the Heart,* nostalgic for a lost New England "community of civic-minded families rooted in two hundred fifty years of tradition" (Bellah et al., 1984: 11).

19. Laslett ([1965] 1973): chap. 3.

20. Guyer (1992); Laitin (1986).

21. Callaway (1987).

22. The prominent Nigerian critic Biodun Jeyifo (1991) makes a similar point in his analysis of *Things Fall Apart.* Jeyifo points out how while the major narrative line and basis for Okonkwo's tragedy is the displacement of one totalizing world (traditional Igbo culture) by another (Western Christian culture), this is offset by a number of subplots and fragmentary stories, often regarding social outsiders, that subvert all such totalities, constituting "a narrative and discursive logic which admits of illogic and which makes *everything* negotiable, including the most sacrosanct values of the culture" (63). Okonkwo's friend Obierika represents the intellectual stance of pondering over and questioning the given conventions even while following them, and of recognizing that the conventions could be different.

23. Nigerian women authors are uncomfortable with the label *feminist,* which they take to imply a separatism, even a hatred of men, that they do not share. One

of the most prominent, the late Flora Nwapa, advocated using *womanist,* a term introduced by African-American writer Alice Walker, who defined a womanist as a "black feminist or feminist of color. . . . Committed to survival and wholeness of entire people, male *and* female" (1983: xi; emphasis in original).

24. See Wilkinson (1992): 56.

25. Foucault (1979) posed this question to deconstruct the artificiality of the author as concept.

26. Cawelti (1976) argues that formulaic fiction sets up moral fantasies whereby social tensions are both expressed and resolved. I am extending his thinking here by suggesting that this concept be applied to genres of nonformulaic fiction as well.

27. While the questionable reliability of Nigerian censuses makes estimation difficult, the Nigerian population is said to be about anywhere from 15 to 35 percent urban. Jarmon (1988: 127) estimates that 14 percent of Nigerians live in cities of 20,000 or more, while the World Development Report (1980), which he cites (p. 19), puts the urban population at 20 percent of the total, with 57 percent of these living in large cities (over 500,000). The *World Almanac and Book of Facts, 1991,* sets the urban portion of Nigeria's population at 23 percent. UNESCO (1993) estimates are on the high end; Table 12 sets Nigeria at 27 percent urban in 1980 and 35 percent in 1990. Comparisons among the UNESCO figures show Nigeria to be less urban than Egypt 44 percent) or South Africa (49 percent), more urban than Kenya (24 percent), Ethiopia (12 percent), or Zaire (28 percent), and about the same as Ghana (34 percent). The Nigerian census of 1991 gave a total population of 88,514,501 in its provisional results, but it did not provide a rural-urban breakdown (Federal Republic of Nigeria 1992). All figures must be approached with caution, particularly since there are no internationally agreed upon definitions of what is "urban" or "rural."

28. I am including the few U.S.-published novels with the British ones in these figures. Recall that only a handful of Nigerian novels have been published anywhere outside of either Nigeria or the United Kingdom.

29. The difference is even greater without the Macmillan Pacesetters, which are published in the United Kingdom but distributed in Africa; these usually have urban settings, thereby inflating the percentage of British-published urban novels.

30. See Bruckner [1983] (1986).

31. An analysis of the relationship between time and place of publication, not shown here, indicates that the two variables operate independently. In other words, the association of British publication with the village subgenre is not just due to an earlier average date of publication; even though a far smaller percentage of novels in the 1980s were published in Britain than earlier, the overrepresentation of village settings among those novels remained evident.

32. This seems a clear case of what has been called "the paradox of constructed primordialism" (Appadurai 1990), with both British editors and Nigerian authors as accomplices in this act of imagining.

33. In 1940 there were six African cities outside South Africa with populations over one hundred thousand, and three of these were in Nigeria. Ibadan and Kano were precolonial cities now taking on new administrative functions, while Lagos was a colonial port (Guyer 1987: 28).

34. In 1830 refugees from the Yoruba wars took shelter there in caves in the Olumo Rock (Peil 1981: 23).

35. See discussion in Jarmon (1988): 124–26.

36. Peil (1981): 13–15.

37. A few pages later, Peil refers to Kaduna as a provincial town; this suggests the tentativeness of any attempts at categorization. Similarly, Enuga would seem to fit this central city category, since it was the capital of the Eastern Region before the civil war, but Peil calls it a provincial town.

38. Jarmon (1988): Table 6:1, p. 127.

39. Onibokun (1989): Table 4.3.

40. Guyer (1987): Table 1, p. 37.

41. Onibokun (1989): Table 4.2, p. 70; White (1989): Table 1.3, p. 5.

42. Onibokun (1989).

43. See discussion in Stren and White (1989).

44. Fapohunda (1981).

45. Jarmon (1988): 134. Migrants working in the informal sector seem especially likely to be male (Fapohunla 1981; Mabogunje and Filani 1981). This may be due to restrictions on women's economic participation in Hausa cities, to women's marriage and (temporary) removal from the labor market, to greater opportunities for women in low-paying levels of the formal economy, and/or to the sampling mechanisms of these studies, which may have underreported both women's trading activities and their participation in prostitution.

46. See Peil (1981).

47. Migration is not the only factor involved in the swelling size of cities; high fertility is another. Contrary to the European experience, fertility rates in Nigerian cities seem to be even higher than in the countryside, while mortality rates have fallen. The urban population growth coming from this combination of young adult migration and high fertility has overwhelmed the cities' employment opportunities and infrastructures. It has produced a dependent group of the very young (along with the much smaller group of the retired), approaching 50 percent of the total urban population; if unemployment is added, the dependent population is around 60 percent of large cities' residents. See Jarmon (1988): 132–34; Onibokun (1989): Table 4.4.

48. Sethuraman (1981): 17.

49. Guyer (1989): 35.

50. Coquery-Vidrovitch (1988): 301; Onokerhoraye (1995): 60.

51. Some discussions, such as that by Sethuraman (1981), have emphasized rural-to-urban migrants as lacking in human capital, but that does not seem to be the case in Nigeria. Fapohunda's (1981) survey of informal sector enterprises in Lagos found that 87 percent of the entrepreneurs came from outside Lagos, with an additional 8 percent coming from outside Nigeria. (The term *entrepreneur* may be misleading here. Half of the enterprises consisted of only one person—"the entrepreneur"—and another quarter had only one other employee, often an unpaid apprentice, so these are not captains of industry.) Three-quarters had some formal education, averaging under six years of schooling (Fapohunda 1981). The percentage of migrants in Lagos's informal sector may be unusually high; Mabogunje and Filani (1981) found only 35 percent of Kano's informal-sector participants

were from outside the city, only slightly higher than the 25 to 30 percent of Kano's population that is migrant.

52. Onibokun (1989).

53. Nigeria illustrates the possibility of a vicious circle in the deterioration of services. Because of regular power "outages" in Nigeria, large firms and wealthy individuals purchase imported generators, which provide power to their factories and compounds when the power goes off. Similarly, wealthier Nigerians buy water storage tanks for their houses as insurance against water shortages, and in some cities individual home owners contract with private waste removal firms for the disposal of household rubbish. In all three cases, wealthy (and presumably more powerful) individuals are able to "buy themselves out" of the system, thereby reducing drastically their personal incentive to try to improve it through political pressure. (I am paraphrasing Stren 1989: 40.)

54. This could change. A recent book speaks of the "coming anarchy" represented by the crowds of disaffected urban youth in West African cities (Kaplan 1996). These young men, with weakened social ties and few economic prospects, are apt to be drawn into the orbits of strong leaders promising both food and a fixed identity. Hence the success of warlords and their teenage gangs in places like Liberia and Sierra Leone. Nigeria has not seen much of this formation of informal armies, but some of the structural prerequisites are present.

55. Coquery-Vidrovitch (1988): chap. 13.

56. One might question how disappointed the young men working in the informal sector actually are. Fapohunda (1981) reports the astonishing fact that 78 percent of the entrepreneurs in his study were satisfied with their jobs, and "very few wanted wage employment" (71 percent; cf. Peace 1979). But his fiindings also indicate that they live at an absolute level of poverty at odds with this reported satisfaction, with a median income well below the minimum wage. It may be germane to note that 80 percent of the entrepreneurs never applied to regular employment offices, often not knowing they even existed, so the reported satisfaction with the informal sector work may be due in large part to ignorance about alternatives. Most important, however, is to note that Fapohunda's survey took place in 1976, the peak of the oil boom, when even individuals on the lower rungs of the urban employment ladder would have been experiencing an improvement in their economic lives and prospects. It was following the "oil bust" that the most bitter expressions of disappointment were heard. It seems likely in any case that those people with the most human capital, particularly education, would be the least satisfied with working in the informal sector.

57. A Njoku (1985).

58. Coquery-Vidrovitch (1988): 313.

59. From the 1950s and 1960s: 34 novels, 8 (24 percent) urban; 1970s: 94 novels, 53 (56 percent) urban; 1980s: 281 novels, 203 (72 percent) urban; 1990s: 67 novels, 47 (70 percent) urban.

60. The decline has been steep and may be continuing. Of the 34 novels published in the 1950s or 1960s, 23 (68 percent) had village (or bush) settings. Of the 94 novels published in the 1970s, 26 (28 percent) had village settings. Of the 281 novels published during the 1980s, 37 (13 percent) have village settings; of 67 coded novels published so far in the 1990s, only 7 (10 percent) have village or bush settings.

61. For the British literary favoring of the "country," see Williams (1973); for the American use of small-town settings, see Griswold (1981).

62. Griswold (1981).

63. Griswold (1992).

64. Interview with Ibe Oparandu in Lagos, Nigeria, September 1990.

65. For example, Charles Lindberg's solo flight across the Atlantic in 1929 made him into a popular hero, but his deed was interpreted in two very different ways: as a triumph of the unspoiled individual representing America's past and as a triumph of America's technology representing her future (John William Ward, "The Meaning of Lindbergh's Flight," *American Quarterly* 10 [Spring 1958]: 3–16; I thank Lawrence Levine, who included this article in his edited collection *The National Temper,* for bringing it to my attention). For a discussion of metaphoric power as depending on a combination of coherence and ambiguity, see Griswold (1987).

66. Not to be confused with the Lagos slum of the same name.

67. See Ike's "Expo 77" for a fictionalized account of this scandal.

68. There were 452 novels squarely set in one time period. Ninety were set in colonial or precolonial times, and of these 19 (21 percent) had city settings. Three hundred sixty-two novels were set in the present (i.e., postindependence) or, in the case of five, the future; 282 (78 percent) of these had city settings.

69. The West Indian novel, which focuses not on social changes but on issues of identity, offers a contrasting case; it is relatively unconcerned with social change because the novel was well established in the West Indies before the rapid changes of the 1930s and the postwar period.

70. For example, First Lady Maryam Babangida's highly publicized "Better Life for Rural Women" program of the late 1980s was cast in terms of offering rural women the same educational opportunities, medical facilities, and social freedom that their urban sisters had enjoyed for years.

71. It is this "two worlds" orientation that Mitchell may have captured in his 1965 survey of Southern Rhodesians (now Zimbabwe) of attitudes toward town and country life. When asked for their self-rating on a five-point rural-urban scale, 56 percent of the respondents indicated they were "partly a townsman, partly a countryman." The rest were fairly evenly divided between "mainly" or "very definitely" a countryman (23.3 percent) and "mainly" or "very definitely" a townsman (20.7 percent). Respondents were secondary school, teacher training, or adult education students, thus among the Africans most in contact with Western and modern ways, and most had substantial experience with living in a city (Mitchell 1987: chap. 4).

72. Peil (1981): 11

73. For example, it is common for a prosperous family head to own two homes— one in the city, one in the village—with various members of the extended family constantly shifting from one to the other as dictated by their employment, business, education, child care, or personal preferences.

74. Wheatley (1971).

75. Zell, Bundy, and Coulon (1983): 439. Grace Ogot brought out *The Promised Land* in Nairobi that same year.

76. Ogunyemi (1996): 132.

77. Stratton (1994): chap. 4 sets out *Efuru*'s unfavorable reception in detail. She attributes the negative reaction to a biased critical stance that regarded masculine themes as universal, feminine themes as trivial.

78. Although she is not writing specifically about literature, Oyeronke Oyewumi (1997) goes even further when she argues that "women" did not exist as a social category in traditional Oyo-Yoruba culture; gender, with its implication of hierarchy and women's innate inferiority, was an imposition of Western thought.

79. Of the fifty women-and-men novels, thirty were written by women, nineteen by men, and one by an author whose sex is not known.

80. Chukwuma (1989): 5.

81. Of the thirty women-and-men novels written by women, twenty-five have money as a central topic, but only eight of the nineteen novels by men do.

82. Of 459 coded novels for which we know the sex of the author, money was significant in 307 (67 percent). Of the 383 novels by men, 67 percent had money as a significant topic, as did 64 percent of the 76 novels by women.

83. See White (1990), who has studied prostitution in Kenya; the term *free woman* used in Nigerian as well.

84. Remi Ilori, *Bisi;* Helen Ovbiagele, *The Schemers;* Richard Akoji, *Teardrops at Sunset.*

85. Four of the nineteen women-and-men novels by men have Witch-Bitch characters, as do three of the thirty novels by women. The novels by men are Akoji's *Teardrops at Sunset,* Atoyebe's *Countdown to Perdition,* Ilori's *Bisi,* and Oyegoke's *Laughing Shadows;* the ones by women are Emecheta's *Kehinde,* Fakunle's *Chasing the Shadow,* and Ovbiagele's *The Schemers.*

86. Seven novels, all by women, deal with the virtuous woman theme: Alkali's *The Stillborn* and *The Virtuous Woman,* Fakunle's *Chasing the Shadow,* Igbo's *Tiena,* Nwapa's *Efuru,* and Umelo's *Felicia* and *Something to Hide.*

87. See discussion in Ogunyemi (1996), 310–13, which spells out the political dimension.

88. Walker (1983).

89. Ken Saro-Wiwa has probably become better known in the West since his execution, although he is regarded as a minority rights activist and martyr more than as a writer.

90. I am grateful to anthropologist Misty Bastian for pointing out that Nnu Ego has had the perfect set of children according to Igbo tradition.

91. An earlier version of the following discussion appeared in Griswold (1989).

92. Examples from British and American literature include the murder mystery, the Wild West adventure story, the family saga, and the romance. Formulaic works make few demands on their readers and offer few surprises. They are entertaining, not challenging or disturbing. They incorporate a "moral fantasy" of how the world ought to be: the good guys win in the end, crimes are always solved, virtuous characters find true love (Cawelti 1976).

93. Most analyses of the romance boom that began in the early 1970s give credit to Harlequin's aggressive marketing strategies, inaugurated by W. Lawrence Heisey, formerly of Proctor and Gamble; Heisey was responsible for the firm's emphasis on product standardization, subscriptions, and sales in retail outlets such as supermarkets, as well as his somewhat notorious promotional device of including

copies of Harlequin romances in boxes of laundry detergent. A second factor contributing to the boom was the unanticipated success of the longer, sexier historical romances, dubbed "bodice rippers" by the industry. For the history of the romance genre, see Radway (1984): chap. 1, and Markert (1985); brief accounts appear in Guiley (1983), Modleski ([1982] 1984), and Rabine (1985); *Twentieth-Century Romance and Historical Writers* (1994).

94. Romances accounted for one-fourth to one-third of the paperback titles issued in the United States during the late 1970s (Radway 1984: 44) and 41 percent of paperback sales in the early 1980s (Guiley 1983: 4). Harlequin novels alone accounted for 10 percent of the U.S. paperback market in 1977 (Radway 1984: 40).

95. In 1979, Harlequin distributed its romances in ninety-eight countries and claimed a regular readership of sixteen million women (Radway 1984: 40).

96. See Falk (1983): 115; Guiley (1983): 11–15.

97. Readership information comes from Guiley (1983), Falk (1983), and Radway (1984).

98. Guiley (1983): 5.

99. Rabine (1985): 182.

100. Modleski ([1982] 1984: 55) has pointed out that this device allows the reader to strongly identify with the woman, while providing enough distance so the author can describe her beauty and the reader can feel somewhat superior to the heroine; for example, the reader knows that the hero really loves the heroine and that his aloof behavior is a sign of his fear of rejection rather than of his indifference.

101. Modleski ([1982] 1984: 45).

102. Radway (1984) stresses this construction of the nurturing male, its psychoanalytic roots, and the pleasure women readers derive from such a character.

103. Bertha M. Clay was the pseudonym for the English writer Charlotte Monica Braeme (1836–84), who wrote a long series of romantic novels. In fact, many of the Bertha Clay novels are believed to have been written by Frederick Van Rensselaer Day (1861–1922) and Thomas Chalmers Harbaugh (1849–1924).

104. Fifteen women authors have written 25 romances, for an average of 1.7 romances each; 33 men have written 37 romances, averaging 1.1 each. Only one male, Ike Ajogu, has written 3 romances; Jide Oguntoye and Bode Osanyin have each written 2. Among the women writers, Bisi Abejo and Helen Ovbiagele have each written 4 romances; Nyengi Koin, 3; and Hauwa Ali, 2. Five romances are by authors whose sex is unknown.

105. Of the fifty-seven romances with a single dominant setting, fifty-three (93 percent) were urban, four (7 percent) village or rural.

106. Of the thirty-seven romances by men, twenty-three (62 percent) have male protagonists and fourteen (38 percent) female protagonists. Of the twenty-five romances by women, six (24 percent) have male protagonists and nineteen (76 percent) female. There are five romances where the author's sex is unknown; four of these have female protagonists.

107. Twenty-three (62 percent) of the thirty-seven romances by men end with the protagonist married or about to be married as do eighteen (72 percent) of the twenty-five books by women.

108. Of the twenty romances with the sequential pattern, seven (35 percent) have male protagonists and thirteen (65 percent) female. In contrast, ten (56 per-

cent) of the eighteen circular plots have male protagonists. For the twenty-nine continuous novels, thirteen (45 percent) of the protagonists are male, sixteen female.

109. For a discussion of these changes, see Orubuloye (1981).

110. Same-sex emotional ties are important in Nigerian novels in general, not just in romances. In the fifty-nine romances, in only twenty (30 percent) are there no such ties; in forty-one (61 percent) these ties are part of the story, and in six (9 percent) they are crucial. Similarly, same-sex bonds are crucial in 18 percent of the Nigerian novels as a whole, part of the story in 52 percent, and unimportant in 29 percent. What makes romances different is not the presence of such ties, therefore, but the specific role of the same-sex friend/relative as facilitator of the couple's getting or remaining together.

111. Fertility problems are an issue in 26 (43 percent) of the 67 romances.

112. Eight of the twenty-one romances with ruptured endings have male protagonists.

113. Armstrong (1987): 8.

114. Maja-Pearce (1992): 3.

115. The Chinese example comes from Link (1992): 14.

116. In his novel *Mission to Kalu,* Mongo Beti has given a searing picture of the returned student who, despite having failed his exams, is accorded immense power and prestige in his home village.

117. My focus will be on intellectuals who have had contact with Western learning. Nigeria also has, and recognizes, its Islamic intellectuals deeply versed in Koranic scholarship, but these men have had virtually no involvement with the Nigerian novel.

118. Emenyonu (1993): 1–3. This high rate of failure even among educated youth has been attributed to the disjunction between English as the language of instruction and indigenous languages as the first language of virtually every student.

119. This is the title of Ben Okri's second novel, which describes an artist struggling against a hostile society.

120. In the nineteenth century, for example, hundreds of would-be writers flocked to Paris; all one needed to become a writer was to declare oneself to be one; see Graña (1964). The phenomenon of calling yourself a writer making it true is also observed by the narrator of Ike's novel-cum-travelogue *To My Husband from Iowa,* an account of a Nigerian visiting the University of Iowa's writing school.

121. Mann (1985): 109.

122. The concept of cultural capital has been used by Pierre Bourdieu (1984) to describe the prestigious resources based on education and familiarity with high culture that are independent of, and often exchangable with, economic capital. The split between the intellectuals and the economic and political powers in Nigeria is also analyzed by Amuta.

123. Mann (1985) describes a ritual in which this sense of loss was articulated in an unusually public and direct way: "In 1983, I attended the funeral of an informant whose father and mother belonged to the early Lagos elite. Descendants of the old elite families packed the church. A popular Lagos clergyman delivered a eulogy praising the deceased for inheriting a good name and preserving it amid the

many less respectable newcomers who have come to dominate key positions in the city" (170).

124. The Eastern Region maintained that thirty thousand Igbo had died in the May–October violence; later and more impartial estimates suggest that perhaps one-third that number died (de St. Jorre 1972:86).

125. The term is taken from a well-known short story by Chinua Achebe.

126. It is also being told by men. Only four war novels are by women, although women authors are not underrepresented more in this genre than they are in general (in contrast to the intellectual novels).

127. This discussion of obituaries draws on the analysis made by Okigbo (1987).

128. Or, as Robert Frost put it, "Forgive, oh Lord, my little jokes on thee/And I'll forgive thy great big one on me."

129. Love stories were next, followed by stories about "social mores and funny incidents"; least popular were more serious topics such as stories dealing with military affairs, science, and political commitment, as well as (surprisingly) adventure stories (Johnson, Nathan, and Rawski, 1985).

130. Cawelti (1976).

131. This Durkheimian line of thought may be found in Symons (1985). Agreeing with this type of analysis but disputing the desirability of the outcome, Marxist critics have argued that crime novels legitimate bourgeois ideology, either through direct affirmation or through the pointed absense of a feasible alternative. Others, like Eric Hobsbaum, suggest that the character of the outlaw allows for the fantasized treatment of that which is forbidden, and that the appeal of such books lies in their representation of the social order defied, not the social order maintained.

132. Prior to 1829, what little urban crime control there was fell to private groups such as the Bow Street Runners.

133. In a study of fiction published in the United States during 1988, Griswold and Hull (1998) found that 28 percent were crime stories. Of these, close to half were murder mysteries, and another third were thrillers of the international intrigue type. There were over twice as many mysteries published as the next largest category, romances. This pattern is identical to that found in the Nigerian novels (see Table 3-1).

134. An extended comparison between the penny dreadfuls and the Onitsha market literature would be most revealing. Both dealt with crime, love, and getting ahead in a changing social environment.

135. Three novels were written by women, and one by an author whose sex is not known.

136. Watts (1987): 103. Watts maintains that is wrong to assume that public-private distinctions were never established in the first place. While African kinship and township responsibilities cast a different light on various forms of nepotism and favoritism than do Western views, traditional life clearly demarcated between public and private responsibilities. These demarcations are no longer adequate, but new ones have not arisen to replace them. An example of the collapse of the distinction between the state and private accumulation comes from Watts's (1987) study of the history of Kano's food supply. Watts writes that during the nineteenth century and the colonial period, the food supply for Kano was highly vulnerable rather than

being smooth and self-regulating—a "brittle trade"—and state interventions were frequent, if not necessarily effective. Nevertheless, there was a clear distinction between state and market. With growth of the state came accommodation and eventually an erosion of these distinctions; by the 1950s Kano had the *yan siyasa* system—an alliance of merchants, bureaucrats, and artistocrats—linking commerce and politics, which "privatised the public purse" (91). See also the discussion of how the oil economy has distorted public life in Karl (1997).

137. Reported in "Where Money Talks," *Time,* June 10, 1996, 24.

138. Newswire report: LAGOS, Nigeria (PANA), May 26, 1996; distributed on naija-women news group from Bebecee@aol.com.

139. Cf. Suberu (1993).

140. Apter (1996).

141. Even without the oil bust, it may be that the hope of petrol states to improve the lives of their citizens was never well-founded, because such states exhibit the deadly combination of creating highly centralized resource flows upon which a wealthy class depends while having only weak penetration into civil society. See Karl (1997) for a persuasive development of this argument.

142. Ayers (1979).

143. Of the 128 novels published before 1980, 48 dealt with corruption; of the 348 novels published later, 169 dealt with corruption.

144. There was one author of a political novel, Biyi Bandele-Thomas, whose sex I did not know for sure.

145. Moreover, some commentators have pointed out that canonization of women renders them as exotic as demeaning them does. On this point see Boehmer (1991).

146. Achebe (1991): 9.

BIBLIOGRAPHY

Aboyade, B. Olabimpe. 1993. "Turning Individual Talent into Public Property—
A Definition of the Book in Relation to Nigeria's Needs." In *Culture and the
Book Industry in Nigeria*, edited by Sule Bello and Abdullahi Augi, 3–31. Lagos:
National Council for Arts and Culture.

Abrams, M. H. 1988. *A Glossary of Literary Terms*. New York: Holt, Rinehart and
Winston.

Achebe, Chinua. [1983] 1984. *The Trouble with Nigeria*. London: Heinemann.

———. 1975. *Morning Yet on Creation Day: Essays*. New York: Anchor Press/
Doubleday.

———. 1991. "African Literature as Restoration of Celebration." In Peterson and
Rutherford, 1991, 1–10.

Adebowale, Bayo. 1990. "The Prose Fiction in Nigeria: Style and Audience." Lecture delivered to the Creative Writing Group, Department of Modern European
Languages, University of Ilorin, Kwara State, Nigeria, May 12.

African Book Publishing Record. vol. 1–. Oxford: H. Zell, January 1975–.

Akinfolarin, W. A. 1989–90. "Economic Reform and the Dearth of Books in Nigeria." *Reading Research Quarterly* 5 (4): 30–35.

American Book Publishing Record Cumulative 1993. 1994. New Providence, N.J.:
R. R. Bowker.

Amuta, Chidi. 1986. *Towards a Sociology of African Literature*. Oguta, Nigeria:
Zim Pan-African Publishers.

Anderson, Benedict. [1983] 1991. *Imagined Communities: Reflections on the Origin and Spread of Nationalism*. Rev. ed. London: Verso.

Anderson, Elijah. 1990. *Streetwise: Race, Class, and Change in an Urban Community*. Chicago: University of Chicago Press

Andrzejewski, B. W., S. Piłaszewicz, and W. Tyloch, eds. 1985. *Literatures in
African Languages: Theoretical Issues and Sample Surveys*. Cambridge: Cambridge University Press.

Appadurai, Arjun. 1990. "Disjuncture and Difference in the Global Cultural Economy." *Public Culture* 2: 1–24.

Apter, Andrew. 1992. *Black Critics and Kings: The Hermeneutics of Power in
Yoruba Society*. Chicago: University of Chicago Press.

———. 1996. "The Pan-African Nation: Oil-Money and the Spectacle of Culture
in Nigeria." *Public Culture* 8: 441–66.

Armstrong, Nancy. 1987. *Desire and Domestic Fiction: A Political History of the
Novel. New York: Oxford University Press*.

Arowolo, Oladele. 1981. "Plural Marriage, Fertility, and the Problem of Multiple
Causation." In *Women, Education, and Modernization of the Family in West
Africa*, edited by Helen Ware, 112–33. Canberra: Australian National University.

Ashcroft, Bill, Gareth Griffiths, and Helen Tiffin, eds. 1995. *The Post-Colonial
Studies Reader*. London: Routledge.

Ayers, Peter K. 1979. "Ogali A. Ogali and *Coal City*: The Pampleteer as Novelist."
World Literature Written in English 18:99–113.

Babalola, Adeboye. 1985. "Yoruba Literature." In Andrzejewski, Piłaszewicz, and Tyloch 1985, 157–89.

Baudrillard, Jean. 1988. *Selected Writings*. Edited by Mark Poster. Stanford, Calif.: Stanford University Press.

Becker, Howard S. 1953. "How to Become a Marihuana [*sic*] User." *American Journal of Sociology* 59:235–42.

———. 1982. *Art Worlds*. Berkeley: University of California Press.

Beckson, Karl E., and Arthur F. Ganz. 1989. *Literary Terms: A Dictionary*. 3d ed. New York: Noonday Press.

Berger, Peter L., Brigitte Berger, and Hansfried Kellner. 1973. *The Homeless Mind: Modernization and Consciousness*. New York: Random House.

Bellah, Robert N., Richard Madsen, William M. Sullivan, Ann Swidler, and Steven M. Tipton. 1984. *Habits of the Heart: Individualism and Commitment in American Life*. Berkeley: University of California Press.

Bgoya, Walter. 1996. "Publishing in Africa: Culture and Development." In *The Muse of Modernity: Essays on Culture as Development in Africa*, edited by Philip G. Altbach and Salah M. Hassan, 151–179. Trenton, N.J.: Africa World Press.

Bhabha, Homi K. 1985. "Signs Taken for Wonders: Questions of Ambivalence and Authority under a Tree Outside Delhi, May 1817." *Critical Inquiry* 12:144–65.

Bjornson, Richard. 1991. *The African Quest for Freedom and Identity Cameroonian Writing and the National Experience*. Bloomington: Indiana University Press.

Boehmer, Elleke. 1991. "Of Goddesses and Stories: Gender and a New Politics in Achebe's *Anthills of the Savannah*." In Peterson and Rutherford, 1991, 102–12.

Bonds, Parris Afton. 1986. *Man for Hire*. New York: Silhouette.

Bonham-Carter, Victor. 1984. *Authors by Profession*. Vol. 2, *From the Copyright Act 1911 until the End of 1981*. Los Altos, Calif.: William Kaufmann.

Bourdieu, Pierre. 1984. *Distinction: A Social Critique of the Judgment of Taste*. Translated by Richard Nice. Cambridge, Mass.: Harvard University Press.

Brewer, John. 1997. *The Pleasures of the Imagination: English Culture in the Eighteenth Century*. London: HarperCollins.

Bruckner, Pascal. 1986. *The Tears of the White Man: Compassion as Contempt*. Translated by William R. Beer. New York: Free Press.

Bürger, Peter. 1984. "The Institution of Art as a Category of the Sociology of Literature." In *The Institutions of Art*, edited by Peter Bürger and Christine Bürger, 3–29. Translated by Loren Kruger. Lincoln: University of Nebraska Press.

Callaway, Barbara J. 1987. *Muslim Hausa Women in Nigeria: Tradition and Change*. Syracuse, N.Y.: Syracuse University Press.

Cancel, Robert. 1993. "African-Language Literatures: Perspectives on Culture and Identity." In *A History of Twentieth-Century African Literatures*, edited by Oyekan Owomoyela, 285–310. Lincoln: University of Nebraska Press.

Cawelti, John G. 1976. *Adventure, Mystery, and Romance: Formula Stories as Art and Popular Culture*. Chicago: University of Chicago Press.

Chinweizu, Onwuchekwa, Jemie, and Ihechukwu Madubuike. 1983. *Toward the Decolonization of African Literature*. Washington, D.C.: Howard University Press.

Chukwuma, Helen. 1989. "Positivism and the Female Crisis: The Novels of Buchi Emecheta." In Otokunefor and Nwodo, 1989, 2–18.

Cole, John Y., and Carol S. Gold, eds. 1979. *Reading in America 1978: Selected Findings of the Book Industry Study Group's 1978 Study.* Washington, D.C.: Library of Congress.

Comaroff, Jean, and John Comaroff. 1991. *Of Revelation and Revolution.* Chicago: University of Chicago Press

Coquery-Vidrovitch, Catherine. 1988. *Africa: Endurance and Change South of the Sahara.* Translated by David Maisel. Berkeley: University of California Press.

Coser, Lewis, Charles Kadushin, and Walter W. Powell. 1982. *Books: The Culture and Commerce of Publishing.* New York: Basic Books.

Coussy, Denise. 1988. *Le Roman nigérian anglophone.* Paris: Editions Silex.

Crowder, Michael. 1966. "Tradition and Change in Nigerian Literature." *TriQuarterly* 5:117–28.

———. 1978. *The Story of Nigeria.* 4th ed. London: Faber and Faber.

Curwen, Peter. 1986. *The World Book Industry.* London: Euromonitor Publications.

de St. Jorre, John. 1972. *The Brothers' War: Biafra and Nigeria.* Boston: Houghton Mifflin.

Diamond, Larry Jay. 1988. *Class, Ethnicity, and Democracy in Nigeria: The Failure of the First Republic.* Syracuse, N.Y.: Syracuse University Press.

Dore, Ronald. 1973. *British Factory–Japanese Factory: The Origins of National Diversity in Industrial Relations.* Berkeley: University of California Press.

Douglas, Ann. 1980. "Soft-Porn Culture." *New Republic,* August 30, 25–29.

Eisenstein, Elizabeth L. 1979. *The Printing Press as an Agent of Change: Communications and Cultural Transformations in Early-Modern Europe.* Cambridge: Cambridge University Press.

Emenyonu, Pat T. 1993. *Reading and the Nigerian Cultural Background.* Enugu: New Generation Books.

Enoh, A. Owan. 1994. "Philosophical Foundation of Nigerian's Policy on Education." In *Basic Issues in Educational Foundations,* edited by Ayo Adewole, G. Owoicho Akpa; E. M. F. Anyi, A. Owan Enoh, Paul P. Lomak, and James D. Urwick, 20–33. Jos: Faculty of Education, University of Jos.

Escarpit, Robert. 1971. *Sociology of Literature.* 2d ed. Translated by Ernest Pick. London: Frank Cass.

Euromonitor. 1980. *The Euromonitor Book Readership Survey.* 5th ed. London: Euromonitor Publications.

Europa Yearbook 1988: A World Survey. Vol. 2. London: Europa Publications.

Ezeigbo, Theodora Akachi. 1997. "Gender Conflict in Flora Nwapa's Novels." In Newell, 1987, 95–104.

Falk, Cathryn. 1983. *How to Write a Romance and Get It Published.* New York: Crown Publishers.

Fapohunda, O. J. 1981. "Human Resources and the Lagos Informal Sector." In Sethuraman, 1981, 70–82.

Federal Ministry of Education and Youth Development. 1993. *Basic Education for All in Nigeria by the Year 2000.* Abuja: Federal Ministry of Education and Youth Development.

Federal Republic of Nigeria. 1992. *1991 Population Census (Provisional Results)*. Abuja: Census News.

Fischer, Claude. 1982. *To Dwell among Friends: Personal Networks in Town and City*. Chicago: University of Chicago Press.

Forgacs, David. 1990. *Italian Culture in the Industrial Era, 1880–1980: Cultural Industries, Politics and the Public*. Manchester: Manchester University Press.

Foucault, Michel. 1979. "What is an Author?" In *Textual Strategies: Perspectives in Post-Structural Criticism*, edited by Josué Harari, 141–60. Ithaca, N.Y.: Cornell University Press.

Frost, Robert. [1914] 1963. "The Death of the Hired Man." In *Selected Poems of Robert Frost*. New York: Holt, Rinehart and Winston.

Frye, Northrop. 1957. *Anatomy of Criticism: Four Essays*. Princeton, N.J.: Princeton University Press.

Gallup, George, Jr. 1987. *The Gallup Poll: Public Opinion 1986*. Wilmington, Del.: Scholarly Resources.

———. 1992. *The Gallup Poll: Public Opinion 1991*. Wilmington, Del.: Scholarly Resources.

Geertz, Clifford. 1973. *The Interpretation of Culture*. New York: Basic Books.

———. 1983. *Local Knowledge: Further Essays in Interpretive Anthropology*. New York: Basic Books.

Goody, Jack. 1977. *The Domestication of the Savage Mind*. Cambridge: Cambridge University Press.

Graña, César. 1964. *Bohemian versus Bourgeois: French Society and the French Man of Letters in the Nineteenth Century*. New York: Basic Books.

Greenfield, George. 1989. *Scribblers for Bread: Aspects of the English Novel since 1945*. New York: W. W. Norton.

Griswold, Wendy. 1981. "American Character and the American Novel." *American Journal of Sociology* 86: 740–65.

———. 1987. "A Methodological Framework for the Sociology of Culture." *Sociological Methodology* 17: 1–35.

———. 1989. "Formulaic Fiction: The Author as Agent of Elective Affinity." *Comparative Social Research* 11: 75–130.

———. 1992. "The Writing on the Mud Wall: Nigerian Novels and the Imaginary Village." *American Sociological Review* 57:709–24.

Griswold, Wendy, and Misty Bastian. 1987. "Continuities and Reconstructions in Cross-Cultural Literary Transmission: The Case of the Nigerian Romance Novel." *Poetics* 16:327–51.

———. 1990. "A Bibliographic Listing of Nigerian Novels: 1952–1990." *Journal of Commonwealth Literature* 25: 214–27.

Griswold, Wendy, and Kathleen Hull. 1998. "The Burnished Steel Watch: What a Sample of a Single Year's Fiction Indicates." In *The Empirical Study of Literature and the Media,* edited by Susanne Janssen and Nel van Dijk, 24–37. Rotterdam: Barjesteh van Waalwijk van Doorn.

Guiley, Rosemary. 1983. *Love Lines: The Romance Reader's Guide to Printed Pleasures*. New York: Facts on File Publications.

Gusfield, Joseph R. 1975. *Community: A Critical Response*. Oxford: Basil Blackwell.

Guyer, Jane I. 1992. "Representation without Taxation: An Essay on Democracy in Rural Nigeria, 1952–1990." *African Studies Review* 35: 41–79.

———. 1994. "The Spatial Dimensions of Civil Society in Africa: An Anthropologist Looks at Nigeria." In Harbeson, Rothchild, and Chazen, 1994, 215–29.

———, ed. 1987. *Feeding African Cities: Studies in Regional Social History.* Bloomington: Indiana University Press.

Hannerz, Ulf. 1992. *Cultural Complexity: Studies in the Social Organization of Meaning.* New York: Columbia University Press.

Harbeson, John W. 1994. "Civil Society and Political Renaissance in Africa." In Harbeson, Rothchild, and Chazen, 1994, 1–29.

Harbeson, John W., Donald Rothchild, and Naomi Chazen 1994. *Civil Society and the State in Africa.* Boulder, Colo.: Lynne Rienner.

Harris, William V. 1989. *Ancient Literacy.* Cambridge, Mass.: Harvard University Press.

Heath, Shirley Brice. 1983. *Ways with Words: Language, Life, and Work in Communities and Classrooms.* Cambridge: Cambridge University Press.

Hill, Alan. 1980. "Publishing in Africa." *TLS* (October 10): 1144.

Hirsch, Paul M. 1972. "Processing Fads and Fashions." *American Journal of Sociology* 77: 639–59.

Hobsbawm, Eric, and Terence Ranger, eds. 1983. *The Invention of Tradition.* Cambridge: Cambridge University Press.

Hummon, David M. 1990. *Commonplaces: Community, Ideology and Identity in American Culture.* Albany: State University of New York Press.

Hunter, J. Paul. 1990. *Before Novels: The Cultural Contexts of Eighteenth-Century English Fiction.* New York: W. W. Norton.

Index to International Public Opinion, 1982–1983. Prepared by Survey Research Consultants International, Inc. Edited by Elizabeth Hann Hastings and Philip K. Hastings. Westport, Conn.: Greenwood Press.

Inkeles, Alex, and David H. Smith. 1974. *Becoming Modern: Individual Change in Six Developing Countries.* Cambridge, Mass.: Harvard University Press.

Isichei, Elizabeth. 1983. *A History of Nigeria.* London: Longman.

James, Louis. 1994. "Marie Corelli." In *Twentieth-Century Romance and Historical Writers,* edited by Aruna Vasudevan, 150–52. 3rd ed. London: St. James Press.

Janowitz, Morris.1952. *The Community Press in an Urban Setting: The Social Elements of Urbanism.* 2d ed. Chicago: University of Chicago Press.

Jarmon, Charles. 1988. *Nigeria: Reorganization and Development since the Mid–Twentieth Century.* Leiden: E. J. Brill.

Jensen, Margaret Ann. 1984. *Love's $weet Return: The Harlequin Story.* Toronto: Women's Educational Press.

Jeyifo, Biodun. 1991. "For Chinua Achebe: The Resilience and the Predicament of Obierika." In Peterson and Rutherford 1991, 51–70.

Johnson, David, Andrew J. Nathan, and Evelyn S. Rawski. 1985. *Popular Culture in Late Imperial China.* Berkeley: University of California Press.

Kaplan, Robert D. 1996. *The Ends of the Earth: A Journey at the Dawn of the Twenty-first Century.* New York: Random House.

Karl, Terry Lynn. 1997. *The Paradox of Plenty: Oil Booms and Petro-States.* Berkeley: University of California Press.

Laitin, David. 1986. *Hegemony and Culture: Politics and Religious Change among the Yoruba*. Chicago: University of Chicago Press.

Laslett, Peter. [1965] 1973. *The World We Have Lost: England before the Industrial Age*. 2nd ed. New York: Scribner's.

Lerner, Daniel. 1958. *The Passing of Traditional Society: Modernizing the Middle East*. With the collaboration of Lucille W. Pevsner, and an introduction by David Riesman. Glencoe, Ill.: Free Press.

Lindfors, Bernth, ed. 1975. *Critical Perspectives on Amos Tutuola*. Washington, D.C.: Three Continents Press.

Link, E. Perry, 1981. *Mandarin Ducks and Butterflies: Popular Fiction in Early Twentieth-Century, Chinese Cities*. Berkeley: University of California Press.

—— 1992. *Evening Chats in Beijing: Probing China's Predicament*. New York: Norton.

Little, Kenneth Lindsay. 1973. *African Women in Towns: An Aspect of Africa's Social Revolution*. London: Cambridge University Press.

Logan, John R. and Harvey L. Molotch. 1987. *Urban Fortunes: The Political Economy of Place*. Berkeley: University of California Press.

Long, Elizabeth. 1992. "Textual Interpretation as Collective Action." *Discourse* 14:104–30.

Lord, Albert Bates. 1960. *The Singer of Tales*. Cambridge, Mass.: Harvard University Press.

Mabogunje, A. L., and M. O. Filani. 1981. "The Informal Sector in a Small City: The Case of Kano (Nigeria)." In Sethuraman, 1981, 83–89.

Maja-Pearce, Adewale. 1992. *A Mask Dancing: Nigerian Novelists of the Eighties*. London: Hans Zell.

Malmquist, Eve, ed. 1992. *Women and Literacy Development in the Third World*. Linköping, Sweden: Linköping University.

Mann, Kristin. 1985. *Marrying Well: Marriage, Status, and Social Change among the Educated Elite in Colonial Lagos*. Cambridge: Cambridge University Press.

Mann, Peter H. 1982. *From Author to Reader: A Social Study of Books*. London: Routledge and Kegan Paul.

Markert, John. 1985. "Romance Publishing and the Production of Culture." *Poetics* 14:69–93.

McKeon, Michael. 1987. *The Origins of the English Novel, 1600–1740*. Baltimore: Johns Hopkins University Press.

Meyere, John W., John Boli, George M. Thomas, and Francisco O. Ramirez. 1997. "World Society and the Nation-State." *American Journal of Sociology* 103: 144–81.

Mitchell, J. Clyde. 1987. *Cities, Society, and Social Perception: A Central African Perspective*. Oxford: Oxford University Press.

Modleski, Tania. [1982] 1984. *Loving with a Vengeance: Mass-Produced Fantasies for Women*. New York: Methuen.

Mohammed, Abdullahi. 1993. "The Arabic and Ajami Culture of Nigeria." In *Culture and the Book Industry in Nigeria*, edited by Sule Bello and Abdullahi Augi, 33–43. Lagos: National Council for Arts and Culture.

Nell, V. 1988. *Lost in a Book: The Psychology of Reading*. New Haven, Conn.: Yale University Press.

Newa, John M. 1990. "Libraries in National Literacy Education Programmes in Africa South of the Sahara: The State-of-the-Art." *International Library Review* 22: 73–94.

Newell, Stephanie, ed. 1997. *Writing African Women: Gender, Popular Culture and Literature in West Africa.* London: Zed Books.

Nigeria: A Country Study. 1992. 5th ed. Federal Research Division, Library of Congress. Edited by Helen Chapin Metz. Washington, D.C.: Library of Congress.

Njoku, Amby. 1985. *Swinging Lagos.* Lagos: Ambrose Editions.

Nugũgĩ wa Thiong'o. 1986. *Decolonising the Mind: The Politics of Languages in African Literature.* London: J. Currey.

Nweke, Ken M. C. 1987. "Promoting the Reading Habit among the Literate in Nigeria." *Reading Teacher* 40:632–38.

Obiechina, E. N. 1967. "Transition from Oral to Literary Tradition." *Presence Africaine* 63: 140–61.

———. 1972. *Onitsha Market Literature.* London: Heinemann.

Odugbemi, Sina. 1995. "Look Back in Anger." *West Africa* No. 4047 (May 1–7): 682.

Ogunyemi, Chikwenye Okonjo. 1996. *Africa Wo/Man Palava: The Nigerian Novel by Women.* Chicago: University of Chicago Press.

Okara, Gabriel. 1991. "Towards the Evolution of an African Language for African Literature." In Peterson and Rutherford 1991, 11–18.

Okedara, J. T. 1981. *The Impact of Literacy Education in Ibadan, Nigeria.* Ibadan: Ibadan University Press.

Okigbo, Charles. 1987. "Death and Funeral Ads in the Nigerian Press." *Journalism Quarterly* 64:629–33.

Onibokun, Adepoju G. 1989. "Urban Growth and Urban Management in Nigeria." In Stren and White, 1989, 68–111.

Oniororo, Niyi. 1968. *Lagos Is a Wicked Place.* 2d ed. Ibadan: n.p.

Onokerhoraye, Andrew G. 1995. *Benin, a Traditional African City in Transition.* Benin City: Benin Social Science Series for Africa, University of Benin.

Orubuloye, Israel O. 1981. "Education and Socio-Demographic Change in Nigeria: The Western Nigerian Experience." In *Women, Education, and Modernization of the Family in West Africa,* edited by Helen Ware, 22–41. Canberra: Australian National University.

Osiobe, Stephen A., Ann E. Osiobe, and J. D. Okah. 1989. "Theme and Illustrations as Correlates of Literature Preferences among Nigerian Primary School Pupils." *Library Review* 38:45–52.

Osundina, Oyeniyi. 1993. "Book Distribution and Book Use: What Progress?" In *Culture and the Book Industry in Nigeria,* edited by Sule Bello and Abdullahi Augi, 59–70. Lagos: National Council for Arts and Culture.

Othman, Shehu. 1989. "Nigeria: Power for Profit—Class, Corporatism, and Factionalism in the Military." In *Contemporary West African States,* edited by Donal B. Cruise O'Brien, John Dunn, and Richard Rathbone, 113–44. Cambridge: Cambridge University Press.

Otokunefor, Henrietta C., and Obiageli C. Nwodo, eds. 1989. *Nigerian Female Writers: A Critical Perspective.* Lagos: Malthouse Press.

Owomoyela, Oyekan, ed. 1993. *A History of Twentieth-Century African Literatures*. Lincoln: University of Nebraska Press.

Oxenham, John. 1980. *Literacy: Writing, Reading and Social Organisation*. London: Routledge and Kegan Paul.

Oyewumi, Oyeronke. 1997. *The Invention of Women: Making an African Sense of Western Gender Discourses*. Minneapolis: University of Minnesota Press.

Palmer, Eustace. 1979. *The Growth of the African Novel*. London: Heinemann.

Paren, Elizabeth. 1978. "The Multinational Publishing Firm in Africa: The Macmillan Perspective." *The African Book Publishing Record* 4:15–17.

Parsons, Talcott. 1951. *The Social System*. New York: Free Press.

Patterson, Orlando. 1977. *Ethnic Chauvinism: The Reactionary Impulse*. New York: Stein and Day.

Peace, Adrian J. 1979. *Choice, Class, and Conflict: A Study of Southern Nigerian Factory Workers*. Atlantic Highlands, NJ: Humanities Press.

Peel, J. D. Y. 1968. "Syncretism and Religious Change." *Comparative Studies in Society and History* 10:121–41.

Peil, Margaret. 1981. *Cities and Suburbs: Urban Life in West Africa*. New York: Africana.

———. 1983. "Urban Contacts: A Comparison of Women and Men." In *Female and Male in West Africa*, edited by Christine Oppong, 275–82. London: George Allen and Unwin.

Petersen, Kirsten Holst, and Anna Rutherford, eds. 1991. *Chinua Achebe: A Celebration*. Oxford: Heinemann.

Peterson, Richard A. 1978. "The Production of Cultural Change: The Case of Contemporary Country Music." *Social Research* 45:292–314.

———. 1992. "Understanding Audience Segmentation: From Elite and Mass to Omnivore and Univore." *Poetics* 21:243–58.

Piłaszewicz, Stanisław. 1985. "Literature in the Hausa language." 190–254. In Andrzejewski, Piłaszewicz, and Tyloch, 1985.

Popoola, Dimeji. 1988a. "Author Interview: Amos Tutuola." *Books* 1, no. 2:15–19.

———. 1988b. "Book Fairs Nigeriana." *Books* 1, no. 2:49–52, 19.

Popoola, Dimeji, Buki Adesanya, and Lolese Adamolekun. 1988. "Nigeria: Not Yet a Reading Public . . . ." *Books* 1, no. 3:5–8.

Rabine, Leslie W. 1985. *Reading the Romantic Heroine: Text, History, Ideology*. Ann Arbor: University of Michigan Press.

Radway, Janice A. 1984. *Reading the Romance: Women, Patriarchy, and Popular Literature*. Chapel Hill: University of North Carolina Press.

———. 1988. "The Book-of-the-Month Club and the General Reader: On the Uses of 'Serious Fiction.'" *Critical Inquiry* 14:516–38.

Rea, Julian. 1975. "Aspects of African Publishing 1945–74." *African Book Publishing Record*, Vol. 1:145–151.

Samuels, Barbara G. 1989. "Young Adults' Choices: Why Do Students 'Really Like' Particular Books?" *Journal of Reading* 32:714–19.

Sanders, Barry. 1994. *A Is for Ox: Violence, Electronic Media and the Silencing of the Written Word*. New York: Pantheon.

Saro-Wiwa, Ken. 1985. "Dis Nigeria Sef." In *Poems in a Time of War*, 36–44. Port Harcourt: Saros International.

Schmidt, Nancy. 1965. "An Anthropological Analysis of Nigerian Fiction." Ph.D. diss. Northwestern University.

———. 1970. "Nigerian Fiction and the Oral Tradition." In *New African Literature and the Arts,* edited by Joseph Okpaku, vol. 2, 25–38. New York: Thomas Y. Crowell.

Scott, James C. 1990. *Domination and the Arts of Resistance: Hidden Transcripts.* New Haven, Conn.: Yale University Press.

Selsky, Deborah. 1989. "American Reading Habits (and Education) on the Rise." *Library Journal* 114, no. 9:22.

Sethuraman, S. V., ed. 1981. *The Urban Informal Sector in Developing Countries: Employment, Poverty and Environment.* Geneva: International Labour Organization.

Shils, Edward. 1975. *Center and Periphery: Essays in Macrosociology.* Chicago: University of Chicago Press.

Simmel, Georg. [1918] 1971. "The Conflict in Modern Culture." In *Georg Simmel: On Individuality and Social Forms,* edited by Donald Levine, 375–93. Chicago: University of Chicago Press.

Smith, Anthony. 1980. *The Geopolitics of Information: How Western Culture Dominates the World.* London: Faber and Faber.

Soyinka, Wole. 1976. *Myth, Literature and the African World.* Cambridge: Cambridge University Press.

Starker, Steven. 1990. "Fear of Fiction: The Novel." *Book Research Quarterly* 6, no. 2:44–59.

Stone, Lawrence. 1977. *The Family, Sex and Marriage in England, 1500–1800.* New York: Harper and Row.

Stratton, Florence. 1994. *Contemporary African Literature and the Politics of Gender.* London: Routledge.

Stren, Richard E. 1989. "The Administration of Urban Services." In Stren and White, 1989, 37–67.

Stren, Richard E., and Rodney R. White, eds. 1989. *African Cities in Crisis: Managing Rapid Urban Growth.* Boulder, Colo.: Westview Press.

Suberu, Rotimi T. 1993. "The Travails of Federalism in Nigeria." *Journal of Democracy* 4:39–53.

Suttles, Gerald D. 1972. *The Social Construction of Communities.* Chicago: University of Chicago Press.

———. 1990. *The Man-Made City: The Hand-Use Confidence Game in Chicago.* Chicago: University of Chicago Press.

Symons, Julian. 1985. *Bloody Murder: From the Detective Story to the Crime Novel.* Revised ed. New York: Viking Penguin.

Thompson, John B. 1990. *Ideology and Modern Culture: Critical Social Theory in the Era of Mass Communication.* Stanford, Calif.: Stanford University Press.

Tuchman, Gaye, with Nina E. Fortin. 1989. *Edging Women Out: Victorian Novelists, Publishers, and Social Change.* New Haven, Conn.: Yale University Press.

Tunstall, Jeremy. 1977. *The Media Are American.* New York: Columbia University Press.

Turner, Margaret E. 1991. "Achebe, Hegel and the New Colonialism." In Peterson and Rutherford 1991, 31–40.

Twentieth-Century Romance and Historical Writers. 1994. 3d ed. Edited by Aruna Vasudevan; consulting editor, Lesley Henderson. London: St. James Press.

Uchendu, Victor C. 1965. *The Igbo of Southeast Nigeria*. New York: Holt, Rinehart and Winston.

United Nations Economic, Scientific, and Cultural Organization (UNESCO). 1991. *Statistical Yearbook*. Paris: UNESCO.

———. 1993. *Statistical Yearbook. Annuaire statistique. 1990/91*. Paris: UNESCO.

Walker, Alice. 1983. *In Search of Our Mothers' Gardens*. New York: Harcourt, Brace, Jovanovich.

Watt, Ian. [1957] 1974. *The Rise of the Novel: Studies in Defoe, Richardson and Fielding*. Berkeley: University of California Press.

Watts, Michael. 1987. "Brittle Trade: A Political Economy of Food Supply in Kano." In Guyer 1987, 55–111.

Weber, Max. 1946. "The Social Psychology of the World Religions." In *From Max Weber*, edited by H. H. Geerth and C. Wright Mills, 267–301. New York: Oxford University Press.

Wellman, Barry. 1979. "The Community Question: The Intimate Networks of East Yorkers." *American Journal of Sociology* 84:1201–31.

West, Richard F., Keith E. Stanovich, and Harold R. Mitchell. 1993. "Reading in the Real World and Its Correlates." *Reading Research Quarterly* 28:34–50.

Wheatley, Paul. 1971. *The Pivot of the Four Quarters*. Chicago: Aldine.

White, Luise. 1990. *The Comforts of Home: Prostitution in Colonial Nairobi*. Chicago: University of Chicago Press.

White, Rodney R. 1989. "The Influence of Environmental and Economic Factors on the Urban Crisis." In Stren and White 1989, 1–19.

Whiteside, Thomas. 1980. *The Blockbuster Complex: Conglomerates, Show Business, and Book Publishing*. Middletown, Conn.: Wesleyan University Press.

Wilkinson, Jane, ed. 1992. *Talking with African Writers: Interviews with African Poets, Playwrights and Novelists*. London: James Currey.

Williams, Raymond. 1973. *The Country and the City*. New York: Oxford University Press.

———. 1980. "Base and Superstructure in Marxist Cultural Theory." In *Problems in Materialism and Culture*, 31–49. London: Verso.

Williamson, Kay. 1993. "Development of Minority Languages: Publishing Problems and Prospects." In *Culture and the Book Industry in Nigeria*, edited by Sule Bello and Abdullahi Augi, 203–29. Lagos: National Council for Arts and Culture.

Yakubu, A. M., ed. 1996. *Western Education in Northern Nigeria: Challenges and Strategies*. Zaria: National Gamji Memorial Club, Ahmadu Bello University.

Zabus, Chantal. 1991. "The Logos–Eaters: The Igbo Ethno-Text." In Peterson and Rutherford 1991, 19–30.

Zell, Hans M., Carol Bundy, and Virginia Coulon. 1983. *A New Reader's Guide to African Literature*. New York: Africana.

Zill, Nicholas, and Marianne Winglee. 1990. *Who Reads Literature: The Future of the United States as a Nation of Readers*. Cabin John, M.D.: Seven Locks Press.

INDEX